America by the Numbers

Infrastructures Series

edited by Geoffrey C. Bowker and Paul N. Edwards

Paul N. Edwards, *A Vast Machine: Computer Models, Climate Data, and the Politics of Global Warming*

Lawrence M. Busch, *Standards: Recipes for Reality*

Lisa Gitelman, ed., *"Raw Data" Is an Oxymoron*

Finn Brunton, *Spam: A Shadow History of the Internet*

Nil Disco and Eda Kranakis, eds., *Cosmopolitan Commons: Sharing Resources and Risks across Borders*

Casper Bruun Jensen and Brit Ross Winthereik, *Monitoring Movements in Development Aid: Recursive Partnerships and Infrastructures*

James Leach and Lee Wilson, eds., *Subversion, Conversion, Development: Cross-Cultural Knowledge Exchange and the Politics of Design*

Olga Kuchinskaya, *The Politics of Invisibility: Public Knowledge about Radiation Health Effects after Chernobyl*

Ashley Carse, *Beyond the Big Ditch: Politics, Ecology, and Infrastructure at the Panama Canal*

Alexander Klose, translated by Charles Marcrum II, *The Container Principle: How a Box Changes the Way We Think*

Eric T. Meyer and Ralph Schroeder, *Knowledge Machines: Digital Transformations of the Sciences and Humanities*

Sebastián Ureta, *Assembling Policy: Transantiago, Human Devices, and the Dream of a World-Class Society*

Geoffrey C. Bowker, Stefan Timmermans, Adele E. Clarke, and Ellen Balka, eds., *Boundary Objects and Beyond: Working with Leigh Star*

Clifford Siskin, *System: The Shaping of Modern Knowledge*

Lawrence Busch, *Knowledge for Sale: The Neoliberal Takeover of Higher Education*

Bill Maurer and Lana Swartz, *Paid: Tales of Dongles, Checks, and Other Money Stuff*

Dietmar Offenhuber, *Waste Is Information: Infrastructure Legibility and Governance*

Katayoun Shafiee, *Machineries of Oil: An Infrastructural History of BP in Iran*

Megan Finn, *Documenting Aftermath: Information Infrastructures in the Wake of Disasters*

Laura Watts, *Energy at the End of the World: An Orkney Islands Saga*

Ann M. Pendleton-Jullian and John Seely Brown, *Design Unbound: Designing for Emergence in a White Water World*, Volume 1: *Designing for Emergence*

Ann M. Pendleton-Jullian and John Seely Brown, *Design Unbound: Designing for Emergence in a White Water World*, Volume 2: *Ecologies of Change*

Jordan Frith, *A Billion Little Pieces: RFID and Infrastructures of Identification*

Morgan G. Ames, *The Charisma Machine: The Life, Death, and Legacy of One Laptop per Child*

Mario Biagioli and Alexandra Lippman, eds., *Gaming the Metrics: Misconduct and Manipulation in Academic Research*

Malcolm McCullough, *Downtime on the Microgrid: Architecture, Electricity, and Smart City Islands*

Emmanuel Didier, translated by Priya Vari Sen, *America by the Numbers: Quantification, Democracy, and the Birth of National Statistics*

Ryan Ellis, *Letters, Power Lines, and Other Dangerous Things: The Politics of Infrastructure Security*

America by the Numbers

Quantification, Democracy, and the Birth of National Statistics

Emmanuel Didier

Foreword by Theodore M. Porter

Translated by Priya Vari Sen

The MIT Press
Cambridge, Massachusetts
London, England

Translated from the original French, *En Quoi consiste l'Amérique ? Les statistiques, le New Deal et la démocratie*, © Editions La Decouverte, Paris, France, 2009

Revised and updated for the English language edition

This book was set in Bembo Book MT Pro by Westchester Publishing Services. Printed and bound in the United States of America.

Library of Congress Cataloging-in-Publication Data

Names: Didier, Emmanuel, author. | Porter, Theodore M., 1953- author of foreword. | Sen, Priya Vari, translator.
Title: America by the numbers : quantification, democracy, and the birth of national statistics / Emmanuel Didier, translated by Priya Vari Sen ; foreword by Theodore M. Porter.
Other titles: Quantification, democracy, and the birth of national statistics
Description: Cambridge, Massachusetts : The MIT Press, 2020. | Series: Infrastructures series | "Translated from the original French, En Quoi Consiste L'Amerique?: Les Statistiques, le New Deal et la Démocratie, © Editions La Decouverte, Paris, France, 2009." | Includes bibliographical references and index.
Identifiers: LCCN 2019022829 | ISBN 9780262538374 (paperback)
Subjects: LCSH: New Deal, 1933-1939. | United States--Economic conditions--1918–1945. | Depressions--1929--United States. | Agricultural surveys--United States--History--1919–1933. | United States. Bureau of Agricultural Economics--Officials and employees. | United States. Bureau of Labor Statistics--Officials and employees. | United States. Bureau of the Census--Officials and employees. | Statisticians--United States--Biography.
Classification: LCC E806.D5725 2020 | DDC 973.917--dc23
LC record available at https://lccn.loc.gov/2019022829

10 9 8 7 6 5 4 3 2 1

Contents

Foreword by Theodore M. Porter ix

Introduction: America's Reflexivity 1

Part I The Decomposition of America 15

1 The America of the Reporters 19
2 The Decomposition of Links between Statistics and Politics 87
Conclusion to Part I: Solidity and Consistency 119

Part II Expression of Random America: On the Rural Front 123

3 From the Political Representative to Statistical Representativeness 127
4 Probable Error 145
5 The Administration and University 163
6 Areal America 197
Conclusion to Part II: Expression and Consistency 227

Part III Expression of Random America: On the Urban Front 233

7 The Paradoxical Decomposition of Unemployment 239
8 How to Transform the Victims of the Depression into Enumerators 255

9	From Participationism to a Government of the Masses	293
	Conclusion to Part III: Series and Consistency	337
	Grand Conclusion: What America Consists Of	341
Notes		351
Bibliography		367
Index		385

Foreword

Theodore M. Porter

The work of statistics might reduce to simple enumeration if the things we wished to count were all just the same. Depression-era agricultural economists laboring to estimate crop yields faced, along with the problem of heterogeneous landscapes and soils, the abundant uncertainties of winds, temperatures, and rainfall from the season of planting to harvest. In this book, Emmanuel Didier takes us behind the curtain of everyday data work, introducing forms of expertise that we may not even have suspected. He observes the world as it was seen by empirical economists and statisticians, traveling from farm to farm or workshop to factory, seeking out information that might be useful to farmers and manufacturers as well as to state planning agencies. Didier writes with rare insight about the mundane work of agricultural and industrial economics.

His topic, the statistics of agriculture and labor from the 1920s to the New Deal, pertains also to practices of observation. He carried out research in American archives and official document collections to comprehend the ethnographic dimension of crop estimates and unemployment measures. His book, first published in 2009, was written in French and addressed primarily to French scholars, who in some respects have taken the lead in social studies of statistics. Didier's research extends beyond agriculture and industrial labor to a thematic focus on the rich and sometimes contradictory relations of statistics to American politics and administration. He came to the United States to investigate the history of agricultural and industrial statistics. The book he has written concerns democracy in America. It interweaves political discussions with the investigation of new tools of probability sampling. Such tools quickly assumed a basic role in defining the ways that America knows itself.

Statistical tools of tallying and sampling had a key role in the New Deal. The perceptive reader may well surmise that the real story here is of a natural alliance between enhanced statistical technologies and the modern state, perhaps extending also to business corporations and other bureaucratic organizations. We could easily find many examples to support this view. Yet the work of statistics, as he insists, takes in a still wider range of activities and purposes than these. His stories of crop estimation illustrate the point in a particularly engaging way. That effort was introduced not as a tool of centralized agricultural planning, but to bring together information that could be valuable for family farmers. The prices they could expect for their crops in harvest season depended on yields from many far-flung locations, about which the farmers knew little or nothing. How were they to know whether the merchant who showed up one day at their doorstep was offering a fair price? An organized network of rural statisticians could go a long way toward neutralizing the knowledge asymmetries. It sounds straightforward, but in fact it was immensely complicated to assemble reasonably disinterested information of adequate quality. Didier illustrates the point in a series of short chapters in which he lays out the somewhat abstracted stages leading from an amorphous "plasma" of formless uncertainty to a precisely coordinated release of aggregated data. This is no planned economy but a foundation of rules for a fair and competitive one.

Alain Desrosières, the French statistician and sociologist whose work has been so important for social studies of quantification in France and beyond, showed how statistics come in diverse forms, each suited to a different form of the state, from technocratic or Keynesian to liberal (free market) or neoliberal. One of the most satisfying aspects of the present book involves the contrasting forms of expertise associated with different kinds of statistics. In the farm example, agricultural economists were likely to depend on prosperous farmers to anticipate harvests on the basis of their experience of crop growth in relation to expected weather patterns. Such estimates depended on the willing participation of local leaders, who were given credit for at least some degree of disinterested wisdom. The more centralized planning efforts of the New Deal depended on a shift to formal sampling procedures, now incorporating some form of randomization. This was especially the case in urban studies of industrial labor. It would be too simple to say that the more mechanized procedures were less democratic. They were, in one basic sense, more egalitarian, since they no longer privileged the views of the most successful farmers. But now, statistical experts rather than dispersed citizens would run the show.

The statistics of survey sampling, worked out through these and other efforts to reckon with populations, emerged by the mid-twentieth century as one of the most basic techniques of the sciences, and especially of human sciences. The book's title in French, which roughly translates to *What Is America Made Of?*, seems to acknowledge the power and generality of these methods. Didier ultimately suggests, in the general conclusion, statistics was able to represent the diversity of a population rather than just those who, for whatever reason, attracted notice. The price of such exactitude, however, was that lay citizens became, in the main, objects of investigation rather than participants.

Didier has written the book in a way that maximizes the accessibility, and with it the fascination, of survey work. He develops his material not as a practical exemplification of mathematical principles but as a series of tactics worked out in a confrontation with specific problems arising in the course of the work. In short, he presents statistical issues from the ground up. He has in mind that statistics can be much more than a form of technical mastery but might even provide a basis for fairer and more participatory politics.

Introduction

America's Reflexivity

> "Notice how the boat stinks, Joe?"
> "It's being at anchor, and the fog stimulates your smellers," . . .
> Paul was changing the subject: "Well, we're back to God's country."
> "Oh, I can't imagine," cried Mrs. Johnson, "what America's going to be like."
>
> —*John Dos Passos,* U.S.A./The Big Money *(1936, 2)*

The Great Depression that hit the United States in the 1930s was so violent that it destroyed much more than the economy. For it was not just an economic crisis, or even a social one, but an acute crisis of identity (Schlesinger 1957). Many feared that the democratic character of the country was in danger. The farmers, symbols of individual autonomy, were ruined and forced to abandon their lands; the workers, earlier the spearheads of liberal capitalism, now formed unemployed hordes living on charity. Consequently, they began to turn against their employers, their hostility sometimes taking a violent turn. The capitalists, models of free enterprise, chose to jump out of windows rather than face bankruptcy. A few socialist mayors and administrators were elected in select pockets, as some felt that the political experiments taking place in Italy and the USSR had some merit (Bucki 2001). In short, it seemed that the Great Depression was threatening the very essence of the federation.

The shock was such that the tools used until then by the federal administration to guide political action proved completely inadequate. A striking example of this governmental myopia is provided by unemployment: between 1932 (the year when differences emerged between President Herbert Hoover and Frances Perkins, who was to become Franklin Roosevelt's secretary of labor the following year) and 1937—that is, during the five worst years of the Depression—no one knew the rate of unemployment prevailing in the United States, nor the number of unemployed, and not even, for the greater part of the period, the trends followed by these indicators! No business, institution, or administrative department was able to make a reliable assessment of the problem, which was, needless to say, very acute (Perkins 1946; Anderson 2015). And unemployment was no exception. This blot on the human condition eluded the analytical tools of the various administrations. At the commencement of the crisis, it was impossible to gauge exactly how many families had migrated, abandoning their farms, or how many people were receiving public relief, or which professions had been most hard hit by unemployment, to cite only those factors whose ignorance seems quite incomprehensible to us today. The Great Depression had shaken the nation so deeply that, for the government, the disturbing question of how to pull the country out of it was intensified by its inability to project a coherent and clear picture of the transformations it was going through.

Various actors carried out experiments to recapture their country reflexively. Some received considerable acclaim (Stott 1973). The first that comes to mind is the *Brain Trust*, the group of academics brought in by Roosevelt to take stock of the situation; they played a decisive role in formulating the reforms undertaken under the New Deal. We can also mention the photographic section directed by Roy Stryker of the Farm Security Administration (FSA), established in 1937. The photographers recruited by

Stryker—including Walker Evans, Russell Lee, and Dorothea Lange—drew a stark portrait of America in crisis (Lange and Taylor 1939; Fleischhauer and Brannan 1988).

Between the theories propounded by the academics and the reality depicted by the photographs, we are less familiar with the decisive role played by the invention of *representative sampling* in statistics. This methodology allowed the administration to get a grip on this new America in the throes of a painful birth, and it was so effective that it became an essential feature of all democracies.

This book, which adopts a sociohistorical perspective on quantification, shows how this new endeavor made a new numerical reading of America possible during the New Deal, how the statistical representativity graft managed to take in this country, how the technique of random sampling was made compatible with the American population, and at the same time, how this scion transformed modes of governance. This book will not bombard readers with figures about how America is n% women, z% unemployed, and p% something else, for these figures are merely the result of what interests us—namely, the process of forging new tools for the quantification of a country and their interrelationship with its social and political evolution. This study is thus situated at the intersection of the history of science, sociology, and political science (Desrosières 1998; Porter 1995; Hacking 1984; Daston 1988; Espeland and Stevens 1998; Diaz-Bone and Didier 2016).

We should point out that representative sampling already existed before the Great Depression. It was first presented to statisticians in 1895 by Anders Kiaer, the director of the Statistical Office of Kristiana (today Oslo, Norway), during the Berne session of the International Institute of Statistics, the most eminent gathering of statisticians at the time. Thus, strictly speaking, statistical representativity was not invented in the United States. Nevertheless, Kiaer's method was little used and soon forgotten—at least in his country (Lie 2002). So, when the American administration first decided to use statistical surveys during the 1930s and wanted them to be *representative* of the nation as a whole, it actually had to reinvent the methodology anew.

Statistics was not something foreign to the administration, however. First, the decennial National Census, praising itself for counting exhaustively all Americans, had been established since the Constitution. Second, the Department of Agriculture, as we shall see in detail, had been using them since its foundation (Blaisdell 1940). And third, the Hoover administration also gave a lot of weight to the use of quantitative data (Alchon 1985). But none of the techniques they used were *representative surveys*, even though they shared a certain number of common points. Their reinvention by the American administration also implied the reform of old habits. To study the reflective function of the state, we will have to narrate the history of the reinvention of the practice of statistics.

Furthermore, we also need to specify that the representative surveys in question here are not "opinion polls," a meaning that is often (but wrongly) attributed to them. Opinion polls were no doubt developed more or less at the same time, and they met with great success because George Gallup, the principal promoter with some others, used them when predicting Roosevelt's reelection in 1936. However, even if they played a role in the history of representative surveys, these "polls," based on the quota technique and used mainly by private firms, were not the ones used by the administrative departments. Without completely disregarding them, opinion polls are therefore not the subject of our study (Converse 1987; Blondiaux 1998; Igo 2007).

The representative sampling that we will focus on here is *random sampling*. On the one hand, it belongs to a subdiscipline of mathematics, the *theory of probability*. Even more specifically, it refers to the theory of sampling and error, which sets the rules for the selection of a subset of the population under consideration, and to the theory of estimation, which enables calculation and correction of the survey results. Let us note that, according to this mathematical definition, random sampling can be applied to any object and not just people. On the other hand, sampling theory makes it possible for random sampling to be concretely implemented. This task includes drawing up a questionnaire, training surveyors, selecting the sample, surveying the sample selected, analyzing the data provided by the questionnaire, and publishing the results. The term "representative sample" understood in this sense has a broader connotation than the term "opinion poll," for the latter is limited to collecting opinions, whereas the representative sampling technique can be applied to many other things, in particular facts, which was precisely the aim of the statistics that we are going to look at (Kruskal and Mosteller 1979a, 1979b, 1979c, 1980).

It is interesting to note that these representative surveys were more recently at the center of heated political debates. In the United States, for example, the Democrats, opposed by the Republicans, wanted to complete the 2000 decennial census using a sample survey of this type to make a more accurate assessment of the number of poor. The Republicans, who considered this procedure unconstitutional, finally prevailed. The discussion centered around the technique that was developed by the American administration during the New Deal, and which is still perfectly valid scientifically. By reviewing its invention we will be able to better understand the present situation and the reasons why it finds itself in the eye of the storm today (Anderson and Fienberg 2000).

Although until this recent controversy, the scientific validity of random sampling had remained unchallenged since the war, random sampling was not instantly adopted by the administration during the 1930s. We will therefore retrace not only the stages of its development and how the method of random sampling was established as sound in the eyes of statisticians, but also how statisticians managed to convince the government of the method's reliability and utility to reflect the nation. In particular, we will look at the concept of *representativity*. It was already well established in the United States, but in the political acceptance of the term—that is, the representativeness of the two houses of Congress (Manin 1997). Imported from democratic theory to statistics, at the end of the period in question representativity came to designate random samples. What we have to understand is how this migration from the political domain to the scientific took place.

The issues that confronted the statisticians, however, largely exceeded the purely technical problem of the elaboration of the tools of measurement; they also had to completely redefine the concept of *population* (Foucault 2007). In statistics, this term denotes the set submitted for examination, which is also the one that the numbers will talk about once they have been generated. If in sampling theory the population can be a cohort of nails or screws, here the population was very often the "United States" or, to use an expression that appeared at the time, "America as a whole." The aim of the investigators was to study America as a whole, but to do this properly an abstract or general definition would not have sufficed. On the contrary, to draw random samples as scientifically as possible, one had to construct what is today called a sample frame—that is to say, a document that enumerates individuals without omission or repetition, in such a way as to select the sample.

Statisticians had to create this frame from scratch. As it happens, a document of this kind did not exist in the United States at the time. Back then, the telephone directory had very few people listed in it to even contemplate using it. There was no other population register (not then and not even now), and the 1930 census, the only tool that came close to it, could not be adapted for this use. We will come back to this point later, but what we can already say is that the census sponsors prided themselves on being able to do an exhaustive count of the population, and the idea of only looking at a sample of it seemed to them at best to indicate amateurism and at worst scientific jugglery, which they refused to be part of (Porter 1986). The investigators had no document that could have served as a sample frame.

Statisticians therefore turned into detectives and anthropologists, searching everywhere for elements that could help them to concretely constitute America as a whole. Humbly, they got down to creating a new base that they could use to portray America. Let us stress the boldness of their gesture: the investigators ignored the remark heard again and again during the Great Depression—namely, that America was too diverse for any general conclusions to be drawn—and they managed to produce documents projecting it "as a whole," incorporating the maize fields situated in the remotest parts of Oklahoma as much as the factories of Chicago, the humidity of the Mississippi bayou as much as the snows of North Dakota, the Hopi Indians of northern New Mexico as much as the New England Congregationalists (Boorstin 1973).

However, the frame alone was not enough to carry out representative surveys. Logistics had to be provided so that investigators could travel to the four corners of the country to ascertain the number of languages spoken and assess the average level of understanding of the population in order to draft questionnaires that were within their grasp, to get an idea of the means of communication in order to centralize all the questionnaires in one place to process statistical data. In short, to conduct the surveys, it was necessary to know a thousand other characteristics of the country without which the experience would fail. In other words, and over and above the problem of the sample frame, although that was essential, the investigators had to reexplore America from top to bottom during the Depression years in order to perfect their technique. We will be observing, as if over their shoulder, how they went about it and the effort they put into the task (Garfinkel 1967; Maynard 2002).

We are going to see through their eyes and hence visit America from a rather singular point of view—an exercise that gives, as we will see, an image that is completely different from the one James Scott (1998) gives with the reduced sight of the state he proposes. Scott's argument is that the state has an interest in natural resources that is very specific and that it needs to create the tools that make these resources legible. In so doing, it simplifies and creates an abstraction of the resource. But then, the state "ignores the vast, complex and negotiated social uses" of these resources (1998,13). It thus sacrifices "local knowledge" for "state administrative routines." Scott explains: "How much easier it then becomes to assess ... property and its owner on the basis of its acreage, its soil class, the crops it normally bears, and its assumed yield, than to untangle the thicket of common property and mixed forms of tenure" (36).

We think that this presentation is true in that the state needs to create the tools that give it a vision on society. But Scott's description is itself a very crude simplification of what the state—and the people—do when they together create tools of reflexivity. We will see that what Scott calls "simplification" appears so only *after* all the massive work that has been done by state officials to establish all these measures of acreage, soil class, and so forth, at the national level. As we will see, immense work is necessary for the state to be able to produce this national information. The state does not simplify; it creates, through a wealth of local arrangements, another measurement, articulated and commensurable to all the others, but, indeed, one compatible with its own interests.

Then we will see that this interest is not necessarily different, nor opposed to and even less imposed on that of the population, as Scott often suggests. On the contrary, the state and the population enter into a constant interaction to define what their relative interests are. And, as symbolic interactionism has shown for a very long time—but only for "members" (as Blumer [1969] used to say) and not for macro actors such as the state—we will see that both the state and the population are redefined in the interaction. The state is not hieratic like the Commander's statue in Molière's Don Juan, but an evolving state that sees with its evolving eyes a population that is also evolving.

The focus on the actual practices of the construction of a reflexive tool also shares Mitchell's interest (2002, 2005) in the construction of a "national economy." But Mitchell's work remains on the abstract level of the discipline of economics. We will see *in concreto* how the national economy has been rebuilt at that time.

Finally, one practical consequence of our interest in the material culture of statistics is that we have added illustrations and photographs of the period to complete and enrich the description provided by the representative surveys.

But while observing how the surveyors observe America, we must keep in mind the purpose of their efforts, which of course was not limited to just a change of scenery, but rather aimed at nothing less than producing an entity that surpassed them completely: America as a whole. We will try and understand how small human beings like them (and us) managed to change the scale and produce one of the most massive aggregates ever possible. To do this, we will follow them step by step, highlight each stage of their work, starting from the beginning of the chain, when they were content to conceive a research subject, then accompany them all along their statistical itinerary—from the conceptual phase of their projects to the publication of the figures, including the relationship between the investigator and the investigated; the processing, tabulation, and analysis of data; and submission of the results to the sponsors—so that we can finally see how they managed to go beyond these microscopic relations to a single unit as macroscopic as America (Latour 1999). Thus, by seeing on the ground how the statisticians concretely produced so imposing an entity, we propose our answer (or, should we say, their answer) to a difficulty encountered by sociology for many years: without breaking the continuity, how does one transition from the local to the global, from microanalysis to macro-sociology, or to "increasing generality" (Boltanski and Thevenot 2006).

But if their technique allowed the interviewers to encapsulate a newly born America, they did it for a specific need that they attributed to their administrative sponsors and to the government. Now the administration was not always prepared to let a technique of this kind make inroads. Therefore, there is another question that arises from the emergence of representative surveys: What transformations did they bring about in the administration so as to carve a place for themselves in it? Or, to say it differently (Lascoumes and Le Galès 2004), how did the administration change so as to adopt them?

Three American administrative units played a particularly important role in the development of representative surveys. The first, chronologically, was the Statistical Office of the Department of Agriculture, founded in 1862, which, during the greater part of the period that interests us, was named the Bureau of Agricultural Economics. Today, agricultural statistics have lost their shine, so we do not realize the importance they once assumed, but until the 1950s or even the 1960s, given the economic weight that this sector still had, this statistical application was one of the most prestigious as well as the most advanced (Ebling 1935; Moulton 1938). The second administrative unit, established at the very beginning of the twentieth century by Carroll D. Wright, a very active philanthropist from New England, was the federal Bureau of Labor Statistics, whose task was to produce data on social conflicts for the Department of Labor (Stapleford 2009). The third was the Census Bureau, which was responsible for conducting and analyzing the decennial census provided under the Constitution. During the whole of the nineteenth century, this bureau was created temporarily every ten years just for this particular task, but in 1902 it was set up permanently and became, during the 1930s, one of the key constituents of the governmental statistical apparatus (Anderson 1988). It was principally—but as we shall see, not only—in these three offices that representative surveys were developed.[1]

Over and above organizational problems, it seems to us that a study of these departments is really of interest only if we extend it to the programs undertaken by them, in order to detect the political effects of the statistical tools opted for (Desrosières 2003). Indeed, we do not believe—and we shall show why—the instruments are transparent in action and the political objectives are independent of the tools employed to achieve them. We shall show that, in this case, the instruments are not simple intermediaries of action but, on the contrary, they have "specific effects independent of the stated objectives and [that] they structure public action according to their peculiar logic" (Lascoumes and Le Galès 2004, 8).

In particular, we will see that representative surveys played an active part in the great turmoil that American democracy went through during the New Deal, the abandonment of the laissez-faire policy, and the introduction of interventionism specific to the welfare state. The initial liberalism was associated with a specific statistical method that was criticized as much as its political counterpart was during the 1930s; at the same time, the emergence of representative surveys accompanied, informed, and confirmed the birth of a new governmental interventionism (Mills 1959; Skocpol and Finegold 1982).

Moreover, the government was not the only one transformed by representative sampling. The situation of the population in the democracy also changed. The old liberal government was bracketed with a popular "participationism," mainly rural—which, as we shall see, had permeated statistical techniques and which today we compare with the *empowerment* of the population. Then, once interventionism and representative surveys became the norm in the various departments, these popular movements became embarrassing for statisticians and politicians, who managed to take advantage of and act on a much more passive population. Representative surveys thus contributed to the birth of *mass democracy* (Igo 2007).

Thanks to the work of scientific legitimization, socio-anthropological exploration, and political articulation,[2] representative surveys became, by the end of the period under consideration, one of the most effective instruments used by the administration to take cognizance of the conditions in which the population was living since the beginning of the crash of 1929. Representative surveys established themselves during the New Deal as one the major tools of America's reflexivity. But in what sense can we talk of reflexivity?

This concept is often understood as if the entity in question—a person, for example, or in our case, America—split itself into two, and one part can be seen while the other part observes its own reflection from a distance, with representative surveys acting as a mirror (Pitkin 1972). The important difference between this model and that which we have outlined in this introduction resides precisely in the distance separating America, which is reflecting itself, from the tool of this reflection. Representative surveys were in no way detached from America; on the contrary, they were a very intimate part of it and constituted one of its components.

In other words, from the outset, reflexivity for us signifies a certain way not of observing an image, but rather of consolidating a great number of initially scattered elements, among which are included the instance of apperception, the entity perceived, as well as the instrument that links them together. As Alain Desrosières has so aptly put it, what counts is to know how to do something that holds together, which has nothing to do with the idea of reflection or a mirror (Desrosières 1998). Reflexivity is not a type of passive contemplation, but an active method of getting a hold on oneself; that is to say, "gathering the pieces." This mechanism is moreover quite similar to the individual experience of reflexivity: he who asks himself who he is feels he has overspread himself and seeks to get a hold on himself in order to forge ahead; if he revels in contemplation, he lapses into narcissism. Hence, reflexivity as it appears to us here refers to the *enhanced consistency* of components scattered by the Great Depression, which, as it happens, covers the whole of America. By clarifying this model of reflexivity as the enhanced consistency of a state, we will try to pinpoint *what America consists of* (Dupréel 1961).

If this book studies statisticians, the procedural arguments on which it is based owe practically nothing to them. We will use only a few tables, figures, enumerations, and quantities. On the contrary, we will present singular facts, portraits of statisticians (including photographic), and unusual events. If quantification depends on the serialization of regularities, its history is made of breakdowns and innovations, which is what we want to show. We will therefore initially focus on the watersheds and the outbreaks rather than on repetitions. It is the history of pioneers, which does not really lend itself to quantification, that we will recount here, and not that of the disseminators.[3]

This book is divided into three thematically and chronologically organized parts. The first presents the American ancestor of representative surveys that was used to make estimates of agricultural production, thereby allowing the administration to conduct an archetypal laissez-faire policy. We will see how these proto-surveys functioned before the crash (chapter 1) and how the Great Depression made them completely obsolete (chapter 2). The second part will show how, at the same time, the government's agricultural statisticians developed the random sampling method. They first worked on the concept of representativeness (chapter 3), then they tried to apply probabilistic formulas to the data they had been collecting over a considerable length of time (chapter 4) before joining forces with a university (chapter 5) to conduct a mammoth representative survey, the Master Sample, which allowed them to project a consistent image of the country (chapter 6). In conformity with a dichotomy that was very active at that time between rural and urban problems, we will leave the countryside to observe in the book's third part how employment experts managed, on the ashes of their old methods (chapter 7), to realize random samples and even surpass their colleagues from the Department of Agriculture. From 1933 onward they launched a great number of very fruitful projects, one of which, the "Trial Census of Unemployment," has been lost, despite the key role it played in the history of representative surveys. Fortunately, we found the archives and are able to include the analysis here. These surveys, where were initially conducted by the victims of the crash themselves (chapter 8), provide reliable measurements on a variety of subjects, including unemployment, and helped to redefine America's relationship with democracy (chapter 9).

Parallel to the chronological presentation, the historical materials analyzed allow us to progressively develop a theory of the consistency of social aggregates whose breakthroughs we highlight at the end of each section.

Part I

The Decomposition of America

In this chronological section, we introduce readers to a method similar to the surveys that carried great weight in the United States in the 1920s. The Department of Agriculture used the method to estimate the total volume of the national agricultural production, and thus it was a crucial socioeconomic indicator. We explain how this method functioned and how solid it appeared in the 1920s—until the Great Depression, which delivered such a serious blow to the country that this fine piece of machinery began to jam. We will examine how this decomposition took place.

1

The America of the Reporters

Up to the Great Depression, an evil figure prowled around America. He could be seen hanging about towns but his choice target was the farmer who, isolated in the midst of his fields, fell for his sales pitch more easily. "You know, Mr. Farmer, this year the yield has been extraordinary in the country. I, who have just come back from neighboring Oklahoma, can tell you that I have never seen the fields so full of corn. The prices unfortunately have slumped. But as I am with you, I am ready to buy yours at 1 cent above the going rate, which this year is 12 cents a bushel." And the deal was struck to the satisfaction of both parties—till the day the farmer went up to town or had a cousin visiting him who said, "Well, business has been good this year, I suppose, with corn at 25 cents a bushel!" And the farmer's face would go slack with shock. This detestable personage was the *speculator* who, not satisfied with tricking farmers and enriching himself by lying, committed a much worse crime: he distorted the market. He played on the information asymmetry caused by the farmers' isolation and, taking advantage of his own connections, rendered the market imperfect. As a result, the government decided to intervene.

The antidote used to combat the speculation fever was statistics. First, it ascertained the total annual yield of the principal cereals in bushels, then the quantity of the other agricultural goods to be sold on a particular date ***t*** and the quantity of those that would be sold at the close of the season (that is, at the end of the period of activity). After this, the series was fleshed out, with data being continuously updated.[1] To counter the ill-effects of speculation, the administration always settled the problem by generating more statistics.

How was this antidote supposed to work? According to Leon Estabrook, chief of the U.S. Department of Agriculture (USDA) statistical bureau during the First World War, the government's objective reports were intended to check the circulation of the false or misleading reports produced by the speculators, whose primary interest was to control and manipulate prices (Estabrook 1915, 8). The administration made the impartial estimates of agricultural yield public and in so doing rendered the speculators' task extremely complicated. The speculators did, of course, continue to manipulate demand (which depended mainly on them), but stage-managing supply became much more difficult. To counter market distortion, the administration realized that *objectivity* was the most effective weapon (Daston and Galison 2010). To make the actual figures of domestic agricultural production public was the most effective means of sanitizing and strengthening the markets (Didier 2005).

How did the administration generate these figures? The question seems quite incongruous today, for numerical information on the United States as a whole now circulates very easily (whether on agriculture or on a thousand other subjects). Numbers proliferate so naturally that we cannot imagine how their construction could pose a problem even if, in general, we do not exactly know how they originate. However, this was not always so. In fact, it was quite the reverse. As late as the end of the First World War, for example, numerical data pertaining to the country as a whole was rare. The statistical techniques that exist today were lacking and data circuits had not yet been centralized. The task was all the more difficult as the area covered was vast: it is not normal for a single standard to apply to tropical Florida and snow-covered Montana, or that actors separated by thousands of miles have to comply with the same rule to produce data and, although living in different time zones, have to send it to Washington, D.C. at the same time. In the beginning of the twentieth century, producing agricultural data several times a year, aggregated to the national level, created many problems.

How did the administration manage to overcome them? To begin with, an agency had to be created to take charge of this operation. Today, this institution is called the National Agricultural Statistical Service (NASS), but it is difficult to say what it was called then, as the agency changed names frequently. In 1917, the name given was the Bureau of Crop Estimates; in 1921 it became the Division of Crop Estimates; in 1922 it was renamed the Division of Markets and Crop Estimates; toward the end of the period we are interested in, it was called the Division of Crop and Livestock Estimates (Taylor and Taylor 1952). In view of this litany of titles, for the purpose of our work we call it simply the "Division." The statistics that concern us were created by the Division.

How did the Division generate the data? To resolve this question, our only way out was to consult its archives, for no specialist on the history or sociology of statistics has considered how statisticians operating at the beginning of the century concretely produced the first national statistics! The archives were a massive jumble of documents. We had before us dozens of cartons, in-house notes, letters, drafts, questionnaires, lists of names, pay slips, rulers, tables of numbers, soil samples, mathematical formulas, and what have you. Everything had been kept.[2] The most striking characteristic of this mountain of archives was its diversity. It made us wonder how items so different in nature had been combined to constitute a single and unique entity, the number. Who does not remember the lessons learned in childhood that said we cannot add pears and apples? To our eternal surprise, the administrative machinery responsible for these calculations used not only pears and apples, but also melons, pineapples, mangoes, and loquats, and even, if we are allowed to spin out the culinary metaphor, included roasts, fattened pullets, spices, the last dregs of sauces, as well casseroles and stoves. As paradoxical as it may seem at first glance, the creation of homogenous numbers (for example, the overall quantity of wheat produced by the United States at a given date) boiled down to amalgamating a multitude of perfectly heterogeneous elements.

To understand this operation, we will start from the time when everything constituted a challenge for statistics and we will advance step by step toward the construction of the final figure (Latour 1999, chap. 2). We will observe how the farmer filled out his questionnaire; we will see who questioned him and how this person classified the questionnaires of all those who replied, how and to whom communications were handled, and so on, until we arrive at the result of this long chain of production: the numbers describing the whole of American agriculture. We will discover in the greatest of detail, on a human scale we could say, the aggregation methods used by agricultural statistics in the time of laissez-faire and, through it, what America was at that time.

The Plasma

To understand the process by which statistics finally managed to generate figures, it helps to ask when this first occurred. At what point did a statistical act take place? Was it when the statistician learned the theory at school? When during breakfast he reflected on unsolved problems encountered the day before? When he took up his pen to do his first calculations? All these answers have some justification and are of some interest. To avoid a long discussion we will peremptorily impose, as in fiction, the stage at which statistics began. This stage we will call plasma.

This name comes from the Greek verb *plassô*, which originally designated Prometheus's task of sculpting man and Hephaïstos's act of creating Pandora with wet clay (Cassin 1995). The linguistic root of plasma is a verb whose meaning denotes "modeling." Substantively, plasma is the raw material that the person modeling and shaping has in hand—which makes the activity of conformation possible. It is something that has its own specific characteristics, insofar as it presents itself for shaping and modifying.

Plasma is what is available to statisticians when they want to initiate something but have not yet started.

The plasma is something that is open to human manipulation; apart from statisticians, others have manipulated it, but the manipulation that it has undergone is not statistics. Thus, a sheet of paper is produced by diverse operators—from the woodcutter to the papermaker—and it has its own specific characteristics (it is perhaps white or cream, A4 or U.S. Letter in size, etc.), but as long the question of printing a questionnaire on it does not arise, we consider that this sheet is plasma. It ceases to be plasma once it becomes part of a statistical project. The plasma is the entire panoply of elements available to the Division or to one of its representatives when it decides to transform them into statistics. It is the realm of suspicion—that is, those elements that interest the Division because it suspects that they will be interesting to transform into statistics, but which still elude it (Didier 2000, 174–178; Latour 2012).

Lists

After having worked in the regional meteorology offices of the Department of Agriculture, Verne H. Church (figure 1.1) was hired by the Division in the winter of 1913. He was asked to survey the state of Michigan and, excited by this new challenge, he immediately set out to explore the countryside, seeking direct contact with the area under his charge. This is how the plasma appeared to this novice:

> In keeping with my instructions, I then shut my office and left for one week's excursion in the country. My apprenticeship was both painful and disappointing. Thanks to the directories and a personal survey, I located the grain, fruit and vegetable marketers. I found that some were cooperative while others were not. Most criticized statistical results and methods. Because of my lack of experience and sketchy knowledge of the subject, I did

1.1 Verne H. Church. One of the first agricultural state Statisticians, he was the son of a farmer and had been a journalist and a meteorologist before. (Wager family)

> not have the results in my head and very few in my brief case. I found that the greater part of the criticism was levelled against State statistics, which at that time I didn't know much about. Those who were satisfied with the reports published by the State thought that the federal invasion of the countryside was a waste of effort and expenditure. Approximately one-third or one-half among them were agricultural county agents; some were friendly and helped me; others were sceptic, critical and antagonistic. The farmers in general knew practically nothing about the service and were inclined to be sceptic about its usefulness. The first few weeks of roaming around was the only period during which I had regrets about leaving the meteorological service (Church 1944, 120).[3]

The initial experience of this statistician was very disappointing—he left full of enthusiasm but met mostly unhelpful interlocutors. Church discovered that most farmers were highly critical of agricultural statistics. However, he soon realized that they were confusing them with the statistics produced by the state of Michigan, which were completely independent at the time from federal statistics, which Church was then heading. He was treated as an outcast. When by chance he came across a rare attentive ear and managed to make clear that he did not work for the Michigan statistics bureau but for the federal administration, the reaction was just as demoralizing. The standard reproach against him, which each federal census had to put up with since the very beginning, was that he was the federal goverment's stooge sent to colonize the last spaces of freedom that the Great Plains still represented. In short, Church's joy of being hired by the Division quickly evaporated because of the frosty welcome that the farmers gave him. And the shock was all the more great as he couldn't figure out how he could improve relations. He produced statistics, but statistics did not appear to be popular.

The way out of this embarrassing situation was a list—a simple list of names. Indeed, rather than weaken the morale of its agents, the Division began to retain the names of its interlocutors who, once they understood the purpose of its questions, agreed to answer them regularly. All that was needed was to convince them just once of the utility of the approach. Recruitment was never easy: "Making long lists of addresses was quite difficult and progress slow" (Church 1944, 9). But occasionally he succeeded. Thus, each time a survey was initiated the Division posted a questionnaire to the farmers figuring on the list, always the same ones, and asked them to complete it and return it within the given time. These interlocutors the Division called *voluntary crop reporters*, because they were like agricultural information volunteers; we call them "Reporters," because they corresponded with the Division by post.[4]

As they were a rare commodity, the Division turned them into loyal allies and tried to forge as lasting a link as possible with them. It used to send them, for example, *Crops and Markets*, a weekly in which the survey results were published. It also sent them guidelines for filling the questionnaires and for using the published figures, and even Christmas greetings at the end of each year! In short, the Division made efforts to remain in close and enduring contact with its sympathetic interlocutors.[5]

But was any person who was willing to cooperate a suitable choice? Apart from willingness, were there any other selection criteria that the Division considered necessary? It seems that two additional directives guided the choice of Reporters. First, the Division chose farmers that it considered intellectually superior. What was the reason for this elitism? Because, unlike the representative surveys of today, the Reporters' task was not to share their feelings or their experience, but to inform the Division about the state of agriculture on the ground in the entire neighborhood. "Their figures were based on their personal knowledge and investigation"[6] and had to "encompass their whole neighborhood and not just their own crops, for their individual yield depended on their ability to farm well or badly" (Taylor and Taylor 1952, 177). In other words, the Reporter had to conduct a personal investigation, observe neighboring agriculture, not be influenced by their personal results (which could differ from those of others), and only after this work had been accomplished, send a memorandum to the Division on the growth condition of the crops. As Reporters were a rarity, they were asked to provide information that was as precise and as broad-based as possible, which required excellent analytical ability.

Let us remember that cognitive elitism is necessarily accompanied by moral elitism. In fact, once the Division entrusted the surveys to its new recruits, it also assumed that they would not misinform. Hence the Division described its Reporters as "intelligent and reliable" and dispensed with the misleading answers "of ignoramuses and those who were worried that truth would lead to higher taxes." The Reporters were as much investigators as investigated. Extremely active, they inspected the land with all their cognitive and moral faculties to transform it into figures. The Reporters "knew" in the place of others, and they were "known for their intelligence and their discernment" (Taylor and Taylor 1952, 186).

Second, they were chosen so that there would be roughly one Reporter per township: "The list [of Reporters] was started in 1896 and contained mainly farmers, the aim being that each township would be represented by at least one Reporter" (Church 1944, 7). The objective was more or less achieved. In 1926, for example, this list contained nothing less than 40,000 names (USDA 1933, 4), which was much more than the number of rural townships. The selection mechanism was thus to find at least one voluntary and impartial representative for each item, which when combined formed the totality.

The first elements that the Division extracted from the plasma to forge America were these people, the Reporters—foreshadowing today's survey respondents—who little by little learned to transform the plasma into statistics. But under what form did they send their observations?

Questioning

To understand how the Division interrogated its Reporters, let us look at the surveys on grain crops, which were the first to be conducted and remained the most important (the most strategic) of all. This example does not of course cover all the questionnaires used. We can easily understand that questions valid for wheat cannot be applied to pigs. However, for more clarity, we prefer to take up an emblematic case rather than a multitude of examples. In the case of surveys on grain crops, therefore, the questions addressed the area farmed and the yield per acre which, when multiplied together, gave the quantity produced. The problem was how to formulate the questions so that the Reporters could understand them.

To estimate the acreage under cultivation, from the outset the Division faced one difficulty that was—dare we use the word—anthropological in nature. In fact, with the help of a certain number of studies that it claimed to have conducted on people in general, the Division had come to the conclusion that it was difficult to estimate absolute values, whereas it was easier to estimate percentages.[7] In other words, when asked for an estimate of the number of acres (which was the agricultural unit in use) under wheat cultivation, the Reporter tended to give a somewhat inaccurate answer, whereas if asked to reply by comparing his observations with other observations, the response was much more precise. Consequently, with reference to a specific crop, the Division decided to ask the Reporter to compare the area under cultivation in the current year with the previous one and to give the answer in the form of a percentage. For example, the answer typically might be that 80% of the acreage under wheat last year is also being sown with wheat this year. Thus, by its manner of formulating the questions, the Division was able to help its Reporter to answer in the best way possible. True, this implied that it had to find a method to transform the percentage variations into absolute values, and we will see when the time comes how it went about doing this. In this way, the Division ensured accurate estimates of the area assigned annually to each crop.

What about the yield per acre? How did the Division go about estimating it? It used a variable, rather surprising from today's point of view, called the growth condition of plants. This condition was taken as the productivity indicator of one acre. For example, if the weather had been very good during the whole season and the farmers had enough reserves of water for their crops, one acre could be said to have been farmed under good conditions and therefore presumably would have given a good yield. On the contrary, if conditions were bad, so too the yield. The condition thus gave an indication of the productivity of the soil.

Like the area, and in conformity with the research already mentioned, yield per acre (the parlance of the division abbreviated it into the simpler word "yield") also had to be expressed in terms of percentage change, but instead of the area, the denominator of the current year condition was not the same as that of the previous year. The condition observed was the percentage of the normal condition of growth of the crops. This concept of "normal condition" was very problematic and gave rise to numerous justifications, explanations, and criticisms, even as it was used. Let us for a moment focus on the definition as given in the questionnaires received by the Reporter.

> 1 - The condition of the crops on the date indicated for mailing the schedule is not a comparison with a condition at any former period, but with a normal condition of growth and vitality such as would be expected at this time in a crop starting out under favorable condition and not subjected afterwards to unfavorable weather, insects pests or other injurious agencies. If condition is asked for any crop that has already been harvested, give condition at time of harvest.
> 2 - In estimating condition of crops in comparison with a normal condition of growth and vitality giving promise of full yield per acre, 100 is the basis; if nine-tenth of a (normal) yield per acre are indicated by the present condition, the answer should be filled in as 90; if one-tenth, or 10 per cent, more [than] a normal yield per acre is indicated, the answer should be reported as 110, etc.[8]

The normal condition was therefore the growth condition of a plant that had not suffered from any harmful external causes; it was the growth condition by which the plant had escaped from all parasites, weather conditions had been good, and the farmer had provided the best care possible, so that it had achieved maximum yield. If the Reporters had observed these conditions—that is, when the crops had not been subjected to any stress—they had to indicate that the condition had been 100% normal. Inversely, however, the normal condition was not the optimal condition either. Indeed, it could happen that conditions, the weather in particular, had been exceptionally good and the yield had exceeded all expectations. In this case, it could not be said that the condition was normal, as it had been exceptional, and the Reporters then had to indicate a condition superior to 100%. Hence, the normal condition was when the crop had grown without experiencing any luck or bad luck.

In contrast to acreage, the growth condition was not compared with the past but with an extratemporal norm. This characteristic constituted an additional difficulty, for it meant preventing the Reporters from automatically taking the exceptional years as normal (this was a normal tendency as their exceptionality made them memorable) and instead explaining the type of data that the Division possessed if it wanted to switch from variations to absolute values. We will revert to the problem of evaluating the norm itself later. Be that as it may, the information that the Reporter sent to the Division was thus of two kinds of percentages: one, the percentage of the area farmed in comparison to the previous year, and two, the percentage of the growth condition as compared to the normal condition.

To conclude this sequence, let us stress that these two indicators resulted from the composition of a great number of elements. Which ones? Among others, there was the "theory" by which the Reporter was better able to estimate percentages in contrast to absolute values; the limits of townships that enabled the distribution of the informers in a homogenous manner; the mountains of letters on which the Division tried to establish a relationship of trust with its Reporters; and the strange norm called "normal condition" of crop growth. Before the survey, all these elements were separate; they were not necessarily linked. The survey established the list of Reporters, dispatched questionnaires to them, wrote out and transmitted the instructions; the Reporter conducted his own inquiry and translated his observations into figures (see figure 1.2). The survey extracted all these elements from the plasma and then reorganized them and reconstituted them into one little number recorded by the Reporter in the box intended for this purpose. The number contained and summarized this multitude statistically and gave a texture—still incomplete—to what America would become at the end of the process. However, at this stage, it was just a minuscule element, only valid for a ridiculously small area. After this it would change scale and

1.2 A farmer filling out a schedule. In this picture, the Division wanted to portray the seriousness (the farmer wears glasses) and the cleanliness (the white cloth) required for the job. (U.S. Department of Agriculture-National Agricultural Statistical Service [hereafter USDA-NASS] Archives of Richard Allen)

become part of a bigger entity, which is the reason the Reporter[9] had to send the questionnaires by post to the statistical head of their state, who received many of them. Let us now see the fate reserved for them.

Touring on the Job

An official from the Department of Agriculture, the agricultural Statistician, whose one representative we have already encountered in the person of Church, received the questionnaires.[10] He was responsible for the figures generated in one of the states of the Union.[11] His task was to prepare reports on the agriculture of his state based on data that the Reporters had communicated to him. For this, he had to gather detailed knowledge of his territory while traveling through it, talking to farmers, and going to fairs. This personal knowledge helped him to interpret and study the percentages passed on by the Reporters in the most constructive way possible. Hence, the initial processing of the questionnaires, paradoxically, consisted of setting them aside while he went out to survey the land directly. Before taking up the questionnaires again, let us first see how these field surveys took place. As we have already seen through Church's example, accumulating detailed knowledge of the terrain was not easy. Let us review some of the additional difficulties that he encountered and see how he resolved them.

First and foremost, knowledge of the terrain necessitated great mobility, and in fact, it appears that this was one of chief attractions of the profession. This explains why Church chose to become a Statistician in 1913:

> During the following winter my health again deteriorated and I decided that I would have to change to an occupation that would take me outside of the office. While debating my future course of action I read an announcement of a civil service examination for field work in the bureau of statistics. I immediately sent a letter to the chief, Leon M. Estabrook. (Church 1944, 5)

Before working with numbers, the most obvious characteristic of the profession of Statistician was that it "would take [him] out of his office" and "to the field." However, if these trips were attractive, they posed a thousand difficulties. The first constraint was that the means of transport were often nonexistent in the 1910s.

> To interview farmers and inspect crops, it was necessary to use horse and automobile liveries for trips into the country. Because the cost of this type of transportation was usually based on distance and time, interviews had to be brief, and the return trip often made over the same route as the outgoing one. Travelling salesmen with privately owned cars were covering much more ground, accomplishing far more work, and at a less cost than I was doing. (Church 1944, 19)

Like the sales representative, the Statistician needed to increase his mobility by getting a car, but it was not easy to obtain the necessary funds.

The second constraint was the administrative boundary of the terrain, which complicated the Statistician's task further.

> The topography and shape of the State were not conducive to efficient operations as it stretched 700 miles from east to west, but averaged less than a third of that north and south. The road system radiated out from Louisville with few [intersecting] roads, making cross state travel a round about, time-consuming, jaunt. Secondary and tertiary roads were simply old buggy pikes that wound around ridges to avoid creeks and rivers and had been plastered over with macadam, or laid with a veneer of gravel. Very little grading had been done and the winding, hilly, high crowned, "hog-backed" roads were dangerous to drive, especially in wet weather, and made for slow travel at any time. (Brooks 1977, 29)

Even if the Statistician had a car, the shape of the state of Kentucky was not conducive to traveling and the infrastructure was poor, which further complicated his movements. Local roads and highways were very far from being tarred and suffered from mudholes and the horse liveries ruts. What is more, it was not until 1926 that the federal system of numbering highways was formally adopted—before then, maps were rare and often reduced to simple trail route books that were extremely misleading (Akerman 1993).

These difficulties, however, made it possible to understand how surveys should ideally proceed: The Statistician had to do long interviews and travel over many roads to inspect different crops. For this, he could mobilize several resources (some examples follow). First, he made use of of an instrument essential for his work: a districting of the territory (see figure 1.3).

In 1932, G. D. Clarck, agricultural Statistician for Texas, describes how he used it for his work:

> In many counties in the State there are well informed men at each shipping point who can give reasonably accurate information as to vegetable acreages in their own locality and often for their entire county. It is possible for a crop estimator to call upon many of these men.[12]

Territorial divisions were useful on two counts: with smaller and smaller subdivisions (the state, then the county, and last, the shipping points), it was possible to identify people who could, first, give accurate information and, second, format the information supplied ("the condition of tomatoes was 100% in my neighborhood/in my county"), which was all the better as the information pertained to vast stretches (the divisions being moreover presented according to increasing size). The Statistician could thus zoom in on "well-informed men," then collect "accurate information" from them.

The county, the key geographical division of this example, seemed more effective when it was used for identifying rather than for formatting. The identifying part is affirmative, whereas the formatting is less so. Terms such as "reasonably" or "often" are used. The reason is that shipping points

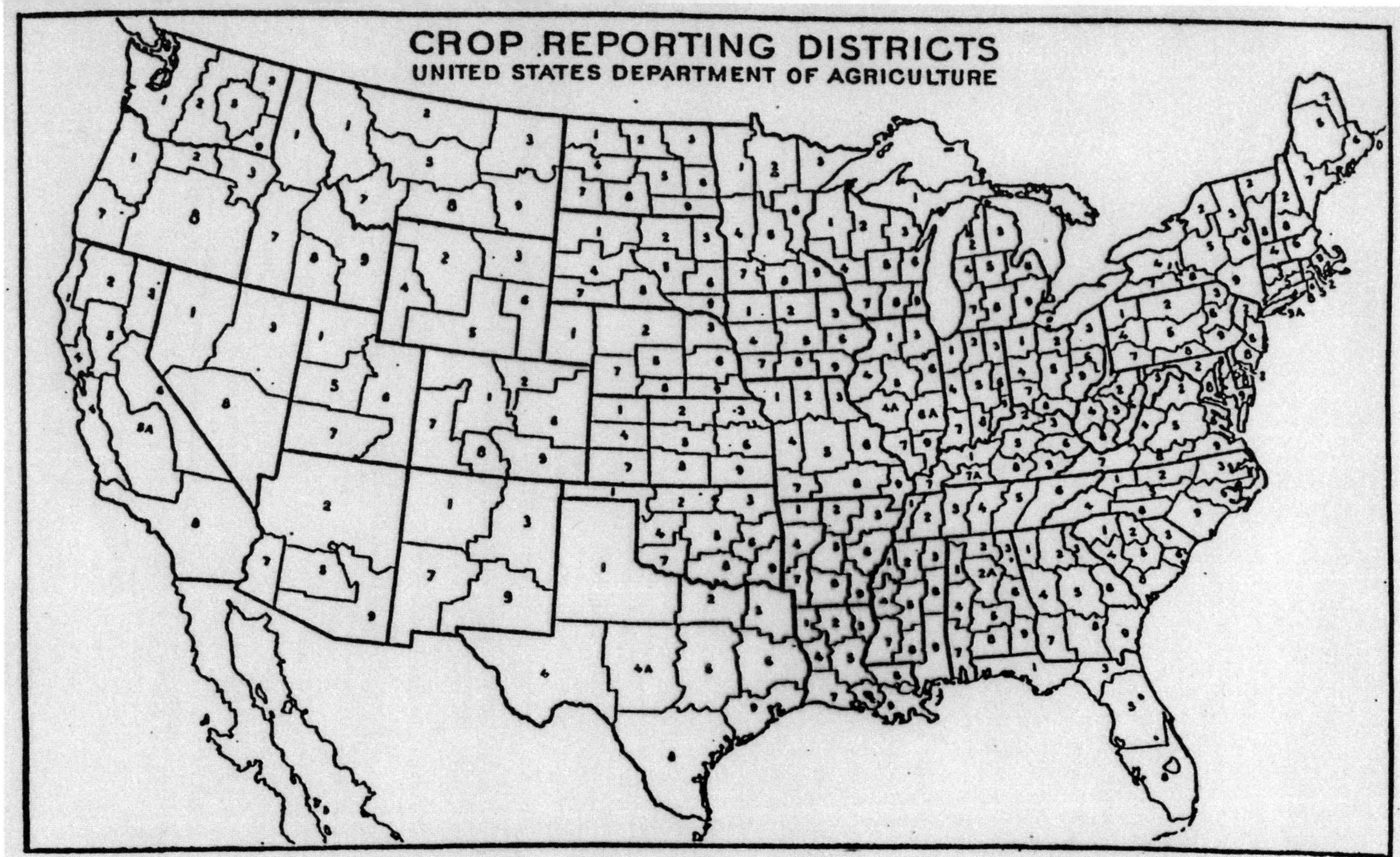

1.3 Map of the crop reporting districts of the U.S. Department of Agriculture. It is a transformation of the U.S. Post Office Department's map of the rural mail carrier routes. (USDA 1933)

were administratively identified by the county, whereas the Reporters' judgment on agriculture had no reason to mold itself to these administrative boundaries. This is the reason why there also existed divisions that made sense only to the Statistician. Let us mention, in particular, the "crop reporting districts" that E. M. Brooks, for example, used in Iowa during his job as "junior" Statistician under the supervision of the state Statistician, Leslie M. Carl.

> In fact, there was a total of nine [corn-hog juniors]—one for each of the crop reporting districts into which, for statistical purposes, the state had been divided on the basis of agricultural and geographical homogeneity. (Brooks 1977, 13)

Here, too, the Statistician started from the limits imposed by the boundaries of his state's districting. But this time, the partition was specific to agricultural statistics: it depended on the "homogeneity" observed in "agricultural yields." The advantage was that, as each district was homogenous, any information pertaining to a given crop was valid for the entire zone.

The Statistician used certain preexisting divisions coming from different spheres of activity and created others for his own use. The advantage, in the first case, was that the division could be easily imported; in the second case, its product was directly usable. To combine these two advantages, the Statistician sometimes constructed hybrid divisions. For example, this is how G. D. Clarck positioned the production of tomatoes in Texas: "There were about sixty counties in Texas that produced a commercial crop of tomatoes in 1931. These counties were distributed over approximately one-third of the state extending from the Oklahoma state line to the Mexican border."[13]

The "tomato farming zone" was demarcated on the basis of the counties, which were initially outside the reach of statistics but were distributed in such a way that the zone lent itself to statistics. Moreover, Clarck clarifies: "Consider then that the tomato crop is only one of nearly twenty vegetable crops covered by the crop reporting service in Texas."[14] This example was not exceptional; the Statistician created a plethora of such hybrid divisions to transform the plasma into statistics.

Apart from the divisions, another very important resource for surveys by agricultural Statisticians was what they called "area confabs." What was this about? Let Verne Church explain: "Bryant, Cochran and I immediately agreed that we could meet together occasionally near the common boundary of our three states, not only to collect information at that point, but to exchange ideas and experiences concerning the work and the problems involved" (Church 1944, 11).

Brooks explains that this experience "inaugurated the practice of Area Confabs where Stats in adjoining or nearby states, get together once a year or so at a convenient time and place to mull over their difficulties, check on the 'grapevine' and get better acquainted" (Brooks 1977, 43). For the Statisticians, the "area confab" was an opportunity to rise above their usual task and share their experiences and synthesize their methods. It was an opportunity given to officials to reflect on the matters at hand.

Lastly, equipped with all these resources, the Statistician directly questioned the farmers he had managed to identify. These interactions, that were generally quite friendly, could also turn out to be incredibly complex. One example we have is narrated by Church. He talks of a survey on the quantity of potatoes that would be put on the market. It was a difficult exercise involving a cash crop—that is, a product grown in order to bring some hard cash to farmers (as opposed, for example, to corn for feeding pigs) and therefore very susceptible to market prices: "Most farmers felt the estimates influenced the market prices, which made them reluctant to give unbiased information" (Church 1944, 223). Despite the difficulty, Church went as usual to Greenville, the capital of Montcalm County, where he had discovered a farmers cooperative and three wholesalers, of whom the most important was Sam Metzger. Following is a brief description of his interaction with Metzger:

> While he pretended to be co-operative in supplying information to me, his talk was mostly generalities about the potato

> situation and the big things he was doing in a business way. The real information I was seeking, he carefully concealed, or it was suspiciously unreliable. I always called on him merely to satisfy his egotism and minimize his criticism of our estimates, although I obtained my best information from the other Greenville dealers. (Church 1944, 223)

Church and Metzger thus found themselves in a very complex situation where they talked to each other each time they met, but to lie all the better, both indulged in half-truths and manipulation. Church knew that Metzger "concealed" pertinent information, but he listened to him nevertheless, not for what he said to him, but to defuse in advance his interlocutor's criticism (insofar as the latter had participated in the production of the final figure, he could not say that it was bogus, unless he confessed that he had lied). Inversely, Metzger cooperated because he knew that if he did not meet Church, he had no way of influencing the numbers that the latter would produce. For the Statistician, learning about agriculture required mastery of manipulation as well as agronomy!

But if the purpose of this in-depth knowledge was initially to enable a judicious interpretation of the questionnaires, it also led to genuine agricultural discoveries for the Statisticians, and sometimes showed that elements globally neglected by the institution could be crucial. Before going back to the questionnaires, here is an example of a case in point.

Proposing

By constantly crisscrossing the state of Michigan, Church realized that a crop hitherto ignored by the questionnaires held an important place in local agriculture: the pickle. No doubt, just the name of this vegetable is enough to raise a laugh. Moreover, its ranking in the vegetable hierarchy is not very high, but do these reasons justify our ignoring it? Was the poor pickle so contemptible that it was not worth considering statistically? This is what the questionnaires distributed by the Division seemed to suggest, as they never mentioned the crop. Nevertheless, the Michigan farmers disagreed with this view, and went on planting pickles. Church ended by taking the farmers' side and put in a great deal of effort to give the pickle "numerical recognition." Let us see how an entity was created through statistics:

> During my early travels I also noted the large number of towns and villages, particularly in the central and northern parts of the state, that had a pickle-station. I began making inquiries of managers of plants which maintained one or more offices within the State. Some of them supplied me with acreage and production data on pickles for pickles; others referred me to their head offices in other states. I wrote to a few of the larger ones and obtained the data I asked for, but there were many lesser companies and I needed a circular letter and questionnaires, for which I had no printing facilities. Michigan produces the bulk of the nation's salt requirements, and I happened to meet a salesman for one of the salt companies in the course of my travels who supplied me with a complete list of pickle manufacturers.
>
> I prepared a circular letter together with the questions concerning needed data, sent them to Washington, and asked that 50 or 60 copies be mimeographed. The reply I received from Washington was to the effect that the crop was considered too minor to bother with. This embarrassed me considerably as I had promised the firms contacted that I would supply them with a report of my findings. I immediately wrote to Washington again, outlined what I had done, the promises I had made, and stated that I had already collected 25,000 acres. I pointed out that, unless the survey was completed, I had wasted considerable time, and I dropped the hint that I would like to know how many acres were required to give a crop recognition. I then concluded the letter with: "Please forward the letters and blanks as previously requested."

> They arrived within a few days and within a short time the survey was completed. I showed that the State raised 40,000 acres for pickles that year, more than any other state, more than all other states combined, as determined the following year from a Nation-wide survey instituted by the Washington office. (Church 1944, 12)

Thus, Church confirmed that the Statistician's work consisted of touring the area to gather information. In the course of his peregrinations, he remarked that the pickle appeared to be an important crop, although it had been ignored by the Division. He then tried to legitimize the existence of this new entity—the "countable" pickle. This demonstration took place in three successive stages: he first undertook a preliminary survey, then he reverted to Washington, and finally he carried out the survey.

During the preliminary survey, he "came into contact" with the pickle of his state in all its various avatars: observations of towns and villages, letters to managers, chance meetings (his travels resulted in providential encounters—luck or something like that seems to have played an important role in his work). Each of his contacts sent him a thousand and one details on pickles in all their forms: "data on the acreage under cultivation and the quantity produced" and the "complete list of factories." He therefore had the plasma he needed to work on, but the elements were very dissimilar and made computing impossible.

At this stage, the state of Michigan for all intents and purposes did not exist. As Church was looking for contacts capable of sending him pickles in all their manifestations, he wanted exact locations, firms, and salt vendors, everything that could help him centralize the information on pickles. It was not important whether the informers were from his state. If they were listed, they became relevant. Michigan too subsisted, as Church continued to visit the "towns and villages … of the State," to seek managers who had "at least one office in the State," and when a "head office" was "in another State," he thought it merited a mention. Even in the negative, the boundaries of Michigan still counted. Michigan was less visible because of the fact that Church restricted himself to collecting worthwhile interlocutors, but it subsisted as the geographical limits of a whole, whether or not it contained these factors. The geographical picture outlined here is that of a whole containing inherently diverse objects.

The second part of Church's survey includes the points already mentioned, in particular the "firms," and Washington. What was happening in Washington? Why did he need to revert to it? The answer is that Washington had a duplicating machine. After the word "mimeograph" in his account, follow the words "crop," "survey," and "acres." Being able to make an identical reproduction of the questionnaire made it possible to change the vocabulary, to switch from the diversity of the plasma to statistics and its stable categories. In Washington, the questionnaires could be duplicated, and in large numbers, making statistics possible. Identical reproduction was thus the first stage, following which one could talk of statistics.

However, there was disagreement between Washington and the Statistician on expenditure. Washington considered that because it involved a "minor" crop, the resources employed were not worth it, whereas Church insisted on the fact that, at this stage, not to complete the survey would be still more onerous. To resolve this dispute, Church used the arguments that he had at his disposal by advancing that he had counted "already 25,000 acres" under pickle cultivation in Michigan, and therefore it was an important crop. He needed mimeographed copies to be able to improve on his approximate assessment in order to "complete the survey"—that is, expunge the "already" in the expression "already 25,000 acres." Washington was the place where the Reporters were *standardized*, thanks to the duplicating machine. But this standardization involved expenditure, and negotiation was needed for the advantages to be greater than the costs—in other words, for the state to finally emerge (Maynard 2002).

This extract from Church's recollections describes the genesis of an agricultural survey, at the end of which the plasma was transformed into statistics. Three phases followed in succession: The first involved visiting the region and determining what was important and what was not among the elements available; the second, the expertise phase, was a discussion with Washington aimed at standardization; the third phase entailed carrying out the survey, which we have merely touched on until now. In the course of these three stages, a multitude of elements, such as the pickle-stations, letters, the list of growers, the mimeograph machine in Washington, and so on, were regrouped in a specific manner and described by Church, which consisted of *listing the informers in order to have all of them fill the same questionnaire*. We can now understand how each word in this sentence is indicative of highly innovative and industrious work on Church's part: "listing" signifies the chance of coming across a promising interlocutor in a train; "informer" refers to meeting people, who are naturally reticent, and winning their trust; "questionnaire" implies drafting a letter of introduction and asking pertinent questions; "the same" denotes an ongoing debate with Washington.

By incorporating all the elements, he delivered a new entity, the Michigan-Pickle, which now became a "countable" plant, occupying a certain space and officially recognized as compared to the other pickle, which was many things but not the Michigan-Pickle. The survey, so to speak, added another characteristic to the original pickle—the quality of being countable and thereby earning its rightful place in the America that was taking shape. But to really understand how, we have to examine the last stage in greater detail. This is the stage that took place after the Statistician had scoured his state and familiarized himself with its agriculture. What treatment did he then reserve for the questionnaires?

Editing

Exhausted by his travels, the Statistician returned to his office at last. His first task was to sort out the questionnaires that had piled up in his absence. To preserve hundreds of loose sheets without letting disorder, and its correlate—error—reign was not a trivial task! The solution was to secure some ordinary envelopes in which he could keep the questionnaires on the various ongoing surveys (one file for wheat, one for corn, one for pigs, etc.).

Once the last date for the fact-gathering phase had passed, the task of processing the questionnaires could commence. He then opened the envelope and what did he systematically discover? That many of the Reporter had made obvious mistakes! What could he do about these errors? How could he fix them? Editing helped to repair the damage.

In some cases, editing was carried out directly on the questionnaire to correct the most obvious mistakes made by the Reporter. A typical error was to confuse the boxes meant for cattle with the ones for grains (heads of cattle were not written down as a percentage but counted) and consequently record figures much greater than 100 in those boxes where, normally, this was impossible. When the error was identifiable, editing consisted of transferring the information to the appropriate boxes.

In other cases, editing often involved eliminating some questionnaires from the calculations. This is how Leslie Carl, the Iowa Statistician, described it during a survey in March 1932 on falling land prices. In this example, he calls both the questionnaires he received from the Reporters and the document produced by him on the basis of the questionnaires the "reports."

> Reports were made in two ways: (a) as given by the reporters and (b) editing out all decreases of 35 per cent or more. Of the 128 reports edited because of showing 35 or more per cent decrease, the frequency is as follows:
>
> 35 per cent .... 17 reports
> 40 " " .... 41 "
> 45 " " .... 2 "
> 50 " " .... 68 "
>
> ... This elimination brought about a net decrease of 19.0% of the land value. This is an improvement for now its level is

> comparable with the 15.6% decrease indicated by 426 pairs of reports and it is also comparable to the direct comparison of the values of this year with those of the previous year.[15]

The edited questionnaires (i.e., the eliminated ones) were those in which the variations, considered too extreme, exceeded 35%. Carl did not offer a justification for choosing this percentage, but he decided to disregard the questionnaires that exceeded it. This operation allowed him to "bring into line" the results obtained with those of the previous year. Or, to put it more simply, the decrease, which became 19% after the elimination of some questionnaires, was comparable, on the one hand, with the 15.6% obtained from the "paired reports"—that is to say, with the reports of the Reporters who had replied for two consecutive years and which the Statistician had collated two by two—and on the other, with the aggregated results of the previous year. The figure obtained after editing was thus "aligned" with the earlier results.

Editing had the advantage of rendering a survey compatible with the totality of the results already produced, among which it came to take its place. It also had one enormous drawback. Selectively eliminating questionnaires implied lack of faith in the authenticity of the information provided by those who had filled them. However, as the Reporters were in fact the Division's principal informers, it seemed highly paradoxical to disqualify them. On what logical basis did the Statisticians choose to doubt their faithful informers rather than disregard the data from the preceding year? Why not simply believe the Reporters and deduce that the growth condition had varied enormously from one year to the next? How was this elimination justified?

Here is an example of the measure of variability of the condition:

> In our editing out of extreme reports, it is possible to rely on first hand knowledge of local condition. Extreme reports which other information does not substantiate, are brought into line or rejected. We do not feel warranted in accepting extreme

> reports which first hand knowledge of local conditions would discount.[16]

The exclusion of some questionnaires was not arbitrary; it depended on "firsthand information"—that is, the personal observations made by the Statistician while touring his territory.

We must however point out that the Statistician did not always go by his own gut feeling but preferred to give priority to the assessments made by the Reporters when they differed from his. Sometimes, when he had certain reservations about the information given him, he was inclined to disregard it but nevertheless decided to trust their choice rather than his own. C. J. West, the Ohio Statistician in 1923, gives us an example of this type of dilemma. In the following report, he informed the Division that the number of breeding sows was the same as the previous year:

> Should data from other sources suggest raising this figure, I should recommend that you give weight to that data. I have carefully weighted my material so that I am certain the figure I am submitting reflects Field Aid's ideas. On the basis of personal observation, I am inclined to the view that there has been a slight increase over last year but the strength of my conviction is not sufficient to warrant a change in Field Aids' average. It is possible that Field Aids are influenced by the lack of enthusiasm among farmers for an increase, tho [*sic*] this dying down of enthusiasm may be an argument in favor of estimating the number the same as a year ago. When enthusiasm among farmers ceases there is a tendency for them to conduct their operations on about the same scale from one year to the next.[17]

According to his initial opinion (as well as information from "other possible sources" that the Division may have received), West could have increased the figure slightly compared to the preceding year. But here he felt that his own judgment had to give way to the "average recorded by the Field Aids," which was the same as the previous year. Why? In the name of what we may term "social theory," which is contained in the last two lines quoted: According to West, the farmers carried on as in the previous year when they were short on enthusiasm. Being pessimistic, they tend not to be innovative and repeat their decisions of the preceding year. Now, according to him, the Reporters seemed to have effectively shown less enthusiasm this year. As a result, West recommended that this theory and the Reporters' response be given priority.

Thus, contrary to what is often believed, statistical work is not governed solely by mechanical rules and procedures. Editing, which was an essential step, is one example. In fact, the data was nearly always self-contradictory. As a result, the Statistician had no other option but to do a personal nonstandardized evaluation aimed at tallying the data as best he could. This evaluation consisted of asking which data could be eliminated, and after that reorganizing the remainder of the data into a *coherent* whole that contained the *maximum number of elements*. To try to include more agricultural data (personal knowledge accumulated by the Statistician, some theories on the farmers, etc.), Carl, the Iowa Statistician, first sought to incorporate contradictory data the same way West, the Ohio Statistician, did, but in such a way as to sacrifice as little as possible. Editing was a delicate operation that *had to be carried out* (mutually exclusive information could not be retained), but it deprived the Statistician of all his anchor points (all sources of information could be called into question). Hence, it was necessarily left to the *discretion* of the Statistician.

Adding

Once edited, the questionnaires were ready for the essential task of calculating the average. There is nothing more mechanical than an average: all it requires is to add all the observations then divide the total by their number. Everyone knows this. But in practice, is it that easy? Has the reader ever taken a hundred loose-leaf pages (approximately the number of questionnaires that the Statistician received from each agricultural district), selected just one of the several columns, and added the numbers that it contained without ever repeating or forgetting any entry? Well, it was not that easy. It was, in fact, so difficult that the Statistician initially started out by copying the columns of numbers on a single sheet to add them. But what a waste of time, and the risk of errors it entailed was even greater! Nothing is more hypnotic than to copy-recopy a hundred numbers, generally between 70 and 100, and nothing is more easy than to forget one number or repeat another; not to mention other, less foreseeable risks that could occur, such as an unexpected intrusion, bringing a draft of air into the office, sending all the sheets of questionnaires flying, and obliging the Statistician to start all over again. Although the formula for calculating the average may be simple, actually computing a hundred questionnaires is far from evident.

Hence, a very ingenious mechanism was developed that resolved all these difficulties:

> I quickly learned that the unusual arrangement of the questions and spaces for answers at the bottom was to facilitate the "shingling" for adding.... The schedules were sorted by crop-reporting districts and "shingled," one district at a time, without reference to counties within the districts.... A blank schedule was placed at the bottom on which the number of reports, sums and averages for each item were entered. (Church 1944, 6)

Before totaling the entries and calculating the average, the questionnaires for each district had to be *physically* rearranged. The statistician did not begin by calculating but by sorting out the questionnaires on the basis of this invention called *shingling*. To understand what this operation consisted of, we must first note that the questionnaires had a strange format: They all ran length-wise like a roll of paper, and the boxes in which the Reporters noted their observations were at the bottom of the questionnaire, in one line. The questions were printed above the small boxes in which the answers had to be filled.

Shingling meant that the Statistician had to take all the questionnaires of one district and make them overlap each other horizontally, just like roof tiles, so that only the numbers were visible. After the last questionnaire at the bottom, he added a blank one, then he used a long wooden ruler—the Peg strip—which resembled a wire hanger for skirts (except that it was more than a meter in length), and tightly clipped together the entire lot of questionnaires.

After shingling or clipping together a large number of questionnaires, the Statistician could then do the calculations directly, without having to copy the reports and without the risk of forgetting some or counting them twice (see figure 1.4).[18]

The totals and the number of Reporters having replied to the question were directly noted in the boxes of the blank questionnaire found at the bottom of the lot. The average then became very easy to calculate: all that was required was to divide one number by another.

Before the introduction of shingling, the questionnaires pertained to the neighborhood; but through the specific shingling arrangement, the integrated report now covered the district (or the district average). The total, however, did not add a new element extracted from the plasma to the preceding ones, except for the new way of organizing the questionnaires. Thus, little by little, the state's elements were starting to become cohesive. Editing had helped to collate certain elements, and shingling had completed the process and produced districts. State by state, America was also in the process of taking concrete shape. But there was still work left to be done before there would be full consolidation.

Smoothing

Once the averages had been calculated, the agricultural Statistician noticed that sometimes, even in neighboring districts, the averages varied

1.4 The Peg strip in use. This photo was taken in 1960, and the hook's direction has been reversed, probably to facilitate its use with sheets of a more standard format. But we can see that the adding operation has become slightly more complicated for the Statistician as the numbers are no longer in the form of columns. (USDA-NASS, Archives of Richard Allen)

considerably, so much so that at times the variation did not seem plausible. What could be done about such disparities? Endorse them on the pretext that they were based on local data, or cast doubt on them because it was strange for two neighboring districts to present such very different conditions? To resolve this problem, the Statisticians carried out an operation called smoothing, which required a geographical base map.

For smoothing, the Statistician pinned a map of his state on the wall on which only the district boundaries were shown. Inside each county he noted the corresponding average. What he thus did was to highlight the distribution of the growth condition—if we take this variable as an example—in the sub-elements of the state. He could now see how they had evolved when he looked from left to right or from top to bottom. In other words, the map allowed him to create a function that combined two variables, space and condition, by making them depend on each other, and solely on each other.

These values could now be smoothed out—that is to say that the excessive differences between neighboring districts could be minimized. This procedure rested on the principle that if two neighboring districts had very different results, it was possible that this difference was imputable not to nature but to an artifact that needed to be corrected. On the map of Kansas (figure 1.5), we can see that the Statistician has circled an odd-shaped zone, which is consistent within itself (the growth condition of wheat is close to 70%) but not with the zones surrounding it (where it is closer to 90%). The Statistician had to decide whether to "smooth" this peculiar variation or leave it as it was. But then he had to provide an explanation.

During the smoothing process, the state in its entirety began to emerge. But it is remarkable that this step, which is really a kind of generalization, is *not* an induction—that is, the whole inferred from its parts, as it uses elements from the totality (the form of the state) as well as from the localities (the values ascribed to the counties), and even certain other factors that fit inside each other (the principle according to which one had to be wary of marked variations). On the contrary, the totality was used to calculate local values as much as local values helped to construct the totality. The emergence of the state is an add-on resulting from an overlapping of the extra elements and not an induction. It is in this way that America was consolidated much more than it was induced (Guibert, Lagagnier, and Volle 1971).

Weighting

Once the percentages had been smoothed out, they formed the basis for the calculation of the state averages. The Statisticians normally recopied the data they had smoothed out on a sheet (here the procedure was easier than in the case of the questionnaires, for there were only a small number of

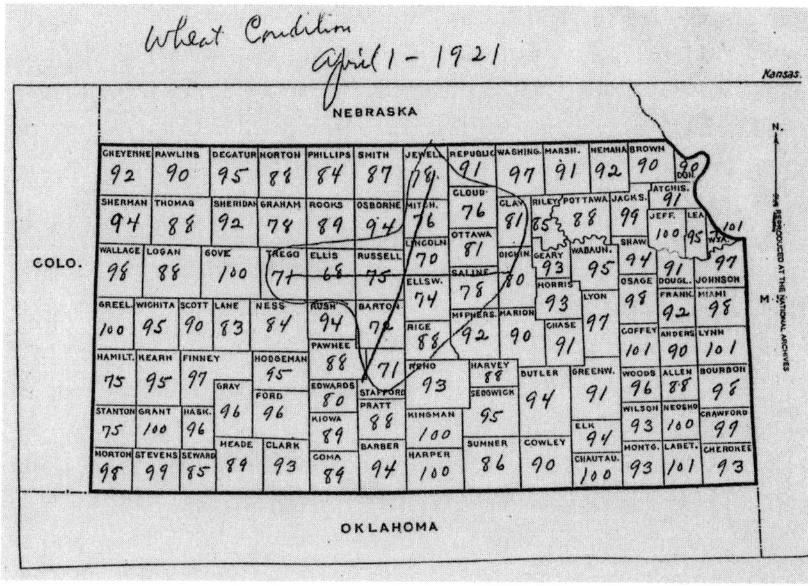

1.5 An example of smoothing carried out on the maps of the different states. In this instance it shows the growth condition of wheat in Kansas in April 1921. The Statistician has highlighted the central depression by circling it. (National Archives, Record Group 83, Bureau of Agricultural Economics [hereafter RG 83])

units), added them, then divided them by their number. However, there were cases where this formula for calculating the average proved inadequate. Let us take the example of the quantity of corn stocked in farms at the close of the season. This variable, introduced during the 1920s, was an important one for it affected the quantity sold on the market during the next season (and thus affected the price). To calculate it, the Division proceeded as it habitually did, by asking the Reporters to give the percentage of the current year's stocked yield. But the Statistician, however well informed he was about this percentage, in no way knew the absolute value of the quantity that remained to be sold. How could he estimate it?

To answer this question, we will study the weighted data sheet reproduced in figure 1.6. Let us look at the column that deals with the percentage of "corn remaining on the farms" (*Corn, Per Cent of 1931, Crop on Farms*)—that is to say, the corn that was not sold—in relation to the total quantity produced the previous year. In district 1, this percentage is 23.3 and in district 4 it is 32.9. While the percentage of district 1 is inferior to that of district 4, it would be erroneous to believe that, as a result, there is less corn remaining in district 1 than in the other district. If district 1 has produced twice as much corn as district 4 then, in this case, the unsold 23.3% represents much more corn in terms of absolute value than the 32.9% remaining in district 4. To understand this asymmetry one has to "weight" the percentage of district 1 more than that of district 4; that is, multiply the percentage of district 1 by a factor greater than that of district 4. It is this pre-multiplication that characterizes the weighted average.

Now the problem was how to estimate these weights. That is, how to assess the relative importance of one observation as compared to another? Here, it was the 1930 census that was used as the base year for computing the weights, as the line at the bottom of the district data sheet indicates: "Variable no. 7 is weighted by data from the 1930 harvested acreage." But it was possible that the reference to the harvested acreage of the census year was no longer valid, for district 1 could have produced an enormous quantity of corn in 1930, which would have given it considerable weight, but 50% less in 1932, consequently rendering the weighting completely obsolete. Other solutions could also be envisaged—for example, to weight on the basis of production not of the census year but of the year preceding the survey. Nevertheless, all solutions necessitated positing hypotheses on the link between the weighting variable and the variable to be calculated. In the first case, we can assume that the relative importance of the districts is constant over ten years, and in the second case, only one year out of two. The weighted average, which made it possible to refine the results by assigning different weights to the units, always led to making additional hypotheses at the same time (in this case, that the relative importance of the

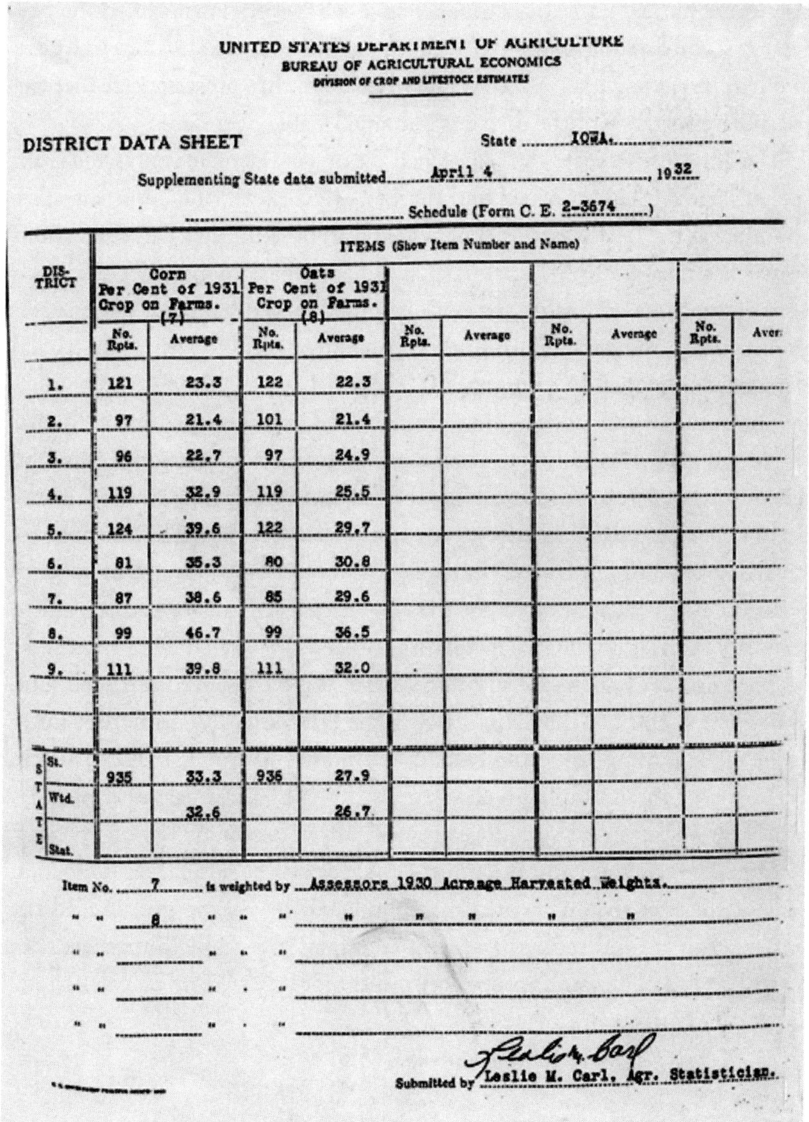

UNITED STATES DEPARTMENT OF AGRICULTURE
BUREAU OF AGRICULTURAL ECONOMICS
DIVISION OF CROP AND LIVESTOCK ESTIMATES

DISTRICT DATA SHEET State IOWA.

Supplementing State data submitted April 4, 1932

Schedule (Form C. E. 2-3674)

ITEMS (Show Item Number and Name)

DISTRICT	Corn Per Cent of 1931 Crop on Farms. (7)		Oats Per Cent of 1931 Crop on Farms. (8)							
	No. Rpts.	Average	No. Rpts.	Average	No. Rpts.	Average	No. Rpts.	Average	No. Rpts.	Aver.
1.	121	23.3	122	22.3						
2.	97	21.4	101	21.4						
3.	96	22.7	97	24.9						
4.	119	32.9	119	25.5						
5.	124	39.6	122	29.7						
6.	81	35.3	80	30.8						
7.	87	38.6	85	29.6						
8.	99	46.7	99	36.5						
9.	111	39.8	111	32.0						
STATE St.	935	33.3	936	27.9						
STATE Wtd.		32.6		26.7						
STATE Stat.										

Item No. 7 is weighted by Assessors 1930 Acreage Harvested Weights.
" " 8 " " " " " " " "
" " " " "
" " " " "
" " " " "

Submitted by Leslie M. Carl, Agr. Statistician.

1.6 Example of a summary sheet. (National Archives, RG 83) districts remained stable over time). Hence the Statistician retained the two averages: the direct average based on the hypothesis that all districts were of equal importance, and the weighted average that presupposed that the relative importance of the districts remained stable over time.

The "summary sheet" thus contained the myriad elements extracted from the plasma by the Reporters and the Statistician (e.g., the administrative boundaries, the trust between a person and an institution, a car, discussions between colleagues, letters, skirt-peg hangers, base maps) once they had been edited, totaled, smoothed out, weighted, and organized. It was itself an element in the general tallying process, incorporating all of the partial elements and meticulous operations.

The summary sheet was then transformed into a new document that contained only the principal results and was immediately dispatched by telegram. These results were telegraphed to ensure that they reached Washington, D.C., rapidly. Moreover, they were coded (see figure 1.7): each number from 1 to 120 (for the percentages) was replaced by a common name to ensure the confidentiality of the data, which, at this stage, had started to seriously interest potential speculators.

Then and only then, the summary sheet (the weighting sheet) was sent, under seal, by post to the main office of the Division in Washington, D.C., as the phrase "Supplementing State data submitted April 4, 1932" indicates at the top of the example given in figure 1.6. Thus, the partial consolidations carried out in each state were eventually all assembled in one place.

Once the telegram and the summary sheet had been sent, an important part of the Statistician's work was completed: he had aggregated all the information at his disposal in a secret telegram on a single loose sheet. But he still had to complete another part of his monthly schedule.

Commenting

After having sent the figures to Washington, the Statistician had to write the "Comments on crop reports," whose purpose was to mention all the

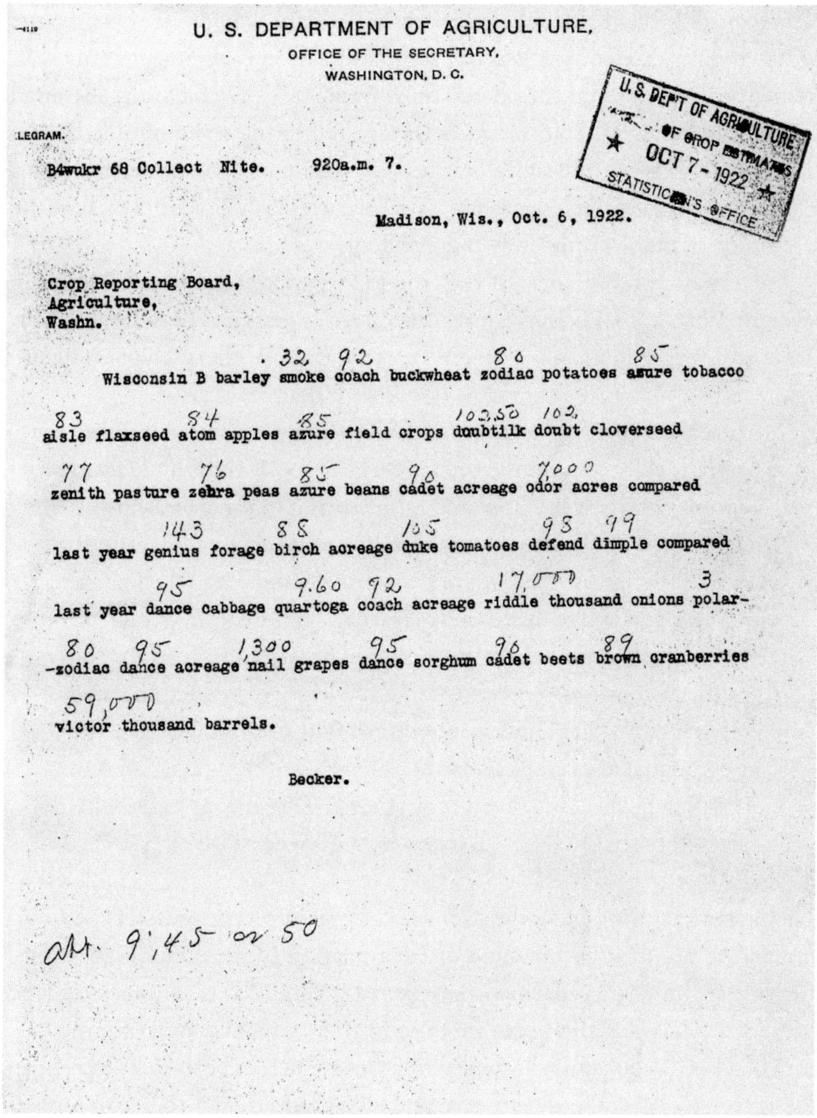

U. S. DEPARTMENT OF AGRICULTURE,
OFFICE OF THE SECRETARY,
WASHINGTON, D. C.

U.S. DEP'T OF AGRICULTURE
OF CROP ESTIMATES
OCT 7 - 1922
STATISTICIAN'S OFFICE

LEGRAM.

B4wukr 68 Collect Nite. 920a.m. 7.

Madison, Wis., Oct. 6, 1922.

Crop Reporting Board,
Agriculture,
Washn.

Wisconsin B barley smoke coach buckwheat zodiac potatoes azure tobacco aisle flaxseed atom apples azure field crops doubtilk doubt cloverseed zenith pasture zebra peas azure beans cadet acreage odor acres compared last year genius forage birch acreage duke tomatoes defend dimple compared last year dance cabbage quartoga coach acreage riddle thousand onions polar-zodiac dance acreage nail grapes dance sorghum cadet beets brown cranberries victor thousand barrels.

Becker.

1.7 Example of a coded sheet. (National Archives, RG 83) elements mobilized during the processing of the schedules. During the 1930s, the list of elements was not standardized, so each Statistician chose to mention the ones he considered most important. We have already cited Leslie Carl, the Iowa Statistician, who referred to the series of older statistics, and C. J. West, the Ohio Statistician, who conceived a social theory. These reports were relevant precisely because each Statistician had the advantage of being completely independent.

Let us look for a moment at the crop report written by Joseph Becker in 1922 for Wisconsin. He shows how certain arguments had been used to confirm the information given by the Reporters, and by others to contradict it.

> Total acreage of all field crops. Correspondents show an increase of 4% as compared to the total acreage in 1921. Individual farm reports, which were tabulated in the spring of the year, showed an increase of 4% which would indicate an increase in acreage, after allowing for the bias, of between 2% and 3%. The normal increase in acreage due to new clearings in northern Wisconsin was partly accounted for in increased acreage of crops. In the southern counties there was some tendency to reduce the area of tame pasture and put it into crops. Our preliminary acreage as estimated at present shows an increase in the vicinity of 4%. This, I believe is somewhat high. Our final revisions in December will probably show an increase of between 2% and 3%.[19]

The Statistician first gave the average calculated on the basis of the questionnaires. He then commented on it in relation to his own observations. Certain arguments confirmed the figures given—for example, that land had been cleared in the north or that, in the south, the area of tame pasture had been reduced and sown with crops, which in both cases explained the increase of farmland. Other arguments contradicted the crop reporters, called here "bias," which suggests that the Statistician had reservations about the degree of growth indicated.

This bias, which is only briefly alluded to here, refers in fact to a very authoritative general theory on farmers that all the agricultural Statisticians seemed to have shared: "Farmers who are willing to report on a complicated acreage questionnaire are unquestionably better-than-average farmers and consequently data for their farms is not exactly representative of all farms" (USDA 1933, 17).

This bias resulted from the fact that the Reporters constituted the elite among farmers. The situation had an advantage, because they were supposed to be "public spirited," which made them more open and more ready to respond, but it also had a disadvantage—namely, that they obtained better agricultural results than their neighbors. Being more intelligent, they were also the more capable among the farmers. This characteristic normally should not have had any effect on their estimates, as they had been advised not to take their own yields into account, but as it turned out, they found it difficult to comply with these instructions, and so their estimates very often were *higher* than the end estimates. It is the effect of this overall competence shown by the Reporters that Becker called bias. At the individual level—for example, at the level of wholesaler Sam Metzger—the Statistician assumed that the correspondent bragging overrode his craftiness, so that he ended by declaring results better than those of his neighbors.

The consequence of this bias for the Statistician was that he had to moderate the Reporter's estimates slightly so that they were representative of the results of all the farmers. The comments made it possible to highlight the elements that had an impact on the construction of the final figure—whether plus or minus—and showed how they fitted in with the Reporter's declarations.

The comments on the crop reports were also useful for presenting other elements that had perhaps not been useful directly for the estimation, but whose knowledge the Statistician considered important for understanding the information supplied by the Reporters. For example, Becker always gave a summary of the latest weather report as a sort of foreword to the data on the growth condition that he had collected. He was convinced that there was a very close link between the weather and the growth condition, so much so that when later he received a promotion and had the necessary authority, he launched a research program aimed at establishing a correlation between these two sets of data.[20] As long as he was merely a Statistician, he did not have the tools allowing him to consolidate this relation. He had to be satisfied with presenting the raw weather data without establishing a direct link with the condition—more like a body of knowledge that one had to have in one's head in order to understand the data on the condition.

The Statisticians thus produced three types of documents: a coded telegram that only contained extremely condensed numbers, a "summary sheet" that gave an exhaustive synopsis of all the results, and detailed remarks on the various stages of production of the first two documents. Between them, the three documents recapitulated the agriculture of the state. They condensed and aggregated the masses of reports sent by the Reporters, discussed and rationalized them when they contradicted each other, and presented the Statistician's personal observations and some earlier statistics. These three modules took different routes (telegraph and the ordinary post), but they left for the same destination—Washington—the heart of the Division where the statistics of the different states would be compared.

Closing

Before 1905, the final figures were calculated by the director of Division independently. But in 1905, one of the deputy directors, Edwin S. Holmes, secure in his personal relationship with his superior, resorted to what is today known as insider dealing. He "took advantage of the advance knowledge of what the government report would show and speculated in the cotton futures market" (Murray 1939, 710). Holmes was able to speculate as the estimates produced by the Division influenced the market prices. The greater the supply, the more the prices were likely to come down; inversely, the smaller it was, the more the prices were wont to go up. As Holmes had advance knowledge of the quantities on offer, he was able to sell or buy before the prices changed, only to resell (or rebuy) after the variation in price. This operation was extremely profitable: "In the trial of Mr. Holmes it was brought out, as I remember, that in one deal alone Mr. Holmes's share of the profits was more than $70,000" (Murray 1939, 710). This affair triggered the cotton scandal (it was on this crop that Holmes had speculated the most), which ended with his and his boss's dismissal. A secondary effect was that it forced the Division to entirely rethink the mechanism for producing the figures.

Willet M. Hays, assistant secretary of agriculture, acting as interim director of the Division, set up an internal structure called the "Board of Crop Estimates," which we will from now on simply call the Board. It was a body that did not have perpetual succession but met as often as deemed necessary for determining the figures for the states and the country as a whole. Its special characteristic was that it met in strict privacy to prevent information from leaking out (USDA 1969, 46–47). To create a space where this information could be kept in total secrecy, "a complete section of the building [of the Department of Agriculture] is cut off from communication with the outside, by disconnecting telephones, drawing window shades, and placing guards at the doors" (Becker 1937).

The "fence" ensured that no eyes, no ears, no voice could carry the figures outside the demarcated space.[21] That was not all. The entire chain used for bringing the Statisticians' reports from their state up to Washington was also subject to extreme caution. We have seen that the Statistician sent two kinds of data: results in the form of numbers in a coded telegram and his written report. The telegram was coded so that no one, not even the telegrapher, could access these figures. As for the reports, they were sent through a special courier and, on arrival in Washington, they were immediately locked up in a safe located in the Secretary of Agriculture's office. Only the director of the Division and the secretary had a key, and it was opened after taking all necessary precautions. Thus no members of the Board could avail themselves of the final information in order to speculate.

With regard to the employees, without whom the Board could not function, they had to be checked against the temptation to speculate. The decoded telegrams were cut into two to delink the quantities from the state to which they corresponded.

> Sheets are cut into two pieces, one containing the name of the state and all identifying marks and the other containing only the figures drawn from the reports. A simple identical serial number is marked upon each of the two portions of the sheet and the portion containing the headings and indentifying marks is placed in a safe.[22]

Hence, the Board's employees could not take advantage of the numbers on which they worked as they did not know what they referred to. All these precautions were institutionalized by a law that levied a fine of $10,000 (maximum) and/or a prison sentence of ten years (maximum) on those who infringed the condition of disinterestedness laid down by the Board.[23]

Experts

The first "things" that entered he sealed-off section of the Board were human. At the time of its creation, the Board had five members plus the staff who did the calculations.

These members were the following: "Mr. Hays, [Chief of the Division], devised the plan of calling together two section chiefs and two special field agents, as a committee, with himself as chairman to go over the crop material." The Board, as a committee in preference to an individual, finalized the official state-wise estimates of the various crops (Murray 1939, 710).

This structure remained unchanged, except for one detail—now a particularly eminent member of the Division, but who was not its head, could become the Board chairman. The five professionals were certified as experts: "The final reports are prepared and issued by a crop reporting board of experts" (Estabrook 1915, 8). And the same term was applied to the clerks: "The necessary computations are made by expert statistical clerks" (USDA 1933, 8).

In view of the Board's responsibility, it was a fundamental point: only experts could legitimately finalize the national agricultural production. But expertise implies in-depth knowledge of a subject; one is expert in a particular field of knowledge. We are going to specify what it means to qualify all these eminent statisticians as experts.

First, and this point is the easiest to illustrate, the clerks were expert in calculation. They applied the rules of algebra with robotlike reliability. But the subject that the five professionals were masters of is not easy to describe because it crosses the academic boundaries that we are familiar with today. They knew how to use statistics, but it was not enough; they were knowledgeable about the agricultural practices of the times, but their knowledge was not limited to them. Perhaps the best name for their subject was simply, perhaps redundantly, agricultural statistics. What does this mean?

The Board professional members knew how to use statistics in its mathematical form. For example, it was necessary to know how to read a table of numbers, to extrapolate from a scatter plot, and to calculate the percentage change. Until the late 1920s, the Board recruited its members from among the employees who had joined the Division ten or twenty years before as ledger keepers without a university degree (Brooks 1977, 320). They acquired this knowledge while working in the Division, for its tools were still pretty basic. But the situation changed beginning in the late 1920s, when it became mandatory to learn statistics at university to get a job as an executive in the Division. Be that as it may, whether they learned it at university or in-house, the Board's executives practiced formal statistics. They were also familiar with the functional statistics applicable to practical and administrative procedures, as a result of which information at the local level obtained by individuals was centralized (Desrosières 1998). This knowledge was just as important as the former:

> College graduates appointed as junior statisticians, in many cases, were unable to make full practical application of their training in statistics to the various steps involved in preparing

> the monthly crop reports. In the winter of 1927 about 15 of these young men were called to Washington and given a month's intensive training in the application of the various statistical methods to our work. (Church 1944, 20)

Mathematical formulas were useful insofar as they could be "applied" to the administrative practices of the Division (the term used by Church). Let us borrow an example from Becker.[24] We have seen that to calculate the quantity produced, the acreage under cultivation had to be multiplied by the yield per acre. But this simple formula was not good enough as the cultivated area never corresponded to the harvested acreage. There was always abandonment because of "the ravages caused by drought or floods, insects or disease." In other words, a part of the land that had been sown with grain was abandoned during the season. As "it is difficult to forecast the probable abandonment,"[25] the Division had decided that, "by custom and practical considerations of its logical fitness, estimates of production are based upon estimates of harvested acreage times yields per harvested acreage."[26] This lesson is obviously not taught anywhere except in-house through familiarity with the workings of the Division. A simple multiplication required Board members to understand how data was manipulated locally. As a consequence, one of the areas of competence essential for all Board executives was knowledge of their own administration:

> One of Ag. Estimates' long standing practice[s] has been to move its professional staff from one field office to another, and into and out of Washington as a means of developing a highly integrated, technically competent and operationally skilled staff, knowledgeable in all aspects of the agency's program, procedure and personnel." (Brooks 1977, 65)

This policy, which consisted of transferring Division members from one state to another and inviting them to Washington off and on to join the Board, allowed them to become familiar with the existing practice. This knowledge was so important that Becker went as far as to say that the Board's problems could not be resolved "without considering the background and historic development of the service."[27] The huge mass of archives left by the Board, the great number of conferences, seminars, meetings that it had organized, whose traces still remain, are other indications of the Division's concern for transmitting its procedures.

As a last point, the Board executives had in-depth knowledge of the terrain. No member of the Division could become permanent in Washington without having worked as Statistician for several years in different states. The Board was therefore constituted of persons who were familiar with the agriculture that they were quantifying.

The Board professionals were expert in agricultural statistics, this strange discipline that ranged from mathematical statistics, administrative statistics, and knowledge of the terrain. In addition, at least three of them were among the Division's finest statisticians. Indeed, one had to be an excellent agricultural Statistician in order to be permanently posted in Washington. Brooks (1977, 66), on the other hand, did not feel he had enough experience to accept the post offered to him: "He felt he needed more field office experience before joining the Headquarter's staff."[28] Hence, to leave the fields behind, one had to be among the best in the department in all the subjects listed.

For their part, the two field statisticians invited to Washington more or less assumed the role of disciples. They accepted this position because "to serve as a member of the Board was good training for them, and helped to increase their efficiency" (Murray 1939, 710). They came to learn by participating in the construction of numbers. At the same time, they brought with them local knowledge from the fields, their skills renewed and honed through experience at the grassroots level.

The Board thus had five executives, called "members," who rotated (three members from the central administration and two statisticians), and as many staff as necessary. How did they proceed during their meetings?

Arbitrating

Behind the closed doors were to be found both experts and information of various types (telegrams, comments, reports, etc.). The Board's task consisted of combining all these elements, numbers and remarks, rules of calculation and estimation, human and nonhuman elements, in such a way as to amalgamate them and produce a single element, a single number indicating the quantity of a particular crop produced in the United States on a given date. After all the manipulations, a single entity would emerge. As with the entire length of the statistical chain, the Board worked toward this end in small successive stages (see figure 1.8).

The first stage consisted of feeding the five members the same *nonnumerical* information. What was this nonnumerical information and how was it shared?

The session began with the chairman of the group reading aloud a certain number of texts. This reading specifically focused on the Statisticians' comments, which were opened and communicated to the Board. Then the meteorological data, provided beforehand by the National Meteorological Agency[29] and processed by the Board staff, was examined.

Finally, the comments and forecasts were completed by "information prepared by the research section," which signifies that the Board worked with information that was less broad-based and more pertinent to the situation at hand. We are going to give two examples of such information. The first concerns the "bias" that we have already talked about. We had said that the crop reporters, recruited from among the farmer elite, were in the habit of overestimating local yields. But this rule was only valid when the condition was below normal. In the opposite case, even if the Reporters were the most reliable possible, their general tendency was to underestimate:

> The tendency of reporters when a crop is normal or above is to understate the condition, as there seems to be an instinctive objection on the part of reporters to report more than 100 at

1.8 Photomontage realized by the Division to showcase itself to the public. The shots in descending order show the Board at work (observe the drawn curtains behind the person standing); during this time, telephone lines are disconnected; Secretary of Agriculture H. C. Wallace examining the report and signing it; the staff photocopying it; the director of the Board leaves with the reports at 3 p.m. under the watchful eyes of the guard; later, journalists rush to the telephone cabins, now reconnected, to transmit the figures to their editorial office. (American Farm Bureau Federation, *The Nation's Agriculture*, October 1937, 6–7)

> any time. This factor must be taken into consideration in interpreting condition report. (Callander and Becker 1923)

When the farmers registered an increase (yield greater than 100%), they had a tendency to reduce the quantity declared from the quantity actually harvested. In such a case, the estimates had to be corrected and the condition increased.

While it was easy for the local Statisticians, who were close to the farmers and in daily contact with them, to do such corrections as suited them, it was much more difficult to do those that put them at a disadvantage. As a result, the thinking was that a distant authority would be better situated to do the final rectifications: "It is the function of the Crop Reporting Board to correct for this kind of bias in making estimates, and it is in better position to do this than is the State statistician, because the members are not so closely in touch with local agricultural affairs in a given State" (Sarle 1932, 28). Hence the Statisticians carried out the rectifications that suited the farmers by decreasing the declared percentages, and, on the contrary, the Board, unaffected by local pressures, inserted the percentage increases that penalized them.

Information on the crop reporters was collected by the research division and transmitted to the new arrivals on the Board, especially to those Statisticians who had been invited especially for the occasion. These details were probably transmitted orally, while reading and commenting on the reports. In this way the Board accumulated a body of knowledge on the strategies that the Reporters used in order to instrumentalize statistics to suit their needs.

The second example shows that the information that entered the precincts of the Board was not always determined beforehand. Sometimes, in fact, circumstances or incidents that occurred on the ground caused such a stir that it reached the doors of the Board and forced the members to think whether or not to let the information enter, even though it had not followed the normal statistical route. This happened, for example, during one season when a worm (the Mexican ball weevil) attacked the cotton blossoms, seriously damaging the crop and resulting in a low yield. The deliberations that took place to decide how to tackle the parasite also gave the Board an opportunity to question the parameters of the information relevant to the Board. Which information was acceptable? Which should be taken into account? Here is the answer given: "[The Board] has taken the position that no known factor having a bearing upon final yield can be justifiably passed by or overlooked while at the same time serving the true purpose of the service, which is to give its best available appraisal of probable yield."[30]

The Board decreed that all pertinent information could be referred to it, even if it was not standardized. But this rule could not be wholly complied with. For example, reacting to the charge levied against the Board because it did not properly represent certain "small segments" of agriculture (crops produced in small quantities, such as pickles, before Verne Church's big coup), Joseph Becker, who had been the Wisconsin Statistician and had become president of the Board, affirmed that "many small details and sources of information can easily be overlooked in the preparation of the thousands of determinations made annually by a national service of agricultural statistics."[31] All information was not pertinent, after all. Arbitration was required for each case.

Comparing

While the Board members were exchanging information verbally, the staff members were not standing idle. Immediately after the introductory work session, they got busy preparing the figures for the Board members to work on. But which numbers? What data was given to the experts? Rather surprisingly, they did not content themselves with the Statisticians' reports and coded telegrams. On the contrary, the Board worked on different data.

The Board's other source of information came from the results provided by a list of crop reporters who were in direct communication with Washington. To simplify matters, we have not up till now mentioned the existence of these other lists of informers. In addition to the voluntary Reporters in contact with the Statistician of their state, there existed "County Reporters" who communicated directly with the Division. (This County Reporter could be, but was *not* necessarily by any means, the same person as the county agent *payed* by the national agricultural extension service.) Historically, this list was made earlier (in the 1860s), with the Statisticians being authorized to prepare their own lists of interlocutors only later (at the beginning of the twentieth century). But apart from the fact that they were in contact with the federal capital instead of their state capital, these County Reporters and the Statisticians' Reporters were very similar. In particular, the attention showered on them and the effort made to secure their loyalty were as intense. There were three federal lists in all. In addition to the County Reporters, who checked the growth condition and acreage in their commune, there were two other much more specialized lists: one of the price paid by the farmers to buy agricultural material, and the other of cotton.

The purpose of these federal lists was to give another perspective on the crops, besides that of the state Reporters, and through another intermediary, other than the Statistician. The response sample was then duplicated and each list served as a counterpoint to the other. The Board thus had two sources instead of one.

In addition to the results obtained from these two sources, the Board used data that it already had—first, its estimates on the same date last year and, second, "the average estimate of the same crop on the same date calculated over a ten year time span" (USDA 1933, 10). Like the Statistician, the Board was not in favor of straying too much from past estimates unless there was a strong reason to do so.

Numerical information on which the Board members were supposed to work were the figures supplied by the Statisticians, the results of federal lists, and ten-year averages. To compare the data, the clerks prepared tables with all the numbers for the members to work on without wasting time and effort. The states were represented horizontally in the table. Each source had its own column. The members of the Board simply had to read the line to *compare* all the estimates for each state. This is the first sketch of America as a whole emerging from the long chain that we have been tracking.

At this point in the statistical chain, the expertise of the five Board members and the numbers still remained to be incorporated.

Estimating

To combine the various data and the five separate expert opinions, the Board proceeded to what it called estimation. It estimated the final quantity. How did it go about this task?

The first stage of the Board's work had been a collective one. Its members had collectively received the data and had all shared the same information, which meant that they were on equal footing. The second phase was then solitary; each Board member studied the tables individually:

> After examination of the data regarding each State, the members of the Board separately and independently, make a definite decision without consultation with any other member; and each enters a figure expressing his conclusion opposite the name of each state in the blank column provided for that purpose. (USDA 1933, 11)

In the course of the second phase, contrary to the previous one, the Board members acted "separately" and "independently." Whereas they had started by putting all the information in a common pool, they now separated, silence reigned (they did not "consult" each other), and each of them retained in his head the data that had been read publicly and examined the tables of numbers given him. Each member weighed every piece of information, then "decided" on the number that fit the data best. The word "decision" is important. It did not involve a calculation governed by a formula, and this was for three reasons at least. First, if this had been the case, the clerks would have, as usual, gone ahead with the calculations. Second, the five members did not come up with the same numbers. For example, on one occasion one of the members decided that the condition in Minnesota was 88% of the normal condition, whereas others preferred to put 87% or 89%. Now, if the progression from the data to the result arrived at by the member had been governed by a mathematical formula, except for a gross error, they would have all found the same thing. Third, it is impossible to do calculations on heterogeneous data. If the numbers do not all refer to the same thing, all algebraic formulas are useless. The only operation that can synthesize such data is therefore a judgment. So, the members did not calculate; instead, they decided (see figure 1.9).

Once the individual decisions were taken, the Board again met collectively: [32]

> After the Board members have made their individual estimates, the chairman of the Board enters them in parallel columns on one sheet. When the individual estimates of all the members are in close agreement the median figure is usually adopted. If there is much difference between the individual estimates all the evidence before the Board is carefully reviewed and discussed until an agreement is reached. (USDA 1933, 11)

During the third phase of the process, each member gave his decision publicly; the chairman noted them in a new table where their names figured in the column, which made them easier to compare. The members were then once again reunited, both on paper and physically, to jointly synthesize their individual decisions. Here, it was possible to use a calculating device, the median, if the members' opinions did not diverge too greatly.[33] But if the disagreement between members was too marked, they reviewed the data again and argued it out in order to arrive at a consensus. Each one justified his decision openly; discussion followed until one person managed to convince the others of the rightness of his decision.

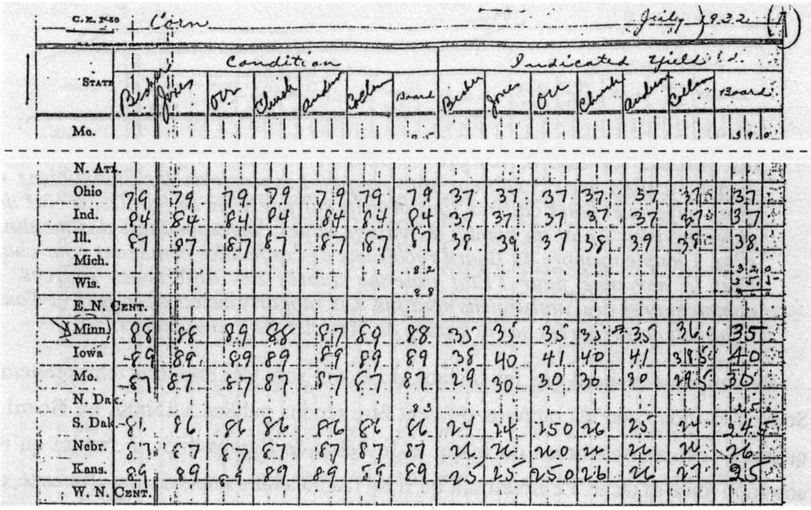

C.E. F-50 Corn July 1932 (1)

State	Condition: Becker	Jones	Orr	[illegible]	[illegible]	[illegible]	Board	Indicated yield: Becker	Jones	Orr	[illegible]	[illegible]	[illegible]	Board
Mo.														
N. Atl.														
Ohio	79	79	79	79	79	79	79	37	37	37	37	37	37	37
Ind.	84	84	84	84	84	84	84	37	37	37	37	37	37	37
Ill.	87	87	87	87	87	87	87	38	39	37	38	39	38	38
Mich.							82							32.0
Wis.							88							35.5
E. N. Cent.														
Minn.	88	88	89	88	87	89	88	35	35	35	35	35	36	35
Iowa	89	89	89	89	89	89	89	38	40	41	40	41	38.5	40
Mo.	87	87	87	87	87	87	87	29	30	30	30	30	29.5	30
N. Dak.							83							25
S. Dak.	86	86	86	86	86	86	86	24	24	25.0	26	25	24	24.5
Nebr.	87	87	87	87	87	87	87	26	26	26.0	24	26	26	26
Kans.	89	89	89	89	89	89	89	25	25	25.0	26	26	27	25
W. N. Cent.														

1.9 A detail of the Board's worksheet; the actual size is 60 centimeters in height and 30 centimeters wide. On the left is the list of all the states, finally reassembled; on top, the name of the variable; and below it, the line for the name of the member who wrote the estimates in the columns (names written diagonally by hand in the box: "Becker," "Jones," etc.). The discussion was then opened and lasted until the estimate of the whole board was noted in the last column. (National Archives, RG 83)

If, for some unfortunate reason, the discussion did not end in consensus and time was running out, the chairman could decide without waiting for unanimity among the members. However, let us stress the fact that, out of the examples we have already given, members were generally very close to each other. Most of the time, the rule of the median seemed to work.

We have to insist on the fact that the estimation process does not work at all according to the "Social Studies of Knowledge" school model (Bloor 1991). According to it, the true reality is twisted by the representations of those who reported it, and the composition of different representations aims at annulling them all. In fact, in the case of the statistics that we are in the process of examining, the various sources did *not* help to prevent the successive biases from occurring. On the contrary, the data submitted to the Board presented the specific fields according to their unique characteristics and was useful in examining the *different aspects* of agriculture. The meteorological data, for example, supplemented the data expressed in terms of condition with data expressed in terms of temperature and rainfall. Similarly, the data of the Washington crop reporters was not used for *correcting* the data of the state crop reporters but was a second opinion. The Board's primary aim was not to correct, but to have pertinent information on agriculture and to fit all the data with the other in the most satisfactory way possible so as to obtain one single piece of information that was the most complete.

Far from lamenting about information considered erroneous by the Edinburgh model, the members of the Board were delighted to have at their disposal the thousand and one *characteristics* of agriculture in order to integrate them. Estimation is an arrangement of elements with different characteristics from which one single number is brought out that has all these characteristics. Once this number was estimated, the Board transmitted its results to its staff, who finally got down to the task of calculating.

Calculating

The example analyzed shows that the Board first took up one crop and then studied it region by region: In this particular case, it deals with the "North Atlantic" and "East North Central" zones. Once it had finished with one region for a given crop, it moved on to the next region. When it had finished with one crop, it went on to the second crop. But before taking another crop, it gave its staff the results arrived at and the staff then, and only then, began the computations, a procedure that is generally considered primordial when working with numbers:

> When the basic State figures for a given crop have been determined by the Board, the necessary computations are made by expert statistical clerks to ascertain the probable total production for each state. State totals are then combined to ascertain

> totals and averages for the United States. As soon as the computations are finished and checked the results are again reviewed by the Board. (USDA 1933, 11)

These calculations were based on data taken from the Census Bureau, which then made it possible to switch from the percentages declared by the crop reporters to absolute values. This stage was crucial in forging a solid America for it combined all the operations undertaken by the constitutional institution of the census.

What calculations did the staff do? The first year after the census-taking, they obtained the cultivated area by applying the percentage variation to the value in acres recorded by the census. The second year, they redid this same calculation but by using the numbers obtained for the first year and so on, from one year to the next, until the next census. But, as obvious as this procedure may seem, it was not enforced readily.

In fact, in 1901, just after the 1900 census, the Division had refused to immediately publish its estimates of the cultivated acreage because it first wanted to compare them with the census results. But the National Board of Trade was keen to do this comparison publicly, for it wanted to judge the quality of the numbers produced by the Department of Agriculture. It thus gained permission for a survey to be conducted, which showed that the census and the Division's estimates differed by more than 10%, and furthermore concluded that it was the Division that had erred and not the census. John Hyde, the incumbent director of the Division, chose to counterattack and showed that the census-taking of the cultivated area in some counties made it out to be larger than the area of the county itself (USDA 1969, 42).

It was not until 1905 that there was an outcome to this issue. The "Keep Commission," named after its chief, Charles H. Keep, by Theodore Roosevelt to identify the administrative best practices, inspected the different federal statistical services, looked into this problem, and reworked the most doubtful portions of the census. It concluded that the overestimates of the Census Bureau were explained because some farms had their homestead in one county and their land in another, and the census had attributed all the land acreage to the county where the building was. But if the census had erred, the error was considered unimportant. The Division was thus put in the wrong (Taylor and Taylor 1952). There was no repeat of this episode for a long time to come; partial statistics had dared to challenge the census and emerged the loser for a very long time. The census had established itself as the ultimate authority, despite its imperfections. A sign of its defeat, in 1933 the Division specified that, "despite everything, the overall policy of the Division is to accept the census as the basis for its series of acreage"(USDA 1933, 16).

The acreage under wheat or corn, however, did not give the yield of wheat or corn during the season. The yield per acre had to be estimated. This estimate was done through the *par* method, which also had to make a detour via the census. As we have seen, the yield was estimated by the crop reporters in terms of variation in the condition compared to the normal condition. The *par* (as in the expression "to be on par with something") was the yield, in bushels, to which corresponded the normal condition converted into yield per acre on the basis of past yields given in the census. For example, if in July 1920 the condition recorded at the time of the harvest was 75% of the normal condition, and if later a yield of 12.5 bushels of wheat per acre had been noted for the year, then it was not difficult to calculate the yield that would have been observed in the current year if the condition had been 100%—a simple rule of three was all that was required to calculate it. If in 1920 the condition had been normal, the yield would have been (12.5*100)/75 = 16.67. This yield deduced for a normal condition was called *par*. The *par* was thus the normal yield of one cultivated acre. It was a key, non-observed quantity obtained by taking census data and doing the appropriate calculation. If the next year, in July 1921, a condition of 68% of the normal condition was observed, the yield in 1921 was easy to deduce: 68% of the *par*, that is, of the normal yield the previous year.[34]

The calculations were carried out by the statistical clerks as soon as the doors were closed. To do these calculations, a major part of their activity consisted of recopying the numbers mentioned in the tables. As it was very easy for errors to slip in with all the manipulations being done, the final tables were verified by the Board. Finally, by means of a fresh smoothing, comparable to what the Statisticians did to estimate the percentages of the counties in their state,[35] the Board came out with the most comprehensive results, those that concerned, on the one hand, the States and, on the other, their grand total—the "United States as a whole."[36]

Thus, it was only at the very end of the run that the conversion of percentages into absolute values was carried out. Something that seemed central when describing the Division abstractly was concretely merely one of the many stages, and certainly not the most select as it was conducted by ordinary employees who helped to produce the numbers.

Be that as it may, thanks to these calculations, the most comprehensive figures were definitely established. They were then recopied by the staff in the Crop Report (figure 1.10). What then happened to this report?

Releasing

As long as that the Board worked in secret, the release of the report became crucial, for privileged access to data would have been tantamount to insider dealing. The Board had to very carefully control the disclosure process of the numbers. How did it go about it?

The first stage consisted of making the results official. What did this involve? That the report was given to the Secretary of Agriculture himself, who then gave approval by countersigning it: "The report as finally approved [by the Board] is multigraphed and after approval by the Secretary of Agriculture is ready for release."[37]

We did not come across any example of a Secretary of Agriculture refusing to sign this report; the exercise was thus a symbolic one that nevertheless retained its importance, for it was the government and not just the administration that assumed responsibility for the numbers that were going to be released to the public. Scientific legitimacy was coupled with the legitimacy of the state.

How was this final information released?

UNITED STATES DEPARTMENT OF AGRICULTURE
BUREAU OF AGRICULTURAL ECONOMICS
WASHINGTON, D. C.

Released:
October 10, 1932.
3:00 P.M. (E. T.)

CROP REPORT AS OF OCTOBER 1, 1932.

The Crop Reporting Board of the United States Department of Agriculture makes the following forecasts and estimates FOR THE UNITED STATES, from reports and data furnished by crop correspondents, field statisticians, and cooperating State Boards (or Departments) of Agriculture and Agricultural Colleges:

CROP	CONDITION			TOTAL PRODUCTION IN MILLIONS			
	Oct. 1, 10-yr.av. 1919–1928 Per cent	Oct. 1, 1931 Per cent	Oct. 1, 1932 Per cent	5-yr av. 1924–1928	1931	Indicated a Sept. 1, 1932	Indicated a Oct. 1, 1932
Corn .... bus.	78.1	71.4	77.2	2,625	2,563	2,854	2,885
Winter wheat .... "	—	—	—	549	789	b 442	b 442
Durum wheat, 4 States "	—	—	—	67	18	45	b 43
Other spr. wheat, U.S. "	—	—	—	213	86	228	b 227
All wheat .... "	—	—	—	829	894	715	b 712
Oats .... "	—	—	—	1,277	1,112	1,245	b 1,265
Barley .... "	—	—	—	219	198	303	b 313
Rye .... "	—	—	—	44.1	32.5	b 42.5	b 42.5
Buckwheat .... "	82.3	77.3	65.1	11.8	8.9	7.2	7.1
Flaxseed .... "	72.4	41.4	48.0	23.3	11.1	13.3	13.2
Rice, 4 States .... "	c 83.8	81.1	79.0	38.8	45.2	37.7	37.7
Grain sorghums d .... "	79.8	70.3	68.4	98.1	105	118	116
Hay, all tame .... tons	—	—	—	73.8	64.2	68.6	b 68.5
Hay, wild .... "	—	—	—	12.0	8.1	b 11.4	b 11.4
Hay, all clover and timothy e .... "	—	—	—	36.2	27.4	b 26.0	b 26.0
Hay, alfalfa .... "	—	—	—	23.0	21.0	26.5	b 26.4
Pasture	80.1	63.5	67.1	—	—	—	—
Beans, dry edible d 100-lb. bags	—	—	—	—	12.7	9.9	b 10.2
Soy beans	f 80.3	82.2	79.6	—	—	—	—
Peanuts (for nuts) lbs. ...	73.8	73.1	63.5	759	1,083	1,026	1,019
Cowpeas	71.6	76.5	67.3	—	—	—	—
Apples, total crop ... bus.	58.2	70.5	48.6	180	202	138	134
Apples, com'l crop .. bbls.	f 60.4	69.3	53.1	32.4	34.6	29.6	27.9
Peaches, total crop .. bus.	g 64.9	g 79.8	g 50.4	h 56.8	h 76.6	h 46.4	bh 46.3
Pears, total crop ... "	68.2	64.3	60.9	21.5	h 23.3	22.2	22.2
Grapes i .... tons	78.2	54.3	74.6	h 2.34	h 1.62	2.09	2.14
Pecans .... lbs.	f 51.2	59.6	48.4	56.8	76.7	51.2	53.7
Potatoes .... bus.	76.1	69.5	69.3	361	376	357	357
Sweet potatoes .... "	75.8	67.8	69.9	57.8	62.9	76.2	74.6
Tobacco .... lbs.	77.4	79.4	65.8	1,299	1,601	1,028	1,012
Broomcorn d .... tons	—	—	—	j 51.2	j 44.6	j 37.1	bj 34.7
Hops d .... lbs.	—	—	—	30.3	25.9	26.0	b 25.3
Sugar beets .... tons	—	—	—	7.39	7.90	8.21	b 8.59

a Indicated production increases or decreases with changing conditions during the season.
b Preliminary estimate.
c 5 States including Missouri.
d Principal producing States.
e Excludes sweetclover and lespedeza For 1931–32 excludes minor States.
f Short-time average.
g Production in percentage of a full crop.
h Includes some quantities not harvested.
i Production is the total for fresh fruit, juice, and raisins.
j Thousands of tons.

Figure 61.—First page of a monthly crop report.

1.10 This "Crop Report" summarizes or contains all the previous stages. It is this sheet that was released to the public. (National Archives, RG 83)

> At about three minutes to 3 p.m. on either the 9th or 10th of each month from April to November a group of newspaper reporters, telegraph operators, messengers and other persons concerned about the nation's crop prospects gather in the release room of the Bureau of Agriculture Economics in the South Building of the Department of Agriculture in Washington. From the crop reporting division, just around the corner of the corridor, the chairman of the board appears with an armful of crop reports for release at 3 p. m. Exactly at 3 o'clock the Department Release Official gives the signal and those who are waiting receive a copy of the report and begin sending a digest of it all over the world by telephones, telegraphs and other means of communication. (Becker 1937, 7)

Becker emphasized the reach of the reports, going as far as to talk of the whole world. If the space was vast, time on the other hand was reduced to a single instant: This whole scene took place between 2:57 p.m. and 3 p.m. Three short minutes when the whole drama was played out and everything hung in the balance. The most varied means of communication at that time, the telephone and telegraph, made it possible to link the unending space with that one instant. Thanks to them, the numbers were available instantly everywhere.

For everyone to get the results exactly at the same moment, an even more subtle mechanism had been set up. In the center of the newsroom, a long white line had been painted on the floor. On one side, the telephones had been hooked above a line of tables and, on the other, the journalists were gathered behind the line, waiting for the signal to cross it. The chairman of the Division himself came to place the packet of final reports on the table "face down," while "those desiring the report are required to remain back of the line marked upon the floor, a distance of a yard or more from the tables until the moment of the release, when upon the signal, each person may step forward and take his copy of the report"[38] (see figure 1.11).

1.11 The race for data. Journalists waiting behind the white line for the signal to cross. (USDA, Archives of J. J. Prusaki)

Thus no one was given preferential treatment before the commencement of the race. All journalists stood at an equal distance from the goal. The race was symbolic of the impartial treatment by the Division—that is, to release the numbers to everyone at the same time.[39]

Using

In spite of the long and complicated maneuvering required to produce it, the report was really a sort of "by-product," as we would say today, of its initial object, which was to fight speculation and speculators as effectively as possible "in the same way that a police or constable force tends to check but not entirely prevent crime in a community."[40] The administration's aim was above all to purify the agricultural market. The use was just as good for producing numbers as the data gathered by the crop reporters or the rules of summation. Utilization was an additional pillar making it possible for the numbers to hold their own.

In the introduction to this chapter, we proceeded as if the connection between numbers and market purity was mechanical; as if, as soon as objective information was made public, the markets would purify themselves. Can we, for all that, rely on this mechanism? Would truth in itself frighten the speculators? This is not what the administration and the farmers thought. The steps taken by the state and the numbers would be effective if and only if they were adopted by other actors. In conclusion, let us now examine the role played by the numbers in relation to economics.

Here is how, according to the Division, the numbers were useful to farmers:

> Farmers are benefited by the Government crop reports both directly and indirectly; directly by being kept informed of crop prospects and prices outside of their own immediate districts, and indirectly, because the disinterested reports of the Government tend to prevent the circulation of false or misleading reports by speculators who are interested in controlling or manipulating prices. (Estabrook 1915, 9)

The numbers brought farmers up to date with agricultural prospects and prices. How was it possible that farmers were unaware of this information? "Prices in [the farmers'] own local market are influenced, as a rule, more by the condition of the whole crop throughout the State or the United States, and even in foreign countries, than they are by local conditions" (Estabrook 1915, 10). As prices depended on global, not local, production, farmers were probably too isolated to be aware of these factors. The Division centralized a certain number of scattered facts and transformed them into relevant information for each farmer. "In a sense the Bureau of Crop Estimates is a form of farmers' cooperation" (Estabrook 1915, 9). The numbers thus kept the farmers informed of the overall state of agriculture.

But this information was only useful, dare one say, for the farmers' edification. Indeed, it did not seem to have a direct effect on speculation. Only indirectly did the numbers neutralize the ill-effects. How? According to the Division, the numbers hampered the circulation of other numbers, "fallacious information" that the speculators published with the aim of distorting the market.[41] Thus, the foe that the numbers had to combat was not men, but other numbers. How did the fight take place? How did the farmers actually use the Division's reports?

Numbers alone could not lead to better "marketing" of agricultural goods; they were not directly useful to the farmer during the sale of the crops because of the complexity of the distribution circuit. Indeed, the harvested crops were collected from the farms by a shipper who delivered them to a cooperative that in turn was responsible for the sales. The cooperative used the government's figures, but not in order to discuss the price with the buyers, for the rates on the market were fixed and it was left with no other option except to agree to them (Miller 1933). The only thing that the cooperative could choose was the date on which it wanted to intervene, and it is here that statistics were useful, as the price depended on the season (prices were higher in the beginning of summer, just before the harvest, than at the end, just after) and projections of the quantities produced (prices were higher if a poor yield was predicted and lower in the opposite case).

> To do a good job of selling at the right time, the shipper needs a full range of information as to the present and prospective supply situation. This does not cost much money because most of this information can be obtained free from governmental sources. But it does take time. It is a full-time job for any man

> to digest, analyze and interpret this information. A farmer who did this job well would have no time left for any other work. (Miller 1933, 88)

Therefore numbers helped the cooperatives, which alone had the time to process the information, to decide the best time to sell. In this way the objective numbers provided by the administration prevented speculation and purified the market.

While the numbers were circulating on the markets, the Division archived them so that they could eventually be reused, for example, for research or calculation of the past ten-year averages. But before archiving them, it carefully verified them. To do this, the Division had a great amount of "check data" that enabled it to check whether its estimates had been correct. The common feature was, first, that the data was sourced from other administrations, such as the Census Bureau or other states and, second, that it was exhaustive (the check data came from surveys covering the totality of a part of the territory). Let us give an example of such data:

> In about one third of the States, the agricultural agencies, with the help of their local assessors, make an annual or biannual enumeration, either at the beginning of or during the growing season, of the acreage to be planted or harvested, or after the close of the season of the acreage harvested. (USDA 1933, 14)

Here, the Division could take advantage of the numerous annual censuses of the acreage harvested carried out by the states themselves. The comparison between the two sets of data allowed the Division to judge the validity of its own figures. But this assessment took time because the temporalities of the various administrations were not the same: The Division had to sometimes wait one year (in the case of biannual surveys) to obtain the data that it required. It had to moreover ensure that the control data was comparable to its own estimates.

Most of the time this additional data was used for making minor adjustments to the Board's estimates, which differed only a little. In rare cases, the data had compelled the Division to undertake a more systematic review of its estimates (e.g., by accepting the intrusion of the various committees of Statisticians who had come to observe its work). This resulted in controversies, one example of which we have given, whereby the Division could either contest the control data to save itself or, on the contrary, accept it and reform itself.

Conclusion: America Consolidated

We have run through a series of stages that have all participated in the constitution of the final number that, at last, said something about "America as a whole." We have seen how the transition from initial diversity to eventual unity was slow and meticulous, which is understandable because the entity ultimately produced, America, turned out to be massive—gargantuan—whereas statisticians remain simple mortals, with little strength and small brains. The problem of scale between these tiny humans and their colossal object was resolved by lengthening the chain of statistical operations (Dupréel 1933). Each operation provided an opportunity to add man-size elements (dare one use the expression!) to this enormous concretion that was in the process of taking shape in such a way as to, little by little, make America appear.

The result of these operations, this grand aggregate of elements, what was it really? Was it truly America or was it simply the crop reporters' method? Despite the humility that is integral to practitioners of statistics, it seems likely that it was both, standing back-to-back like the two sides of a coin. If we look at this aggregate from one side, we see statistics: questionnaires, categories, averages, enumerations, tables, tables, tables, tables (not always the same ones, however), numbers, and percentages. In short, we see a statistical method. But seen from the other side of the coin, this aggregate is nothing other than America itself: its farmers, its press, its cultures, its states and their internal boundaries, its meteorology, its inventiveness, its past captured in the weighting, its postal service, its secret codes, its guards, its experts, its market and legal theories, the types of state action, and so on. All these elements the statisticians found in the plasma, and they amalgamated them with the help of their modest tools of quantification. What is solidly held together by the numbers is well and truly America or, if we play it down a little, agricultural America in its totality (Latour 1998).

This duality associated with the aggregate explains why the methodological appendixes of statistical surveys, which everyone avoids looking at, yawning in advance, in reality are fascinating to those who know how to read them: they speak as much of the object as of the numbers themselves. When statisticians explain how they have constructed their categories, what methods they have used, and why they have done it, they explain, to whosoever knows how to read them, how they have statistically determined their object.

Finally, this America was not just a collection of elements extracted from the plasma—it was also the manner in which they were configured that conferred a certain solidity to the aggregate. How can one say of a nation or, symmetrically, of a method—elements oh-so abstract—that they are solid?

To answer straight off, we can say that solidity seems to be the capacity of an aggregate to resist the assault of unforeseen circumstances, of plasmic attacks; for if the aggregate was not solid, it would prevent the internal process from being realized. We can moreover add that it is obtained locally, through the insertion[42] of one element between two others that preexisted it and which ensures the transition from one to the other.[43]

The Board's organization for determining the final figures can be given as an example of such consolidation between a preliminary situation, where the Statisticians' reports are all collected in the Department of Agriculture, and a final situation, at exactly 3 p.m., when the aggregated numbers are released. Initially—that is, before the Board was institutionalized—the interval between the two situations (aggregation of the reports) was indifferent because it was left to the good offices of the director of the Division, who was so little concerned with it that he had delegated it to a subordinate.

But it turned out that there were, in this apparently indifferent space, forces that were against the smooth functioning of the chain of events; indeed, the "insider dealing" by the subordinate—namely, short-circuiting the release of the figures by violating his pledge of secrecy—nearly put a wrench in the whole mechanism. To ensure that the initial situation would carry along with it the chain of events leading up to the final situation (the uniform sharing of information), the interval between the two was structured in a very specific manner, which isolated the experts, bringing them together, then separating them only to bring them together again, which gave more weight to one in comparison to the others. Thanks to this organization of the interval, simultaneous revelation was ensured. The agricultural Statisticians thus consolidated the series of stages.

Each stage that we have crossed was not just a way of incorporating elements of the plasma within the aggregate "America as a whole," but at the same time it was an operation B that made sure that operation A would well and truly be followed by operation C. Generally speaking, we can say in consonance with the Belgian philosopher Eugène Dupréel, unjustly ignored, that consolidation takes place when "intercalary phenomena, however insignificant, which fill the interval between two periodic repetitions, tend to organize themselves in such a way as firstly not to hinder, secondly to promote, in order to ensure by themselves, the said repetition" (Dupréel 1931, 493).

Consolidation is the organization of the interval that ensures a more determinate link, in a word, more solid, between two preexisting elements. It ensures "either the regular production of a fact B as a sequel to a fact A, or the periodic repetition of the same fact A, A', A'' ..." (Dupréel 1931, 488). That is why we have retained the word "method" to designate this invariable repetition of stages: statisticians sought to consolidate the stages of their work so as to evolve a method, a series of procedures that invariably start all over again. It is not surprising, then, that this method has often been called the "Crop Reporters' method." Consolidation allowed American agricultural Statisticians to methodically process millions of questionnaires that they received over a period of time. Symmetrically, this method was also the stabilization of what America consisted of at that time. All the elements that we have mentioned were, because of these statistics, held together, stable and lasting, so that we could say that they gave consistency to America.

But if consolidation helps to produce repetition, predictability, one of its characteristics is to be specific at each interval. True, there exists a general theory that we have summarized in this brief conclusion, but the interval between "editing" and "smoothing" is called "summing up," and this summing up occurs only in this place. Each stage of consolidation had compelled statisticians to resolve a singular problem, having irreducible properties and posing specific problems. Statisticians had to be, as much as possible, ingenious and inventive, cunning even, consolidating each operation, finding the most satisfactory, adjustable response possible. Each stage was thus a special case but critical for producing an America that held together. It is the specificity of consolidation: it is difference that produces repetition.

This idiosyncratic aspect of consolidation moreover explains why we, who have been retrospectively observing the work of our astute predecessors, have had to go through all the stages, one by one, in order to understand their work. Although this chapter may seem long, it is still too short in view of all the stages that we have passed over in silence and that the statisticians, on the other hand, must have consolidated. If this chapter is long, it is so precisely to show the lengthiness of statistical work.

If statisticians finally managed to give consistency to America as a whole by aggregating its parts, what was its degree of solidity? The Great Depression that unexpectedly struck America will allow us to test the resistance of the method of unforeseen events.

2

The Decomposition of Links between Statistics and Politics

While the Division worked methodically to produce numbers, the 1929 stock market crash, followed by the Great Depression, threw everything into sudden and total disarray. To begin with, the Statisticians were not particularly affected; during Herbert Hoover's entire tenure at the helm, no one asked them to change their way of working. But on March 6, 1933, the very day that Franklin D. Roosevelt and his team took over, the President asked his Secretary of Agriculture, Henry A. Wallace, to set up a meeting with the principal agricultural stakeholders of the country. Roosevelt intended to shut himself in a room with them and come out only after a "plan for immediate action" had been decided on (Lord 1947, 327). This was done, and very quickly, on March 16—barely ten days after the new government came to office. The resulting Agricultural Adjustment Act, which would put into motion the first recovery program, better known as the New Deal, was submitted to the Congress.

In the course of this economic revival policy, agricultural Statisticians played an underrated yet crucial role. As the adjustment program consisted of coordinating a reduction in the supply of agricultural goods and adjusting it to demand, they had to first statistically estimate the level to which production had to be reduced to meet this demand. Thus, the New Deal provides us with an exceptionally good example—although particularly neglected in this context—to study how politics and statistics re-create their links and interact during a political crisis (Desrosières 1998; Stapleford 2009; Tooze 2001).

Historians of statistics generally envisage this operation in one of three ways. The first group tries to see how a new politico-administrative arrangement transforms statistics (Duncan and Shelton 1992). It therefore opts for political or administrative determinism whereby technical change is explained by politics or its administrative forms. The second group asks itself how Statisticians can keep working without letting political upheavals affect their independence and disciplinary autonomy (Blum and Mespoulet 2003); this larger group favors science that is safe from interference by political or social interests. The third, more radical group, questions the capacity of statistics to influence political action by itself. It adopts the position of the "performativity" of the social sphere by science (MacKenzie, Muniesa, and Siu 2007). These three options differ on what, in short, we can call the real cause of social change: the first thinks the answer should be sought in politics, the second in unadulterated science, the third in science for politics.

But the America of the Great Depression forces us to reject all three options. Indeed, the crash was above all a vast destruction, a general undermining of the system. This affected first, the farmers and, of course, agriculture as a whole, but also the Statisticians, as the methods they had been applying until now turned out to be totally unsuitable for the new government policy. The data that they held had been useful in the laissez-faire policy conducted before the arrival of the Democrats; now, suddenly they were being asked for new data more adapted to the recovery policy, which they did not have. Initially (for at least the first few years of the New Deal), they went through a complete reassessment and their established methods suffered a setback—or rather, they were trashed.

The situation thus contradicted the hypothesis common to the three models, which consisted of assuming that the forces involved were constructive, and supposing that what came out of the interface between science and society was something more organized, more ordered than before. Historians only very rarely ask themselves "how things fall apart"; they work on the productivity of the articulation between the world and science, giving very few examples of disintegration, of decline. The theoretical resources needed to conduct a study of this type are missing, whereas the instances of disintegration are as frequent as cases to the contrary. Anyone would think that historians and sociologists fear, given the likelihood of failure of this phenomenon, that it may rub off on their own work.[1]

This chapter is going to describe the two main political objectives delineated by the New Deal administration, then show that each depended on the development of new statistical instruments. But we will see that the links initially established between the population, statistics, and political action did not become solid: they were not able to stand the test of reality and eventually collapsed. This chapter tells the story of two successive failures, two unfinished attempts to articulate politics and statistics, and puts forward a thesis that converts these failures into a theory of the decomposition of social linkages.

The "Prefects" of the AAA

The meeting held in March 1933 led to the creation of the famous Agricultural Adjustment Administration (AAA), under the aegis of the Secretary of Agriculture (whereas the other New Deal programs came under the direct authority of the President). The AAA was flanked by two other older bodies of the Agriculture Department: One was the Federal Extension Service, created in 1914, whose task was to disseminate technological innovations in agricultural circles through a network of "county agents," which included a representative in each agricultural county of the country. The second was the Bureau of Agricultural Economics, founded in 1922, to which our "Division" (the very one whose history we have been following) was attached on this date. At that time it was called the Division of Crop and Livestock Estimates and was designated in full in the AAA's organization chart (Nourse, Davis, and Black 1937).

How was this machinery supposed to function? The principle, as it was spelled out by Washington, was simple. Its aim was summed up in a slogan coined by Wallace: "Equality for agriculture." It signified that the prices paid to farmers were too low, compared to industrial prices, to allow farmers to live with dignity, and that this disequilibrium affected the entire economic system. The incomes of the farmers needed to be increased, putting their purchasing power at par with that of the industrial workers.[2] Hence it was a necessity to implement an action plan with twin objectives: On the one hand, to do what was necessary for agricultural prices to rise, which would curb production; on the other, without further delay, to grant subsidies to farmers in proportion to the reduction in production, for the economic stranglehold they were in was so strong that they would not have been able to survive till prices rose again. Controlling production and granting subsidies was therefore supposed to augment farmers' incomes, but only until "equality" was attained with the purchasing power of the industrial sector, but not to the extent of exceeding it, which would have been harmful to consumers of agricultural goods. Such was the government's aim. Under these conditions, the difficulty consisted of finding a method of "adjusting" supply to demand, making them tally without creating an imbalance. If this principle seems relatively simple, its realization was complex. To explain it, we are going to start from the top—that is, from the Secretary of Agriculture—and move down to the farmers. Then we will explain the situation from the farmers' end and move up to the Secretary.

It was initially decided to intervene in the first year only on the five main crops (wheat, corn, cotton, tobacco, and rice) and on pork.[3] Each of these activities would be handled in Washington by a special "Commodity Division." For each item, it had to be decided by how much the production was to be lowered to adjust to demand. The question of "how much?" made it possible for Statisticians to enter the arena.

In view of this new way of conceiving economic flows, the traditional statistics of the Division turned out to be inadequate. Indeed, the issue was no longer speculators and cheats who were skewing the market forces, but an economic situation that was destabilized by its own logic. The classic remedy was quite useless.

William F. Callander, the then Division chief, seemed to have realized very early on that major statistical problems would arise from the New Deal and immediately made preparations to find a way for the Division to participate in the new setup.

> Callander had anticipated this development and on March 22, 1933 sent a Crop Estimates Memoranda (CEM #55), marked "strictly confidential" to all Statisticians in charge of a State office, alerting them to the impending demands that they provide county estimates. This was followed on April 27 by CEM #64 confirming the role of the Crop Reporting Service as the primary source of statistics needed to formulate plans and to establish quotas essential for operating the production adjustment programs. (Brooks 1977, 12)

The Secretary of Agriculture and the principal officers of the AAA had retained the task of deciding the percentages that needed to be reduced for each product on the national scale, as well as the allotment of the "quotas" between the different states. The Division supplied the production estimates for each of the five crops for the country and for the states, in terms of volume, for the years 1932 and 1933. It is on the basis of the data supplied by the Division that the quotas were fixed for the states.

Once the state-wise quotas were decided, they were transmitted to the Division's Statistician in each state (represented by the box "State crop and livestock offices" in the organization chart), who then transmitted them to a committee created specifically for this purpose—the State Allotment Committee in the organization chart. On this committee sat a member of the AAA, a member of the Extension Service, the Division's Statistician, and a few farmers. This committee was supposed to allot the quotas to the various counties, in proportion to the average output recorded by the

Division in 1932 and 1933. The responsibility for the allotment of quotas in the counties seems to have fallen not so much to the committee as the Statisticians of the Division. For example, Verne Church wrote: "From that basis, quotas were set up for each county, the major responsibility for which fell upon me personally. The totals of the county quotas must not exceed the state quota set in Washington" (Church 1944, 255).

It was thus the Statistician himself who allotted the quotas for his state to the different counties. At this stage, we know how the reduction quotas were attributed to each county. But how were they used in the county? To answer this question, we are going to go to the other end of the chain, that of the farmers.

Rightly or wrongly, the administration expected a strong reaction from the growers against an excessively planned or excessively centralized government intervention. At the same time, Wallace himself was hesitant about imposing too bureaucratic a system; it was important for him that the New Deal not be a parenthesis in the democratic process, but on the contrary, that it stimulate democracy. Washington may have decided to play a bigger role in the nation's economy, but Wallace believed that citizens should not become passive as a result.

In concrete terms, this democratic requirement took the form of a contract based on voluntary service: only those who were willing participated in the adjustment program by signing a contract with the Secretary of Agriculture himself. This contract was limited to one crop (so that if the grower wanted to reduce his pork, wheat, or cotton production, he had to sign three contracts) and specified the area that the farmer undertook to leave uncultivated (or the percentage of hogs that he would not breed) and the amount of subsidies that the Secretary of Agriculture pledged to give him. It was a long contract, about ten pages, that detailed the grower's obligations, those of the Agriculture Department (see figure 2.1; we have highlighted it on the page given as an example), the different quantities contracted and the sums remitted, and at the bottom of the document were affixed the signatures of the grower and the Chief Treasury Officer of the

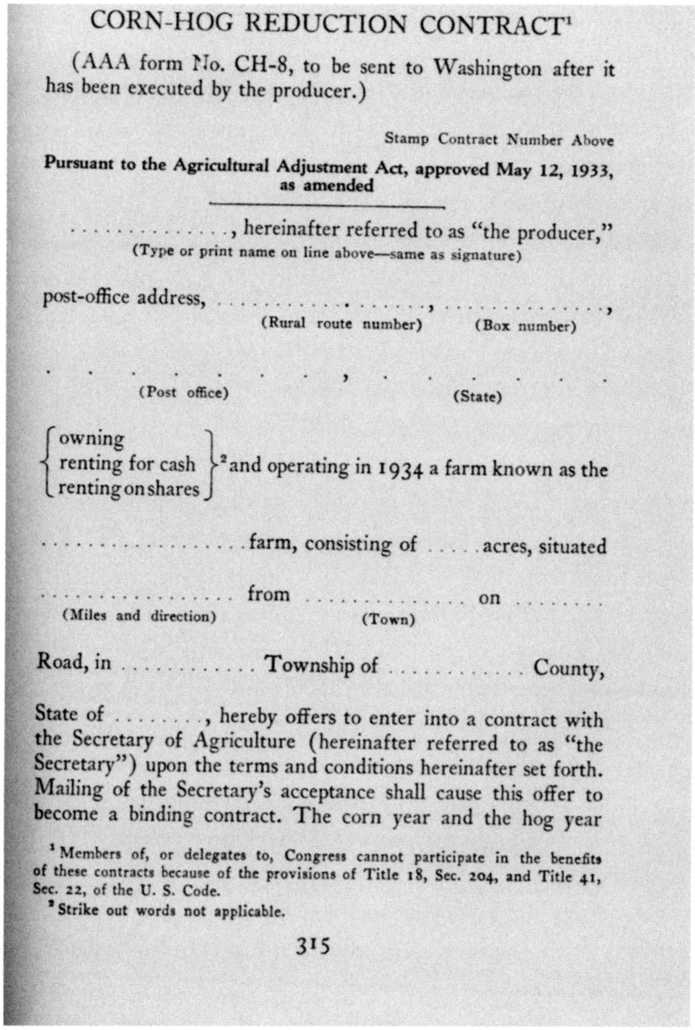

CORN-HOG REDUCTION CONTRACT[1]

(AAA form No. CH-8, to be sent to Washington after it has been executed by the producer.)

Stamp Contract Number Above

Pursuant to the Agricultural Adjustment Act, approved May 12, 1933, as amended

. . . . , hereinafter referred to as "the producer,"
(Type or print name on line above—same as signature)

post-office address, ... , ... ,
(Rural route number) (Box number)

. . . . , ...
(Post office) (State)

owning / renting for cash / renting on shares [2] and operating in 1934 a farm known as the

. . . . farm, consisting of . . . . . acres, situated

. . . . from . . . . on . . . .
(Miles and direction) (Town)

Road, in . . . . Township of . . . . County,

State of . . . . , hereby offers to enter into a contract with the Secretary of Agriculture (hereinafter referred to as "the Secretary") upon the terms and conditions hereinafter set forth. Mailing of the Secretary's acceptance shall cause this offer to become a binding contract. The corn year and the hog year

[1] Members of, or delegates to, Congress cannot participate in the benefits of these contracts because of the provisions of Title 18, Sec. 204, and Title 41, Sec. 22, of the U. S. Code.

[2] Strike out words not applicable.

315

2.1 Facsimile of the first page of the contract signed between a voluntary farmer and the Secretary of Agriculture himself. The contract emphasized the importance of the Agricultural Adjustment Administration. (Fitzgerald 1935)

United States. Hence, the program, the primary democratic factor of the recovery policy, was contractual (Nourse, Davis, and Black 1937).

At this point, we can better understand one of the complexities of fixing quotas, both for the states as well as for the counties. As participation was voluntary, it was not possible to know in advance how many farmers were going to join the scheme. The quotas could therefore not be given as percentages of past productions (e.g., each grower must reduce the cultivated area by 20%) but had to be an absolute quantity (e.g., so many acres are not to be sown) to be divided between the number of participants, fixed afterward. So, the Statistician had to calculate the area sown in 1932, in absolute terms, in order to determine the 1933 quotas. The question that now arose was how should the contractual quantities be determined between the participants within the county?

The answer to this question provided another opportunity for local democracy to experiment. Indeed, by signing the contract, the farmer automatically became a member of a County Control Committee, as indicated in the organization chart (which was an aggregation of local committees called the Community Committees). This committee, composed of all the growers who had signed up for the local committees, was self-monitoring. Indeed, it was supposed to "check data furnished by individual contract signers as to their acreage and production in base years, and to see that the reduction undertaken by each and the benefit payments claimed therefore conformed equitably to the estimates for the county as a whole" (Nourse, Davis, and Black 1937, 74).

Wallace had devised a very clever plan for allocating the total subsidies of each county to these committees, whereby it was the growers themselves who, within each county, divided the subsidies paid by the federal government and monitored each other, which ensured democratic justice. Moreover, Wallace had reason to feel satisfied with a setup that constituted the first example of "economic democracy in action" (quoted by Brooks 1977, 11).

When the Committee dealing with the allotments had fixed the quotas for the growers and the latter had distributed them among themselves, a final body had to verify whether the reduction quotas that the farmers had agreed to and those that they had been allotted actually tallied. It was toward this end that a Board of Review (mentioned in the organization chart) was created.

> For clearing the work of the allotment committee, there were established state boards of review. The work of these boards called for a membership technically competent to pass on difficult and delicate questions of adjusting individual and county base and production figures in line with official state totals. The state committee was expected to check the quality of work done in the several counties and assist in bringing any inefficient or apparently biased committees up to standards. The state crop and livestock statistician served on these committees; also, ordinarily, one or more representative of the state extension service, and a farmer or farmers. (Nourse, Davis, and Black 1937, 74)

In this way, the Board of Review completed the adjustment process—a process designed to collect the declarations of the counties with regard to the reduction in their outputs and then verify that they actually corresponded to the sums and quotas allocated by the AAA.

In short, the Secretary of Agriculture fixed the reduction targets for each crop; these targets were thereafter communicated to the states, then to the counties by the Division's Statistician. The farmers who wished to participate organized themselves into committees and divided the quotas and subsidies that had been allocated among themselves, and the Board of Review, still controlled by the Division's Statistician, verified that this allocation corresponded to the initial specifications of the government.

Hence, in this local process at the state level, the Division played a crucial role through the intervention of its Statisticians. Why were the latter chosen to play this role? First, it was because they apparently possessed the numbers that were necessary for establishing the quotas. Second, for this task, an institution was needed that had a network in the states, and preferably also in the counties. From the outset, because it would have been very time-consuming (among a thousand and one other reasons), the AAA had given up on the idea of setting up a new structure of this type. What remained was, first, the Division, which along with its Statisticians already had such a setup, and second, the Extension Service with, supposedly, its reputation of being very Republican. Wallace, who did not want to be embarrassed by this fact, chose to confine the Extension Service to the role that it was familiar with—namely, explanations and presentation of public policy at the local level (Church 1944, 11). The Division was thus the obvious choice to concretely help in articulating the link between the government's objectives and the decisions of the growers, with its agents supposedly being the best source for the agricultural data accumulated over the last two years. The Division possessed the best tools—its statistics—to carry out, in practical terms, the adjustment between the federal government and its farmers.

Each agricultural Statistician of the Division, because he was "technically competent" on the subject of the quotas, thus assumed the role of the "prefect," in the sense that is familiar in Europe in keeping with the blueprint developed by Jean-Antoine Chaptal, Napoleon Bonaparte's Interior Minister. The prefect transmitted "the law and orders of the government to the lowest subdivisions of the social order with the rapidity of electric fluid," as Chaptal explained to the French House of Representatives as he was defending the law of Pluviôse 28, year VIII of the Revolution instituting the prefects (which means February 17, 1900 in the Gregorian calendar). He was the intermediary between the central government and the local bodies. True, he was the prefect of only those who had signed the contract, but the signatories were by far the more numerous. Like the prefect, the Statistician executed the decisions of the federal government in his state (Mackenzie 2006).

Fragilization

However, what really transpired was that the supposedly effective link between the AAA and the Division turned out to be the source of a veritable disaster.

First, the government was acting under pressure as time was running out. In agriculture, it was necessary to act ahead of the seasons and intervene before the harvest at the end of summer. One of the consequences of this pressure was that the county quotas were in fact often established by Statisticians *before* the federal government communicated the quotas for the state to the central government, and not after. The Statisticians tried to gain time by relying on the figures that they had, and they worked confident in the fact they would be *in fine*—that is, in agreement with the national figures. But reality decided otherwise: the federal figures were often lower than the Statisticians' hypotheses. For a Statistician, it is not surprising and is even predictable for estimates calculated in two different places to differ, but when it is a question of using these figures to distribute incomes, statistical oddities are more difficult to accept.

Moreover, the AAA vehemently refused to go over its own work again. By so doing, it laid the whole responsibility of the blunder on the Statistician, who was obliged to revise his calculations. Hence, many Statisticians were forced to go back to the farmers and sign new contracts, and what's more, compel them to contract less land (and get smaller subsidies)! For example, Brooks, a Statistician (from 1931 to 1966) initially in Iowa and then in Washington, D.C., who, like Church, wrote his professional autobiography, recounts that in Iowa, he had to make fresh contracts in nearly all the counties. Imagine the farmer's reaction when he was not only obliged to renegotiate but, on top of it, negotiate downward. "A very unpopular enterprise," he says, in an obvious understatement (Brooks 1977, 21).

Second, as we have seen, Roosevelt and his team established the AAA office in March and the initial measures were ready by March end. As it happens, on this date, seeding had already taken place for the majority of crops in most states and the sows had freshened. So, in the first year, the problem was not controlling production but destroying the crops already sown and even slaughtering full-grown piglets. This was quite traumatic for the farmers, and also for the consumers.[4] For example, in the case of cotton, Brooks recounts how mules became an unexpected source of opposition: All their life, they had been taught to walk *between* the rows of cotton and *never* trample them; now suddenly they had to unlearn everything and, on the contrary, walk over the cotton plants to crush them. They found it enormously difficult to accomplish this barbaric ritual. Books comments:

> Although it has been said that a mule is an animal without pride of ancestry or hope of posterity, mules, as compared to horses, are highly intelligent and their opinion of this destructive operation may have coincided with that of many outraged critics and thought it a sinful waste. (Brooks 1977, 3)

Fortunately, the growth condition of wheat and corn, catastrophic in 1933, excluded these two crops from the destruction program. All the other producers participating in the program were, nevertheless, critical of the Statisticians. According to them the program was a complete waste, and it was the Statisticians who were responsible for the quantities to be destroyed or slaughtered.

Lastly, and this problem was the most serious for the Statisticians of the Division, whereas the government and the AAA projected themselves as the ones distributing the funds, the Statisticians were seen as dashing the farmers' hopes, of reducing the quantities declared, of curtailing their demands, of setting limits to the distribution of subsidies. It was always they who had to make the county committees, which systematically tended to exceed the quotas, fall in line with the limits fixed by the government (and in fact fixed by themselves because they had converted the state-wise quotas into county-wise quotas). In Michigan, for instance, the particulars that the County Control Committees gave to Verne Church, the Statistician, exceeded his own estimates by 2% to 45% of the total! In other words, the area of one crop, let us say wheat, declared by the farmers participating in the program of a particular county exceeded the total area devoted to this crop in the county, as estimated by the Statistician, and by a percentage that was as much as 45!

Of course, everyone, including the committee members, thought that the farmers had lied in order to obtain additional subsidies. But the County Control Committees did not know who was lying and thus did not know how to go about comparing the statements with the estimates given by the Statistician. Their task was so tough that some committee bureaus even preferred to resign rather than investigate. How was one to visit his neighbor and accuse him of falsehood without starting a local conflict? It was practically impossible. Brooks recounts:

> Tough decisions had to be made with consequent lower benefit payments for old friends and good neighbors already hard pressed by adversity—decisions that often were difficult to defend on plausible grounds. The unsung heroes of the Corn-hog program of 1934 and 1935 were the county and local committeemen. (Brooks 1977, 23)

Brooks well realized that if the decision was, according to the government, "democratic," it was above all locally very *hard to take*. That is why, when writing his autobiography much later, he continued to praise the members of the committee. But Church relates another version, just as credible, according to which the committees actually abandoned this impossible task and off-loaded the responsibility to the Statistician:

> These were hectic days for me and I did not relish fighting from one to four or five committees each day of the week.... Their stock argument was that our data, being in the nature of estimates, could not be relied upon for establishing equitable quotas. They could not comprehend our highly technical methods

> of statistical analysis and, in the beginning, we had no other tangible proof to submit in rebuttal. (Church 1944, 256)

The Statistician's position was difficult not only because he had to dash the hopes of the farmers but, on top of it, he did not have good arguments to justify his action. With regard to "methods," Brooks simply explains that the Division did not have exact data for the counties. We saw in chapter 1 that the Division served to calculate the estimates for the state, but in no case was this done by the addition, purely and simply, of this partial data. The Statisticians had estimates for each county, but these figures were part of the mechanics of the production of data in the state and were constantly revised for correction of bias, smoothing, and comparison with past data or direct observations. In other words, data was entered in the production of the final figure for the state but, paradoxically, remained very inaccurate for the county that it described:

> As has been indicated, all of the New Deal farm programs required county estimates and it was the task of the Crop Reporting Service to provide them. Resources available for this purpose were scant everywhere … for the job of preparing county estimates of what John Wilson called "serviceable accuracy." Much imagination and many hours of strenuous endeavor went into conscientious efforts to achieve relative accuracy. It was not an academic exercise. The results were used for determining payments to farmers, a matter of critical importance to hard pressed people in those stricken times. Try as one might, the official county estimates bore the scars of blemishes inflicted by crude tools, meager and wobbly data, overworked clerical staff and pressures of taut time-frames. (Brooks 1977, 31)

While the administration and the government distributed the resources eagerly awaited by the growers, the Statisticians found themselves in the thankless role of being the only ones stifling farmers' hopes; moreover, they did not have a strong argument to justify their position. Statisticians who have given an account of this period have all affirmed how intolerable it was for them because they were used to joking and laughing and exchanging information with the farmers. It is here that the storm becomes a tornado, that we shift from solidity to total ductility, because as the Statisticians opposed the farmers, the farmers lost no time in holding it against them and soon saw no reason to cooperate anymore and give them the precious information necessary for producing the Division's statistics. This is what Walter Ebling, the Wisconsin Statistician, has to say about his experience:

> Because of the extreme pressure of other work, the sampling machinery on which much of the Crop and Livestock Estimates data have been largely dependent has suffered during the past few years. [It] has caused lists to be neglected, and the returns from the samples have frequently declined. In addition to that, the workers are confronted with new forms of bias arising out of the adjustment programs to say nothing of ill will which has sometimes been engendered among correspondents as a result of the AAA activities and has caused sample data from voluntary reporters to decline. (Ebling 1936, 115)

From the moment the Division opposed the crop reporters, it obviously risked losing their support. As a result, many of them either stopped replying or started to lie (to give a rather undiplomatic interpretation of what Ebling calls "a new form of bias"). In one year, an analyst of the Brookings Institution estimated that the number of respondents to the survey on hogs had decreased by 12% (Fitzgerald 1935, 108). Losses were heavy! What is more, the "voluntary" crop reporters (if we can still call them that) not only stopped replying but they verbally attacked the employees of the Division during their information-gathering field missions; they went as far as to humiliate one Statistician who had come to lend a helping hand to a colleague by having him forcibly escorted by the sheriff to the border of the state (unnamed) "with the injunction not to return if he wished to escape bodily harm" (Church 1944, 257). Thus, by taking action against its own source of information, the Division was turning off the tap.

In other words, statistics and Statisticians cannot permanently be the government's prefects, performing for the world rather than describing it. For nothing obliges those who supply information necessary for the very existence of statistics to shoot themselves in the foot and continue to serve an administration that, according to them, is doing them a disservice. The Division was thus given—and accepted—the villain's role (without, moreover, its leaders seeing the danger looming) against the good government that was giving subsidies and the poor farmers who deserved them. As the very basis of its primary mission was being undermined, the prefectorial delegation of Statisticians turned into a double failure.[5]

Fortunately, we would like to say in support of the Division that on January 6, 1936, the Supreme Court invalidated the first AAA, giving as reason that it was not constitutional for the government to manage markets and that quantitative contracts constituted such management. The law instituting the first Agricultural Adjustment Administration was revoked, and on the occasion, the Division was relieved of this "administrative" task, as both Church and Brooks call it.

How should this relationship between statistics and the action it took to achieve its goals be described? What should we call something that seems more like destruction than construction? We would like to say that the effect of the AAA on the Division was to *fragilize* the method of the crop reporters and increase the risk of the link between the Statisticians and the crop reporters breaking down. An intercalation—namely, the "production quotas"—took place between farmers and Statisticians, and this occurrence, instead of strengthening the link, as Callander had hoped (when he tried to get his Division to participate in the New Deal program) rendered it enormously fragile by inducing a breakdown of the relationship of trust between the Division and its informants.

This fragilization did not lead to a change in the "Crop Reporters' method," which in 1934 and 1935 remained the same as in 1929, in the sense that at no point were the successive stages of statistical production called into question. Whatever the number of respondents, the Statisticians continued to stock the reports and go out into the field, then on their return to process the questionnaires they had received. In 1934, the Statisticians had fewer reports than before, but they processed the smallest number that they had in the same manner as they had processed the large number. The method was as predictable and solid as before, the order of the stages was also the same, but this did not prevent one of the links from running the risk of a breakdown. And when this risk became fact, what was rejected was excluded: it disappeared from the aggregate and was thrown back into the plasma (Didier 1996).

This risk was such that the AAA and the Division had to completely revise their reports. After the first agricultural adjustment law was repealed, the reaction of the government was extremely clever: it had a second law passed on "soil conservation," based on the fact that intensive cultivation of arable land was the cause of severe erosion that put the land itself at great risk. To protect it—which was a constitutional function of the government—the AAA financially incited the farmers to reduce the area planted with soil-damaging crops (which not surprisingly were the five that had been listed during the first AAA) and increase the area planted with crops that restored it (which were under-cultivated). Thus, by changing the justifications for its action, the government managed to reinstate itself within the constitutional framework while maintaining its interventionist policy, which it considered important. But for its new mission, the AAA had preferred to hire "crop adjusters," whose job it was to measure the declared areas, like tax control officers, and who freed the Division's members from this "administrative" responsibility (Church 1944, 258). Although relations between the two institutions had been allowed to shrink to nothing, a new attempt to articulate statistics and public action rapidly followed.

Planning

After 1936, the measures taken by the Department of Agriculture for promoting agricultural revival became less monolithic than in the first three years of the Roosevelt government. In particular, another method used in the context of the New Deal, parallel to the AAA, assumed importance in 1936. Surprising though it may seem today, it was planning. It was very different from Russian planning, or the fascist plans of the same period, and even French planning in the postwar era. American planning, especially between 1938 and 1941, was an extremely powerful trend in the Agriculture Department that explicitly addressed the issue of the relationship between the exercise of democratic power and research in the social sciences—a question which was also put to statistics. We are thus going to see how planners made use of statistics and how they conceived the relationship between public action with this mode of description.

We are first going to broadly outline the objectives of agricultural planning, then we will concentrate on its specific link with statistics. We will see the great hopes that it had pinned on statistics and how it brought only great disillusionment.

Since the commencement of the New Deal, and consequent to Roosevelt's setting up the "Brain Trust," the Department of Agriculture had appointed an impressive number of academics to top jobs. This migration of intellectuals was explained by Kirkendall (1962) as the result of two converging movements. On the one hand, in view of the magnitude of the 1929 crash, Roosevelt and Wallace (along with several politicians) had become skeptical about the different kinds of knowledge that had traditionally guided the actions of the U.S. government as well as the big industrialists and the great administrators, because not only had such knowledge been unsuccessful in averting the crisis but also, until then, in resolving it. As a result, universities now featured as a second storehouse of knowledge, likely to replace the earlier one, despite the typical reservations existing in the country (Curti 1955). On the other hand, Kirkendall saw that the government's interest in academics was the result of a pragmatic outlook, largely inspired by the philosophy of John Dewey and his work on the *service intellectual*, in which they had been trained (Kirkendall 1962; Gruchy 1939). We can, moreover, note the extent to which the participationism proper to this philosophy, already quite dominant in the Agriculture Department, was congruent with the method of relying on voluntary crop reporters. It was these academics—and among them the more influential economists often identified with the institutionalist current—who developed American-style planning (Wallace 1934). Politicians in search of new knowledge and intellectuals eager for action thus met in the ministries, and in particular in the Department of Agriculture.

Among these intellectuals, we can especially cite Professor Rexford Tugwell, who gave up his chair of economics at the University of Wisconsin to become Deputy Secretary of Agriculture in 1933 and later resigned in 1936. He was replaced by another very well known professor of economics, Milburn L. Wilson, who became the chief administrator of the AAA and retained the post of Deputy Secretary until Wallace's departure in 1941. We can also mention Dr. Howard Tolley who, after having taught economics at the University of Wisconsin, administered one of the most important bureaus of the AAA, called since its inception the Bureau of Planning; after 1938, he came to head the Bureau of Agricultural Economics (BAE), the organization to which the Division was attached (see Wilson and Tolley in figure 2.2). Thus, in the Department of Agriculture, economists were appointed to key posts.

What were these "agricultural planning programs"? What did a "plan" signify in the United States before the war? Planning initially had a rather vague connotation and could refer to practically any component of the adjustment policy of the first AAA in its entirety.[6] But beginning in 1938, this concept of "planning" took on a more specific meaning because a group of specialists took charge of it. Indeed, during a general reorganization of the Department of Agriculture, Howard Tolley who, as we have seen, was already heading the Bureau of Planning in the AAA, was offered the post of

2.2 If Rex Tugwell was a confirmed "urbanite," here we see H. Tolley (left) and M. Wilson (right) who, brilliant as they were as an academic and a powerful administrator, respectively, liked to project themselves as being "close to the soil," comments Kirkendall (1966, 116).

director of the BAE by Wallace, with the aim of making it the central planning agency of the Department (Moulton 1938). His bureau came directly under the authority of the cabinet Secretary for Agriculture. He therefore did not depend on any other administration, and especially not the AAA, from which, on the contrary, the Bureau of Planning was detached, aggregated to the BAE. The task of the new BAE was to draft plans for the entire Department and specifically for each of its sections.[7] The aim, on the one hand, was to synchronize the various activities of the Department, which had been combined under fewer heads and, on the other hand, to articulate these various activities with the more local plans, initiated in the states or even the counties. The "plan" was that the central operator would enable this articulation, and the extended BAE would be the facilitating agency responsible for it.

The specific tool on which Tolley was relying to achieve this aim was a planning method that he had been experimenting with and whose success he had great hopes for. This tool was called "land-use planning." O. V. Wells, who had been part of the BAE since the 1920s and had even been Tolley's student, described it in very clear terms, particularly with regard to the role that researchers and academics were supposed to play (Wells 1938). Let us follow his four-step presentation.

The first phase involved the "farmers' recognition" of the problems, the particular situations that needed remedial measures. During this phase, the farmers formed local committees (mostly at the county level) that specified the problems needing resolution and the goal to be attained, but without reflecting on the means to be employed. This phase was crucial for all involved, and in particular for Tolley, Wilson, and Wallace, because it ensured that planning was democratic, something that was of concern to all the stakeholders. Even if the meaning that they gave to "democratic" varied enormously (see, for example, Tolley 1939; Gruchy 1939; Wallace 1934), democracy signified, for them at least, that the public had to first identify the problems they were beset with. It was the farmers who, at the grassroots level, identified a need, an objective (Dewey 1991).

The second phase consisted of the "recognition of the demand" by all the other stakeholders in the agricultural field: for example, the state's agents, federal agents, journalists, and agricultural workers. This recognition was not easy. According to Wells, the initial reaction of the different groups was often to ignore the farmers' demands, which they felt were not important. But, Wells adds, the pressure exerted by the farmers eventually resulted in their making themselves heard. It also happened that in reality it was the other groups that identified the problem and "sold" it to the farmers. It was a less direct, more complicated process but, after all, acceptable. The recognition of the demand consisted of specifying the different methods and measures necessary for the goal to be realized, while redefining it. Researchers, and in particular, agricultural economists who surfaced at this juncture, made their investigations, established and explored the alternative solutions, and nearly always concluded—perfidiously, adds Wells—that they did not have the required data and needed to ask for additional funds to continue their investigations.

The third phase was that of "agreement." Everyone had to agree on the approach to be followed among those outlined in the preceding phase, an approach that would necessarily be modified again in the process. Many discussions took place to arrive at a consensus, which meant that more players joined in: representatives who were for or against, financiers who provided the numbers to the solutions, lobbies that had a stake in the game.

The final phase involved bureaucrats having to find an administrative method for implementing the plan and agricultural economists to establish and identify the socioeconomic results that could be expected. The author notes that there was again potential in this phase to introduce substantial changes in the program, which then ran the risk of opposition by the farmers, who had initially launched the process. He also indicates that economists outside the process had a tendency to limit "planning" to these final amendments, which were actually only a stage in the process.

There were innumerable such plans. Let us give two examples. Donald Blaisdell, Wilson's assistant, cites the case of Quay County, in New

Mexico, where the road network was particularly bad and where planning brought about changes making it more practical and practicable (Blaisdell 1940). Tolley gives the example of Teton County in Montana, where land use had been inappropriate, leading to exhaustion of the soils (Tolley 1943, 151–156). A plan was implemented that redefined land use in a more sustainable manner.

Organizations at all levels—from the county to the state level—could participate in finding a solution. This point is important because it shows that planning had been conceived as not only having local consequences but also having the capacity to legitimately affect the federal level as well. For example, certain plans transformed federal laws, especially those relating to land use. Moreover, these plans mobilized and helped to develop the expertise and tools available with the federal department alone: for example, in the case of Teton County, crop distribution maps for areas lying beyond Montana and covering the entire northwest of the country were needed and could be furnished only by a federal agency. Tolley proudly indicated that 200,000 people were members of one of the agricultural planning committees in 1942, whether at the level of the state, the county, or the community (Tolley 1943), a number that because of its strength, began to assume importance at the federal level (Gilbert 2001).

Thus, in the course of these four stages, which were really the summarization of a long process—very much like the public participation theorized by Dewey (1991)—the farmers continued to be involved. First, no doubt they sometimes realized that the initial sweeping and indeterminate goals had eventually been transformed into specific and attainable ones, and this may not have been to their liking; nevertheless, farmers continued to participate fully in the entire process and therefore, according to the promoters of this planning, in the transformation of the nation (Skocpol and Finegold 1982). American-style planning thus consisted of fixing objectives and achieving them by insisting on following procedure, and as much as possible in a democratic manner.[8] Second, research by economists—with a few exceptions, such as Milburn Wilson, the Deputy Secretary of Agriculture, for whom the other social sciences (sociology, anthropology, political science, and psychology) played an important role (Wilson 1940)—also had a constant and specific role in this process, which to a great extent tended to be interventionist. Let us note, however, that the specific form of intervention by academics in the process remained controversial and could be resolved only by nomenclatures of colleagues and established categories of economists, depending on their greater or lesser propensity for action (Tolley 1939; Wells 1938).

Planning thus constituted an experiment for promoting a political relationship between the farmers and the academics. We can picture the vast building of the Department of Agriculture as the political setting for the encounter between the steady flow of farmers from the countryside and the long line of professors from universities, who formed a great experimental, noisy multitude together with the hordes of administrators already in place.[9] But, in this melee, where were the Statisticians and statistics? Is it possible to specify the role that was expected of them and that they effectively played?

Deliquescence

To understand the encounter between planning and statistics, let us study the comments made by planners about the Statisticians. In fact, the government was very interested in statistics. However, rather strangely, this interest went hand in hand with jokes, caustic remarks, and even as far as the Division's statistics were concerned, open criticism. This ambiguity can be illustrated by a short passage in the rather clipped style of Robert Lynd, author of the famous *Middletown*, a book that met with great success in the Bureau of Agricultural Economics after its publication in 1939—so much so that, it is said, Tolley made it mandatory reading for his collaborators![10]

> Statistical manipulation is the spearhead of current empirical research. It has been remarked that it is almost impossible to overestimate the significance of sex in human affairs, but that

> this impossibility Freud has achieved. In much the same sense, one may say that it is almost impossible to overestimate the significance of refined statistical procedures for social science, but that some current researchers are achieving that impossibility. (Lynd 1939, 126)

We frequently come across this paradox—at once a fascination with and reservations against statistics—among the planners of the time. Let us try to analyze it. First, the old statistical methods from the time of the crop reporters were no longer appropriate for planning. The planners did not completely disown this method, but this great ancestor had become obsolete. Although the point was also taken up by Wells (1938), Tolley offered a fervent homage to Henry C. Taylor, who had founded the BAE early in the 1920s around the statistics of the Division (Tolley 1943). He showed that the crop reports had been one of the first instruments of planning, for they had allowed the farmers to coordinate their actions. Indeed, according to him, by relying on the Division's estimates, the farmers could together decide whether to sell or stock their crop. Retrospectively, Tolley brought out a new characteristic of this data, which had been conceived very differently in the 1920s—namely, the data was not originally meant to help in the coordination of the various actions but to fight speculators, which is not the same thing. The fact remains that, for Tolley, "crop reports" had played a crucial historic role.

But the 1929 crash had shown that the coordinating ability of these statistics had ceased to be effective: "They do not smooth out the production cycles, eliminate undue spreads between farm and city prices, or prevent agricultural depressions that result from the periodical collapse of buying power," wrote one of the BAE officers (Chew 1937, 66). In one word, when the economy became seriously ill, they were no longer able to heal it. True, everyone agreed that statistics continued to describe the economy. Hence, Tolley states that one of the great past merits of Statisticians had been their ability to compile empirical data and analyze it through quantitative methods, in particular with regard to crop reports and cost analysis (Tolley 1939, 14). But these statistical descriptions were no longer like the earlier ones that had helped to correct economic flaws when it proved necessary; the jolt given by the AAA experience had demonstrated that direct action did not suit them. "A thermometer cannot in itself cure the fever," concluded the same officer (Chew 1937, 66).

Therefore, when the BAE was transformed into the Department's powerful planning bureau in 1938, the Division, the one that we have followed up to now, was separated from it. Under the name of the Agricultural Statistics Division, it was attached to a new Agricultural Marketing Service, which was created as a sort of consolation prize for its new head, A. G. Black, who had steered the BAE before Tolley's arrival and who was a close associate of Wallace (Kirkendall 1966). The Division was thus considered outmoded and was clearly excluded from the BAE and from policy planning.[11]

In the administrative language of organization charts, BAE economists had clearly indicated that they could no longer see what use they could make of the Division's statistics. Even if statistics had played a crucial role in the past and no doubt continued to describe the economy, this description was no longer of much use. They thus weakened the link between numbers and their earlier role in policy making, going as far as to sever it. The Division's method was endlessly reproduced according to the same procedure, yet, on the one side, its link with the crop reporters was dangerously fragile and, on the other, its link with politics had been broken. Like a fossil, the method remained solid but was plunged into an isolating limestone bath.

Did this break, however, signify that planners were rejecting statistics? Far from it. On the contrary, statistics in general remained a tool of prime importance for them. Regardless of the difficulties that the Division had encountered in the early 1930s, its past aura had all the same left the impression in everyone's mind that statistics could be very useful and had already proved their worth. Other, more recent experiences also made people realize that statistics could be useful.

One example of the fascination that statistics continued to exert came in the form of an article very often referred to by members of the BAE because it talked of "social engineers" (Davis 1937). According to this article, state intervention in economic and social affairs, especially planning ("the word *planning* has been dinned into our ears," the then-president of the American Statistical Association said), entailed the training of better and more engineers of a new kind—social engineers—capable of "repairing" appalling economic situations, like engineers are capable of repairing bridges. Obviously, planners were delighted by the argument. And yet, insisted the article's author, "at all events, statistics is basic to social engineering. Perhaps nowhere else, even in business and government, is the proper use of statistics more truly vital" (Davis 1937, 5). Statistics would thus form the basic equipment of social engineering, which was starting to see the light of day.

In the same vein, we can cite Tolley himself, who explained that, for planning, "high quality work stands for the development of more effective theoretical analyses, improvement of statistical techniques, additional and more advanced research" (Tolley 1943, 244). That is to say that for him, too, statistics remained important, not exclusively but among other activities. He had remarked on the phenomenal success that George Gallup's polls had met in 1936 by predicting, contrary to other quantitative prediction methods like straw polls, Roosevelt's reelection (Igo 2007). Tolley thought: "If it worked for Gallup, why would it not work for us?" (Converse 1987), meaning that if Gallup had managed to statistically understand the opinions held by Americans, there was no reason that they could not repeat this feat in the Department of Agriculture. In 1939, Gallup thus came to deliver a series of talks on opinion polls in the in-house ongoing training organized by the Department.

Similarly, M. L. Wilson too defended statistics. As he was first and foremost a great supporter of the social sciences apart from economics (Wilson 1940), in 1935 he created within the Department a small "Division of rural attitudes and opinions," inspired by the Chicago School, which initially comprised only six interviewers who did "semi-direct" interviews, if the term is not anachronistic. The investigators talked casually with the farmers about their attitudes in relation to various problems. Thereafter Wilson sought to quantify his methodology. In 1939 he appointed Rensis Lickert as head of the Division (which now became known as the Division of Program Surveys). Lickert was already recognized for his work on partial surveys (in this hiring, Wilson was following the advice of Robert Lynd, the author of the comparison between Freud and statistics). Lickert standardized questionnaires and conducted surveys and, in so doing, clashed with his investigators who found their new task lacked prestige (Converse 1987, 51). Wilson had thus noticed the emergence of this new clearly statistical "research through surveys," whose history is exhaustively related by Converse (1987), and attempted to develop them in the Department.

The misfortunes that befell the Division did not stop statistics in general and especially the partial investigation methods—the Chicago surveys, Gallup polls—from being sought after by planners. Nevertheless these statistics remained, within the framework of the Department, in the realm of the potential—of what could happen or could no doubt be constructed. Social engineers had to be trained, pre-electoral polls did not yet have their place in the administration, and Lickert's surveys were in the process of being transformed into statistics. Be that as it may, planners expected a lot from statistics.

Now the results that statisticians offered them rapidly gave rise to reservations, and even disappointment. Davis, for example, who ranked statistics very high in the training of social engineers, went so far as to write: "I doubt if any group of workers has a larger representation of experienced gnat-strainers and camel-swallowers than those who deal with or dabble in statistics" (Davis 1937, 6). For Davis, statisticians were so involved in methodological quibbling that they lost sight of the real objective of this discipline, which consisted simply of describing reality.

Similarly, Tolley was unhappy over the fact that statistical data was so ill-adapted to its political objectives. He criticized the researchers who "postpone acting until they have developed a complete theoretical framework, compiled and analyzed more statistics, undergone advanced training in social engineering schools which yet remain to be opened." According to him, researchers always want to investigate further, statisticians want to produce more statistics, and this stopped them from acting. He concluded bitterly that, "in their attachment to the most abstract stages of their discipline, some economists lose sight of the essential connection between theory, research and public policy" (Tolley 1943, 243).

As for Wells, he compared the hardworking group of "researchers," whose "answer to every problem is to gather more facts, whose vision of agricultural economics is limited to schedules, interviews, tabulations, and the conclusion that more research is needed" (Wells 1938, 761), to another much more worthy group, that of the "administrators," "who are interested in statistics and research only to the extent that such activities serve toward the development of a practical program." He "must be able to marshal the relevant facts, to separate the wheat from the chaff" (Wells 1938, 763). For Wells as well as for Tolley, statistics too often went around in circles, postponing the time for action.

What is highlighted in this criticism is that the response of statisticians to the interest that planners had for them rarely satisfied the latter. Not only were the responses often considered very slow, but, even when quick, it seemed that they were rarely useful.

Statisticians did not manage to make themselves relevant in the eyes of the administrators. Planners no longer wanted reports on crops. They still wanted statistics, but at this stage did not know which ones; also they had not made their expectations clear. Most of the propositions made by the statisticians did not satisfy them. The planners could not figure out what to do with them, for they did not answer their unformulated questions.

It seems to us that this strange relationship between an answer that was not suitable and an unformulated demand can be qualified as deliquescent (Roux and Magnin 2004). Just like two molecules of heavy oil, statisticians and planners slid against each other without managing to connect and interact, even when they met each other in meetings and exchanged commissions and results. Statistics did not fulfill the promise of the political use that was expected of them. The lack of relevance prevented the stabilization of the link between planners and statisticians.

Conclusion: The Disintegration of America

There have not been many studies on the processes through which an aggregate comes apart, but in the case of the Great Depression, which caused such phenomenal destruction, it is difficult to skirt the issue. How did the old America, characterized by laissez-faire, crop reporters, a statistical method, and a certain type of public action disintegrate? We can answer this by reviewing the three principal stages of the process that we have just observed.

First, even though the Division continued to generate the old data, which still retained a serviceable degree of accuracy, it soon became clear that it was no longer very useful, at least for combating the Great Depression engulfing America, especially as there was no stopping its destructive force. What statistics captured of the population and conveyed to politicians had become outdated and useless. Which is why the earlier statistics were filed away in the white elephant category.

Instead of the old statistics, the administration first and foremost needed fresh and accurate data for the counties. Hence, in the second stage of the process, the Division attempted to collect the same. It thought that the task would be simple because it had produced figures for the states, and the counties were simply an extension of the state-wise administrative units at a lower level. But it proved difficult to break the global figures down to geographical subparts, so this attempt turned out to be a massive failure (Desrosières 1993). One of the unexpected consequences of this failure was that the old method based on a stable relationship of trust between the administration and the crop reporters collapsed.

In the third stage, for changing policies and carrying out "land-use planning," planners needed statistical results. But they found it very difficult to obtain results that were relevant for them and that captured the characteristics of an America that could serve as the basis for their projects. They were not questioning the validity of the numbers that they were given, but these numbers gave them information on things that did not interest them. Once again, statisticians were not able to capture those aspects of the population that would have been useful for public action.

At the end of the day, whereas in the time of laissez-faire there was a predictable and useful continuity (i.e., solidity) between the population, statistics, and public action, the Great Depression widened the gap between the interstices that separated the elements. It is these gaps between the people hit by the Depression, statistical techniques, and public use of these numbers that we call "disintegration." The nice and solid aggregate of the laissez-faire era comprising these three entities was in the process of disintegration. Let us stress the fact that it was not just a question of a change in the administrative requirements that statisticians, bound by their old practices, failed to satisfy. Change not only concerned administrative requirements but also the population itself, the object of statistics, which the statisticians were trying to describe and which was so out of step and displaced, and hence eluded the tools that were too antiquated.

We have identified two different mechanisms of this disintegration: first, the disintegration, or at least the weakening, of a link in the statistical chain and, second, the deliquescence of the relation between these two links. But how do these two mechanisms relate to one another? To answer this question, we now have to systematize, in the conclusion to the first part of this book, our observations in the first version of the theory of consistency.

Conclusion to Part I

Solidity and Consistency

To begin with, the history that we have just traced has shown, with the Crop Reporters' method, how the links between a statistical technique, its object that we call the population, and political action were consolidated. Every year, and all the summer months of every year, in each of the states of the Union, the administration sent a representative to meet with the crop reporters, those faithful volunteers spread over the territory, who replied to the same questions, whose answers were processed in the same manner, till they reached the Board of Crop Estimates that also always followed the same procedures. This stability, this predictability allows us to qualify the links between the population, statistics, and politics as solid.

But, because consolidation processes exist, it also means that links can be broken. How can one describe this phenomenon? Let us start with our second example, which concerns planners once they had taken hold on the Agriculture Department's policy. They had great expectations of statistics for their project on land-use reform. But what was produced by the agricultural Statisticians never satisfied them: their data always needed more in-depth processing, the results always arrived late, and methods changed too often, so that, instead of being predictable and productive, the relationship between political action and statistics was unpredictable and often lacked relevance. We have named this process "deliquescence," and we will qualify its resultant aggregate as viscous.

We note that the values of the terms of this opposition were very clearly denoted: solidity was qualified positively and viscosity negatively. However, if these values were obvious during the 1930s, today they are much more open to debate. Martuccelli (2005), for example, praises the positive qualities of flexibility, elasticity, malleability, whereas Bauman (2000), who also shows how these characteristics reached their peak at the end of the twentieth century, on the contrary, emphasizes their detrimental effects. The respective values of *solidity* and *ductility*—a term that does not have the pejorative significance of deliquescence—have not been stable since the 1930s, but this does not affect the existence of these two concepts, or the constancy of their polarity.

But where do we place *fragility*—the name that we have given to the risk of rupture between two segments of the aggregate—on the solidity-viscosity axis? To answer this question, it should be first noted that a solid aggregate as much as a deliquescent aggregate can break up. We witnessed the first example of rupture when, faced with the 1929 stock market crash, and realizing that the earlier statistical procedures were far from adequate, the government tried to use Statisticians as prefects charged with implementing national policy at the local level. This role did not suit them at all, for it met with strong resistance on the part of farmers, so much so that very soon there was conflict, with several of the Reporters ceasing to respond to questionnaires, the very foundation of statistics. The aggregate remained solid since there was not an iota of change in the methods used for producing the earlier figures, but nevertheless the likelihood of a break existed, as suddenly, from 1934 to 1935, a large number of Reporters stopped corresponding with the Statisticians.

The aggregate became viscous when statisticians began to work for planners. In this state too it ended up by breaking, although not in the same way as when the aggregate was solid. The split was not sudden, because that would have led to a very serious conflict, but it was staggered over a long period in an imperceptible manner. The Division found itself attached to a unit other than the Bureau of Agricultural Economics, of which it had been the nucleus, then, gently, without there being any hint of a scandal, an attack, or a rebellion, the Division was separated from its initial administrative unit.

Thus, there are two types of rupture (Roux and Magnin 2004): one corresponds to the solid state of an aggregate, to a violent clap of thunder, with discontent, cries, and resignations; the second corresponds to the deliquescent aggregate, in which the break is silent, difficult to date for it occurs over a long period, during which the players tire out rather than flare up and consequently do little to explain their motives and reasons.

Fragility thus has a dimension that is perpendicular to the solidity-viscosity axis. Instead of describing a change in the texture of the links between the elements of the aggregate, it describes the risk run by some elements of breaking up with the others and hence, finding themselves excluded. It highlights the fact that whatever the degree of solidity of the aggregate, some of these elements can be isolated and thrown back into the plasma.

These three concepts—solidity, deliquescence, and fragility—of which the first two are opposites and are both independent of the third, thus constitute the beginnings of a repertory making it possible to speak about the consistency of an aggregate. We have seen an America go from great solidity to a state of complete deliquescence. The links between statistics and its object, on the one hand, and its users, on the other, were initially well under control, repetitive, and foreseeable, then became loose, unpredictable, broken, inadequate, and irrelevant. The Great Depression had unquestionably pushed America into a slump, and the big question was whether it would be able to pull itself out of it. Today we know that it did, but to know how, we are going to have to go back a little and discover how the random sampling method made this possible.

Part II

Expression of Random America

On the Rural Front

At the end of part I, we left the agricultural Statisticians in a deadlock. The Great Depression had resulted in the people going through a very severe *human erosion*, to borrow the telling title of one of the first books of that period combining photography and sociology (Lange and Taylor 1939), leading to such an astounding situation that statistical tools proved incapable of capturing it and government action appeared to all but overlook it. Statisticians no longer seemed to have either users or a clear objective.

To break the deadlock, they had to search for methods better adapted to the post-Depression scenario, and they opted for a singular survey technique: random sampling (Didier 2002). Initially, this option was not at all obvious, especially as it was very different from the traditional methods of the Division of Markets and Crop Estimates. Whereas the old method relied on the crop reporters, who volunteered to collaborate with the Division, one of the central features of randomness was that those interrogated were drawn at random—that is, the willingness factor was not taken into account. The question that we need to understand and ask—as it was asked by the actors—is how this transition was made.

In this case, the option proved to be extremely enriching. From the moment that the Division introduced randomness, everything was restructured around a new nucleus: the *Master Sample*. The Statisticians managed to put together a new population, perfectly compatible with the random method, and the politicians found use for the data generated by this new method. In other words, gradually America gained consistency around randomness and this new consistency was long-lasting. The new method was patently very solid and frequently copied all around the world, including in France by the Institut National de la Statistique et des Études Économiques (INSEE),[1] and even today it remains the standard in statistics. Of course, we have to understand why the Statisticians retained it, but also how it enabled America to find a new yet solid consistency.

However, rather than rushing to the end of the story, we will take the time to present the resources available to the supporters of randomness. The concept of statistical representativeness and the bits and pieces of the theory of probability, which were central to its development, were imported and discussed as early as 1920, and even before, within the Department of Agriculture, even if they did not have an immediate effect on the aggregation methods described in chapter 1. We will therefore backtrack and try to understand how these two essential features were captured by the agricultural Statisticians, before accompanying them in their efforts to consolidate random sampling.

Part II is composed of four chapters, or the four historical stages following which agricultural statistics became random. They describe how the population was made compatible with this method and how the data was rendered functional for the Agriculture Department's users. From each stage, we have extracted elements pertaining to the theory of the consistency of an aggregate, which will be summed up in part II's conclusion.

3

From the Political Representative to Statistical Representativeness

The story goes that the first statistics on American agricultural actually date back to 1862. They were produced not by the state but by a journalist, Mr. Orange Judd, the managing editor of *The Agriculturist*, who proposed to "let the readers of the *Agriculturist* in every town counsel together, and select some man who may be relied upon for good judgment and general ability to estimate [the condition] with some degree of accuracy in regard to the leading crops, wheat, corn, etc."[1] Thus, the very first concern of the very first person who thought of compiling agricultural statistics was to know who to question, how to choose the informants, and what criteria to use. Judd's solution was to rely on the persons *designated* or *elected* by their fellow citizens.

This very year, 1862, the Department of Agriculture was created in America. It immediately took responsibility for this task and for the production of figures, so that farmers could sell their produce in a more equitable manner (Ebling 1939). It seems, moreover, that the Department retained Judd's methods, but sources do not agree on *which* representatives were questioned. For a historian of agricultural statistics, it appears that members of Congress selected future crop reporters among the local representatives (Vogel 1995), whereas, according to the memoirs of a former practitioner, "monthly questionnaires sent to township supervisors provided the basic information for the published state reports. There were about 1,200 townships each having a supervisor who was elected by popular vote annually in April" (Church 1944). It is not important which of these two sources is right (in fact, they may both be right, for the initial surveys had not been standardized so that they could be applied to the whole territory). What is important is that when the government took over the publication of the figures, it also believed that the best sources of information were the elected representatives.[2] The first statistics thus borrowed their mode of representation from the political sphere—more precisely, the democratic sphere: the good representative in statistics was a good representative in the political sense.

The Division then expanded the group of potential crop reporters to include people who were not necessarily elected representatives but who nevertheless had several points in common with elected representatives: they were volunteers, the most capable farmers, and driven by the spirit of public service, just like American representatives are thought of as being volunteers, the best among us, and motivated by the desire to serve.[3] In other words, the Division's conception of crop reporters was deeply influenced by its conception of the people's representatives, at least until the end of World War I. But this method had to be radically modified in 1921, following a crucial error. Let us see how, on the basis of this initial reform, successive changes resulted in the idea that representatives could be replaced by a *representative sample*.

Individual Farm Inquiry: Objectivity of Informants

In 1921, after a brief controversy, it became clear that the estimates of the acreage planted with cotton were far below actual production. In February 1922, a "Committee of Consulting Statisticians," composed of three eminent professors from major East Coast universities, went to Washington, D.C., to try to ascertain the reason for the error and to come up with a solution that would ensure that it would not be repeated. The methods hitherto used were explained to the Committee, which was given the files containing the principal documents used by the Division. The consulting statisticians then left, promising to come back in three weeks with the results of the analyses.

According to the Committee, the people behind the 1921 campaign had been afraid that overproduction would lead to a fall in prices. The government therefore instilled that the acreage under cultivation be substantially reduced in order to lower the volume of production. The crop reporters, who were "public spirited," responded to this appeal by reducing their yields; similarly, all the other farmers told the crop reporters that they were complying with the recommendations. The latter thus reported a general decrease in production, which was reflected in the statistics. The Committee thought that in reality only the crop reporters had produced less. As the other farmers did not have a public service mentality, they had probably deliberately given the impression that they were complying with the government's instructions, but in reality had not lowered their production, resulting in an error of estimation. The Committee therefore deduced that the crop reporters had been victims of "collective panic": They had been influenced by discussions with their neighbors (they had reported a decrease in the farmed acreage, real in their case, and in the declarations of the other farmers), but not by the neighbors' fields (where no decrease had taken place). They had been misled by a mechanism of a "psychological" nature.[4] Psychology was identified as being the cause of error in the figures.[5]

The problem now was to find "new methods to obtain reliable data" (Taylor and Taylor 1952, 238–242) free from psychological factors. This was not easy to resolve: What could be done so that people were unaffected by psychology? The Division came up with a very clever solution: it simply no longer questioned people but machines, which, as everyone knows, have the definite advantage of being devoid of psychology. These machines were called *crop meters*. They were the descendants of another machine that Verne Church was proud to have invented, the bean box, which was simply a small box with compartments, one for each type of crop (one for wheat, one for corn, etc.), and which he used while driving. To count the number of fields devoted to a particular crop, he put a bean in the compartment corresponding to the crop alongside which he was driving. The crop meter was an improvement on this first machine and was directly connected with the car's speedometer, which it moreover resembled, the only difference being that it had a certain number of push buttons (see figure 3.1).

To use it, when the Statistician passed a maize field, for example, while driving on the roads of his state, he pressed the button corresponding to this crop and the crop meter automatically measured the length of the field. This machine created enthusiasm among the Committee members because the data that it helped to mechanically produce was necessarily more objective.

However, if the machines had the advantage of being unaffected by psychology, they also had major disadvantages: they were not interested in the results, and the "loyalty" dimension in the relationship was missing. In short, they destroyed the old link that the Division had painstakingly and slowly established with the farmers. Nat Murray, who was the Division head at that time, vigorously opposed doing away with the crop reporter services and replacing them entirely with the machines. He reiterated that the crop reporters were "public spirited representatives" and rejected any criticism against the "faithful reporters who have always been and must continue to be [the Division's] principal reliance for securing data."[6] He believed that it was *not* the crop reporters who had been misleading, but that they had been misled by their neighbors. Therefore, there was no question of giving the impression that they were being penalized by relieving them of a task of which they were the raison d'être. To preserve the usefulness of the numbers, it was necessary for farmers to continue to supply them and to participate in their own defense by producing them. There was thus no question of abandoning the Crop Reporters method.[7] But what could be done so that they would no longer be taken in by their neighbors?

The remedy was apparently quite simple and consisted of looking only to farmers for information. Initially, the crop reporters' profession was not relevant; what was important was that they had to be thoroughly familiar with local agriculture. They were thus farmers, but not exclusively. For example, we read about a retired army officer or a postal employee (Church

3.1 H. L. Collins, agricultural Statistician of the state of Kansas, using a crop meter.

1944, 8) serving in this role. But after 1921, it was decided that only farmers should "give actual facts as to the acreage":

> Instead of asking the reporters to give their opinion as to the change in acreage from year to year, a large number of farmers in every locality are now asked from time to time to give actual facts as to acreage in various crops and numbers of livestock on their farm. (USDA 1925, 14)

This development had the advantage of "saving" almost all the crop reporters since most of them were farmers, and at the same time the Division was able to change the statements of the voluntary correspondents described as "opinions" into answers of farmers capable of reporting "real facts." How was this possible?

> In the early days of the crop reporting service "judgment" inquiries concerning acreage changes were the principal indications used concerning acreage changes. In these inquiries a crop correspondent was asked to express his judgment of changes in acreage of crops in his locality by reporting the current acreage as percentages of the corresponding acreages of the previous year. Analysis of the results from this type of schedule indicates that it is difficult for a farmer or anyone else to report with sufficient precision as to the acreage changes that have occurred within the locality for which he is reporting. … Analysis of the results obtained from the record of actual acreage of crops on sample farms from year to year indicates that this method is much superior to the use of judgment inquiries. Consequently the inquiries requiring the judgment of the correspondents concerning acreage have been practically discontinued. They are replaced by sample farm acreage data—records of the actual acreages of crops on farms of crop reporters. The change to this basis was a definite forward step towards increasing the accuracy of the reports. (USDA 1933, 16–17)

The reason a farmer gave "facts" whereas a crop reporter expressed his "judgment" was because the former managed to be more precise than the latter. It was the accuracy of the response, confirmed by subsequent studies and analyses, which had transformed an assessment into facts. But why was the farmer who was talking about his farm more accurate than the crop reporter who was talking about his locality?

Apart from the fact that a farm was smaller than a locality, the nature of the two spaces was different. The farm was controlled by its farmer whereas the neighborhood encompassed it. Hence, during the initial surveys, when the question concerned the entire locality, the instructions written on the questionnaires were as follows: "Report ONLY on such crops named as are grown in your locality. Report for the part of the country around you which comes under your personal observations."[8] By contrast, the individual farm inquiry specified: "Can you fill in the schedule below for your farm or plantation?" (USDA 1933, 69).

Why did the fact of owning a farm allow the farmer to give the "real surface area of crops"? The Statisticians seem to have assumed that the crop reporters could only have definite knowledge of something they had direct control over. The reality of their statements was thus supposed to reside in the bond between each individual and his *property*, as John Locke as well as the entire Anglo-Saxon liberal tradition subscribed to. According to them, objectivity was achieved only in relation to something on which direct influence could be exercised.[9]

In addition, a study presented in 1920 in Madison (Wisconsin) confirmed the validity of this option. It showed that "the degree of bias [of the individual farm inquiry] could be measured" (Becker and Harlan 1939). As we have seen, the bias is the difference between the values obtained by Statisticians with the help of their instrument and the "real" values—in other words, with other values in which they had confidence. In this case, it had been possible to measure the bias because of a very recent agricultural census of Wisconsin, with which the figures obtained in the survey of individual farmers could be compared. The new form of the survey thus made it possible to calculate the error, which was considered the principal advantage of the method. In the previous method, the bias could only be measured with great difficulty as there was no simple geographical commonality between the census and the survey which made comparison possible (if the census took the farms into consideration, it completely neglected the "neighborhoods" that Reporters had to observe). This inability to compare in the older method was considered a weakness in itself (i.e., not including the results, which the comparison would have helped to obtain); therefore, the second method was considered the better of the two.

In addition, two years later, after considerable effort to make the Crop Reporters' method compatible with the census, this same bias calculation was finally applied to two methods simultaneously, and it is the method of individual farms that turned out to be the more accurate: "In 1923, another bias study was made of the individual-farm data on cotton acreage, by states, which were available as far back as 1915. This study disclosed the superiority of the individual farm inquiry over the judgment inquiry" (Becker and Harlan 1939).

Hence, for acreage surveys to be more objective, the Statistician would ask farmers for details of their own farms and discontinue asking crop reporters to provide data on their locality. Since the Statisticians had initially identified psychology as the cause of error, the best means of getting rid of it was to rethink the bond that linked the informant with the land. As it had been demonstrated that psychology was inseparable from the neighborhood, whereas it spared the farms, it was enough to replace the one with the other to do away with the troublesome element. The Statisticians had managed once again (as with the crop meter) to do without people and their weaknesses, this time by asking farms directly what acreage was attributed to different crops (is not the new method called "survey of individual *farms*," not "survey of individual *farmers*"?), without however completely giving up the idea of asking the farmer himself, reappointed as spokesperson for his farm. It was thus hoped that the Division would not commit the 1921 error again.

The new method was more suitable for determining the *acreage* than determining the *growth condition*. In fact, in the case of the second variable, the information concerning the neighborhood was still pertinent. The crop reporters thus did not need to limit themselves to their "own farm" when observing the condition. The reason was that the condition depended mainly on geographical factors: soil type, topography, climate.

The method, which eventually was used only for determining the acreage, had two related consequences. The first consisted of transforming the observations (which, together, were exhaustive) into a series of examples. In fact, initially each township was represented by at least one crop reporter, so that if the township was equated with the neighborhood (as the Division did), the crop reporters together constituted a sort of parliament of the entire agricultural territory. But after the survey of the individual farms, those the Division did not solicit were no longer *represented* by the crop reporters, because their responses were limited to their own farms. The latter were henceforth considered *examples* of other farms. This new characteristic of the respondents can probably be illustrated by the appearance of a new word in the statistical system: *sample*. Even if the statistic manuals of the 1920s, including American, used this word without ambiguity in the sense of a group of individuals, at the same time, in the Division, *sample* designated a single person. For example, in the formula noted at the back of a 1923 questionnaire addressed to farmers, it was specified that each individual was considered a *sample*.[10] Here, each respondent was by himself a sample.

The second consequence was that those agricultural Statisticians who were *employed* by the Division found themselves being given additional responsibilities. Indeed, from the moment that the answers were no more than examples of farms that had remained silent (and not their spokesperson), someone was needed to check the exemplariness of their answers. Because of this new responsibility, the Statisticians were easily able to weed out the odd questionnaires, carry out the rectifications, and in short do what was needed to evaluate the answers of their informants and express doubts about them.

Despite the advantages of the new method, the Division soon encountered an unexpected difficulty: it now lacked respondents.[11] We can cite here a small in-house newspaper, the *Omnibus*, which states that "Koenig [an agricultural Statistician] from Pennsylvania reports that he has had some very favorable returns.... Of the schedules sent to farmers on the pig survey card, he received a 20% return."[12] What is now known as the rate of nonresponse was thus extremely high, as Koenig was satisfied with only 20% returns. This lack of information was a problem, since too few examples rendered generalization hazardous. This problem reached a critical threshold in 1924, forcing the Division to realize that a solution would have to be found which, unknowingly, took it a step closer to randomness.

Numbers and Representativeness

For the estimates to have an acceptable degree of accuracy, the Division had planned to increase the number of respondents. But what could be done to induce more farmers to put their names on the lists? This objective was already difficult to realize when the crop reporters were dealing with the whole neighborhood, but from the moment the Division asked them for information on their own farms, it risked scaring off farmers, who would have been wary of leaks to the tax authorities. The Division was thus faced with a serious difficulty.

A solution emerged, as the story goes, in the felted drawing rooms of Washington's administrative buildings. It happened that the incumbent Secretary of Agriculture, who from a distance was following the developments of his statistics department, was a personal friend of the Postmaster General. Now, in the course of a conversation, they discovered that there were several points in common between the duties of the agricultural Statistician, going to the remotest corners of his state to collect information, and the duties of the mail carrier who distributed the mail. They reached a partnership agreement on this basis with crucial consequences (Taylor and Taylor 1952).

The first was that it secured "crop reporting districts" for the Division, an essential territorial division, based on postal distribution zones (see figure 1.3).[13] These zones were transformed by the Division according to the "homogeneity" observed in "agricultural production," which facilitated the work of generalization of the observations (because a single observation carried out in a homogeneous space was valid for the whole space). The first advantage of this agreement, then, was to provide the Division with a definition of the whole of America that it could quite easily reutilize.

The second consequence of this agreement was that it considerably increased the number of respondents. As the mail carrier had to visit many letter boxes, he could distribute several questionnaires. Now experience showed that when the number of persons who received questionnaires was multiplied, the number of people who sent back a filled-in questionnaire was also multiplied. To increase the number of respondents, all it took was to increase the number of persons questioned. Hence, the relationship of loyalty between the farmer and the statistical system, which had earlier ensured the returning of the questionnaires, was no longer necessary. The crop reporter did not need to claim the status of volunteer; it was enough that he was one, as and when consulted.

The Division had, however, taken the precaution of replacing the initial agreement of voluntary participation with three different inducements for getting a response. First, it hoped that the mail carrier would enter into direct contact with the farmers. The recommendation made to mail carriers was that "the best results will be secured if the carrier will question the farmers and fill in the answers himself."[14] Indeed, this method had an advantage over the farmer knowing how to read and write; the farmer was supposed to be capable of filling out the questionnaire himself thanks to information given to him orally, and the discussion with the mail carrier was supposed to incite farmers to cooperate. The second inducement was that the Division explained the advantages of the survey to the farmers in the questionnaire: "The farmer himself will be benefited most by the results of this inquiry; therefore it is to his own interest to furnish data. Those who refuse to furnish information stand in their own shade."[15] As a third inducement, the Division concluded its little text with a polite request: "Your aid and your cooperation is earnestly solicited.'[16] The reply could also be made graciously, out of politeness, because the Division had asked the question. As a substitute for loyalty, the Division had thus come out with other inducements for replying which, via the mail carrier's mediation, considerably increased the number of respondents.

But were the large number of answers enough for the Division? Was the aim simply to have as many as possible? No, the instructions recommended that each mail carrier distribute ten questionnaires per postal round (USDA 1933, 68), which represented far more questionnaires distributed than the number of names on the list of crop reporters, but mechanically restricted the number of replies that it was possible to receive. The aim, therefore, was to distribute not the maximum possible but only the "right number." For example, Henry Taylor, the Division head in 1925, wrote that "careful studies have been made to determine the number of farms that are necessary to give an accurate picture of each area" (USDA 1925, 15).

Moreover, the mail carrier was not supposed to just get rid of the questionnaires, he had to *choose* ten farmers to give them to. The criteria according to which he had to choose were explained as follows:

> The farms reported upon should be such as to give a good average picture or "sample" of all farms on the route. The surest way of obtaining a fair "sample" would be to get reports from every farm along a portion of the route—owned and rented, large and small, rich and poor, etc. Just as they come—care being taken to select a portion that will be fairly representative of the entire route.[17]

First, he had to obtain replies from each postal route, which together corresponded to a partition of U.S. territory (in reality there were zones where mail was not distributed, but the Division made an approximation). The idea therefore was to obtain good data from each one and then simply add the partial information together. This first recommendation did not contain anything particularly new. The originality of these instructions lay in the idea that relevant information was to be obtained not from any superior individual, or from some good examples, but from "every farm along a portion of the route." In what way did a portion of the route advantageously replace the crop reporter?

The portion allowed the Division to calculate a "good average picture" of the route, an expression on par with the word "sample." The meaning of this term was thus comparable to the meaning given in the manuals of statistics; it no longer denoted a single observation but constituted an entire group of observations. This meaning was still approximate, but considering that the word was put in the instructions given to the mail carrier, it started to make a mark: within a few years "sample" no longer referred to an observation but to a group. This detail, however, tells us very little about the properties of the "average picture" the mail carrier was supposed to construct. What other characteristics was "sample" supposed to have?

The word "average" has a double meaning in this sentence. It signifies first that a subset of the route had to be constructed whose average could be calculated. This implied that the mail carrier had to carry out an *exhaustive* survey of that portion of the route. Thus, minor and incidental differences between the various farms of the subgroup selected would cancel one another out (which is why the mail carrier had to take the precaution of surveying "large" and "small," "rich" and "poor" farms, etc.) and the result of this calculation would indicate an average that would be real. This relation between average and exhaustiveness has been established by Adolphe Quételet (an average is meaningful only if it has been calculated on the basis of all the elements in the set) (Desrosières 1998b); this was the Division's aim.

But the Division complicated matters because the "average picture" *at the same time* signified that the portion of the route had to have a certain connection with the rest of the route, which had not been taken into consideration while calculating the average. This special connection was the concept of "representativeness" that appeared in the Division's vocabulary at this time: the "portion" had to give a "good average picture" that would be "fairly representative" of the entire route. What did this relation signify? Its meaning was not yet very precise; it only corresponded to the idea of a group—in other words, the sample, which would represent the totality.

Conclusion: Expression

During the 1920s, the Division was forced by two successive difficulties to review its methods and upgrade them to meet the criteria of accuracy of the findings. Thus, the Division moved from its reliance on the crop reporter deputed as *representative* to an *objective* farmer who owned a farm, then to a small group representing all the other farmers. What is common to these two evolutions? We are going to use the concept of *expression* in response to this question (Didier 2007). We will first see how it can help us understand the process of innovation, then what it is opposed to, and finally we will examine one of its important properties, which also explains how certain things are rendered obsolete.

In reality these two evolutions are part of a ternary process. First, the Division teamed up with two entities in succession: the Committee of Statisticians in 1921 and the Post Office Department in 1924. Second, it established a certain type of relationship with each of these entities: a *consultation* with the Committee and an *agreement* with the Post Office. Third, from this specific relationship a new element emerged each time. We propose to call this entire process statistical *expression*. The Division and the Committee expressed the method of individual farms; the Division and the Post Office expressed postal surveys.

Where does the word "expression" come from? Very often it refers to the mathematical tradition that goes back to Leibniz, for whom one thing expresses another when there is a constant and regulated relationship between what can be said of one and what can be said of the other. In this case, expression signifies a certain structural analogy between two elements, an important characteristic of which is that structure exists prior to their interconnection. We speak, for example, of the algebraic expression of a geometrical form (the algebraic expression of a circle is thus a second-degree equation). But even if this meaning is most widespread and has the advantage, for our purpose, of referring to mathematical and hence statistical entities, it is not the one that we will retain. On the contrary, we prefer another tradition, highlighted by Deleuze (1990) and going back to Spinoza. The advantage that we find in this second tradition is that expression is not understood as a specific kind of relationship between preexisting things, but as the mechanism by which something new—really new—occurs during the encounter with something that is not new.

The philosophical argument is highly technical, but the use that we make of it is much simpler: the elements constituting the Crop Reporters' method (i.e., the crop reporters, their psychology, the area, the condition, the questionnaires), articulated in the special relationship that has been described, gave rise to this *new attribute* of farmers responding more *objectively* than in the past. Objectivity is the expression of the elements in the list in the sense that it is the outcome of their specific articulation. Similarly, the elements enlisted in the second venture organized by the Division, jointly expressed as the postal survey, are characterized by the great number of responses. The central point about expression is that what comes into being is new and what is expressed did not exist earlier or, in the language of philosophers, was at best virtual. Expression produces a novel characteristic.

Expression, as we understand it here, is different not only from the meaning that the Leibnizian tradition gives it, but also from two other simple ideas. First, it does not have the limited day-to-day meaning when we say that someone is giving free rein to his instincts or, when replying to a survey, that he is expressing himself and exteriorizing something. The meaning that we give to it is not the simple formulation of something that preceded it (i.e., a feeling or something internal). It is, on the contrary, the production of a novelty, of something unforeseeable.

Second, we will say that "expression" is undoubtedly, as Bruno Latour puts it, a *meaningful articulation* (Latour 1999, 187), because the process that we have described includes a stage, during which the players take up a certain number of elements and try to assemble them and articulate them in the most satisfactory way possible, that produces properties and characteristics. But the word "expression" signifies more than just "articulation" (to which one has to moreover tack on "meaningful" to make oneself heard), particularly because of its aesthetic connotations, On the one hand, expression implies the inventive, surprising aspect of the activity, which also consists, effectively, of articulating the elements. Statisticians no doubt do not create their objects, but they nevertheless invent a thousand and one surprising ways of getting them to cohabit; their activity thus has, like that of artists, an inventive dimension, which the word "expression" allows us to bring out more than the word "articulation" does. On the other hand, and this time from the point of view of the objects and not the players, expression also signifies the sudden appearance of something during the process. The term implies this emergence, this something extra. On the contrary, the word "articulation" is suggestive of a simple Meccano, simply putting things together, without any indication that either thing is modified by the coupling. Expression thus resembles the "articulation" defined by Bruno Latour, because the former contains the latter, but it also encompasses in one word other aspects of the process—invention and emergence—which articulation alone does not imply.

Now that expression has been defined, let us highlight one of its important properties. Expression is not only the characterization of something that is trying to establish itself; it is also the retrospective characterization of methods that have been rejected as outdated and archaic. The expression of new characteristics not only concerns the nascent wonders but also, and inseparably, the methods that are at the same time rejected as obsolete (the paradox between coming into being and obsolescence being entirely voluntary on our part).

Let us elaborate by going back to the transition from reliance on the crop reporter to the individual farmer. We can see that the new method was often considered capable of producing "true facts" and dealing with "real facts." In one word, it was considered "objective"—as the Division's members insisted on several occasions—even if they used the term in place of what we simply call accuracy today (Sarle 1927). But it should also be noted that the earlier method at that point was at the same time newly qualified as survey "by assessment," in which the crop reporters merely gave "opinions." The terms "assessment" and "opinion" were never part of the professional vocabulary of the Statisticians before the appearance of the said "objective" survey. Until then, the method applied to the neighborhood simply *never qualified* under the objective/subjective criteria. The epithets used for the crop reporters were their commitment, "spirit of public service," "accuracy of reports," but never their objectivity. When the new survey method was developed, it was accompanied by the new criterion that devalued the old method (for there is no doubt that here subjectivity was pejorative). The process of expression thus not only spawned properties in the new survey, but also those pejoratives in the older one.

This point has a very important outcome—namely, that Statisticians never know exactly which elements to include in their work, for it is only at the end of their experiments that the characteristics of what they had included become clear. Before the appearance of new properties, they never know precisely what the earlier ones were; for example, the characteristic "representativeness" has to be expressed in order to say with certitude whether the earlier methods had been or had not been representative. To put it in another way, the new characteristic that commends a method is also the one that devalues the older one. Thus, expression effectively constitutes one of the mechanisms of innovation.

In this way Statisticians and their allies of the moment had, during the first quarter of the twentieth century, expressed statistical representativeness and discarded political representation in statistics as passé. But this representativeness was still entirely theoretical, if one can so put it, which is to say that it was without any mathematical justification. This articulation with the theory of probability remained to be done in order to make the concept more valid.

4

Probable Error

While the initial experiments to select crop reporters were being carried out in Washington, in a remote corner of Iowa, in Ames, an obscure agricultural Statistician, Charles S. Sarle, was diligently preparing his debut. He was a cut-and-dried person who, in contrast to his colleagues, had a degree from Cornell (Brooks 1977). Hired as a Statistician in 1922, he was fascinated by statistical methodology and his work caught the attention of J. Becker and W. Callander, who had just been appointed, respectively, as director of the Board of Crop Estimates and head of the Division. As a result, soon afterward, in 1926, Sarle was called to Washington, D.C. Once there, without losing time he published (in 1927 and 1932) two brochures that represented two minor revolutions in the Division by introducing a major methodological innovation, *probable error*, which was not even remotely on the Division's daily agenda (Sarle 1927, 1932), although it had been invented some twenty years earlier in England by Arthur Bowley.

It would seem that Sarle had simply *applied* a classic tool (unknown in America) to his own data. He had learned to use a mathematical formula with unknowns and variables (x's and y's), put the numbers produced by his department through this mill (replacing each x and y with actual numbers), then observed the results that he got. In this he had been neither creative nor innovative, but had just done things mechanically, repeating the same gestures, the same reasoning, a thousand times. But this rather tame description of the application does not take into account certain difficulties that Sarle encountered from the outset, in particular the fact that the Division's data was constructed according to its own methods—that is to say, based on crop reporters who had *volunteered* to respond. This point made the Division's surveys very different from the ones created by Bowley, who had *randomly* selected the observations to construct his tool. We can thus straightaway say that there is an initial contradiction between data collected from voluntary respondents and random selection, for randomness is the negation of willingness: something which was selected randomly is precisely something which had not chosen to be selected. How did Sarle manage to use a tool that was not meant for his specific purpose? How did he reconcile this new tool with his data, which from the outset was completely dissimilar?

To answer these questions, we are going to undertake a more cognitive study than what we have done until now and follow Sarle's thought processes, which he published in the two brochures he produced. We will see how a reading of European specialists allowed him to ask a new question of the Division's data and thereafter examine the solution he provided (Bjelic 1996).

An Unexpected Object

Sarle had very extensive knowledge of statistics. The bibliographies attached to his articles show that he was familiar with the works of renowned statisticians in Europe, such as Karl Pearson (1911), Ronald A. Fisher (1958), and John Maynard Keynes (1921), whose *A Treatise on Probability* was frequently cited in the United States at this time,[1] and Frederick C. Mills (1924) and Robert Emmet Chaddock (1925) in America. Among his sources, he considered George Udny Yule (1911) and Arthur Bowley (1926) particularly significant, for both had directly worked on probable error. Sarle was also familiar with the discussions on the "representative method" initiated at the very end of the nineteenth century by the Norwegian Anders Kiaer, at the International Institute of Statistics, and which after many fresh developments were taken up by Bowley and Adolph Jensen, the director of the Danish Institute of Statistics (Jensen 1926b, 1926a).

Sarle wished to be recognized by his colleagues as a graduate. For example, he liked to accentuate his difference by using the word "sample" in the sense of a group of individuals whereas at that time his colleagues used it to denote a single example. Similarly, by endorsing probable error, which no one in the Division had heard of except him, Sarle was able to demonstrate the extent of his knowledge. "Use of its probable error as the sole basis for interpreting the average of a sample is an important forward step" (Sarle 1927, 38). He thus showed that he was the only one to have access to resources from far off shores, unconnected with American farmers and their problems, believing that they would help to rethink and improve the survey procedures of the Division. But what advantages did he associate with this tool? Why did he want to introduce it into the Division?

The concept of probable error had allowed Sarle to detect a problem thrown up by the data that till then had escaped the notice of his colleagues. Sarle knew that Bowley had stressed the fact that his own data bore on a small group of interviewees, a sample, but that he still could give estimates for the *whole* of England; as a result, his works at best—in Sarle's words—gave "evidence that a certain construction is reasonable, but not that it is true" (Sarle 1927, 13); that is to say, that the final figures could only be *reasonably close* to reality but never entirely correct. In other words, Bowley was confronted by the huge problem of *induction*: he claimed that observations made on a sample could be generalized to apply to all the population. Logically speaking, this operation posed serious problems, but probable error was the one tool likely to provide a solution.

This issue, which is at the center of the current theory of sampling and which all statisticians use today, was new for Sarle and *a fortiori* for his colleagues in the Division. In fact, they had some grounds for ignoring it, as the past methods used by the Division had simply got around it by interrogating crop reporters who represented the *entire* neighborhood, so that the initial figures were constructed from data provided by a few spokespersons whose aggregate was supposed to represent *all* of America, just as the Senate represented the will of *all* Americans. The preliminary sampling methods in America thus initially had this surprising particularity of bypassing the problem of induction. But Sarle realized that this logic did not apply if the data was based not on the judgments of the crop reporters but on the new method of making individual farm inquiries. This method resulted in more accurate data, but the linkages with European research established by Sarle showed that it implied the question of induction, which no one had thought of in the Division.

After this first step, Sarle reverted back and nonetheless questioned the Crop Reporters' method. Indeed, he remarked that it was by reason of an unverifiable approximation that we could call these reports noninductive; it was only if a hypothesis had been posited that the various localities on which the Division had information were all contiguous to one another that they could effectively constitute a partition of the territory. But, according to Sarle, there had never been any indication that where one neighborhood ended another began; nothing proved that the limits of a territory surveyed by the crop reporter merged with his neighbor's. So, strictly speaking, one was forced to the conclusion that the data on the neighborhood was also inductive. To prove the second point, in 1932 Sarle published his second work, which was much more dangerous because it concerned one of the two central series that the Division had been working on: the one on condition and yield, which were still largely produced from data on the neighborhood.

In view of the problem caused by the inductive nature of the Division's data, the advantage of probable error was that the risk of error during the selection of the sample could be measured. Probable error is first based on the concept of sampling error, which was a concept fairly well established in European research. It indicated the gap between the average calculated from the sample and the real value (i.e., that of the entire population). In fact, no one observes, as by definition the sample was drawn when the whole population was not known. So sampling error remained a risk, a probability. Which is why it is called probable error—the risk of error was measured in terms of probability.

The calculation of this probability was an old problem, and here too Bowley had something to contribute: He had supposed that the difference between the estimated variable (on the basis of which he calculated the average) and the theoretical variable followed a normal distribution (generally called a "bell-shaped curve"), a hypothesis that was justified as this law was already very well known and the tables of significant values had already been calculated. He could thus affirm that there was a 50% chance that the error would be less than 0.6745 units of this distribution's average. Thanks to this hypothesis on the shape of the distribution of the data, the probability of being wrong (i.e., probable error) was easy to calculate.

Sarle had borrowed this tool but kept the definition practically intact. He explained that "this is found by dividing the standard deviation of the sample by the square root of the number of reports and multiplying by 0.6745," a more mathematical formulation than ours and one that is in line with Bowley's definition—except that while determining the factor 0.6745, he fixed the probability of error at one out of two, whereas Bowley had not fixed it.[2] Apart from this, Sarle's interpretation of the tool was similar to Bowley's: "probable error signifies that the chances are 50 out of 100 that the average of an infinitely large sample collected in the same way as the given sample would not vary more than the amount of the probable error from the average of the sample we have" (Sarle 1927, 25).

Probable error was of immense interest because it allows one to calculate the error committed when inferring from sample to population. Thus the *accuracy* of the estimation could be measured, and probable deviation between the real value and the observed value could be calculated. It was not exactly a palliative for the weaknesses inherent in induction, but a way of measuring and therefore, despite everything, of controlling the inexactitude of this inference.

Yet Sarle, who owed so much to Bowley, had introduced a statistical innovation. He wrote that probable error compared the observed average to the average of a "sample of infinite size calculated in the same conditions as that of the sample that we have" (in other words, a census, which was conducted according to the same method—same questionnaire, same interviewers—as that of the survey). For Bowley it was completely different; the 0.6745 factor, which Sarle used, was only justified, according to Bowley, if the sample had been drawn randomly, and definitely not if the sample had been drawn "in the same conditions" as the census that Sarle was referring to. This inversion of the mode of selection of the sample was proposed by the American statistician. As we have seen, the samples of the Division were not at all drawn randomly, which made them incompatible with Bowley's probable error, whereas it was possible to compare the observed averages with the total observed population "under the same conditions as those of the sample that we have." This probable error reformulated so as to forgo randomness could then be used by the Division. But even if we understand this limitation, even if we realize that this transformation was necessary for probable error to be used in the Division, we still need to understand how Sarle justified this adaptation.

Adapting the Assumptions

Sarle was interested in probable error because it made it possible to calculate the risk of error, but he found it problematic because of the preconditions attached to it. In particular, to calculate Bowley's probable error, data had to be taken from a random sample, a condition that the Division's data did not fulfill. To be able to use probable error, therefore, Sarle decided to test the robustness of the presuppositions underlying the tool. He wanted to see which one would be easier to adapt to his own data. For this purpose, he started by listing the conditions that the data had to verify for calculating probable error. He took help from the work of his former professor, F. Mills, and found five:

The assumptions that underlie the normal use of the concept of probable error are the following:

(1) There is a reasonable degree of homogeneity in the population from which the sample is drawn.
(2) The sample is representative.
(3) The observations in the sample are exact measurements of the phenomenon, that is, not subject to errors of observation or compensating errors.
(4) The observations are free from bias or noncompensating errors.
(5) The standard deviation of the sample measures the amount of dispersion in the universe from which the sample is drawn. (Sarle 1927, 30)

He then tested these hypotheses to see if they were verified by the Division's data. For those that the data did not verify, he had to find a way to render the data and the statistical tool compatible.

Stratification

The first hypothesis—namely, that data should be homogeneous—was validated by the Division's samples, for the latter were *stratified*. This word and the procedure that it designated were again borrowed from Bowley: stratification consisted of dividing beforehand the total population into a certain number of subpopulations (for example, according to the principal crop cultivated in a zone) and selecting a sample from each of the subpopulations; the final sample being a combination of the subsamples (Bowley 1915). This operation thus consisted of forming groups in the population contingent on the regularities observed (because of the formation of groups, the variation in the principal crops was less in each stratum than in the total population).

For Bowley, stratification could be done with any variable—which is the current thinking among statisticians—but this was not the case with Sarle who used *geographic* variables only. He did not confer the same status on these variables as on the others, for according to him, in agriculture, geography was explanatory whereas the other variables were consequences. Indeed, the yields depended above all on "the local topography, geography, soils, etc." (Sarle 1927, 15) and much more directly than, for example, the sociodemographic characteristics of the farmer. The sample thus had to contain representatives from each geographical type. As these zones did not always correspond to the political subdivisions of the territory, the Division used the famous "crop reporting districts," established by the Post Office Department, which fulfilled these requirements. Thus the homogeneity of the sample was ensured because territorial partitions were one way to stratify the universe.

Representativeness

The second hypothesis of probable error, according to which the sample had to be "representative," was the most problematic of the five. Indeed, for Bowley, the sample had to be "drawn randomly," but for Sarle it was more important for it to be representative. For him, randomness was only way of obtaining something that he considered the true prerequisite of probable error: the representativeness of the sample. But this argument was extremely long and difficult to expand on for Sarle, for he also wrote (especially) for his colleagues in the Division, but they did not know either of the two tools that were being weighed against each other. To show that representativeness was better than randomness (an argument that he addressed to an absent Bowley), he first took the trouble of defining, in detail, each of these operators (for his colleagues who were very much present).

First, Sarle explained how he understood representativeness and how he connected it with randomness. According to him, if the sample was representative, then, by the definition of representativeness, error tended toward zero. "Perfect" representativeness—if we can call it that—ensured that the sample could be used "in the absolute sense," as he said; in other words, in place of the universe. The less the sample proved to be representative, the greater the error. Error thus depended on representativeness; it was a consequence. Hence it was representativeness that gave its meaning to probable error.

With representativeness thus being instituted as an evaluator of samples, the selection method was only a means of obtaining representativity; and in particular, randomness was nothing more than one of the possible methods that made the construction of representative samples possible, a method that European interlocutors no doubt used profusely but was not essential to the process.

To use probable error in an optimal manner, it remained for Sarle to compare randomness to the Division's methods, and to only retain the one that was most representative. Now, randomness did not seem to be the best method: "Although random selection is the foundation of all sampling theory, certain departures or improvements can be affected that will insure a sample [is] not only more representative, but more stable than one selected purely on the basis of randomness" (Sarle 1927, 19).

It seemed to Sarle that even though statisticians in universities had always based their reasoning on randomness, the representativeness of this method of selection could be enhanced. He gave the example of a card game, in this instance bridge, to explain himself:

> The limitations of random selection are well illustrated in dealing four hands of cards in auction bridge. Each hand of 13 cards is a random sample made up of 25 per cent of the 52 cards and yet one player may get a hand worth several times as much as the hand of some other player from the standpoint of taking tricks. The composition of this especially good hand is not at all representative of the whole deck of cards. (Sarle 1927, 20)

The randomly selected sample of cards could be any sample among those of 13 cards. The number of points contained in this sample could thus vary enormously from the 25% of the total number of points. According to Sarle, there were therefore chances that a random sample would not be representative of the universe from which it was drawn—that is to say, it would not resemble it.

After this general elaboration on representativeness and random selection, he wondered where in all this did the Division's data fit. Was it representative? Was it more representative than a random sample was? He began by comparing the Division's method to the "four methods of selecting a representative sample" that, according to him, had been established during the 1925 meeting by the International Institute of Statistics (Sarle 1927, 19). In fact, the Institute had defined only two, which Sarle does not cite, but which deserve mention as he had come across them frequently during his readings.[3]

> The International Institute of Statistics
>
> I. Calls attention to the very considerable advantages which can be obtained by applying the Representative Method under the following conditions. The results of a partial investigation should only be generalized provided that the sample used is in its nature sufficiently representative of the totality. In such respects the sample may be selected in different ways; the following two main cases, however are to be distinguished:
>
> A - Random selection: a number of units are selected in such a way that exact equality of chance of inclusion is the dominant rule.
> B - Purposive selection: a number of groups of units which together yield nearly the same characteristics as the totality. In order to have any knowledge of the precision of the estimates, it is necessary that sufficient groups should be included to allow the variations between the characteristics of the groups to be measured.
>
> II. Recommends that the investigation should be so arranged as to allow for a mathematical treatment of the precision

> of the results, and that with these results should be given an indication of the extent of the error to which they are liable.
>
> III. Repeats the wish that in the reports of the results of every representative investigation an explicit account in detail of the method of selecting the sample adopted should be given.
>
> (Bowley 1926, 62)

The two representative methods were thus, first, and whatever Sarle may say, random selection, and second, purposive selection, which consisted of selecting groups of units which together resembled the totality.

But Sarle had also understood Bowley's point according to which it was always more profitable to stratify the samples. He had composed it with the Institute's conclusions, which resulted in differentiating between *four* modes of representative selection. "Random selection or simple sampling," "stratified random selection," "purposive selection," and "stratified purposive selection" (this last category was justified because Sarle continued to think that a pertinent stratification was geographical).

But none of these four methods perfectly corresponded to the Division's sample because none made allowances for the fact that the Division's crop reporters were volunteers. This characteristic of the Division's data was its most original feature and the most incompatible with representativeness: first, because the voluntary aspect of the crop reporters made them superior to their neighbors (i.e. different, therefore not so representative), and second, because it also signified that they were not entirely selected by the Division, that in one sense they selected themselves. As it happens, the case of a sample selecting itself was nowhere to be found among the definitions of representativeness.

To take this characteristic into account, Sarle proposed a new name for the type of selection practiced in the Division:

> With Bowley's classification in mind, the judgment inquiry on crop yields may be designated a "stratified voluntary-judgment

> sample of crop yields per acre." The sample is not random, nor does it fall under the heading of purposive selection, as returns are only from those who are willing to reply. (Sarle 1927, 22)

The exercise of their judgment by the crop reporters was a characteristic of the Division's data, which became under Sarle's pen much more prominent than in the past for it was the main cause of their divergence from the standard characteristics: "This limitation of lack of representativeness is serious with all the sampling work of the department," stated Sarle, specifying that eventually the Division would have to change to purposive selection: "A careful and intelligent application of stratified purposive selection as suggested by Bowley and herein developed, would go a long way toward obtaining a really representative sample of American agriculture." But as this was not possible before a reasonable period, Sarle considered the Division's sample such as it was, to have some great qualities, despite everything:

> The use of weighted State averages is an excellent and practical substitute for "proportional stratification." Instead of having a random sample within the district, the sample is further stratified because of the fact that the reports are distributed by townships. The use of county or districts weights helps to improve the geographic representativeness by distributing the influence of the sample in proportion to the acreage of the crop.

In any case, added Sarle—and for him this was the crucial factor—the Division's sample was better than a random sample: "In fact, this departure from random selection tends to improve the representativeness of the sample." With this final comment Sarle had made his point: It was essential for the samples to be representative, and those of the Division were, and more so than random samples in particular, because they were geographically stratified and weighted (all citations Sarle 1927, 22–23).

Thus the first two assumptions of probable error (reformulated by Sarle) did not disqualify the Division's data from being used for the calculation of probable error. The data was homogeneous because they were stratified; the sample was representative because it was properly stratified and weighted.

Restricted Interpretation

If the two first conditions of the application of probable error to the data were finally fulfilled, the last three were not. In fact, it was difficult to verify them in the context of the Division's surveys (exact measurement and absence of bias especially) as the statements in the questionnaires were full of errors. It was a serious problem for, "unless the statistician can use one of Bowley's four methods of selecting a sample and can be sure that the observations are the result of unbiased measurement, he is not justified in using the probable-error concept in the ordinary manner" (Sarle 1927, 22).

Finally, after a hard-fought struggle in which Sarle had been able to ensure conformity of the surveys with the first two hypotheses of probable error, something that had aroused great expectations, he instead found himself before an insurmountable obstacle. To use probable error in a bona fide manner, the sample had to be purified of all the other errors, especially errors in the statements that Sarle could not ensure with regard to his data. Persistent as always, he however found a solution that resolved in one go the problems posed by the three last hypotheses:

> In this study the probable-error concept will be used for comparing the average of the sample with the more stable average which would have been obtained from an infinitely large sample taken at the same time and under the same conditions. … This restricted interpretation of probable error eliminates all assumptions concerning representativeness of the sample, and of bias in the individual observations, and permits the statistician to proceed on the practical assumption that the infinitely large sample would be subject to the same limitations as the one in hand. (Sarle 1927, 31)

The restricted interpretation of probable error was that if the universe had been studied according to a method which would have subjected it to the same distortions as the observed sample, then all the hypotheses were verified because there were no other differences between the sample and the population except those emanating from the process of selection. Probable error therefore measured sampling errors as, with regard to the rest, this sample was biased in exactly the same manner as the universe. All the deviation that the observed sample experienced was in exactly the same proportion as in the hypothetical sample that served as a comparison. From the moment that the two surveys were carried out in the same manner, the only difference between them came solely from errors of selection. Probable error measured the error committed by the process of selection.

Thus, to use probable error, Sarle had to bring the assumptions of this tool in line with the Division's data. He had identified what he called the five hypotheses of probable error, then he had shown stratification, representativeness, and what he called "restricted interpretation" enabled a bridge to be built between the British tool and American data. He had thus managed to calculate probable errors in the Division's data; he had become the master of error.

Conclusion: What Does Applying a Formula Mean?

At this stage it is probably important to point out for the benefit of present-day statisticians that Sarle's work should not be assessed on the basis of judgments which *consequently*, much later, they will be subjected to. In particular, what one thinks *today* of these innovations, which are surprising because the question of the representativeness or the critique of randomness are no longer topical, is not very important. What we are trying to define, in fact, is how these transformations took place *at that time* in the Division and how they affected those who worked there *at that time*. These transformations took place independently of the present criteria of validity, because they had not been determined. In short, our problem is not to understand if Sarle was wrong or right, if he had outstripped Bowley or had slipped up, for this judgment would be nothing more than an anachronism. Our problem is to understand how the endeavors of this particularly dynamic statistician transformed the statistical landscape in which he evolved (Bloor 1991). To come back to our initial question, we are actually seeking to measure the extent of the transformations brought about by the "application" of a new tool to his data.

First, in order to "apply" the formula of probable error, Sarle was not content to import bits and pieces of the theory of probability into the Division, which was already a great innovation because no one had done it before him, or to put his data in the grinder of this formula. The operation was neither mechanical nor predictable. On the contrary, here, the "application" resembles the process that we have called "expression" (Didier 2007). Indeed, Sarle initially took two elements: the Division's data and the formula of probable error. He tried to arrive at the most suitable articulation between the two (a search that meant going back, first, to the definitions of the "assumptions" of probable error and, second, to the methods of construction of his data) and then, from this interaction, a new probable error with its limited interpretation was formulated. Probable error, invented by the great Bowley, did not remain unchanged during its treatment; Sarle transformed it to make it compatible with his data.

Moreover, even as Sarle was reformulating Bowley's probable error, new properties of the Division's data emerged. In particular, Sarle showed that it was inductive, homogenous because it was stratified, and, above all, representative—three essential characteristics that had been entirely virtual till then. "Applying" a formula for Sarle, therefore, did not even remotely translate as mechanically repeating a calculation; above all it meant finding the adequate expression of this formula for his data. This inventiveness was in fact the condition *sine qua non* of repetitive calculation (Callon and Muniesa 2003; Weber 2013).

As can be observed—this point probably needs to be made by a sociologist—Sarle the person, the individual, did not remain passive in this process. He was not, of course, able to do everything, and we have seen that it is the special articulation between probable error and the Division's data that can be said to be the source of the new innovation. However, Sarle's energy, his tenacity, and his knowledge were not indifferent to this process.

This "restricted probable error" did not remain inert, either; in turn it too influenced the Division. The reception to Sarle's work can be gauged in many ways. The schedule of publication of the articles is a good indicator. The first article, written in 1927, was published very quickly after its drafting, but the second, of which a first draft was ready in 1929, encountered numerous obstacles. Sarle had to convince practically the whole Division that his text was interesting and carry out thousands of corrections and modifications in order to publish it. The points of disagreement concerned, first, Sarle's language, which was often faulty, and second—the more interesting argument as far as we are concerned—the discrepancy between the highly theoretical part involving the definition of restricted probable error and the very descriptive part, in which Sarle effectively calculated the probable errors—according to his own interpretation—in the Division's data. In a few words, he was criticized precisely for putting his theory into practice. But his perseverance, and the modifications he introduced, paid off and his text was finally accepted and published in 1932.[4] The process of publication of his articles in itself, then, constituted a platform for Sarle's works, which were considered as significant methodological advances. Thus, all the actors who intervened later would cite them systematically.[5]

Second, Sarle, in addition to his normal duties, played an important role as instructor in the Division. He spent a great deal of his time instructing the agricultural Statisticians who had been newly hired in their future profession. He never stopped pointing out the advantages of probable error and the methods of representative selection. He thus influenced the generations who succeeded him.

A final consequence of Sarle's work, and not the least important, was to promote relations between the Division and Iowa State University, with which a collaboration was established. Sarle, by initiating an ink-and-paper link with European statisticians, created another, more direct relationship with the academics of his country, who had already been working with tools that were new to the Division. What role did these academics play in changing the methods used by the Division?

5

The Administration and University

If it is a well-known fact that the *Brain Trust* attracted many academics to top government jobs; it is a less well known fact that the New Deal experienced a brain drain, a reverse movement from the government to the universities. This is, however, what happened, at least as far as the agricultural Statisticians were concerned. The entrance of a new actor—the university—accelerated the rhythm of the methodological reassessments that the Division had to deal with. The classic history of these events informs us that the Division evolved radically through its contacts with the university and the discovery of the great authors, especially European, who helped sampling theory to develop and concomitantly helped the Division to modernize itself by applying their methods to its problems. The power of theory, of truth, facilitated this progress.

This argument was put forward by several historians of statistics, for whom the work of a renowned statistician, Jerzy Neyman, revolutionized sampling theory by demonstrating the superiority of one of the methods, stratified random sampling, over all the others. Frederick Kruskal and William H. Mosteller (1980), for example, wrote that "Neyman's [1934] paper brought us into modern thought." The Division thus tied up with an intermediary, the university that introduced it to Neyman's work; as a result, the Division was able to improve its own methods.

However convincing it may seem, this account is very similar to the trite, uninspiring version of "application" that we have discussed earlier. The idea that theory was responsible for the progress of statistical procedures simply because it was true and the Division's members accepted it seems doubtful, given that this is not what Charles Sarle did when he "applied" the formula of probable error and does not take into account the innovative aspect of activity (Latour 1987; Desrosières 1998, chap. 5 and 6). Was it any different with stratified random sampling theory?

Formalization of the Ties between the Division and the University

Why did the Division, when it decided to team up with a university, choose Iowa? The question is all the more relevant because in the early 1930s, one of the most prestigious universities in the field of agricultural studies in the United States was Cornell University in New York State. Once the Division, which was located in Washington, decided to collaborate with academia, its excellent reputation could have brought them together. Yet the Division finally chose the plains of the Midwest.

To understand this choice, we have to give a brief introduction to Iowa State University before its association with the Division. In the early 1920s, it had only a rather skeletal "Mathematical Statistics Division" (David 1984), whose name indicates that it was not well endowed with funds and also that the statistics practiced there were less like the Division's statistics and more akin to pure mathematics, consisting mainly of equations, logical implications, and formalisms rather than surveyors, questionnaires, or *crop meters* (see figure 5.1).

The statistical procedures of Iowa State University were, moreover, largely inspired by the work of the British statistician Ronald Fisher, who had spent time there in 1931 (the joke that made the rounds was how Fisher, used to the foggy chill of England, had sweated out all the water in his body in the muggy

5.1 The entire Statistics Division of the Mathematics Department of Iowa State University on January 31, 1930. The paucity of both staff and equipment is obvious. (ISU Library, University Archives, Special Collections Department)

Iowa summer). Fisher was a mathematician by training and produced highly formalized results (Box 1978). An example of the early use made of Fisher's work in Iowa can be found in an article written in the 1930s by George Snedecor, the director of the university's statistics division, together with Gertrude Cox, his first graduate student in statistics, on the analysis of the covariance of two agricultural variables, cultivated area and yield (Cox and Snedecor 1936). Iowa State University and its statistics division was thus comprised of the followers of Fisher, whose statistics were highly mathematical.

In 1933, Snedecor converted the statistics division within the mathematics department into an authentic Statistical Laboratory, which now became "the first statistics center of its kind in the United States" (Box 1978, 314), the first full-fledged laboratory to use mathematics for generating agricultural statistics. Stephen Stigler (1996) in fact jokingly fixed the birth date of mathematical statistics—"stats-maths," as it is called today, and which he defined as a subdiscipline that only statisticians with solid mathematical training could understand—as 1933. Hence, in the early 1930s, Iowa statisticians used mainly formal mathematical tools. As a result, for the Division's statisticians to turn to them was like going to people who practiced a different discipline. It was very unlikely.

Yet, even though the first concrete steps of this collaboration seem to have been forgotten, it is possible to identify two reasons why the Division and the Statistical Laboratory at Iowa State University decided to set up a partnership. First, Henry A. Wallace, Roosevelt's famous Secretary of Agriculture, came from Iowa and had in his youth been very close to Sarle and Snedecor. During the winter of 1923–1924, Wallace gave a series of ten talks on statistics at Iowa State University, a subject that fascinated him. Sarle, who was then the agricultural Statistician for Iowa and a friend of Wallace (to the extent that both did some field surveys together), attended these talks, as did Snedecor, who had just joined the university's mathematics department (which at that time did not have the statistics division). The understanding that developed between them was such that in 1925, they jointly published a research article (Wallace and Snedecor 1925).[1] Once Wallace became Secretary of Agriculture, he reiterated his interest in agricultural statistics by closely following the work of the Division and frequently signing the reports himself rather than send his vice-secretary, as was the practice before him—in fact, it is always Wallace who figures in the photographs showing the secretary signing the reports. It is therefore possible that it was he and Sarle who brought to the notice of the Division the advantages of working with the Statistical Laboratory of Iowa. In any case, Leslie Carl, the Iowa Statistician who succeeded Sarle in this state in the early 1920s, had established excellent relations with the Iowa State University.[2] On the one hand, he had arranged the transfer of data to the Statistical Laboratory that wanted to "apply" its mathematics to actual data, something that was too costly and complicated for this small structure to carry out on its own. Carl also transmitted to the Division certain results obtained in Iowa (see, for example, Beyleveld 1929).

The second justification for the collaboration with Iowa was that the Division had reasons for staying away from Cornell. If this university had a high standing in the field of rural studies at that time, it was because it had become the bastion of a very active research group, "the Farm Economists" (Taylor and Taylor 1952, 92–100), a group formed in the beginning of the century that assumed more and more importance between the two world wars. It specialized in everything concerning agriculture from the point of view of the farms: it included, for example, farm "management" specialists, as well as marketers, whose main focus was how to take maximum advantage of the yields (once harvesting had been done), and also economists specializing in different agricultural markets.

But these studies did not take up issues that were relevant to the Division, in particular, representativeness, and even less, randomness. This is shown, for example, on the Cornell side, by Stanley W. Warren who, when writing on statistics useful for "farm management," talks exclusively of multivariate breakdowns and correlations but never of representativeness or confidence intervals—words that he does not even use (Warren 1936; Hill 1941)—and on the Division's side, by Sarle's criticism of their methods, which he calls "subjective" (Sarle 1939). Thus there was nothing incongruous about choosing Iowa.

Thanks to a new piece of legislation, an initial collaboration and funding agreement was signed in 1935 between the Iowa Statistical Laboratory and the Division. The Bankhead-Jones Act had an annual budget of $5 million, two-fifths of which was allocated to the Department of Agriculture and the rest to the states (on the basis of their size and rural population), which distributed the money to their agricultural experimental stations. The aim was to develop collaboration agreements between the federal government and local research centers in all the fields of agronomic activities, especially the social sciences (including economics and statistics). Toward this end, it had been ruled that the sums allocated by the federal department could not exceed those that the state governments had agreed to allocate to the projects; a state first had to obtain local support before applying to the federal agencies and showing that the scope of the project transcended local interests (Blaisdell 1940). Now Snedecor, the head of the Statistical Laboratory, was also the head of the experimental station. He therefore decided to finance the initial projects carried out jointly by the two institutions.

Then an event, independent of those already described, caused the officials to intensify this collaboration. Since 1929, the Division had been petitioning Congress to finance a big survey of American agriculture using the questionnaire method. It convinced Texas Senator Pat Buchanan to defend the bill carrying his name before the Senate. This bill encouraged the development of agricultural research by authorizing "the Secretary of Agriculture to make surveys of representative farm areas each year in each State for the purpose of obtaining and publishing information upon the economical conditions of agriculture throughout the United States and for other purposes" (Nourse, Davis, and Black 1937, 477). It had been presented before the Congress for the first time in 1929, then in 1930 and again in 1935. On this last date, it was rejected for the third consecutive time by the Senate, in favor of more urgent issues.

The Division then got the idea of tying the two strings together, the Buchanan project and Iowa State University, in order to derive a double benefit. The Division felt that the collaboration with the Statistical Laboratory would increase its legitimacy in the eyes of the politicians and speed up the Buchanan bill, and give it an important ally to carry out the eventual survey. At the same time, in order to develop a relationship with the university, the Division felt it would be wiser to go with a big project in hand, possibly richly endowed (the project thus taking on a much more academic complexion than when it was mainly administrative). The combination of the ISU Statistical Laboratory and the Buchanan bill would enable the Division to make a double hit (Ben-David 1984).

The formalization of the links already established between the Division and the Iowa State Statistical Laboratory took the form of a joint meeting, held at Ames in 1936, to discuss the best way of preparing and eventually managing a prospective survey. Organizing a meeting was not enough, however. For a meeting to be something more than a marriage between a carp and a rabbit, not only should it effectively bring together two institutions, but also the substance of the discussions must be rich, the arguments interesting.

A Conference and Three Conceptions of Representativeness

After having studied Sarle's articles and the formalization of the relations between the university and the Division, we are going to observe a third classic ingredient of academic and administrative life: a conference. In this case, a conference was to discuss the best way of conducting a major survey whose budget would be voted by Congress. The contributors were many and came from three different backgrounds. First, there were members of the Division, which included civil servants from the central administration and agricultural Statisticians speaking about the experience gained in their states. Then came members of Iowa State University, some from the Statistical Laboratory and others from the Department of Economics. Lastly, there were the potential users of statistics, external to the Division and the university, such as the Farm Credit Administration.[3] The Census Bureau also made the effort to attend. The conference was then heavily attended, including by Fisher, who however did not present a paper.

The proceedings of the conference show that the operational aspect of this survey centered around the problem of the construction of a representative sample (Bureau of Agricultural Economics 1936). In other words, how to select a sample that would give results that would be valid for the country as a whole. The three most important positions were taken by the three most famous speakers, who were the three organizers of the conference. Let us examine them one by one.

The first to speak, T. W. Schultz (future Nobel Laureate in Economics in 1979), was the head of the Sociology and Economics Department at Iowa State University. He was born in 1902 and had obtained his doctorate in 1930 from Wisconsin University. He had hence been taught by the first generation of Farm Economists. However, very soon after he joined Iowa University, Schultz became deeply interested in the works of Snedecor and the Division. He had even coauthored with a statistician colleague an article on the analysis of variance, a question that was typically Fisher (Schultz and Snedecor 1933), and a second article, written alone, on the same subject in which he gave a detailed analysis (although critical in some respects) of Sarle's articles (Schultz 1933). Schultz was thus an economist, but pro-statistics.

Schultz's stand on representativeness was similar to what Arthur Bowley called purposive selection at the conference organized by the International Institute of Statistics in 1925. According to Schultz, in a statistical study, the subjects of the survey (farms, for example) were above all *different* from each other for a certain number of *reasons*. As the aim of the survey was to highlight these differences, the farms had to be selected according to the *cause* of for their differences—what he called "control factors."

> The following factors were controlled: (1) Type of soil, (2) topography, (3) degree of erosion, (4) size of farms, and (5) character of tenure. The one hundred and one factors, in addition to these, which tend to make each individual farm a unique institution, were not controlled. The additional sources of variation weren't classified—not enough information was available to isolate them, and thus we could not take them out of the total variability. The remaining bundle of variations is what, I assume, the theoretical statistician dignifies and glorifies as the unknown behavior which is the very bone and blood of randomness. (Bureau of Agricultural Economics 1936, 12)

According to Schultz, the sample will be representative—that is, it will behave like the universe, on the single condition that it be constructed so as to respect the "control factors" of the various observations. The statistician should thus establish the modalities of the causes (for example, list the various types of soil, cross-compare them with the various topographies, etc.), then select the units (the farms) in each of these modalities; in this way he obtained all the possibilities in the universe and could then compare them.

Schultz then took the trouble to explain that as it would be impossible to take *all* the factors into account, the less important could be regrouped under the *name* random. But this randomness was merely ignorance, which is why Schultz was being ironic about the concept. If the knowledge had been more extensive and if all the factors influencing the observations could have been identified, it would not have been necessary to make do with this stopgap concept. Further down in his presentation, his opposition to randomness was even more explicit, less disparaging:

> Should we proceed and select the farms to be enumerated at random? I believe not. If, to the best of our knowledge, all the farms in the universe were essentially homogeneous, then I would subscribe to a design that gave us a sample, and the only characteristic would be that it was strictly at random. But since we have objective measures of a substantial amount of the heterogeneity that prevails among farms, it is important, in fact essential, that this information about the farms in our universe be employed in deciding which farm to record and which to exclude.... It seems to me folly to attempt to force this heterogeneous material into a single pattern.... Accordingly, the sample selected should be such that we know that we are going to obtain farms that are representative of various subuniverses that we know exist. The feature of randomness is attained in that it is a matter of indifference which farm of many within each

> of these subclasses, or subuniverses, we enumerate. (Bureau of Agricultural Economics 1936, 13)

In simple language, Schultz insisted that the most important thing in the process was first to stratify the universe, which was of course incompatible with simple random selection that forced *the real to enter a one-of-its-kind mold*. It was only then, after stratification, from within the strata, that he envisaged random selection, although if we go back to his first sentence, we can see that he was not in favor of randomness even at this stage. This was, according to him, the best way of obtaining a representative sample.

George Snedecor's position was very different from his colleague's. He was so deep into random mathematics and laws of probability that he presupposed randomness; he could not in fact imagine working without it. According to him, the problem of selection was really to know which units or which elements the statistician should select for sampling.

He nevertheless took the trouble to explain, citing Fisher, the use of random selection (Bureau of Agricultural Economics 1936, 38). To determine if two kinds of plants really had different yields, Fisher conceived the idea of planting in conditions that were as homogeneous as possible and observing whether, in (practically) identical conditions, the two varieties would give different results. If this was the case, it was then necessary to find out if these differences were significant (if they were really *caused* by the varieties) or if they were not (in which case they could be attributed to chance or experimental error). To answer this question, Fisher had recommended random experiments, which means randomly selecting the plot of land on which each variety would be planted. This allowed comparison between the results observed and those which would have been obtained if the differences in the yields were a result of the random selection of the plots (calculated through the laws of probability). Randomness only came into play when testing the significativeness of the results; it alone made it possible to know if the differences were due to chance or not. Thus the real objective of the statistician was not randomness, a simple enough tool, but rather discovering the differences between the causes of the different effects.

Consequently, for Snedecor, the causes were intrinsically obscure, unknown—in one word, *suspect*—and had to be *confirmed* by the statistician. Randomness was a tool that helped to *ascertain* the differences and their causes, which were considered *dubious*. This is an important point on which Schultz and Snedecor differed: both concurred that statistics was useful for studying the causes underlying the phenomena, but the Schultz started from the principle that certain causes were known and hence effects should be attributed to them, whereas the Snedecor supposed that the effects were observable and the statistician should infer the causes that explained them. Under these conditions, according to Snedecor, how should one go about selecting a sample?

> Exactly as the biologist did, by studying and experimenting with population data. In crops, such data are derived from "uniformity trials." In economics, you have the general census to work with. By trying various ways of sampling, each based on some set of known principles, you can choose one that gives promise of satisfactory results. (Bureau of Agricultural Economics 1936, 38)

For Snedecor the main problem was to test a series of sample units (households, buildings, addresses, villages, etc.), all according to the same selection protocol, which would definitely be random ("uniform experiments"), and see which gave the most "satisfying" results by comparing the averages calculated from the samples with those of the census survey. Above all, it was a question of determining the unit that would provide results that would best tally with the census findings.

It was Sarle who, on behalf of the Division, expounded the last concept of representativeness at the conference. Although he derived the principal arguments from his 1932[4] paper, the novelty of his presentation resided in the fact that he placed purposive selection and random selection on an equal footing, as compared to his previous articles where randomness was clearly devalued. It should be pointed out that in the past he had worked on data that was, despite his best efforts, clearly not random, whereas this time there was a distinct possibility of constructing data randomly. He concluded by leaving it to *experimentation* to decide between these two solutions:

> The question regarding representativeness can be answered only on the basis of considerable intensive research and experimentation in the taking of actual samples.... Much depends on the ability and ingenuity of the statistician in developing a sampling technique for selecting a representative sample that will be economical and simple to administer. (Bureau of Agricultural Economics 1936, 21)

His idea was to ascertain the best method of selection through experimentation, with the outcome being judged not merely by the yardstick of representativeness, but also taking into account the material constraints of cost and simplicity of administration.

At the conclusion of the conference, Sarle summarized the various points that, according to him, had been highlighted. This text is thus the concrete "expression," in the technical sense that we have given to it, of what the Division and the Iowa State University together had achieved through collaboration.

Sarle's principal argument was that he had identified "two schools of thought on this fundamental question" (Bureau of Agricultural Economics 1936, 75) about the modes of representative selection: that of random selection and that of Schultz (it should be noted that Sarle had humbly withdrawn his own propositions). We will again reiterate the fact that random selection, by competing with the other method, had made an important breakthrough in the Division. In view of this alternative, Sarle, and through him the entire Division, now campaigned in favor of initiating experiments to compare the two methods. With this aim in view, he put forward the four recommendations: First, Sarle proposed setting up an "annual sample census" in response to the demand for figures, a specific survey that would thus justify methodological research. Second, "it [was] essential that the appropriate sampling design be found to insure such adequacy in the results." This was the important point: one had to continue to weigh the relative merits of the two methods by means of a series of experiments (Bureau of Agricultural Economics 1936, 80). Third, administrators and field staff had to be trained in modern statistical techniques so that they could carry out the experiments and turn them to good account. Fourth a committee had to be set up to see that the recommendations were carried out.

At the conclusion of the conference, it became clear that to conduct a fresh survey, a method had to be chosen for selecting the sample and, for this, it was necessary to compare the two principal methods that had been presented. What was the outcome of this comparison?

The End of Comparisons

A classic model used for describing a comparison is the model of the "weighing scale." According to this model, the statistician puts one method on each pan of the weighing scale. The beam would tilt on the side of the method that prevailed over the other. However, if this mode of comparison is what comes immediately to mind, it is not the one that our statisticians used (Labrousse 2010).

Indeed, the weighing-scale model assumes that there is a decisive moment when the experimenter removes his hands from the pans and anxiously waits to see which side the beam will tilt. But here there was no such moment of truth. On the contrary, comparison proved to be a long and zigzagging process. At least six different experiments succeeded each other, with research on the population being carried out in between to find elements that would add grist to the mill.

To understand how the agricultural Statisticians chose between the two methods, we will study a series of experiments conducted by the group composed of the Division and the Statistical Laboratory at Iowa State University. We will see that these experiments were numerous and innovative, especially because the Statisticians had to "step out" and look for elements of America that they could bring into their laboratories to enrich their research (Frankel and King 1996, 71). We will then see whether a comparison is a long process or a dramatic turn of events without which a gigantic America could not have been recaptured (Marks 1997).

Too Many Degrees of Freedom

The Statisticians began by asking if certain experiments conducted within the Division but carried out independently by any of them could be linked to the issue in question. Two employees of the Division, J. B. Shepard (1937) and H. Schutz (1937), were asked to look into this possibility. They found three examples that were likely to prove useful.

First, there was an experiment conducted by Leslie Carl, the Iowa Statistician, who had tried to carry out a survey using purposive selection in two counties of his state by structuring the sample according to types of soil. Second, H. L. Collins, the Kansas Statistician, conducted an experiment (in collaboration with the Economics Department of the State College) using the same method, but in this case designed on the basis of types of farms. Last, in Alabama, a third experiment was conducted randomly with the aim of determining whether townships could be used as a sampling unit in surveys on the county to which they belonged. This question overlapped two different concerns: On the one hand, there was the recommendation made by Snedecor during the 1936 conference, namely, to begin by identifying units that would yield the best estimators (an experiment that sought to test whether the township was not one such unit). On the other, the Statisticians needed to find effective methods for obtaining good estimates at the county level after the trauma over the controversy with the Agricultural Adjustment Administration (see chapter 2, especially

"The 'Prefects' of the AAA") (an experiment that could then be used to test whether the township fulfilled this objective). The second issue was clearly the more burning one.

But how could one evaluate these experiments? Shepard and Schutz, quite classically, had initially compared the results of these experiments with the federal decennial census and, when it was possible, with other agricultural censuses carried out by the states, especially those that were part of the Corn Belt. Indeed, agriculture being an important component of the output of these states, they conducted on their own initiative annual censuses along with the tax collection exercise: a team of full-time assessors, who were listing farm incomes, also gathered data on the farms. This data was not always immediately comparable with the Statisticians' data, especially because it was collected by tax assessors, which obviously introduced a bias. The Statisticians, however, managed to use it.

They considered that, with regard to the censuses, the results of these three experiments were not very satisfying. First, the two sampling experiments carried out according to the purposive selection method had produced very different results; second, township samples did not represent their county adequately. How could these discrepancies be explained? Statisticians wondered if this was because the purposive selection method was not very reliable or because it had not been applied with the right "control" variables? If the sample had been slightly bigger and if the Statisticians had established their choice by combining types of tenure with types of soil, would the experiments on purposive selection have given more accurate results? Did the experiment on the townships not come up to expectations because of the size of the unit or because of the mode of selection adopted?

It was not easy to answer these questions. Sometimes, it seemed to them that the method should be rejected outright; at other times, on the contrary, they identified only one of the shortcomings and then suggested improvements. So their final conclusions had the very defects that the planners criticized statisticians for: they argued *in fine* in favor of continuing the research so as to be in a better position to identify the elements that were worth testing. However, the statisticians considered that despite everything, these experiments were sufficiently interesting to be presented at a joint meeting of the American Statistical Association and the American Farm Economists Association in December 1936, which was published in 1937.

The picture painted by the Division's staff was twofold. First, the material available leaned toward purposive selection; indeed, it is specially this method that had been experimented on, whereas mostly the defects of randomness were highlighted in the publication (mainly because it made the survey very difficult to carry out). Second, the task of making comparisons was very problematic. The authors were not able to decide if the flaws identified came from the methods or from the practical and specific modalities of their application. If the census seemed a stable and rock-solid reference point, the characteristics to be compared were not established firmly enough to determine which were worth weighing. In order to compare it was necessary to reduce the degree of freedom available to statisticians and stabilize the properties of the methods to be studied.

Topographical Survey "Sections"

This was the task that had kept Sarle busy since January 1937. To start with, he had increased the number of institutions interested in the issue. Whereas Shepard and Schutz had mainly put together the experiments internal to the Division (sometimes conducted in collaboration with state colleges), Sarle had managed to get the Central Statistical Board (a New Deal organization that we will discuss in detail later), the Census Bureau, the experimental stations of Kansas and Iowa (which signified that Snedecor was kept informed of Sarle's experiments), as well as the secretary of the American Statistical Association interested in the work he was doing.

More determined and more confident than his colleagues, he had established two criteria that he considered crucial for assessing the different methods: first, the administrative cost of the future survey and, second, the reliability of the results. Moreover, with regard to Shepard's and Schutz's experiments and the questions raised therein, he had managed to establish strong links between, on the one hand, the choice of the sample unit (in keeping with the definition given it by Snedecor during the conference) and the cost of the survey and, on the other, the choice of the sampling method (randomness or purposive selection) and reliability. For Sarle, the sample unit determined the cost of the survey and the method determined its reliability.

On the basis of these two criteria, he worked on two studies. The first was the one Shepard and Schutz had identified in Alabama, for it gave a good idea of the respective costs of the different sample units. Because of this Sarle decided to use one and only one selection method, otherwise the comparison of the units would not have been possible, and he chose randomness. As the best elementary unit, randomness tipped the scales, while purposive selection was eliminated.

Which sample unit did he choose? The "minor civil division" (i.e., smallest political division), in this instance almost always the townships that were used before at that time, had been rejected by Shepard and Schutz because they felt it was too large to provide accurate estimates of their county. Sarle thus looked for smaller units. He tested four. The first two were normally used by the Division: a sample of farms and another of roads. To determine the other two units, he turned to the long history of American townships. During the Independence era, in 1785, Congress had decided that all American territory would be sold to individual farmers. The political objective was to colonize the continent and, toward this end, promote settlement by giving colonizers proprietorship rights to a plot of land.[5] The government therefore decided to proceed with a topographical survey of the entire territory, which would enable it to demarcate the "plots." The measuring unit of this survey[6] was the township, defined as a square with each side measuring six miles. This was further divided into thirty-six "sections," with each side of each section measuring one mile or 640 square acres (Stewart 1979) (see figure 5.2).

Those responsible for the topographical survey had to specifically note the special features of the land in order to identify the corners of the townships and the sections. This task required so much effort that in 1954, a

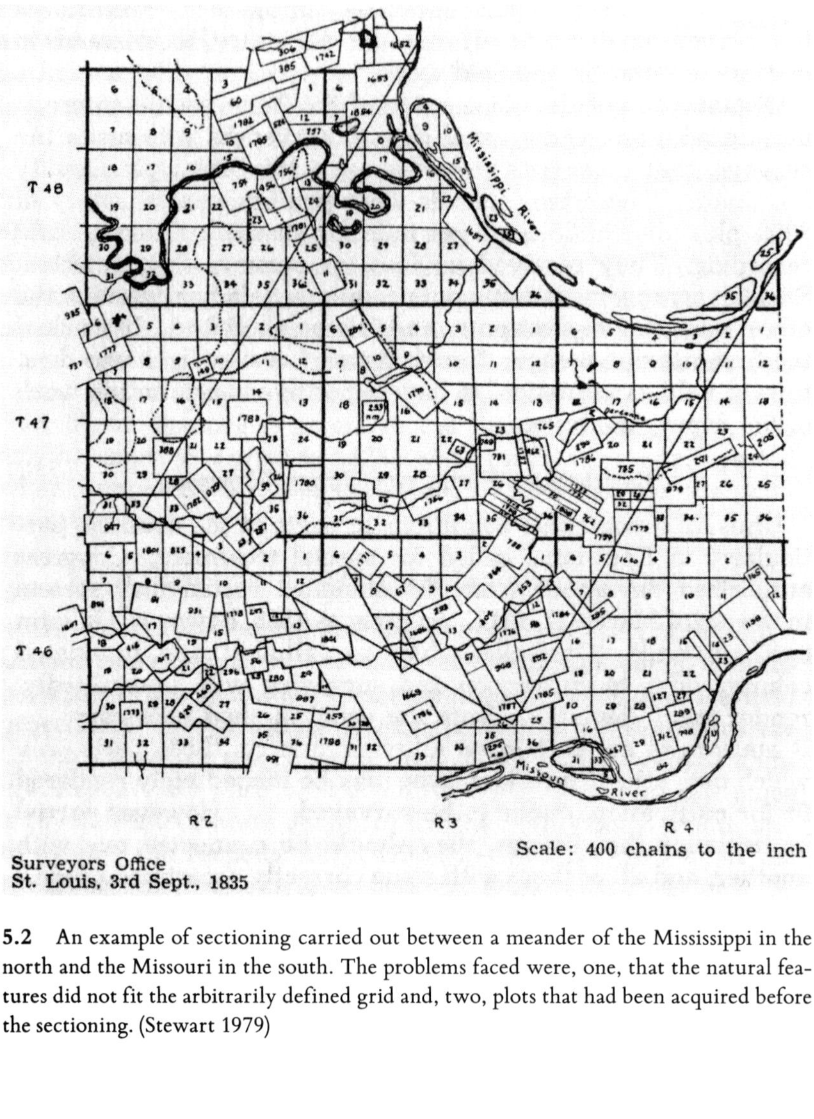

5.2 An example of sectioning carried out between a meander of the Mississippi in the north and the Missouri in the south. The problems faced were, one, that the natural features did not fit the arbitrarily defined grid and, two, plots that had been acquired before the sectioning. (Stewart 1979)

hundred million acres in the western states had still not been surveyed (Harrison 1954).

Hence, when statisticians were seeking sample units smaller than a township, they suddenly remembered that the townships had been divided into subunits called *sections* and speculated whether these sections could be of use to them. To test them, Sarle had to devise a way to concretely select sections. Should he use the farms or the fields that sections contain? He put together a first random sample of sections in which each section was represented by the farms located on it, and then a second random sample represented by the fields that a section it contained. One initial conclusion drawn from this study was that, in the context of random selection, the smaller the unit, the more expensive it was to study it. Using small units implied that a great number had to be drawn, which increased the travel expenses of the investigators between the locations. This additional cost had to be estimated. Comparison therefore also had to factor in a standard criterion: the dollar.

The second study that Sarle conducted was supposed to test the different selection methods and consequently their reliability. It consisted of choosing between "fifteen to twenty" counties in six states whose census had been satisfactorily conducted by the assessors. The Statistician wanted to construct experimental samples according to two different selection methods and compare their results with those of the censuses: on the one hand, purposive selection applied by means of a geological map of the soils and, on the other, the random selection of farms. But, as in the other experiment, he had to identify a unit to serve as the basis for comparing the selection methods. He decided to retain the farms grouped into units of three different sizes (farms by themselves, all the farms of one section, all the farms of a group of sections). Again, he was obliged to make a blind choice—this time, of the unit he would use—to determine the best method of selection, which happened to be farms and sections. But Sarle did not have the time to pursue this further and sought to hand over the study to a colleague.

In the meantime, all this activity showed that Sarle was not very keen on purposive selection in contrast to his colleagues in the Division: Even if he had tried to do a comparison between this method and randomness, the fact that in Alabama he had tested different units using just random selection indicated that he already developed more confidence in it. In addition, although the comparison of the units to be tested was conceptually distinct from that of the selection method, they were increasingly interlinked on the experimental front (Sarle 1938).

Combining the Sections

The survey on the "fifteen to twenty" counties was entrusted to Irvin Holmes, a young employee of the Division who at the time was assistant to Verne Church, the Michigan Statistician who had shared his experience of counting "pickled" cucumbers. Holmes inherited the two issues raised by Sarle, the comparison of the sampling units and the comparison of the selection methods. What solution did he come up with?

He first took Sarle's idea of taking samples from four different units. First, he used a farm sample; then, he used two different samples of the township sections, but they posed serious problems because their contours were not always clearly defined on the ground and because the sections came in groups of thirty-six (a number that did not have simple dividers), so he eventually constructed a sample whose units comprised four contiguous sections and a second sample of four sections drawn randomly from the township. Then, besides the first sample of farms and the two samples of sections, Holmes conceived the idea of constructing a fourth sample of (postal) routes, mainly because they were straightforward units and not expensive to enumerate and because it was an option favored by the Division's Statisticians. It should be pointed out that it was the only unit in which the agricultural Statisticians continued to play an important role—Holmes asked them to decide on the routes to be surveyed, using purposive selection, and then select the portion of the route to be surveyed according to the same procedure. The routes sample was thus the only concession made both to the purposive selection method and to the Statisticians, who were the only ones left to defend it vigorously at this juncture. In fact, Holmes seemed to bitterly regret the exception constituted by the routes sample for he thought that it partially invalidated the comparison since, not being produced in the same way (randomly), it could not be legitimately compared to the others. Thus in reality, Holmes had already eliminated the possibility of doing a survey with purposive selection.

But among the three units that remained, the question was which one to choose? From the outset Holmes found it difficult to decide on the yardstick for comparing the samples. He felt that the censuses carried out by the tax assessors had plus points, especially the fact that they were annual, but they were available only in five of the six states initially retained and their results were uncertain. Hence, he started by assessing the reliability of these censuses by comparing their results from one year to the next and then comparing them with the 1935 decadal census. Finally, he came to the conclusion that the quality of the census was sufficient in only 19 counties out of those initially retained, and therefore only these could be included in the study.

At this stage, he had managed to compare the acreage under the various crops and the cattle population as estimated by the different units (in all four cases, according to the 10% and 20% samples) and as inventoried by the fiscal agents. He had drawn several conclusions from this experiment (he had listed eight), but we will only discuss three. First, the various units did not really give very different results. Second, a 10% sample seemed optimal as regards the desired accuracy and the cost of the operation: indeed, by doubling the size of the sample, probable error had decreased only by one-third (and not by half), which did not justify the expenditure. Third, the road sample needed to be reviewed.

As far as we are concerned, the conclusions that we can draw are slightly different from those of Holmes. In reality, the comparison was no longer between the two sampling methods initially retained but between the different ways of administering random selection. Only the Division's Statisticians, responsible for one state of the Union, who were especially in favor of purposive selection, remained committed to it. Instead, it was the units formed by the sections that all other statisticians seemed to find most interesting: they were less concerned with comparing them with other units than seeking an optimal manner of using them.

Available Knowledge

The fate of this project was exceptional because of the fact that Sarle chose it to showcase the work done by the entire group working on sampling in the Agriculture Department, at the annual conference of the American Farm Economists Association in 1939 (Holmes 1939). This conference was of enormous importance. It took place subsequent to the restructuring of the Department of Agriculture, which led to the redefinition of the Bureau of Agricultural Economics (BAE) as its planning body headed by Howard Tolley who, taking advantage of this opportunity, presented his program (Tolley 1939). The conference was thus an opportunity for the agricultural economists to take stock of the new direction taken by agricultural policy since 1938. By asking Holmes to present his work, Sarle's team wanted to show planners what they could expect from sampling, give an idea of the statistics that it would eventually produce, and describe the services that it would be capable of rendering.

In addition, Sarle also wrote a paper from a more general perspective to complement Holmes's presentation in which he explained the different leads that the Division's statistics would follow in order to "improve" (Sarle 1939, 356). In other words, he decided to present to this much larger public, and not just members of the Division and the Iowa Statistical Laboratory, the work of comparison that had been carried out since 1936. And as it meant being heard by all the reformers in the Agriculture Department, which included the principal political decision makers and planners, who did not necessarily know much about current statistical practices, Sarle did not limit the comparison to the two methods that had been presented during the 1936 conference. He did a sort of recapitulation of the different techniques that existed at the time.

He first criticized the Division's traditional method of surveying only voluntary farmers and dared to point out its "limitations." He pointed out that as volunteers, the crop reporters were the best farmers, which skewed the sample, Second, he explained that it was more and more difficult to amalgamate samples of a suitable size because the farmers were unhappy with the Division (as we have seen in chapter 2). Third, the last defect of this method emerged shortly before the talk: It was not possible to measure the abandoned acreage, for the Statistician did not have the wherewithal to determine the reasons for the lack of response; if he did not receive a questionnaire from a particular county, how could he know whether the silence meant the farmer had not wanted to reply (whatever the reason) or whether he had left because of the crisis? Consequent to the rural exodus, the area of the abandoned lands had become a crucial issue for the Department's adjustment policy, for it had undergone several changes. These three points considerably undermined the Division's normal practice. Sarle went as far as to write: "In view of the serious limitations of the voluntary sample as a basis for current estimates, it is time that a more objective method of sampling be developed" (Sarle 1939, 359).

After having criticized the Division's methods, Sarle also vehemently attacked certain partial surveys conducted by other sections of the Agriculture Department and by some universities (among which the informed reader can easily identify Cornell) that did not concern themselves with representativeness and were only valid for the farms studied: "No matter how carefully one's judgment is used in selecting a sample, the sample usually is badly biased from the standpoint of representing the larger universe of inquiry" (Sarle 1939, 360). He called this method "subjective" and rejected it out of hand.

Finally, after having rejected the two older methods, the alternative he presented was between random sampling and purposive selection. His choice was indubitably made. On the one hand, he maintained that the purposive selection method was full of defects: It had never been defined explicitly, and until now research had not been able to identify a control factor that could be correlated with more than one or two variables pertinent to the survey, which was too little. On the other hand, random selection presented several advantages:

> It is possible to use available knowledge about an area, region or State to stratify the area geographically into subuniverses before selecting the sampling units nearly at random as possible within each stratum. This method of sampling is known as stratified random selection. It seems to be a happy combination of the systematic application of the principles of purposive selection and purely random selection. (Sarle 1939, 364)

The great advantage that Sarle perceived in random selection was that it could be stratified. For him the procedure in this case was above all geographical but in addition, it allowed the use of "all available knowledge" about the area, which meant any available variable. In other words, the supplementary knowledge pertaining to a geographical zone could be used instead of excluding it, as in the case of simple random selection. "Obviously, no useful information should be ignored," he affirmed (Sarle 1939, 364). By using supplementary knowledge, the Statisticians did not simply settle for measuring the error that they could have committed; they ensured, as much as it was possible to do, that their estimators would be as close as possible to the quantities of interest. They therefore increased the "effectiveness" or the "accuracy" of the sample: "precision depends primarily on size of sample, dispersion, and effectiveness of the stratification process" (Sarle 1939, 361). Stratification was thus the clinching argument for Sarle, but only if it no longer applied solely to geography and was extended to all available knowledge. Finally, it was the stratified random method that Sarle in this paper declared as being undoubtedly the best.

In conclusion, we can say that to compare the methods, Sarle identified the defects of those he wanted to eliminate (the Division's traditional methods, "subjective methods," the purposive selection method) and the advantages of those he wanted to promote. He thus did not conform to the weighing-scale model at all. He simply pointed out the advantages of one method and the defects of the other. In other words, he chose not to be "symmetrical," to use David Bloor's terminology (Bloor 1991); Sarle was not interested in developing a unique dimension through which both methods could be scaled. At this stage, Sarle was clearly in favor of randomness, but a stratified randomness.

The Tradition

In November 1939, a special issue of the *Journal of Farm Economics* had been planned to commemorate the centenary of the first agriculture census in the United States in 1840.[7] Agricultural Statisticians immediately seized the opportunity presented to complete the comparison between methods. That was all that the members of the Division, as well as their friends at Iowa State University, required to steer the issue toward the progress of agricultural statistics during the preceding century.

The introductory article was by Henry Taylor, the person we credit with creating legends about the Division, the founder of the BAE, who stressed the importance of statistics as a source of information for Farm Economists. This was followed by others writing on the principal methodological stages that the Division's statistics had gone through ("internalists" articles, which we have discussed in earlier pages) and, finally, by Sarle's (1939) and Snedecor's (1939) articles on the latest developments in statistical methodology.

Sarle's commemorative centenary article was a little slapdash; it should be said in his defense that he had only a few months, from February (when he published his latest paper) to November, to complete this assignment. It is not as clear and cogently argued as the previous paper (a work, moreover, that he asks the reader to refer to). We will thus not dwell on it. On the other hand, we will focus on Snedecor's article, the last one to weigh the two methods—randomness and purposive selection—that had been retained at the 1936 conference.

Snedecor followed a classic but nonetheless necessary procedure: he framed the question within a tradition, and it was this tradition that he used for comparing the two methods. The difference between his speech in 1936 and his 1939 article can therefore be described, to put it bluntly, in one word—bibliography. At the time of the conference, his head had been full of Fisher's ideas; this time, he took all the articles published on sampling in the major journals in order to follow its evolution and show how it helped to adjudicate between the two methods.

Snedecor began by recognizing the Norwegian, Anders Kiaer, as the father of the "representative method," which Kiaer had first presented in several issues of the *Bulletin de l'Institut International de Statistique*, between 1895 and 1905, though he felt that Kiaer's definition of the term was not very clear. He then cited the works of Bowley on representativeness which, except for minor points, he still considered relevant. "Bowley considered representative sampling as being accomplished by either of two methods, random or purposive selection" (Snedecor 1939, 849). Snedecor thus accepted the possibility of drawing representative samples in two distinct ways, just as Bowley and Jensen had done at the International Institute of Statistics conference in 1925 (paper published in 1926), as did the Division and Iowa State University during the 1936 conference.

He now proposed three arguments to show that purposive selection was not really representative. The first was that if Bowley had arrived at this result in theory, in practice he had never used this type of selection: "Professor Bowley never used nor recommended the use of purposive sampling.... His definition of representative sampling [is] reduced in practice to that of stratified random sampling" (Snedecor 1939, 851).

The second argument was that sampling, all sampling, only gave estimates of the quantity sought and not the quantity itself: "From a sample the population mean can never be known but only an estimate of it" (Snedecor 1939, 851). The estimates thus had significance only to the extent that there was a theory of their accuracy. In other words, the theory of accuracy of the estimates was nothing other than the sampling theory itself. This theory inevitably presupposed randomness: "There is no theory of estimation for sampling other than random" (Snedecor 1939, 852). The degree of confidence that a Statistician could have in an estimator was essential, and only random selection made this degree possible. Thus, randomness, which was merely fortuitous for Sarle in 1932, now became a prerequisite (Latour 1987).

Snedecor's final argument was that purposive selection could normally be reduced to a case of stratified random sampling. This time he based his case on the works of Jerzy Neyman (we will see soon why this remark is important) which, although cited by Sarle in an earlier edition of the *Journal of Farm Economics*, were presented here for the first time in detail to readers. The point that had interested Snedecor was not the intervals of confidence, so prominent today, but representativeness, which was also the aspect that Neyman wanted to highlight. This argument went as follows: "If it is to yield unbiased results, purposive sampling must ordinarily be designed as a special case of stratified random sampling" (Snedecor 1939, 853). Neyman showed that purposive selection samples were only a neglected subclass of stratified random samples. Thus only randomness could lay claim to representativeness.

Hence, the experience that was the basis of Snedecor's comparison of the methods of selection was nothing more than to immerse them into tradition, his predecessors, and existing literature. He had established the contours of a bibliography and through it—its authority as well its arguments—he had been able to show that it was randomness that had the best claim to representativeness.

Asymmetrical Comparison

Consequently, there was no question of choosing between the two methods anymore. On the contrary, all the energy went into the development of the random method. Comparison had thus succeeded: the Division and the Iowa Statistical Laboratory had shown that stratified random selection was more representative than purposive selection. But was this comparison, for all that, based on the weighing-scale model? We can without hesitation reply in the negative and list the differences between what we have observed and this model (Galison 1987).

First, no "great moment of truth" had dawned, with the result suddenly appearing in complete clarity to the Statisticians, as if, after a drumroll, they had withdrawn their hands from the scalepan and seen the beam tilt to the side of randomness. On the contrary, comparison was a long process that took place between 1936 and 1939. This process transformed the compared elements themselves in the sense that their characteristics did not remain stable at all. The Statisticians expressed various successive properties of randomness and purposive selection. The two most important changes were, one, that both methods were associated with different sample units (roads in the case of purposive selection, sections in the case of randomness) and, two, that simple randomness was rejected in favor of stratified randomness.

But the methods alone did not change during this process. Comparison also consisted of a series of consecutive persuasions, of successive and as much as possible cumulative "interestments," as Bruno Latour (1987) would say, that also changed the public of the experiments. We can start with the hypothesis that the members of the Iowa Statistical Laboratory, as a group, were in favor of randomness from the beginning. It should, however, be pointed out that, loyal Fisher followers that they were, they initially considered randomness not as a method of selection, but as a way of randomizing the experiments; later they changed their stand and perceived randomness as a means of selecting the units. The members of the Division, however, were less unanimous (Jatteau 2018). Sarle, it seems, was initially quite hesitant, but he became convinced by randomness after realizing that stratification allowed him to use the available knowledge accessible to him for the survey. He then developed random methods that would actually yield results. It now remained for him to convince the Statisticians, probably the most reluctant of the lot. With this objective, it was clever of Sarle to designate one of them, Holmes, to do the comparisons. Hence, just as there was no unique experiment that constituted a "moment of truth," similarly there was no unique group, the Statisticians, who suddenly all converted to randomness.

Finally, if the weighing-scale model is contradicted by the fact that there was no single weighing operation, nor a public that was common to all weighing operations, the very idea of weighing comparable characteristics is also to be rejected. Indeed, the initial problem was that there were too many potential variables, which made it difficult to judge whether a method was better than another or if it had simply been badly implemented. After this Sarle identified two principal dimensions of the comparison: the selection method and the units. But, as they were inseparable from one another, to compare the units, only one method of selection had to be chosen, and for testing a method of selection, only one unit was needed. The effort involved in testing the four boxes of the square was much too important, especially as in reality there were many more than two methods to be decided between (purposive selection could be used according to different criteria whose relevance needed to be tested, and the same with stratification, etc.); similarly, there were more than two units to be compared (the sections, combinations of sections, secondary units within the units, roads). Thus, in reality, it was not just four solutions that had to be compared, but many more. Consequently, the authors decided to retain only one method of selection for comparing the units, and a minimal number of units for evaluating the method.

But these practical choices had important consequences on the rest of the process. For example, Sarle had tested different units on the basis of random selection only. In so doing, he furthered his knowledge of this method at the expense of purposive selection: he knew that the smaller the unit, the more accurate but also the more costly it was, and there was no equivalent conclusion for purposive selection. One of the two methods had thus clearly taken the lead in the selection race, while the other had stayed put.

Now, if the experiment was successful—as was the case when Holmes managed to show that random sampling of various combinations of sections representing 10% of the population gave results that were similar to the census results—why make the effort to "save" the other method that had fallen behind? The issue tackled by Statisticians was neither that of justice, nor equity, but of finding a method that worked. In this case, to start all over again with the other method represented a waste of time for returns that were uncertain: either they obtained less interesting results, and the additional research would be of no use, or they got results that were as, if not more, interesting, and the chances were that all that had already been achieved would again be open to question. Rather than put new irons in the fire, it was much more effective and better policy to reinforce the results already achieved, study them thoroughly, and fine-tune them. This is just what the Statisticians did by presenting them to politicians and framing them within a tradition. Reciprocally, rather than running two champions and taking the risk of seeing them turn against each other, it was advisable to curb the development of the other method. Here, too, like Sarle and Snedecor in 1939, it is precisely what the agricultural Statisticians did.

The fundamentally asymmetrical nature of comparison, the fact that only the qualities of one element are expressed for comparing with the defects of another, induces us to develop a more theoretical, or shall we say, a more "bibliographical" link with what in the history of science is called a "strong program." David Bloor (1991) advises historians and sociologists of science to study the scientific controversies in a symmetrical manner. The "symmetry postulate" signifies that the historian or the sociologist should treat scientific failure and success in the same way and use the same analytical grid to study the method that has emerged victorious in a controversy (which can very well remain at the pacific comparison stage), as well as the one that was eliminated. In fact, as Bloor advises equality of treatment of the participants and the issues involved in a controversy, the strong program recommends studying science scientifically, according to the weighing-scale model. In other words, the strength and the appeal of the strong program lie precisely in the contrast that it presents with the way scientists generally operate, as they seldom treat their objects equitably.

Conclusion: The Expression Model versus the Force of Truth Model

We have seen how the comparison of the two methods retained during the 1936 conference swung in favor of stratified random selection. It now remains for us to wrap up the issue we introduced at the opening of this chapter—namely, the nature of the process by which statisticians arrived at this result. Should one, as most statisticians do, award the victory to Neyman's work on randomness, or should we look for another explanation?

Historians who rank Neyman very high can be qualified as "internalists": by training and by profession they are specialists working in the field whose history they are relating. We term them so because their point of view on their subject is internal to their discipline. Surveyors by profession and by ethos, they have devoted their time to writing about the past of a group that they have influenced from the inside.[8] We cited the example of Kruskal and Mosteller in the introduction to the chapter, but all internal histories of sampling also give Neyman the same status (Seng 1951; O'Muircheartaigh and Wong 1981; Sukhatme 1966). A. J. King, for example, who had been a member of the Division and was later assigned to the Statistical Laboratory, stresses the influence exercised by the new sampling theory on the Ames group: "Jerzy Neyman in his paper published in 1934 recommended: (i) that in general the stratified random selection of sampling units is preferable to purposive selection and (ii) that the sampling units should be small and widely scattered for maximum sampling efficiency" (King 1945, 41). Then he goes on to indicate the way in which these recommendations were followed in Iowa. This explanatory tradition is continued, for example, by Wayne Fuller who, in his more recent history of the Statistical Laboratory, states that "most [of Neyman's paper] is devoted to empirical comparisons that demonstrate the superiority of random sampling over purposive selection" (Fuller 1984, 584), a demonstration (the word is important coming from statisticians) that, according to him, is one of the reasons for the adoption of randomness by the actors.

Thus, the historical model that these historians have in mind is that theories or methods assume importance for the good and simple reason that they are true. This is what happened with the random method. In this process the role of humans is limited to being the first to glimpse these truths, as in the case of Jerzy Neyman. The history of statistics is not very "social." If there is a place for society in this kind of history of science and technology, the only role reserved for it consists of opposing innovations. For theory to come into its own, Statisticians had to give up their social resistance: "The impact of Neyman's 1934 paper on United States sampling was not immediate. There was still the need for communication, understanding, acceptance, and the adaptation and extension of the results he had presented" (Hansen and Madow 1976, 82). The historical process to legitimatize randomness seems to have consisted exclusively of a more or less rapid succession of approbations of Neyman's theories by practitioners of statistics. The internalists thus explain scientific practices by first presupposing a theoretical discovery, which would supposedly become the norm because it was true, and second, by using a social context averse to innovation, which would gradually change its stance by recognizing the truth.

This explanation seems to largely account for at least one detail in the history that we have just narrated: the delay in acknowledging Neyman's work. The publication of the 1934 article elicited no response from the players we are concerned with here because, in the entire corpus that we have compiled, no article mentions Neyman before 1939. Neyman thus initially did not exist, neither in Iowa nor in any of the Division's offices. Then, from 1939 onward, the article began to be cited more often, especially by Sarle and Snedecor. Its impact really made itself felt after Neyman's visit to the United States:

> [Until 1937] Neyman's 1934 article on the representative method had had relatively little influence on US Government statisticians. But W. Edwards Deming … arranged for Professor Neyman to come to Washington in April 1937 to hold a conference on Sampling Human Populations. This series of meetings and discussions had important influence on Washington Statisticians not only directly, but by calling attention in a forceful way to Neyman's foundation article.… Probably it was Neyman's ability to relate theory to practice from personal experience in

> the economic and social fields that caused the lasting impact. (Duncan and Shelton 1976, 74)

The findings of these U.S. lectures and conferences were published (Neyman 1938).

Neyman also took advantage of this trip to America to visit several universities, including Iowa. Hence, it would seem that, as the model of the propagation of theories demands, Neyman's article alone did not have the power to convince American Statisticians, but he reinforced it by his presence and it interested a lot of people (Latour 1987). But if the tardiness of the process in disseminating Neyman's article is effectively well described by internalist theory, it is about the only thing that is. On the one hand, Neyman in no way triggered a sort of swing in the preference shown by the players for randomness and, on the other, his propositions were re-expressed by the agricultural Statisticians when they used them.

First, it is evident that they raised the issue of randomness independently and differently than Neyman. Sarle did so through probable error in 1927; Snedecor worked on Fisher's findings, completely unrelated to those of Neyman and yet steeped in randomness, from the mid-1920s. The randomness issue clearly preceded not only the cognizance but even the publication of Neyman's article by agricultural Statisticians. Thus it was not Neyman who was responsible for introducing randomness to the Division.

Second, Neyman's article cannot claim to have finally established the only true theory of random selection. On the contrary, it became part of the mix of objects already existing in the Division, and it contributed with all the others in expressing some new elements. As in the case of the survey on individual farms, or Bowley's work used by Sarle, or Fisher's propositions in Snedecor's hands, Neyman was also re-expressed by agricultural Statisticians. As usual, the past was re-expressed by the innovators.[9]

Moreover, Snedecor found a way to amalgamate, instead of choosing among, Neyman's theories and Fisher's propositions on inference, which however, at this time, were at loggerheads with each other.[10] The title of

Snedecor's 1939 article, "Design of Sampling Experiments in the Social Sciences," is a perfect illustration. He shows that the positions of the two men—Neyman, who claimed authorship of the words *sampling in the social sciences*, and Fisher, who had proposed *design of experiments*—could be of mutual service to each other, instead of competing with each other. Snedecor's work was an expression of this collaboration between the two camps. Snedecor facilitated the meeting of the two camps.[11]

Thus there was a definite marriage of interests between Neyman and his article and the Division-Laboratory setup; it played a role and the players referred to it. But they gave it a role to play only to the extent that they found aspects that could be used in their own interrogations using their own resources. Neyman in no way changed the agricultural statistics landscape; he was incorporated into it as an ingredient. In this vast, long, and slow articulation, he contributed to the defense of stratified random sampling, which was expressed on this occasion. The interface between the Division and the Iowa State University Statistical Laboratory expressed a truly novel survey method, stratified random sampling, which was new both for the Department of Agriculture and the university statisticians, and also for the person that historical tradition considers as the inventor. Thus the sampling method was new for everyone. But, at the time, they were only experiments, local endeavors. Let us now see how investigators extended their results to this intimidating object that was America as a whole.

6

Areal America

Around the year 1939, agricultural Statisticians in Washington as well as academics from Iowa State University, agreed on the fact that the best statistics they could provide to the government were representative surveys, which could be obtained through the stratified random sampling method. But at the time, this method was only valid if the Statisticians worked on "fifteen to twenty counties" or on a single state such as Iowa or Alabama. It was another matter to cover the whole of America. Going from one to forty-eight[1] was not just expanding the universe; it was changing the scale radically.

We will see how these new representative surveys that asked for a radically new description of the United States were carried out. The Statisticians had, in fact, to find a solution to make the entire population compatible with the random selection model. They had to find a way to materially transform America into a vast urn containing small areas of land from which to draw samples (Desrosières 1998, chap. 7). Let us first see how this was done, and then how politicians managed make use of the results; that is, how a long chain linked together a new population, a new method of observation, and new political actions. In other words, how statistical representativity consolidated areal America.

Chapter 6

Road Maps and Aerial Photographs

The very first endeavor that agricultural Statisticians had to tackle to achieve a representative—thus random—sample of the United States as a whole was to find an element composing the nation that would have this very rare characteristic of staying unchanged all over the country. They were looking for a unit that could metaphorically be put in an urn for random selection. They needed an element exhaustively covering the nation, without repetition. This quest had no simple solution, that is the least one can say.

In 1938, the Department of Agriculture and the Statistical Laboratory at Iowa State University (ISU) had decided to further reinforce their ties by signing a new and more comprehensive collaboration agreement whose main objective was "the development of efficient methods of sampling individual farms" (Fuller 1984, 584). The agreement included a very important clause about the personnel working in the Iowa Statistical Laboratory. It first stipulated that a certain number of staff from the Agriculture Department (seven in number) would go to work in the Midwest and also that funds would be given to the Laboratory by the Department so that it could employ new researchers and research students. One of the students, Raymond Jessen, was a strapping fellow capable of tackling any American football player (he himself played football) or felling a tree with a chain saw (he had been a woodcutter). He had just completed his bachelor of science in agriculture from Berkeley and had been recruited by the Laboratory to do a thesis in statistics precisely on the development of a random sampling method.[2] The fate of Jessen's thesis is particularly interesting to follow because it gave rise to one of the most impressive experiments in representative sampling that ever took shape in American agricultural statistics.

Jessen's initial experiments, presented by him in an article published in the special centenary issue on agricultural statistics of the *Journal of Farm Economics*, dealt with the very township sections that Charles Sarle and Irvin Holmes had worked on. Since his first study was on Iowa exclusively,

Jessen felt that his purpose would be served by taking quarter-sections, with sides measuring half a mile, and he called these small areas of land "geographic zones" (Jessen 1939).

These little areas had the great advantage of giving more accurate results than the Agriculture Department's classic surveys. This was demonstrated by Jessen in a table in which he compared the results of his survey with those of the Iowa tax assessors and the Department's standard estimates.

But these units also presented two difficulties. The first was that, although they gave satisfactory results as long as the interviewers were graduate students or teachers from Iowa State University, as had been the case, Jessen thought that less qualified interviewers would find it difficult to identify them on the ground in a larger survey (Jessen 1939). In fact, it was often very difficult to locate the physical landmarks determining the section corners because the new roads constructed in rural areas often eliminated them without replacing them (Johnson 1976).[3]

The second difficulty, as problematic as the first, was that the nonexhaustive topographical surveys could not be applied to the entire country. In fact, they were valid only for "public lands"—that is, those belonging to the twenty-nine states in 1954, and even in their case, there was no topographical survey for one million acres of land in the west, excluding Alaska (Harrison 1954). This nonexhaustiveness made it very difficult to use the units for a survey on the United States as a whole; hence Jessen preferred to explore other avenues of research.

He did not give up constructing "geographic zones" and searched for territorial divisions that would be easier to manipulate. One obvious alternative was to turn to the Census Bureau. Since it also sent surveyors to the field, it had to necessarily provide them with maps. In fact, the Census Bureau had a Geography Division but was content to centralize all the maps that it found, without producing any of its own (Struve 1940). Therefore, the census agents ventured into the field, equipped with incomplete and outdated maps, having to manage on their own. In other words, Jessen could derive no benefit from it and preferred to try his luck elsewhere.

He suggested a third solution, using the road maps published by a private company, Rand McNally, and not the state maps (Jessen 1945). Their maps were legendary, and especially their "Road Atlas" of the country, which claimed to be absolutely exhaustive and, as such, could have constituted a valuable resource for Jessen. But this map was really meant for cyclists and, subsequently from 1910, for motorists so that they could use it to get their bearings. Only rarely were farms and other cultivated areas lying *between* the roads indicated on these maps, which is what the Statisticians were interested in (Akerman 1993). Hence, it was difficult to use the Road Atlas for surveys.

In keeping with the Rand McNally model, he eventually came up with the idea of using road maps, but those published by the states (see figure 6.1). In particular, the example readily available to him, the Iowa State map, was especially well suited for this purpose. In fact, it was not difficult to construct small geometric forms, almost as simple as the townships and sections, whose sides were defined by the physical features existing on the land that interviewers could easily identify. All buildings unmistakably figured on the maps.

However, despite these three undeniable attributes, the maps did not exactly meet Jessen's expectations. The maps were the states' responsibility, and at the federal level no instructions or norms had ever been given to build a common standard model: "There is no single source from which the best available maps may be obtained. This causes great expenditure of time and money to bring them together" (King 1945, 43). In order to use them, the Statisticians had to standardize them, which involved considerable time and money. Worse still, in some states, "such maps were not always available" (King 1945, 42). Thus, as unbelievable as it might appear today, Jessen confirmed what others before him had already complained of—namely, that at the beginning of the 1940s, the United States was not uniformly mapped to a small enough scale so that routes and farms could figure exhaustively and thus enable random selection.[4]

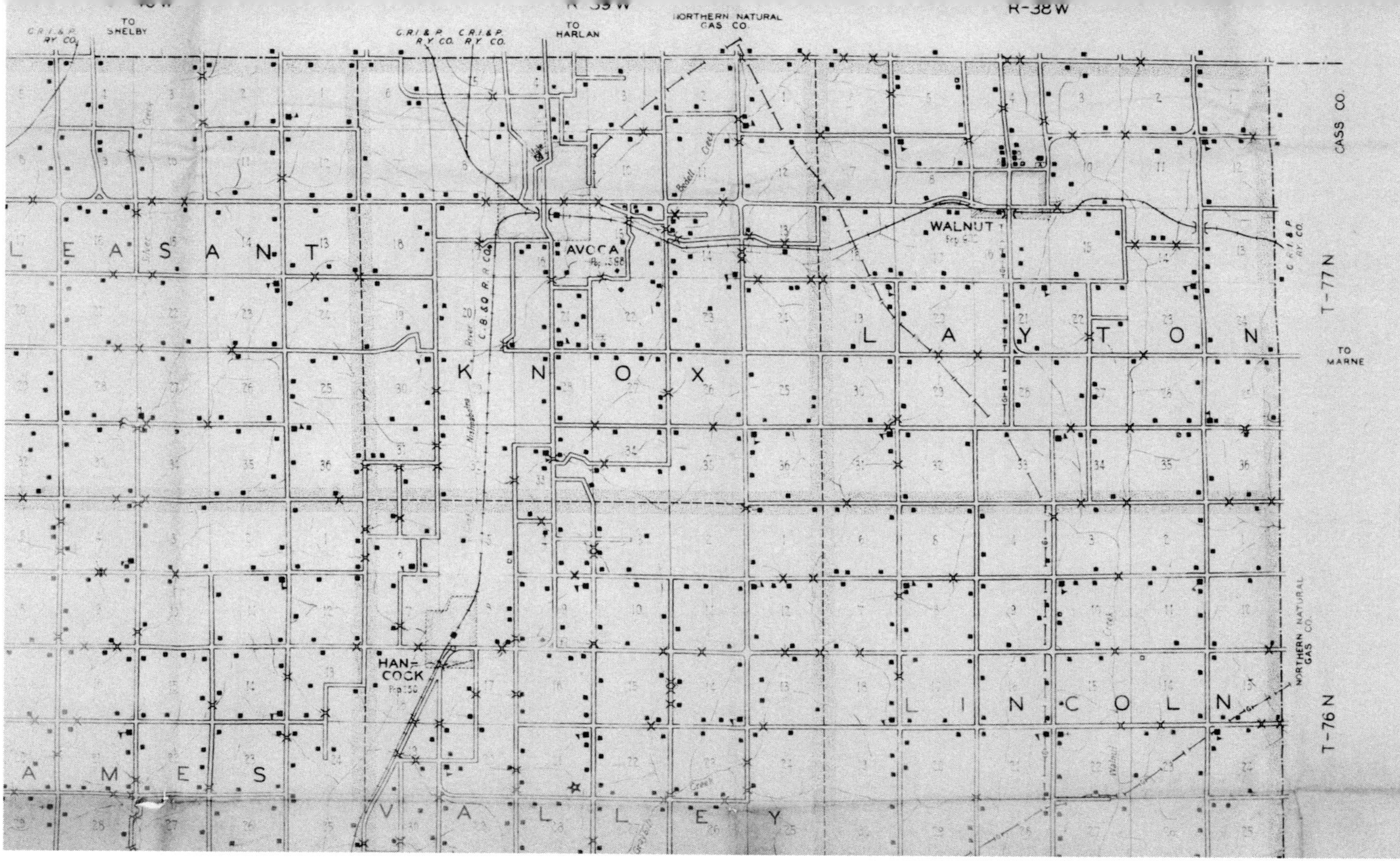

6.1 A section of a road map of Pottawattamie County, published by the state of Iowa. It measures approximately 1.5 × 1 meters. We see small black squares, each representing a farm; roads and other "natural features" (two pipelines, a railway line), which help in plotting the different areas; a dotted-line marking the boundary of the townships, each bearing a name (Layton, Knox, Lincoln); and inside, sections numbered in serpentine fashion from 1 to 36. (Map shown was given by the Statistical Laboratory to Raymond Lévy-Bruhl in 1946, who gave it to me; photo by Yvan Clédat)

Consequently, he searched for an alternative solution. He recalled that Z. R. Pettet, head of Agricultural Statistics in the Census Bureau, had proposed at a conference (Bureau of Agricultural Economics 1936) the use of aerial photography as a means of identifying tracts of land.[5] Jessen used this idea of observing the countryside from the sky, which allowed him to distinguish a large number of relevant features in a specified area, including farms, and thereby draw samples easily.

However, these photographs had the disadvantage of being very costly since one had to pay for the airplane as well as the photographer and, on average, it required at least one-and-a-half prints per sample unit (Jessen 1942). Jessen therefore decided to combine them with the state road maps and only use photographs to compensate for the defects in the maps.

In this way, after great difficulty, Jessen managed to put together 3,070 county maps, one for each county in the United States (Jessen 1945), which when joined edge to edge, formed a complete map of the country measuring close to 3,000 square meters. Jessen decided to make use of the county divisions and assigned an envelope to each county, in which he put all the documents relating to that particular county (see figure 6.2). The United States had thus acquired the singular profile of a series of envelopes containing these maps, which were arranged in thirty-eight drawers of several cupboards (Fuller 1984).

Within a period of ten years, between 1938 and the end of World War II, the agricultural Statisticians in the government and at Iowa State University, without having explicitly set this target for themselves, had nevertheless rewritten the practical history of American cartography. Using random selection as their guiding light and the initial topographical surveys from the era of the conquest of the American West as their starting point, they discovered aerial photographs to make the conquest from the sky. They covered this history while looking for a way to express those small areas that had the dual characteristic of being *small* enough to designate individual farms and *standard* enough to cover the totality of the vast American territory. At this stage, after enormous effort, they had finally

6.2 Raymond Jessen posing for a photo in 1946. In particular, he showed us the envelopes on his desk, each containing a map representing a county.

created a base that exhaustively captured the population. But this was still not sufficient; a selection process was yet to be developed that would allow them to construct a representative sample.

A One in Eighteen Chance

Now that the Statisticians had transformed America into an urn composed of identical elements, the problem was to actually draw representative samples—that is random samples—from it. If utilization of the maps thus obtained appeared *a priori* easy, the Iowa Statisticians soon realized that there was a problem of scale. How could a small laboratory, composed all in all of approximately twenty members, handle the mountains of paper that would be piling up? It would require centuries of work, not to mention the risk of error occurring. Consequently, they had to resolve two interconnected riddles: first, they had to basically understand how a map, any map, could help in drawing a random sample, and second, they had to be able to handle the gigantic map that they had at their disposal.

The solution to the second part of the problem took the form of an agreement with the Census Bureau in 1943. Pettet, who had presented the aerial photographs to the Agriculture Department, acted as the go-between and was later replaced by Morris Hansen, who afterward played a key role in the development of sample survey techniques (Hansen 1987). The Census Bureau wanted to have access to the maps put together by Jessen, and the agreement ensured that the survey frame bore on the totality of the United States (not just rural America); in exchange, it provided money, and a lot of it. For example, for the year 1946 (the only year for which we found data), the university contributed $53,000 toward the Statistical Laboratory's budget, the Agriculture Department, in conformity with the 1938 agreement, contributed $47,000 and private firms $41,000, whereas the Census Bureau alone gave $91,000.[6] At the same time, the random sample survey project acquired a name, the Master Sample, which henceforth applied to the United States in its entirety, including urban America.

The grants received were spent on recruiting an army of clerks, who in 1945 were some 200 in number (Fuller 1984) (see figure 6.3). Arnold J. King, an officer in the Agriculture Department deputed to the Statistical Laboratory since the 1938 agreement, was appointed project director and hence found himself heading the Laboratory's operations while Jessen continued as chief methodologist.

While the staff was being recruited, the Statistical Laboratory, with the help of the Department of Agriculture, succeeded in getting a new building built by the Public Works Administration for housing the growing number of permanent staff (Jessen 1945).

In this way, the project, originally just a thesis in a small statistics laboratory, was adapted to the scale of this huge map of America on which it was based and was transformed into a large bureaucracy, well endowed with

6.3 The Master Sample staff at work. Almost always in statistics, the employees are young women. As a result, very little is known about them (Fuller 1984). (ISU Library, University Archives, Special Collections Department)

institutional linkages, including funding, workers, and buildings. But how did this new and enormous machinery, organized around maps, function?

The first phase of the work consisted of tracing the contours of a series of overlapping components directly on the map. At the outset, Jessen and his team thought that they should not treat towns and countryside alike. The populations were too different to be sampled using the same criteria. They therefore defined three different strata. The first comprised the "urban zones" or "incorporated areas," cities with more than 2,500 inhabitants. The second stratum comprised villages or "unincorporated areas," defined as zones with more than 100 persons per square mile, but which were not considered towns by the Census Bureau. The third and last stratum was designated "open country" and included the remaining areas. Hence, the clerks used the information read on the map to form the strata—in other words, "to designate them properly on the work maps" (Jessen specified that stratum 1 had to be in yellow and stratum 2 in green).[7]

Next, the employees had to draw what Jessen had defined as *counting units*. Because they were different for each stratum, we will confine ourselves to the counting units pertaining to the third stratum, the open country. In this case, the counting units had to first mold themselves to the boundaries of the "minor civil divisions" (which for the most part meant townships); second, the units had to consist of six to thirty farms each, a number that was dependent on the accuracy of the maps; and third, they had to include the boundaries of the "naturally demarcated areas"—that is, those indicated in the key to the road maps (Jessen 1945, 49).

These counting units helped to determine other, even smaller, units, which eventually, effectively, formed the sample called *sample units*. How? Jessen theoretically determined that each counting unit (the previous ones) had to contain a certain number of sample units. This number depended on the estimated accuracy of the counting units. In the most accurate counting units (those for which there were good recent road maps), sample units consisting of four farms were traced, with a tolerance limit of more or less two farms. In the second group, there had to be five farms, with a tolerance limit of more or less three farms; and in the least exact of all groups, there had to be eight farms, with a tolerance limit of more or less six farms, except when there were aerial photographs for the area, in which case the number was reduced to six, with a tolerance limit of more or less four farms.

Jessen estimated that this represented 1,200,000 sampling units (Jessen 1947)! And even with his army of employees, he considered that it would prove a gargantuan task to draw all of them on the maps. He therefore came up with an extremely clever detour "which saved considerable clerical time" (Jessen 1942, 51). By definition, the employees knew how many farms there were in each counting unit. So, by an approximate division and with the help of the rules stated above, they could calculate the number of sampling units that each counting unit contained. They then noted this number, and only the number, in the counting unit directly on the map. Then they recapitulated the *total number* of sample units and their size county-wise in the counting units' list (and not the map), in such a way as to finally obtain the complete strata (see figure 6.4).

It was only from this list that the selection as such could be carried out. So, transforming a map into a list was at the same time fairly complicated *and* crucial. For this purpose, the Statisticians used what we today call a systematic draw of 1/18 sample units. That is, they randomly drew a number *n* from 1 to 18, noted the code identifying the *nth* sample unit, then *systematically*, the next 18th unit and again the next 18th, and so on. Why the number 18? What did it signify? Brooks (1977), who at the time was a Statistician in the Agriculture Department, explains that the initial objective was to draw a sample corresponding to 1/20 of the population, or 5%, but that 1/18, which was close to 5%, had the great advantage of corresponding to half the sections of each township (36/2 = 18). This figure seems to suggest that one would be drawing sampling units from roughly two sections per township. However, the technique that helped select the random number from 1 to 18 is not specified anywhere.

Next, they had to revert to the maps to identify the counting units because of the fact that one (at least) of their sample units had been selected, and then draw inside the identified counting unit the sample units, as many as had been decided earlier on the basis of the most easily identifiable boundaries. Finally, a random number between one and the total number of sample units plotted in the counting units had again to be drawn to know which would be retained. This represented around 67,000 units consisting of approximately 300,000 farms: the average size of the units used in the Master Sample of Agriculture was five farms. In Indiana, the areal extent of these units averaged 0.71 square mile; in Nevada, 108 square miles; and in the whole United States, 2.5 square miles (Jessen 1947, 534).

The final sample was composed of all the selected sampling units put together. Following this, all the lists and all the maps on which the strata,

Bureau of Census
Stat. Lab., I.S.C.
Form 6008
6/24/47

Statistical Laboratory
Iowa State College
Ames, Iowa

MASTER SAMPLE - REVISED
Listing of Open Country Counting Units
Outside of Metropolitan Districts

State Iowa
County Pottawattamie
Sheet 2 of 7

Line No.	MCD No.	CU No.	INOF	INOD	SU's	Cum. INOF	Cum. INOD	Cum. SU's	Line No.	MCD No.	CU No.	INOF	INOD	SU's	Cum. INOF	Cum. INOD	Cum. SU's
101	4	23	7	7	2	530	547	148	151		28	2	2	1	812	831	224
102	5	1	7	7	2	537	554	150	152		29	5	6	1	817	837	225
103		2	2	2	1	539	556	151	153		30	3	3	1	820	840	226
104		3	3	3	1	542	559	152	154		31	4	4	1	824	844	227
105		4	5	5	1	547	564	153	155		32	4	4	1	828	848	228
106		5	5	5	1	552	569	154	156		33	6	6	2	834	854	230
107		6	4	4	1	556	573	155	157		34	2	2	1	836	856	231
108		7	7	7	2	563	580	157	158		35	6	6	2	842	862	233
109		8	13	13	3	576	593	160	159	7	1	4	4	1	846	866	234
110		9	3	3	1	579	596	161	160		2	3	3	1	849	869	235
111		10	4	4	1	583	600	162	161		3	11	12	3	860	881	238
112		11	7	7	2	590	607	164	162		4	3	3	1	863	884	239
113		12	6	6	2	596	613	166	163		5	3	3	1	866	887	240
114		13	4	4	1	600	617	167	164		6	10	10	2	876	897	242
115		14	10	10	2	610	627	169	165		7	10	10	2	886	907	244
116		15	11	11	3	621	638	172	166		8	3	3	1	889	910	245
117		16	7	7	2	628	645	174	167		9	3	3	1	892	913	246
118		17	8	9	3	636	654	177	168		10	5	5	1	897	918	247
119		18	4	4	1	640	658	178	169		11	9	9	2	906	927	249
120		19	5	5	1	645	663	179	170		12	14	14	3	920	941	252
121		20	3	3	1	648	666	180	171		13	8	8	2	928	949	254
122		21	7	7	2	655	673	182	172		14	7	7	2	935	956	256
123		22	7	7	2	662	680	184	173		15	5	5	1	940	961	257
124	6	1	7	7	2	669	687	186	174		16	9	11	2	949	972	259
125		2	3	3	1	672	690	187	175		17	8	9	2	957	981	261
126		3	5	5	1	677	695	188	176		18	9	9	2	966	990	263
127		4	7	7	2	684	702	190	177		19	3	3	1	969	993	264
128		5	8	8	3	692	710	193	178		20	6	7	1	975	1000	265
129		6	2	2	1	694	712	194	179		21	2	2	1	977	1002	266
130		7	5	5	1	699	717	195	180		22	3	3	1	980	1005	267
131		8	6	6	2	705	723	197	181		23	10	19	2	990	1024	269
132		9	2	2	1	707	725	198	182		24	9	9	2	999	1033	271
133		10	8	8	2	715	733	200	183	8	1	4	4	1	1003	1037	272
134		11	8	8	2	723	741	202	184		2	14	15	3	1017	1052	275
135		12	9	9	2	732	750	204	185		3	6	6	2	1023	1058	277
136		13	5	5	1	737	755	205	186		4	2	2	1	1025	1060	278
137		14	8	8	2	745	763	207	187		5	13	14	3	1038	1074	281
138		15	4	4	1	749	767	208	188		6	5	5	1	1043	1079	282
139		16	4	4	1	753	771	209	189		7	12	12	3	1055	1091	285
140		17	5	5	1	758	776	210	190		8	12	12	3	1267	1103	288
141		18	10	11	2	768	787	212	191		9	10	10	2	1077	1113	290
142		19	5	5	1	773	792	213	192		10	6	6	2	1083	1119	292
143		20	3	3	1	776	795	214	193		11	12	20	3	1095	1139	295
144		21	9	9	2	785	804	216	194		12	8	10	2	1103	1149	297
145		22	7	7	2	792	811	218	195		13	6	6	2	1109	1155	299
146		23	4	4	1	796	815	219	196		14	7	7	2	1116	1162	301
147		24	3	3	1	799	818	220	197	9	1	2	2	1	1118	1164	302
148		25	4	4	1	803	822	221	198		2	3	3	1	1121	1167	303
149		26	4	4	1	807	826	222	199		3	5	5	1	1126	1172	304
150		27	3	3	1	810	829	223	200		4	3	3	1	1129	1175	305

6.4 List for Pottawattamie County in Iowa. The first column gives the serial numbers; the second column indicates the beginning and the order number of each minor civil division (here we have townships from 4 to 9); the third column indicates the number of the counting unit; the fourth column, the number of farms in the counting unit; the fifth column the number of dwellings; the sixth column, the crucial one, indicates the number of sample units contained in the counting unit, after which follows the cumulative totals (cumulative sums of farms, dwellings, and sample units). The second half of the sheet (vertically) repeats this format for the subsequent units. The whole of America was thus transformed into a statistical table of this type, running into several thousand pages. (ISU Library, University Archives, Special Collections Department) the counting units and a few sampling units, had been plotted were put in envelopes, which were then stored in the cupboards. At last one could move on to the field survey.

A copy of the map was again used in this new phase. At the time of questioning, with the help of the respondent and the key given in the map, the interviewer used the map to demarcate the area of the land under scrutiny.

The new method was stabilized very quickly under the name of *area sampling*.[8] It consisted of two novel and important points. The first involved the decision-making bodies. In the past, the state Statistician was required to show initiative in his job. He had to constantly find new informants, sometimes depending on luck, besides which he had to have a general idea of his state to select representative portions from it, and so on. With the new method, much less initiative was required because most of the initiatives were taken *at the time of selecting a sample*. Hence, in respect of the plotting of the strata and the counting units, Jessen writes that "a considerable number of new situations required the quick and ready answers of judgement" (Jessen 1942, 50).

In fact, the main problem was determining where to demarcate the boundaries of the strata on the map and how to estimate the number of farms and houses in each unit. After that, all the Statistician needed to do was to question the respondent and follow the selection's instructions. All the decisions that Sarle had talked about in relation to his comparisons, at least all those connected with the selection, were now taken not in the field but in this beautiful brand-new rectangular building housing the Statistical Laboratory, which truly lived up to its name. Thus, the changes in the selection methods led to changes in the profession of the various agricultural Statisticians.

The new method also helped to resolve a very old problem faced by the Agriculture Department's staff, which constituted its second important novelty. In the past the sampling unit and observation unit were not distinct from each other: reporters auto-selected themselves at the moment they declared being volunteers. This was a problem since, as we have seen, the farmer's response was biased *by virtue of the fact* that he had agreed to reply. This relation seemed impassable and inevitable: it is obvious that those who respond are also those who are willing to take the trouble to respond. However, by making this distinction between the sample units and the observation units, the problem was posed differently when it came to random selection (King 1945).

Once the selection method was in place, some units were meant for selection (e.g., geographic zones demarcated with the help of maps) and others for observation (e.g., farms whose main building was located in these zones). The random draw was carried out in the first group and the questionnaires were circulated in the second. Consequently, the selection process was no longer in the hands of the respondents. Not only was the *selection* mechanism thus free from the old relationship of fidelity, but also from the respondent's will. The Department of Agriculture now selected a certain number of individuals—who no longer had a say in the matter—simply because they happened to be located, unbeknownst, on a particular map. Each one of them could be selected and had the *chance of being enumerated* independently of their willingness to respond (Snedecor 1939, 849). The new selection method not only transformed the profession of the agricultural Statistician (see figure 6.6), but also the profession, dare we say, of the respondent (see figure 6.5).

The respondent who had thus emerged through random sampling had also become a representative independent of his choosing, which, we must again emphasize, signified a revolution in the history of the concept of representativeness. Earlier, whichever way we look at it, the representation of people had always been a problem of the will of those who represented and of those who were represented (Pitkin 1972; Manin 1997). Once selection was randomized, randomness took the place of volition and eliminated it from the process. In fact, the method did so well without the will factor that the respondent could henceforth stop being a person. For example, in an area survey carried out by King and Simpson (1940), it was the interviewers themselves who went to the fields, collected samples of the crops at

6.5 This photograph was probably taken in Arkansas in 1951 and shows how new interviews began over a discussion with a farmer about the map to determine where the area to be investigated ended and where his farm ended. (USDA-NASS, Archives of Richard Allen)

random from those ready for harvesting, and sent them to a laboratory in New York that assessed the yield from their fields—all this, without having any contact with the farmers. True, this practice was exceptional, but it shows that the nature of the respondent had changed drastically: there was no parallel between the sample unit and the observation unit (Jessen 1947). The task of selection was delegated to the Statistician, and only the answers were left to the respondents. It is at this point that the problem of "nonresponse" was born: the respondents could refuse to answer, but they could not refuse to be selected. Statistical representativity had thus completely transformed the relation between the population and statisticians. This had to have important consequences on the political level.

6.6 The entire history of the Master Sample can be seen in this photograph, which was probably taken in 1943. Three statisticians meet: on the left, George Snedecor, the director of the Iowa State University Statistical Laboratory; in the center, P. C. Mahalanobis, a great Indian statistician, close to Jerzy Neyman, who was there as an invited fellow; and on the right, Arnold King, an employee of the Department of Agriculture, responsible for administering the Master Sample. Together, they are looking at a road map on which the new sample units had been traced. On the wall, we catch a brief glimpse of an aerial photograph. (ISU Library, University Archives, Special Collections Department)

A New Population

Finally, after much effort and with the help of their new base and random sampling, the agricultural Statisticians were able to produce data with entirely different qualities on America as a whole. They hoped that this time, the data would meet the politicians' requirements and, instead of being bogged down in a deliquescent relationship as in the past, would consolidate their actions. That is why in1939, while presenting the research conducted by his team to the entire Bureau of Agricultural Economics (BAE), Sarle had specified that the Master Sample would provide the "better statistics" to the government, and he had taken the trouble of defining what he meant by "better."

> The need for better and more timely statistics relating to agriculture is so well recognized by this audience that all we need do is to define what is meant by better statistics. By better statistics is meant those that have: 1. Higher degree of accuracy (published statistics); 2. Wider scope, that is, including information not now covered or only partially covered by the Federal Census; 3. Greater geographic detail, especially in basic statistics used in administration of national action farm programs. Furthermore, greater emphasis is needed on dynamic changes taking place in agriculture, including more frequent statistics than are now available from quinquennial and decennial censuses. (Sarle 1939, 356)

Hence, Sarle thought of four crucial points to meet the needs of the government: a wide range of issues, good geographical detail, a new rate of statistical production, and finally, greater accuracy. In other words, Sarle explained that the new statistical tools could interface between the new population and the new policies in order to consolidate the aggregate that they formed (Mitchell 2005). Let us discuss these four points in detail, which in the last analysis effectively characterized the Master Sample.

Issues

The first problem faced by the administrators of the New Deal was to gather information on specific research issues, which had undergone change as a result of the Great Depression. Taking the examples of farm incomes and the fight against poverty, we will see how the Master Sample and surveys in general helped to rethink these questions; we will then focus on one of the properties of the surveys that greatly facilitated this renewal.

The measurement of "farm incomes" formed the basis of the policy on agricultural recovery to the extent that one of its credos was that there was an unjust disparity between agricultural and industrial incomes (Wilson 1936). One reason, among others, frequently cited to justify government intervention was that modern economic conditions prohibited farmers from earning enough money to enable them to continue working the farm, since the price at which they sold their produce was not at par with the price they had to pay for industrial goods. This was the thesis––dear to Henry Wallace, for example—"of equality for agriculture."

To ascertain whether "equality for agriculture" existed, the farmers' incomes obviously had to be assessed; however, it was extremely difficult to resolve this issue using the conventional methods. The census method was absolutely incapable of carrying out this task because the questionnaire in a census survey has to be brief and an income survey can only be long (income sources are usually numerous, and farm incomes are often nonmonetary—two reasons that make the assessment horribly complicated). In fact, the most apt suggestion was given by the economists at Cornell University, who asked the farmers to maintain their books of account as scrupulously as possible so that they could then analyze them in detail.

But the criticism leveled by the Iowa group was severe. According to them, the farmers who had agreed and were capable of keeping precise accounts did not necessarily represent all the farmers. On the contrary, just as the correspondents or crop reporters were necessarily the "best" among the farmers, those who were capable and possessed the required knowledge to keep accounts were inevitably the most educated. Therefore, for the members of the Agriculture Department and the Statistical Laboratory, the books of account could only be used together with an analysis of representativeness:

> Workers in the field differ in the value they place on the individual case studies. Such research procedures and informal statistical methods are most likely to be fruitful when employed by workers of wide experience. Their fruitfulness is also greatest

> when employed in conjunction with some statistical analysis of a representative sample of the universe of which they are a part. (Goodsell, Jessen, and Wilcox 1940, 759)

In response to this criticism that they had themselves expressed, the surveyors from the Department of Agriculture decided to use the Master Sample, or any representative survey, because it allowed them to select a representative group of farmers for whom a fairly long questionnaire could be prepared. Thus, by controlling the representativeness of the results, this tool helped reexamine old issues. Whereas in the past, research had been based only on case studies, now statisticians were in a position to generalize the results for the whole of the United States.

Case studies on poverty highlighted another fundamental aim of surveys. This is how Jessen and two administrators from the Agriculture Department proposed such a study:

> This body of data would supply requisite background information for more detailed studies; for example, a tabulation of the schedules obtained from a sample-census survey may indicate that a number of farms having similar characteristics in several major variates definitely fall into a group which might be called low-income farms. These farms may be revisited with a view to obtaining additional information on operations and management and perhaps complete information as to the use and distribution of resources. Characteristics of these farms may be compared with those of other farms. It is hoped that studies of this sort might suggest the remedial measures needed. (Goodsell, Jessen, and Wilcox 1940, 759)

According to them, the survey made it possible to link two sets of variates, separated into two surveys here, but which were generally incorporated into a single questionnaire: on the one hand, a set of *conditions* describing the "characteristics" and the "context" of the farms, which allowed the formation of "homogenous" farm groups, including those of the poor; on the other hand, a complete set of *behavior patterns* describing the farmers' actions, how they managed their farms, and how they used and divided their "resources." These two sets of conditions and behaviors affected each other, the conditions supposedly controlling behavior and, inversely, behavior supposedly creating or at least sustaining the conditions. These two sets associated in this manner constituted "an established fact" that had been completely transformed by the Great Depression. The surveys were supposed to help in understanding the new articulation between conditions and behavior, which had appeared after the Great Depression.

As poverty was obviously seen as a problem, the survey was subsequently required to "suggest remedies" for it—that is to say, other possible articulations between variables apart from those that had been observed. This is a very important point: with the help of surveys, the administration was finally able to identify the precise ways in which its intervention would be most effective.

The last issue that the surveys helped to observe was precisely government action. Leslie Kish, who later lent his name to a technique (still in use today) for selecting individuals in a household, relates:

> At the Division of Program Surveys, under [Rensis] Likert, we did surveys that were stimulated and supported by Elmo Wilson and Henry Wallace, the Secretary of Agriculture. Wallace said that if we have all these agricultural programs, we ought to have an agency independent of any of the programs to survey those programs. The idea of an independent survey agency was a vital new concept for evaluations, so our division took samples to survey the ongoing work and reported directly to Wilson and Wallace. (Frankel and King 1996)

The surveys thus helped study the causes and effects of government intervention before it was implemented, to give it direction, and once it was over, to assess its action. At the same time that state interventionism was being revolutionized, tools were being forged to help devise tests for it.[9]

In addition, these three problems constituted only some of the difficulties that the government was to subsequently face. For example, Howard Tolley listed about ten new issues that he had to confront: the price of agricultural products, farm incomes, agricultural production for self-consumption, distribution, packaging (especially for meat), agricultural consumption, animal feed, agricultural jobs, rural population, and finally, farmers' attitudes and opinions (Tolley, 1939). As it happens, the survey method, and especially the Master Sample, had a distinctive characteristic that greatly facilitated the transition from one issue to another.

In fact, the Master Sample was only composed of small geographic zones, and from these zones the user was free to choose the final unit that constituted the samples and adapt it to the issue he was addressing. Depending on whether a study of a more economic, demographic, or geographic nature was needed, one could choose any of the units proposed by King (and the list was not exhaustive), whichever corresponded best to the issue. Thus, at the time of actually carrying out the survey, contrary to the earlier methods, statisticians and users could decide what it was going to be based on. The users were not restricted *ab initio*: "This [the Master Sample] should provide more adequate background information for subsequent surveys and will also provide a basis for more efficient subsampling to meet the special objectives of particular field surveys" (Tolley and Taeuber 1944, 423).

Thus, the Master Sample, and surveys in general, enabled the study of a large variety of issues that *de facto* eluded the Crop Reporters' method. It is especially this variety that was missing in the Department of Agriculture's conventional method for, after all, one could conceive that with the necessary investments it could have dealt with each one separately. But the facility with which one could draw several samples meant that it was possible to commission very different surveys in keeping with the objective fixed. Also, this was not its only virtue.

Zones

If we remember correctly, in 1933 and 1934, the first Agricultural Adjustment Administration (AAA) had asked the Department for a whole series of results at the county level, which it was unable to deliver. This episode had traumatized the agricultural Statisticians so greatly that, since then, they had continuously tried to produce results on these units. Would the representative surveys help in achieving this?

Given its exhaustive and gigantic size, the Master Sample of course did not serve to study just one American county. That would have been meaningless. On the contrary, whether it was used for "national or state" surveys or for "small-sized field surveys," a county-wise distribution of results was definitely possible since the sampling process ensured that each county was represented (Tolley and Taeuber 1944). In fact, we may recall that the county was the unit that defined each envelope containing the counting units, from which the in-sample units had been drawn. Hence, for each observation, it was very simple to record the reference of the county in which the observation had been made and to distribute results according to this division.

Having said that, from the late 1930s, the issue of zones based on useful and relevant information gradually saw a shift. In fact, the county was important as long as the administration used this particular channel for its transactions—for example, for the distribution of subsidies—but soon government action began to depend less on political zoning (states, counties, and townships) and more on other, specifically economic zonal divisions.

> Men in farm management have realized that the research in the field would be more useful if the farming universe were divided into broad geographic or physical units in which the patterns of farming were similar rather than into political units in which there is seldom any relationship between the important farm characteristics and the political universe. Area or group delineations that delimit groups with broadly similar production

> opportunities and, therefore, groups of farmers who could make similar adjustments to changes in external forces is what is sought. By assembling certain physical, biological, economic and sociological data the farm management specialists have subdivided broad heterogeneous regions into type-of-farming areas. Each type-of-farming area exhibits certain general characteristics which differentiate it from other areas. General physical conditions are similar within areas and the boundaries follow closely physical rather than political boundaries. (Goodsell, Jessen, and Wilcox 1940, 756)

Consequently, with regard to surveys, political boundaries gradually began to be called into question and were replaced by other more explicitly economic boundaries. The reason, as explained in this long passage, was that the survey helped to understand how farmers would "adjust" to state intervention. However, Statisticians and administrators seemed to realize that they were more likely to do so because of "external forces," such as physical, biological, and other phenomena, rather than the political entity to which they belonged. Statisticians thus prepared a series of zones based on "types of tenure," which they felt were more relevant than the political boundaries inherited from the past.

As a result, because of a paradox that was merely apparent, the *political* action of the government was no longer based on the boundaries defined in view of political representation but on new and specifically economic boundaries, more in keeping with the new "conditions" and the new "context" mentioned earlier. Politicians were taking to economics. Of course, that's not to say that government action was finally free of politics and was now founded on real facts. On the contrary, the point is that economics had become politicized, that a new politico-economic relationship expressed new entities that were political and economic at the same time. Government action was no longer restricted to the old boundaries and former political entities but was based on these new entities and new "actors" that had emerged from the New Deal. Statistical representativity and its uses had expressed political properties on these new issues and relegated the earlier ones to the icy realm of inactive facts.

Rhythm

Another question raised by the administrators of the New Deal and the agricultural Statisticians referred to the frequency of statistical studies in relation to changes in the pace of economic activity caused by the Great Depression. For example, Shepard, who was a member of the Agriculture Department working in Iowa, had brilliantly highlighted this problem. He had made a retrospective table of the correlation between the number of head of cattle—other than milk cows—remaining in the farms and the purchasing power of the farmers. The conclusion drawn by him was that the latter was at its maximum not, as one would have expected, when the head of cattle was at its minimum (the rarer the commodity, the more it is valued), but a little later when the farmers started to keep and rear milk cows:

> Here then is a clear-cut cycle which vitally affects 51/2 million cattle producers, and which affects all of us as consumers. It is based on the normal search for larger profits but it is timed by biological factors. If we had adequate statistics on cattle numbers and marketing and particularly if we knew accurately how much farmers were holding back or how much they were liquidating breeding stock, the basic factors of this cycle could be measured and plotted from month to month as the Weather Bureau plots the hourly progress of a hurricane. This cycle moves so slowly that any farmer would have time to trim his sails if he knew when it would strike him. Our Bureau sends out economic storm warnings from time to time, but with the present limited sources of information we cannot measure current changes accurately enough to do what we know ought to be done." (J. B. Shepard 1937, 456)

In the above paragraph, Shepherd visualizes statistics as being, rhythmically speaking, so well adapted to the bioeconomic movement of agricultural production that it would allow farmers to react advisedly as soon as a reversal in the situation was noticed. The agricultural movements would be like those of the clouds and the winds, and agricultural statistics would be nothing more than meteorology, capable of warning the actors of an imminent disaster—for instance, the sudden depreciation of a product. But the pace of the old agricultural statistics was no longer in tune with that of agriculture. Representative statistics was a means of accelerating the pace of data production, of putting it in back in sync with the observed phenomena and thus enabling government actions to become more reactive.

The attribute that allowed representative surveys to be rapid was the result of all the preparatory work that had gone into it. A major part of the task of sampling—whose progress we have been closely following since the beginning of this chapter—was realized even before any survey was planned or requisitioned. It is this characteristic that allowed surveys to be completed quickly, much faster in comparison with past methods.

Implicitly, Shepherd stresses a very important point—because it is very general—regarding the American government's interventionism: the government was never really "laissez-faire." Before the 1930s, it reacted *slowly*, "from time to time" as Shepherd puts it, using slow instruments, as were the old statistics, but it would be wrong to say that it did not act. The New Deal was not an invention of state interventionism, but that of a more sustained pace of the state's response to economic "upheavals," reactions that were consistent with the accelerated pace of the new economic processes born of the Great Depression, and it needed statistical tools adapted to this new reactivity.

Accuracy

The last characteristic of the surveys, repeatedly stressed by agricultural Statisticians and especially Sarle, is accuracy. A strong point of representativity was that it facilitated the construction of accurate estimators with the help of stratification and, in addition, helped measure the estimators' accuracy through the use of random selection and the calculation of confidence intervals. We have seen this in chapter 5.

The data had the advantage of being sufficiently correct for the government. But most of the time this question is thrown into the agricultural Statistician's "cooking pot," if we can call it that, and what really counts for the administrator, as Sarle very often says, is simply that the data has "serviceable accuracy" (Sarle 1940; King and Simpson 1940). Essentially, the administrators took this accuracy for granted; the new thing was that this time it was the Statisticians who had given it to them.

Satisfaction of the Planners

The characteristic qualities that Statisticians could now claim, thanks to representative statistics and the random surveys associated with it, satisfied the government and the planners with the result that their relations were freed from past viscosity and, on the contrary, were consolidated. Why were they satisfied now?

The reason was that the instrument was considered useful, especially during the second stage of the *planning* programs (such as presented earlier)—that is, during the stage of information and determination of the alternatives, which followed the identification of the problem by the farmers themselves and preceded the initial decisions on the approach to be adopted. For instance, Tolley considered the Master Sample as offering the most apposite response to the expectations of planning:

> The need for quick surveys providing reliable information for a representative cross section of the entire United States, regions, states or other areas focused attention on sampling procedures and field enumerations. Moreover, it has been increasingly apparent that the conduct of numerous field surveys, each using its own sampling procedures, made for lack of comparability

> of results, and, consequently, for inefficiency in the conduct of such surveys. Therefore, work was undertaken to develop some uniform and integrated sampling scheme for surveys in rural areas. It was decided to develop a sample of farms which in effect would be a small replica of all farms in the United States. This sample is designated the "Master Sample." (Tolley and Taeuber 1944, 145)

At last, Statisticians and politicians knew what to expect from each other. The characteristics of representative statistics that Tolley found interesting in the Master Sample were practically the same as those upheld by the Iowa State University group. First, because of the extensive preparatory work that had gone into the Master Sample, it was considered "quick." With the sample frame now ready, samples could be drawn extremely quickly. Second, it was "reliable," which had been the Statisticians' chief concern the whole time: it was possible and even easy to calculate the confidence intervals of these samples. Third, "geographic zones" of all dimensions could now be studied, and this was crucial for planning. The problems that the farmers faced had nothing to do with the administrative or political boundaries: a drought, for example, is no respecter of a county's borders. The Master Sample was based on units—the sample units–which were so small that one could construct a sample of any geographical size with no predetermined contours. Fourth and lastly, surveys could be carried out on a "large number" of subjects that were now "comparable," because there was no compulsion to sample the farms (as we have already seen).

Thus, because these four characteristics made it possible to carry out "realist studies on living conditions and their evolution," to use the words of John Dewey (1927), who had so greatly influenced the planners (see chapter 2, "Planning"), representative statistics were able to "serve as a guide in the formulation of policies and program," as Tolley writes in the same article. The surveys, by acting as the link between a conditioned population and a new federal interventionism, had finally consolidated the whole.

For the planners this argument was still too general, too abstract; the principal advantage for them was that it was sufficiently flexible (in short), both temporally and geographically, to be incorporated into the process of construction and resolution of problems by the farmers. The gigantic size of the Master Sample was precisely the reason why it had achieved this quality. In order to carry out *quick and precise* surveys on *small* or at least *varied* areas, an extremely accurate, and therefore huge, sample frame was required. (For an excellent example of a local plan in Georgia, see Raper 1943.)

Finally, the Master Sample helped establish relations between the federal government and the farmers, which suited planning perfectly. Indeed, the federal government was not absent from the process of governance because, in view of the specialization that was needed, it could only be the federal Department of Agriculture (and the university) that was in a position to operate the Master Sample. But the statistical tool was adjustable enough to produce results that the farmers could get hold of and incorporate in their own decision-making process. The state was seen as an additional resource for the farmers, certainly not a dominating power.

However, immediately after the war, certain events, beyond the realm of surveys, made planning obsolete. Voices were raised criticizing planning for not being truly democratic: on the one hand, mobilizing the poorer farmers was extremely difficult, and on the other, the established elites (trade unions and town officials) had taken over the new deliberative planning bodies to their own advantage. This criticism was leveled at that time (Gross 1943) and again later (Gilbert and Howe 1991). The farmers were gradually excluded from the planning process. As a result, these programs were indiscernibly replaced with simple "economic development," under the sole responsibility of the administrators, while the practice of meetings with farmers was discontinued (Leparwsky 1948).

But the surveys showed that they remained perfectly compatible with this democratic interventionism in an altogether different sense. For example, Rensis Likert, while in the BAE, defended the arguments in favor of the interdependence between surveys and democracy (something we are much more familiar with today), according to which by consulting surveys the administrator was acting democratically, for he was respecting the desires and motivations of the respondents expressed in them:

> Recently, the Department of Agriculture, through a small staff of specialists, has started securing for administrators, the information needed to make decisions in accordance with the desires of the people. (Likert 1940, 999)

The way Likert saw it, it was definitely the administrator who acted and made decisions; the people—to use his words—did not participate directly in the process. But the administrator behaved in a democratic manner to the extent that he paid attention to the statements made by the respondents in the survey—which in a way acted as their spokesperson.

It is possible that the relative failure of the planners explains the shadow under which this nonetheless glorious experiment "of participative democracy" had fallen. Be that as it may, the surveys established a strong foothold in the democratic administration that continues to use them today: the new method helped capture the new characteristics of the entire American population, which could at last be observed anew, and so provided relevant information useful for national-level policies.

CONCLUSION: REPRESENTATIVITY REPLACES PARTICIPATION

By creating handy representative statistics—especially with the Master Sample—the agricultural Statisticians had at last succeeded in reconsolidating an America that had crumbled under the Depression: America had regained consistency.

Thus, the principal characteristic of the now-tabulated population has to do with the volition of its members. Initially, the crop reporters/correspondents were independent farmers whose performances depended first and foremost on their own decisions—in the Jeffersonian way, to use the word of Wilson (1936; see also chapter 5, note 5). At the end of the period things had changed. On the contrary, a set of conditions was thrust upon the farmers and greatly influenced their results. The Great Depression itself had been the most striking and violent example.

Relations between statistics and farmers also changed in the intervening period. Initially, the Department of Agriculture had appealed to the voluntary crop reporters, whose volition was fundamental to this process. They in turn interrogated their neighbors in order to provide the federal administration with information on individual performances. But all this changed. First, the surveys were conducted in small geographic zones, defined by all the "natural elements" listed in the keys to the maps collected by the Statisticians. Second, in these zones, farmers were selected at random, regardless of their wish, unbeknownst to them, and were questioned on their reactions to forces that they did not control. To sum up, at the end of the period, not only the people constituting the population had changed, but also their space, their temporality, the issues they were familiar with, and the accuracy of the numbers that described them.

Toward the end of the 1930s, planners tried to restore the population's "initiative"—"control" is the word Dewey uses—which they considered fundamental for democracy and which they feared the farmers were losing out on. They discovered an earlier use of statistics according to which the enumerated population was also a direct user of the figures. During the 1910s, a farmer who had participated in the construction of the data could consult the data himself and use it to commercialize his produce; toward the end of 1930s, the planners had made it possible for the very same farmer to study the results of surveys of which he was the subject and subsequently implement his "land-use program" in light of the results. However, gradually this use proved ineffective and, by the end of World War II, it was the administrators who exclusively—or practically exclusively—used these studies. Representativity had replaced participation.

Conclusion to Part II

Expression and Consistency

In this conclusion of part II, let us review the twenty-odd years that have been studied and during which we have seen a random America assume consistency. In passing, we will recapitulate the mechanism of expression—the key operation that so often took place before our eyes—and its properties.

We started from the plasma and its properties, and we learned that a great number of elements, initially indeterminate, successively came to disrupt the statistical routine: the psychology of farmers, the post-conference recommendations of the International Institute of Statistics, the high cost of manufactured products, and election results, followed by the arrival of a new political class. We can go on giving examples, moving to smaller and smaller elements, less and less striking, but their common point is primarily that they are not part of the Statisticians' standard equipment but are strange, plasmic. Plasma is hence not always passive, waiting to be captured as a resource by Statisticians. On the contrary, we have often seen its active side.

At the same time, this activity does not take anything away from the fact that, as Simmel (1894) clearly reminds us, actors taking care of an aggregate should either try to push back the elements that shock and destabilize it, so that it does not need to evolve, or find a solution to articulate external elements when they become less and less indeterminate. We have seen an example of the first option, when, after asking themselves if they should or should not take into consideration the information they had on the *Mexican ball weevil* (cotton worm) that had invaded the southern states, the Board of Crop Estimates eventually rejected it. Charles Sarle's intention to integrate probable error in the Division's protocol gives us an example of the second option. Elements of the plasma can thus strike the aggregate more or less violently and encounter either the guards who try to exclude them or the ushers who try to integrate them.

But this second alternative can itself be divided into two possibilities. Indeed, an element can provoke a shock of such intensity that human beings may have no other choice but to suffer its effects, and we then have the impression of "following the course of events," as they say, and these are passive ushers. At other times, on the contrary, an individual may have a very strong desire to influence the course of events—that is, to "take things into his hands," as is rightly said—and here, the usher is active. The mechanism by which the plasma is incorporated into the aggregate appears, *in fine*, like a continuum between two poles: "following the course of events" and "taking things into one's own hands."

The mechanism through which the plasma modifies and renews statistics is what we have called *expression*. As we have often insisted, this process is divided into three stages: first, the regrouping of a certain number of elements (of which some come from the plasma and others from the aggregate already known to statisticians); second, their specific interconnection; third, the coming into being of a new term, one that is compatible with the aggregate and finds its place in it. Through expression, something indeterminate shocks the aggregate and is transformed into a compatible novelty; articulated with the rest of the structure, it confers consistency on the latter. If we agree on the fact that that which is initially indeterminate is also what is foreign and strange, we can then say that expression is the movement that transforms something strange into something new. The long, complex, and difficult process whose stages we have followed in part II of this book is the expression of random America. To begin with, there was the Division and its Crop Reporters' method, which was gradually articulated with the random selection of the sample and the theory of probability; from this a new aggregate was born, areal America, a new description of the population compatible with postwar political action.

Let us recall the principal stages of this expression: first, the term "representativeness," a political term, had to be adapted to statistics; then it had to be demonstrated that the random selection of the sample could be a representative selection; associates had to be identified in the university who could conduct experiments and show that random selection was not just one of the ways of drawing a sample but the best method of doing so; further, random selection had to be enshrined in the old and noble statistical tradition; lastly, the results had to be applied to an object as gigantic as America as a whole. Between the early 1920s and the end of World War II, this process of expression lasted twenty years all the same.

Finally, expression can either add elements to the aggregate, thereby making it either more solid or more deliquescent, or else provoke a rupture, an exclusion, which we have presented in part I.

Let us clarify that this concept of "expression" is similar to "capture" or "appropriation" used by Alfred N. Whitehead (Debaise 2006). Indeed, both describe the same process by which something original comes out of a completely new articulation between two initial resources, but from two different perspectives. Capture is considered from the point of view of the aggregate, which captures, whereas, in the case of expression, the initially indeterminate elements come closer to one another, then hit the aggregate and become part of it. Hence, we may as well say that America has captured surveys in order to become areal, or that Dewey's service intellectual/intellectual service and random sampling have together expressed areal America. The difference lies in the perspective from which we consider the process.

We have established three important properties of expression.

1. Retrospectiveness: Novelty is not only something that emerges at the end of the process. What was put into it initially is also recharacterized

by expression. In other words, even what was "invested" is transformed, enriched with new characteristics. We have thus seen that expression was especially against the idea that the "application" of a formula or a theory would be a servile activity, reduced to complying with the prescriptions of these formulas or theories. Each is itself transformed and retrospectively expressed again through the use it is put to. This explains the mechanism according to which the something new that is produced also serves as the criterion on which what was there before is qualified, and which as a result gets devalued. Let us mention the example of objectivity given in chapter 3. Expression not only creates new objects, it at the same time creates new characteristics in what existed before.

2. Symmetry: We have explained expression by emphasizing the changes in statistical technique. Now, its properties are also valid for the objects of these methods—that is, for the population. The symmetry argument held true for consolidation and remains so for expression. If we say, for example, that by articulating democratic representation, such as conceived by the federalists (the "best among us"), with a certain conception of objectivity (one is objective in relation to what one possesses), we get better accuracy in the answers to questionnaires. We can also say that we have expressed a new characteristic of America, a new characteristic of federalism, and also of a certain Lockean liberalism. Over and above statistical methods, it was effectively America itself that was being renewed.
3. Specificity: All statistical methods can, *in abstracto*, be articulated with all economic policies, but the articulation between a particular policy option and a method is specific and is more or less easy to consolidate. Despite the effects considered beneficial by politicians, articulation between surveys and planning will not last for long, for example, and will be quickly replaced by articulation between surveys and "economic development," which, however, continues to subsist practically till today.

We thus conclude a history of America between the two wars. But one must understand that the America in question here was mainly agricultural, which does not quite correspond with the industrial picture that we have of the Great Depression. There were, of course, the migrant farmers of the *Grapes of Wrath*, but there were also many unemployed industrial workers. In the same period, the statistics on employment and industrial activity were also in turmoil, both because of the Depression, which increased the number of unemployed, and because of the invasion of the random sampling method. To complete our picture of America and highlight the urban and industrial conditions prevailing at that time, we are going to compare the history of agricultural statistics with that of labor and unemployment.

Part III

Expression of Random America

On the Urban Front

In *Nature's Metropolis*, W. Cronon gives a fascinating account of how nineteenth-century colonizers extracted from America's Great Plains the various commodities (wheat, meat, wood, etc.), then used different circuits to transport them to one central hub, culminating in the birth of a metropolis, Chicago (Cronon 1992).

Each of the circuits was specific and could not be used for any other commodity. Thus, to bring wheat into the city—solid matter, which however acts like liquid when it is in its granular form—a remarkable technology was invented, the gunny bag, even if today there is nothing exceptional about it. This became the primary vehicle for transporting grains, thus allowing Chicagoans to eat and grow rich. In the case of wood used for constructing houses, a "peavey," a tool with a hook and a protruding spike at the tip, was required by loggers to drive the massive logs downstream from the forests along the Canadian border and into the Great Lakes. The third major commodity, meat, necessitated the invention of the refrigerated railroad car to transport pork cuts, which otherwise would have rotted. Cronon shows how each commodity, because of its unique characteristics, required the development of a singular method by which it could be transported to one center and stocked with the others in order to create a megalopolis.

The third part of this book poses a similar question, but a century later, only not about the building of Chicago but the rebuilding of America as a whole after the Great Depression. After having explored the American countryside, we are ready to move on to urban America and to ask what it meant in statistics to collect urban information.

One specificity of towns, in comparison with the rural world, which was blindingly obvious in the 1930s, was the magnitude of unemployment. True, unemployment was also rife in the countryside, but since this notion was associated with wages and industry and, therefore, labor, it was first perceived as an urban reality (Schlesinger 1957). In any case, this scourge raised other issues, apart from those addressed by agricultural statisticians, and consequently mobilized other specialists.

An additional argument impels us to take up the study of towns through the prism of unemployment. If during the entire 1920s, and often even during the 1930s, agricultural Statisticians were said to be the most advanced of all, the history of sample surveys today gives credit to the statistics on unemployment and urban poverty for being the most innovative. "The Unemployment Survey was the first national probability sample of households in the United States," Leslie Kish strongly stresses in his testimony (Frankel and King 1996, 70). "The first field of application of the random sampling method … was unemployment," write the undisputed historians of American government statistics, Joseph W. Duncan and William C. Shelton. An experiment carried out in 1933–1934, called the "Trial Census of Unemployment"—shortened later to TCU—was the first, they note, following which random sampling was used massively by the federal government (Duncan and Shelton 1992, 337). Thus, the Great Depression was also the moment when statistics on employment stole methodological supremacy from agricultural statistics.

These arguments suffice by themselves to justify devoting a section to the study of employment by American statisticians, but a historiographical discovery gives us an additional reason. Duncan and Shelton specify that although the "revolutionary" TCU experiment influenced the actors greatly, it "was never published," and except for a short article that escaped their vigilance (Clark 1935), we have in fact not found any publication on this survey. On the other hand, we have found a great number of federal archives that the TCU left behind. These materials allow us to discuss the experiment in detail.

Although it is necessary to highlight the differences between the rural and urban situations, the question that will guide us is similar to the one we asked in the case of agricultural statistics: How, subsequent to the shock of the Great Depression, did random sampling establish itself in the federal administration to tackle the problem of urban unemployment, and how did it influence policies formulated to fight this scourge in order to finally give consistency to the whole of America? This question, however, entails a nuance that is almost automatically explained by the fact that we are presenting it in the book's third section, as part of a story in which we identity and analyze the common features and differences inherent in the urban and rural experiences.

7

The Paradoxical Decomposition of Unemployment

According to Christian Topalov (1994), it was during the 1880s that unemployment first raised its head in the major industrial countries. Economic variations by themselves do not explain its emergence; in fact far, from it. Unemployment as such does not exist because the economy is faring badly, or because there are jobless people. To talk of "unemployment," we need, among other things, social reformers and philanthropists who visualize it as the goal of policy, as well as statisticians and sociologists who construct categories to study it.

The Great Depression threw a great number of workers on the street; it lengthened the queues in front of soup kitchens, impoverished white-collar workers, and caused numerous hardships, symptomatic of a dramatic rise in unemployment. However, statistics, the official tool for measuring unemployment, was rendered completely inoperable during this period. In fact, while some indicators remained more or less stable, others were alarming and yet others reassuring (Anderson 1988). Scenes of hardship and suffering, similar to unemployment, could be seen all around, but there were no instruments to help sum up these situations. How could this paradox be understood? To answer this question, we are first going to present the instruments used for measuring unemployment in the laissez-faire period, and then show how they countered each other in the early 1930s.

Unemployment in the Time of Laissez-Faire

At the beginning of the twentieth century there existed three models of statistics on employment. The first, the earliest one, was associated with the long tradition of censuses; the second, characteristic of trade union statistics, was introduced in the second half of the nineteenth century and used in particular by the Labor Department; the third was used specifically by academics and certain firms. Let us briefly give an overview of these models in this order.

The Census

This method for measuring unemployment was first developed by the U.S. Census Bureau, which prepared the questions in relation to each census between 1880 and 1910 (i.e., every ten years), and then by the Massachusetts bureau in 1885, 1895, and 1905.

To appreciate this method, we must remember that in 1780, the year the first census was held in the United States, a network capable of covering the entire territory—even if it was clearly much smaller than it is today—had to be identified in order to do an exhaustive count of the "noses" (according to the expression used at that time); the data was then centralized in Washington, D.C. The solution consisted of assigning the task to the federal marshals—an administratively and geographically well-established network—who were responsible for hiring deputies locally to conduct the surveys and transmitting the results to the nation's capital. The attributes that the deputies were supposed to have were apparently not specified, but it seems that the marshals retained three principal recruitment criteria (Anderson 1988; Scott 1968; Falkner 1898).

First of all, they had to be capable of reading the questionnaire, which was quite simple during the first census (Lunt 1888). Then they had to visit each and every farm: "The assistants were required to make the returns by a personal visit to each dwelling-house," without faking (Falkner 1898).[1] Finally, the selection probably involved political patronage: the administration used volunteers for the census in order to provide temporary employment to those loyal to it (Anderson 1988, 33). As for the reliability of the survey, the results were first put up locally: "The assistants were required to prepare two copies, which were to be posted for the inspection of the public" (Falkner 1898, 37). Thus, to start with, it was the public itself that verified the figures concerning the census.

During the 1880 census, the marshals were relieved of this task, for in some cases the districts had become too unequal in terms of population and therefore in terms of distribution of workload (Falkner 1898, 37), whereas in others, the federal officer in charge of the census planned to reorganize his network of canvassers by appointing local supervisors and endorsing the appointment of the census agents that the supervisors recruited (Anderson 1988).[2] This practice served to raise the standard of the interviewers, which had become necessary as the questionnaires had become more and more complex with each census, especially the 1880 census, which was the first to include questions on unemployment. One unexpected consequence of this evolution was the feminization of recruitment: "[The canvassers] were chosen largely among schoolteachers, town clerks, and others familiar with record keeping, and—for the first time in history—they included at least 200 women [in 1890]" (Scott 1968, 33).

It should however be pointed out that this new organization did not put an end to patronage. Quite the opposite. In 1937, that is fifty years later (as we shall see), during a heated debate on conducting an unemployment census at the earliest possible time, without waiting for 1940, Stuart Rice, vice president of the Census Bureau, again alluded to a recurring suspicion: "the administration wants a census because it would provide more patronage."[3]

As Topalov (1994) shows, until the Great Depression the definition of the unemployment indicators presented three difficulties. The first was regarding duration: Should the figures reflect the duration of unemployment of each individual or the number of unemployed at a given time *t*? The answer finally retained in 1910 was the reverse of the one that is customary today: the census calculated the "time lost" by workers—that is, the time the person was out of work during a specific period (generally a year) and not the number of unemployed at a given date. The second difficulty was occupation: Should people be considered unemployed if they did not have a job in their usual line of work but found employment elsewhere? The answer given in 1910—despite enormous difficulties (we will come back to this point later)—was negative. The last problem concerned the type of employment: Should unemployment apply only to salaried workers or should it include, for example, seasonal workers or self-employed workers during the slack season? It was decided, in this case, to exclude a certain number of professions from the count, in particular all types of self-employment. As for the rest, the definition retained is familiar to us: an unemployed person was a member of the workforce; that is to say, a person capable and desirous of working but who was not able to find work, without idleness being imputed to him.

However, if the criteria seem to have been established by the census bureaus, it was only with great difficulty that they were converted into a questionnaire. Indeed, at the federal level, questions relating to unemployment were not used in 1880 or in 1910, and if they were used in 1890, it was immediately and severely criticized by the American Economic Association, which managed to sow strong doubts about the data. Similarly, the Massachusetts results were only partially used in 1895 and not at all in 1905. Each time a certain number of questions on unemployment had been asked during the survey phase, but the answers could not be presented in tabular form. Why?

If the official reasons for these failures were basely practical ("lack of time for processing the data"), Topalov gives another explanation. According to him, they were caused by the *discrepancy between the statistical definitions and common sense* (Topalov 1994, 344). The statisticians had established the criteria and drawn up the questions, but during each operation they realized that the interviewers did not fully understand the requirements and in turn interpreted them badly for the respondents, who in turn modified the questions. In particular, the question on the "normal" occupation of the workers continued to pose a problem: both the interviewees as well as the census enumerators found it difficult to convince themselves, for example, that a qualified metallurgist, forced to work temporarily as a garbage collector, was not unemployed, which however was what the designers of the questionnaire had decided.

Thus, in 1910, though the statisticians had established the unemployment criteria during the earlier censuses, they found it difficult to consolidate them into a series of unequivocal questionnaires capable of withstanding the test of the interviewees. This difficulty moreover explains why they abandoned the section of the questionnaire dealing with this point in the 1920 census. Unemployment was an aggregate whose validity could not stand the ordeal of the census.

Trade Union Statistics

From the close of the nineteenth century, a new method of generating statistics on unemployment met with even more success. Devised by the newly emerging Bureaus of Labor, these statistics were produced by the more important among them. They accompanied the account or chronology of work-related conflicts, especially strikes that the administrators spotted in the newspapers, for instance. Statistics made it possible to quantify certain aspects of these conflicts.

The Bureaus of Labor sent the questionnaires to the local authorities (e.g., the town councils) and also to the local police and philanthropic associations that conducted their own surveys of destitute families to help them to get out of their present situation. They asked them to estimate the number of unemployed in the localities that they were familiar with. As we can see, this is something common to both urban and rural surveys, for in the case of the initial surveys on agricultural statistics, the voluntary crop reporters were also prominent individuals conducting their own surveys. Topalov explains, for example:

> The difference is not always clear between individual count of unemployed persons and mass estimation by local authorities. Wright's 1878 survey bears on this technique, which he defends arguing that "estimates come from intelligent officials," each "for its own locality of which he has a personal knowledge." (Topalov 1994, 276)

Carroll D. Wright, the man in question here, founded the federal Bureau of Labor Statistics, after the Massachusetts bureau, and was one of the first to launch a major survey aimed at enumerating unemployed workers. He began by asking "intelligent officials" to count the unemployed in their locality. As in agriculture, the advantage was that these town councillors and other dignitaries had "personal knowledge" of the terrain and could therefore easily distinguish between genuinely unemployed individuals and, for example, regular beggars and vagabonds, or between the underemployed and genuinely unemployed individuals, a task the census agents found extremely difficult.

In the case of unemployment, the method had the additional and unexpected advantage of exempting statisticians from the task of specifying unemployment criteria which, as we have just seen, was very difficult as long as the census categories remained badly consolidated. Thus, until the very late 1900s, the problem of the categorization of unemployment was left to the correspondents of the Bureaus of Labor.

This method worked well between 1880 and 1920, but with certain modifications. The most important of these changes took place rather suddenly between 1906 and 1908 when statisticians replaced the earlier informants—who could be anyone as long as they were eminent and closely connected to the world of work—with trade union leaders. Initially, the union secretaries were entrusted with transmitting individual questionnaires to the members. But this technique was quickly abandoned, and it was the secretaries themselves who gave information on behalf of their members. The unions were thus no longer surveyed by the administration;

they surveyed themselves. The similarity with agricultural data is again striking, as practically at the same moment the voluntary crop reporters were being replaced by farm owners for the purpose of collecting data.

The questions that they were asked were numerous and diverse, such as the number of union members, the wage levels of the employed, the number of those without jobs, and of these latter, the number that were really unemployed, as per sector and locality. These questions were asked on a regular basis, initially every four months, and then every six months.

What purpose did these surveys serve? Just like agricultural statistics, which were used for sanitizing and perfecting the markets, the aim of statistics about labor disputes was to make the markets more fluid and more flexible. The idea was to inform the public about the reasons for the strikes, the number of days without work, the wages demanded, or any other information that would help align the demand and supply of labor. Unemployment was thus conceived as frictional unemployment (to use an anachronistic but telling term). That is to say, it resulted from the friction in the markets owing to adjustments between the demand and supply of labor.

Speaking generally, these statistics also helped to provide information on certain overall rates for the United States as a whole. Indeed, when pieced together, as was done by British statisticians who were the first to get the idea, the statistics enabled the development of a new tool characteristic of this period, the *index number* (i.e., the fluctuation index).[4] This index was calculated by dividing the number of unemployed by the total number of union members, the only denominator that was easily available to the correspondents of the Bureaus of Labor. It was thus possible to plot the variation curve of this strange unemployment ratio as a function of time.

But as the union members constituted a minority among the workers, we could ask ourselves what the variations really represented. Topalov seems surprised that statistics resisted this obvious objection. He accounts for his amazement by explaining that the actors were more interested in variations in unemployment than in its level. The idea was that if they could rightly question each quantity entering into the construction of an index, their ratio would more readily be considered reliable. The administrators could then infer that the variations in the ratio of unemployed unionists to total number of unionists was comparable to the variations in the ratio of unemployed workers to total number of workers. This initially implicit hypothesis was later made explicit by means of curves that connected a variety of indexes, which showed how they varied in the same manner over time. By plotting income, marriage, and beer consumption indexes on the same graph, the English statistician William Beveridge, who would soon be emulated in the United States, showed that all of them varied more or less in the same fashion over time (Beveridge 1907). Together they "measured the pulse" of the nation. These indexes in no way indicated how many people were unemployed, but they implied that the rate of unemployment in the unions was the same as this pulse rate, and the same applied to the overall unemployment rate.

This index of variation was supplemented by the index of the number of persons hired, which gave a good approximation of the rate of unemployment, for it is simpler to count the number of employment contracts effectively signed than *potential* job offers, even if it is clear that the number of people hired is in no way functionally linked to the rate of unemployment.

University Statistics

The third and last model of statistical surveys on unemployment was followed mainly in universities and in research departments of private firms. The technique relied on young recruits, a part of whose training consisted of getting people to participate in the questionnaire. For example, William F. Ogburn, professor of sociology at Chicago University (Chapoulie 2001), and Harold Gosnell, who did huge quantitative studies in political science in Chicago (Converse 1987), got their students to work on the questionnaires. Incidentally, these students had to slog their guts out, for they were few and had a gigantic number of questionnaires to process (nearly 6,000 in the case of Gosnell's study). The surveys, however quantitative they were, remained completely local.

Thus, at the end of the 1920s, three models of statistical surveys on unemployment could be identified—censuses, union indexes, and university surveys—and they were not mutually exclusive. For example, a study undertaken in 1930 by the Federal Reserve Bank of Philadelphia to enumerate the number of unemployed in the city (a study that corresponds more to the third model as it was conducted by a company) was done in collaboration with the janitors of the city's schools, who were asked to canvass their respective blocks. This corresponded more to the first and second models, as it concerned an existing organized network, with a major advantage being the familiarity of the canvassers with the terrain (Bureau of Labor Statistics 1930).

Conflicting Models

During the 1920s the statistical methods for measuring unemployment overlapped, then in 1929, just after the stock market crash, they began contradicting each other to the extent that no quantified statement on unemployment could be made without immediately being countered. This is shown by the sensational controversy that took place in January 1930 between President Herbert Hoover and Frances Perkins, the incumbent Secretary of Industry of the state of New York, whose governor was Franklin Roosevelt.

The controversy erupted when in a radio interview Hoover affirmed that "all the evidence indicates that the worst effects of the crash upon unemployment will have passed during the next sixty days" (quoted by Anderson 1988, 160). This was something that the stabilization of registrations in the U.S. Employment Service (USES), the federal employment agency, seemed to suggest. For Hoover, the number of job hunters had stabilized, which showed that adjustment between demand and supply was taking place and would hopefully lead to a decrease in the unemployment rate.

But Frances Perkins declared before the press that President Hoover was wrong. Indeed, she thought that the USES index used by Hoover did not include among the unemployed those who searched for jobs independently, and hence an entire contingent of unemployed workers was not accounted for. Now, the "employment and wage index," calculated by the Department of Labor (the successor to the trade union series that we described earlier) indicated a deterioration in the situation. The number of jobs had not increased; on the contrary, it seemed to have shrunk (Perkins 1946).

Hoover immediately retorted that if admittedly the USES indexes did not include those searching for jobs independently, they included people who had a job—who were therefore not unemployed—but were looking for a better job. It was therefore not illogical to suppose that these two figures canceled each other out. Besides, the employment index that Perkins was referring to was based on the number of appointments and not on the number of unemployed; in a period of growth it was perfectly possible for the employment rate to stagnate. Perkins's source was therefore not reliable, either. Hence, the existing indexes did not help to put an end to the dispute; in 1930, it was not possible to ascertain the number of unemployed people.

Later the controversy only intensified. As the year 1930 was a multiple of ten, a census was carried out. Were questions on unemployment going to be included? Both the American Statistical Association and the American Economic Association had strong reservations, easily explained by past failures. But at the last minute, the officials in charge were allowed to include questions on the subject (Anderson 1988, 165). Eventually, at Hoover's special request, the results were tabulated and soon published: the census announced that there were between 2.3 million and 2.5 million unemployed in the United States in 1930.

But these figures were immediately challenged because the definitions used considerably reduced the scale of the phenomenon. The critics, who believed that the number of unemployed was between 4 million and 6.6 million, specifically pointed out that those who had been laid off and those who sought entry into the labor market for the first time (former students and housewives seeking employment) had not been counted.

As Jean Heffer writes: "No one knew exactly how many unemployed persons there were during those dark years; figures differ widely from one source to the other; government agencies sailed in obscurity" (Heffer 1991, 137). He cites Walter S. Gifford in support of this statement, who was appointed by Hoover to chair the "presidential organization for unemployment relief" and was called to a senatorial hearing in 1932:

> SENATOR COSTIGAN: How many persons are there without a job or on the edge of destitution?
> MR. GIFFORD: I don't think anybody knows it.
> SENATOR COSTIGAN: You don't know precisely how many are unemployed or need relief, now, inside the borders of the Union?
> MR. GIFFORD: No, and no one can know it. (Heffer 1991, 137)

Thus, at the time, unemployment was characterized by uncertainty and ignorance. We need to stress this point for it seems as if the existing books on history and economics that try to explain the Great Depression dare not admit this ignorance. However, the figures that they give are either estimates disputed at the time or retrospective calculations, replete with all the anachronisms that this implies. Between 1930 and 1937 (we will soon see why we have retained this date), the number of unemployed in the United States was not known. How can this incredible paradox be explained, for although the tools for measuring unemployment already existed in 1910, no one had been able to determine the rate of unemployment in the beginning of the 1930s, when the problem had become so critical and so visible?

Anderson suggests that, as these series were all caught up in controversies associated with partisan politics (Hoover was a Republican and Perkins a Democrat), they were often *ipso facto* discredited (Anderson 1988). Maybe. But there are also scientific oppositions, even mixed with politics, that end in the blatant victory of one side (Shapin and Shaffer 1985; Latour 1988; Mackenzie 1991). Hence, we have to find another explanation.

If we review the controversy, we notice that the indexes undoubtedly helped to grasp certain aspects of unemployment. Characteristically, the USES index, which had been conceived with the aim of combating frictional unemployment, showed that unemployment was decreasing. But it seems that the Great Depression had engendered an increasing number of situations that resembled frictional unemployment in the sense defined earlier, in particular because its victims wanted to and could work but were unable to find jobs, and these situations were sufficiently different to elude enumeration: for example, those who had lost faith in placement agencies and tried to seek a job without the help of these institutions, or the nonworking population—students and housewives—who for the first time were postulating for a job on the labor market. These were borderline cases of frictional unemployment that did not really fit the category.

Moreover, the ferocity of the crisis had rendered these situations omnipresent. Everyone could see them in ways other than as an aggregate; for example, when walking in the street, during a family dinner, or when looking at photographs printed in newspapers, it was difficult to ignore them (Thévenot 2006). It was the omnipresence of these situations that resulted in their clashing with the previous statistics.

In our terminology, we would say that the shock of the Depression had rendered the relationship between the population and statistics deliquescent. In the plasma, many new situations had emerged, so many in fact that they had collided with the old statistics and slipped in between the old unemployment categories. Put another way, they had certain points in common but also certain divergences with them, so that it was with difficulty that statistics was able to capture them; the new elements slipped between the old statistics.

This situation corresponded perfectly with the one foreseen by Dewey in *The Public and Its Problems* (1927), in which he pointed out the fact that a serious crisis was always accompanied by self-delusion on the part of the government. Indeed, the form of government, he explained, was necessarily shaped by the previous crisis that had hit the nation; the aim of its different services was to provide a solution for the problems created by the preceding crisis; the administrative procedures also corresponded to these outdated problems. As a consequence, the government is inevitably caught napping by the onslaught of a fresh crisis and its complexities, and therefore the government is ill-adapted to respond to it. In this case, just as President Franklin Roosevelt was obliged to create a new agricultural administration—the Agricultural Adjustment Administration (AAA)—he had to set up another one to deal with the urban problems.

The Call of New Unemployment for New Statistics

Initially, an appeal was made to statistics to capture this new but nevertheless devastating level of unemployment at a less macro level than that of the federation, for statistics alone seemed capable of providing a useful representation.

To understand this, it should first be explained that traditionally, until the late 1920s, the problem of unemployment was resolved directly and mainly through case studies. The unemployed worker asking for assistance met a welfare worker (often a woman) employed by a philanthropic association (almost never the state, whatever the level), who along with him analyzed his budget and his lifestyle. Together they tried to discover where he had gone wrong, or what aspects of his behavior could explain the unfortunate situation in which he found himself. The unemployed individual was thus always considered as being personally responsible for his fall from grace. This method was used *in fine* to monitor his life. For example, if he needed temporary financial assistance to buy shoes, his demand was deemed to be the result of the mismanagement of his budget, and he was given a gift in nature rather than the money needed for buying a pair of shoes, for the jobless individual was not considered capable of spending his money wisely and economically (Abbott 1940).

But as the Great Depression intensified, unemployment became widespread and social workers realized that the old maternalistic attitude was ill suited for the unemployment problems they had to deal with. Indeed, more and more often the average relief applicant "was so obviously competent and accustomed to managing his own affairs and supporting himself in a normal way that it was utterly useless and absurd to pretend that he was at fault." It was increasingly clear that these people were not asking "for a helping hand" (top down) to rescue them from their blunder, but wanted to act "hand in hand, not handing down" and on an equal footing with the welfare workers (Brown 1940, 227). The unemployed very rarely had the profile of people who had come down in the world for personal reasons that needed to be identified; on the contrary, they constituted an ever-growing, impersonal mass with a few blindingly obvious common characteristics: they were going through a difficult economic situation and did not have a job, but desperately wanted one and needed help urgently.

The social workers very soon realized that this new objective required new tools. Josephine Chapin Brown, whose extensive experience in public assistance made her the ideal candidate for the post of assistant to Harry Hopkins, Director of Public Relief during the New Deal, gives a few examples. First, and the most important according to her, was to find new colleagues to take on the increasingly enormous task. Along with the new recruits, a new "philosophy" of aid to the unemployed had to be initiated, something that she knew had already been implemented by the more progressive charitable organizations, which she called "democratic," for "each person in need had a right to share in the provision made by the government to meet the ravages caused by the breakdown of the American economic system. Because of this right, an applicant for public relief incurred no stigma, asked no favor, and was expected to express no gratitude" (Brown 1940, 228). In practical terms Chapin supported the idea, which we will take up later, of providing this aid in the form of public employment, which would allow the jobless to preserve their dignity, use their skills so that they did not become rusty through inactivity, and most important, earn a wage just like any other worker.

Finally, she makes a last point that is of special interest to us: "The social workers broadened their education and deepened their insight in observing the work of the engineers, accountants, statisticians" (Brown 1940, 230). And indeed, statistics seemed the obvious choice for dealing with this new unemployment. First, it was impersonal, which ensured that the person receiving assistance would not be considered personally responsible for his condition, and second, it captured this new population en masse, something that the earlier personalized procedures did not permit. The interactions with the unemployed, who no longer wanted to be stigmatized, and the change in the scale of unemployment called for new techniques for processing unemployment, which necessarily meant resorting to statistical tabulation.

This appeal was relayed so forcefully that it was taken up politically. Indeed, in 1930, Robert Wagner, the famous senator of New York State (a Democrat, of course) during the New Deal, sought to have three bills passed to combat unemployment (known as the Three Bills), and one was precisely aimed at "the need for collecting more adequate statistics concerning the extent and character of joblessness" (Huthmacher 1968). Wagner was a self-taught man, completely ignorant of statistics, but a true political animal, groomed at Tammany Hall, the building that housed the Democratic Party in New York. These three bills it seems were prepared by Isador Lubin, who, as we shall see, later became the director of the Bureau of Labor Statistics (Unofficial Observer 1934). Even though the efforts of the future senator took time to bear fruit, the fight against unemployment henceforth explicitly trod the path of statistics.

The unemployed had sounded a muffled protest but nevertheless a very powerful one, demanding that their new common characteristics be taken into account, which did not include responsibility for their condition. This protest was first relayed by the social workers, who had transmitted it to at least one academic specializing in unemployment-related issues, Lubin, who in turn reformulated it for an influential politician, stressing, among other things, the necessity of quantifying these characteristics. The encounter between the new "democratic" welfare relief philosophy and the unemployed masses, who did not consider themselves responsible for their situation (in the sense defined above), had resulted in a vehement and powerful call to statistics.

Conclusion: The Desire to Count Oneself

As in the case of agricultural production, the Great Depression had loosened the link between the unemployed population, statistical measures, and government action. Paradoxically, the heightened kaleidoscopic visibility of unemployment in the beginning of the 1930s did not help to consolidate the old instruments of measurement; on the contrary, it made them loose and ineffective, so thatthe administration found itself groping in the dark. But, at the same time, the scale of unemployment became so massive, so omnipresent, that the new common characteristics of the victims could no longer be ignored: the jobless could not all be responsible for the situation in which they found themselves. They were moreover in need of money and work and required assistance. These common features bear a close resemblance to what Gabriel de Tarde would not have hesitated to call "a desire to count oneself"—he, who dared to attribute desires to entities such as unemployment and statistics (Tarde 1999).[5] When the Roosevelt administration came to power, it tried to prolong this desire.

8

How to Transform the Victims of the Depression into Enumerators

Before Roosevelt's election, the debate on unemployment statistics and the need to update them had attracted considerable attention. At the time of his election all the government agencies of the United States were asked to collect the desperately needed statistics. Thus, Stuart Rice, the then president of the American Statistical Association, declared during his inaugural speech at the 1933 meeting of the association that fresh "opportunities and responsibilities in statistics" were on their way to being born. According to Rice (1934, 2), "The precise forms of future organization are not now visible. But we cannot turn back and I am sure that statistics will be essential in finding the way forward. The industrial era was built upon natural science. The era of social control will rest upon factual information about economic and social structures and processes."[1] Similarly, according to his colleague, Willard L. Thorp, professor of economics at Amherst College, statistics was being transformed into "public works" (Thorp 1934). It seemed as if American society wanted to be quantified, and the federal state was especially well placed to respond to this apparent desire.

The fact remains that it was not enough to want to generate all these statistics; concrete means were also needed toward this end. One difficulty that immediately surfaced was finding the manpower to circulate and fill out the questionnaires, for there was a severe shortage, whereas statistics is a big consumer of manpower. Indeed, as we have seen in chapter 7, the sort of surveys being conducted at the time required only a small number of enumerators—voluntary crop reporters and students—or, in the case of the census, a larger number whose work was restricted to one questionnaire. A much bigger group of enumerators was now required, capable of meeting the demands of statistical inquiry and adapting to the aims of the diverse surveys. Where could this manpower be found?

The answer came as a surprise to everyone: the victims of the Depression, and especially the unemployed forced into inactivity. Thanks to them it was possible to guide and fine-tune government policies! All that was needed was to harness the enthusiasm of the hungry masses queuing up in front of the soup kitchens. They were available, they wanted to act, and they were completely familiar with the ugly face of the crisis. Thus, those very people who had had no other option but to suffer the damaging effects of the economic system took things into their hands and produced the knowledge necessary to combat this curse.

This reversal is surprising because one is used to thinking that the practice of science, even science as "impure" as statistics, and even at a level as humble as that of the canvasser, requires a certain technical expertise, which you cannot take for granted that people have, least of all the unemployed. It does not follow that because one is experiencing a problem one becomes a good scientific observer of this very problem (Maas and Morgan 2012; Daston and Lunbeck 2010).

Therefore, a solution had to be found so that the amateur enumerators could master the difficulties associated with the filling of a questionnaire. We will see in this chapter how this army of dropouts learned to comply with the demands of statistics (enumerators hired for the first time had to systematically undertake training courses, for example). We will then see how the results of this work were evaluated and how the people, for whom the statistics were intended, appropriated them. We will show to what extent this largely forgotten experiment constituted an important turning point in the course of which America was "statisticized."

Relief Administrations

An event initially unrelated to the government's statistical problems took place precisely on November 9, 1933: President Franklin Roosevelt created the Civil Works Administration (CWA), whose role was to provide paid relief work to the most needy. The problem was urgent. The 1933–1934 winter was forecast to be particularly severe and the work would help people bear the rigors of an American winter. The connection with statistics was not at all obvious or necessary. Yet this administration made the link. Let us see how.

The CWA was set up after the creation of two other bodies that defined its contours. First, there was the Federal Emergency Relief Administration (FERA), responsible for direct aid to the most impoverished, which depended directly of the President. It was headed by Harry L. Hopkins who, born into a religious Methodist family of Iowa, had discovered his vocation during his studies when attending a summer course at a relief center in New York State. He remained in this field till he joined the Roosevelt administration, when Roosevelt was still governor of New York State (Schlesinger 1958, 265). Hopkins was known for his dynamism, his determination to find solutions to the problems before him, and also for his ironic and sarcastic temperament (as he was also apparently generous, some of his biographers feel that this irony was defensive) (Charles 1963).

The FERA was thus charged with distributing relief (sometimes in cash, but more often in the form of vouchers), nearly always without expecting anything in return and commensurate with the needs of the poor. This aid was called the *dole* and had a pejorative connotation. The FERA normally did not provide jobs, or if it did, they involved tasks known as *made works* that were looked down upon because they were of little social utility and paid according to the *minimum needs* of the beneficiary and not according to one's skills or the market price. While it received praise, especially from those who benefited, the FERA was also sharply criticized, first because it was considered immoral to support the poor without their doing genuine work in exchange and, second, because generally FERA's paternalistic and condescending actions had a tendency to maintain the poor in their condition. Hopkins himself, in conformity with the democratic spirit mentioned above, sought to get rid of this paternalism, which he had inherited, and restore the dignity of the poor. He opposed payment in kind as much as he could because it did not allow the beneficiaries to decide what their own needs were and was moreover humiliating. He argued that *relief work* should be provided to the applicants rather than simple subsidies, for work, according to Hopkins, remained the best means of restoring one's dignity and pride.

Roosevelt had also set up the Public Works Administration (PWA), headed by the Secretary of the Interior, Harold L. Ickes. This was essentially a public investment program focused on civil engineering works and not a social program. Of course, it was also expected to generate jobs for the unemployed, but this objective was conceived as secondary. Moreover, these works were commissioned by the administration to private firms; employment was market driven or at least came close to it. This program was also highly praised, but very soon it became apparent that drafting tenders and analyzing bids took time—too much time—and that nothing would be ready before several months.[2]

In autumn, when things were going from bad to worse with the onset of winter, it dawned on Hopkins that something had to be done in all urgency. He managed to convince Roosevelt to create the CWA, taking care to steer clear of the weaknesses of its sister agencies. The idea was to create a federal agency of "civil" works that would finance socially useful projects and could be rapidly set up so as to provide jobs to the most needy, and as quickly as possible. Thus, the employees of the CWA would receive real wages, paid in exchange for work having genuine social utility, and could live through the winter with dignity.[3]

Of course, this administration was criticized by the conservatives in the name of the sacrosanct market: it seemed to them that these jobs would necessarily interfere with the market's normal functioning and would thus make even more employees and workers redundant, moreover replacing real jobs with relief jobs (Lester 1934). Against this attack Hopkins did *not* justify his politics by mentioning Keynes's thesis of stimulating recovery by boosting demand, as there is a strong inclination to think today.[4] His logic was patrimonial: For Hopkins, winter threatened to destroy both the morale and the skills of the workforce, which would be forced into destitution and idleness, and it also endangered the country's infrastructure, abandoned to the rigors of winter. To do nothing was to let the national asset base and the population deteriorate and lose their worth: "Realistically viewed, expenditures by the government for these purposes are *investments* that will increase the wealth of the nation in both human and materiel terms," wrote his deputy director (Gill 1939, 168). In addition, direct aid anyway had a cost, so the marginal cost of projects, where the beneficiaries were really productive, was practically nil.

Therefore, when choosing his staff, Hopkins decided against employing social workers, who were accustomed to doing simple case studies and lacked the imagination to create useful jobs, and instead opted for progressive engineers from private firms, or "corporate liberals" (Schwartz 1984, 46). These engineers responded with enthusiasm and, taking advantage of the opportunity, developed a large number of projects. They brought with them the planning mindset advocated by Henry Taylor—that is to say, holding regular audits, unifying accounting practices, and introducing security regulations at work.[5]

Several statisticians and economists were thus hired as the principal administrators of the CWA. Let us mention Corrington Gill (see figure 8.1) in particular (1898–1946), a young freelance economist with journalistic experience who had been hired by Hopkins for his statistical abilities to work in the FERA (Myers 1946). As early as October 1933 he organized a census of the people on relief—by asking each local office to fill a questionnaire on the number and characteristics of the persons receiving aid—and

8.1 Corrington Gill, 1940. (FSA/OWI Collection, Library of Congress)

discovered that it came to 12 million persons (Gill 1934)! When the CWA was created, he established its Research and Statistics Division,[6] and he named Emerson Ross head of economic analysis and Paul Webbink head of the statistical department (Ross 1934). The FERA and the CWA thus constituted a den of "liberal statisticians."

The change in the mental outlook induced by Hopkins and his staff in the relief work being done seems to have been immediately and easily discernible.

The Statistical Projects of the Civil Works Administration

The CWA had been established first and foremost to help blue collars, for it was mainly they who lengthened the queues in front of the soup kitchens every day. Therefore, they were recruited *en masse* to work in the initial projects:

> Activities included the construction, improvement, and repair of old schools, hospitals, libraries and other public buildings; streets, roads and highways; water supply plants, sewers, airports, etc. Parks, forests, community golf courses, beaches, and swimming pools were established or improved with CWA labor, and pest control and sanitation projects were also undertaken. (Gill 1939, 166)

However, manual laborers were not the only people who were destitute; many white-collar workers were also affected by the crisis, but their suffering was more difficult to identify because of the sense of shame in broadcasting their poverty. However, Hopkins wanted his program to reach out to this category of the population. The problem was finding employment to suit them. To specifically help white-collar workers, "[Hopkins] frantically made the rounds of all government agencies and solicited ideas for projects" (Schwartz 1984, 134).

And what came out was a grand, loud, and clear call for statistics from all the "social" administrations—mainly the Departments of Agriculture, Commerce (to which the Census Bureau was attached), and Labor (Rice 1934, 2), but also from some of the counties and states[7]—demanding statistical studies.[8] All needed to get their bearings in the debacle of the Depression so that as soon as they were offered trained workers to man the desks, they responded by asking first and foremost for statistics (see figure 8.2).

To see how these projects were concretely formulated, let us take the example of the "Trial Census of Unemployment" (TCU), the first random sampling experiment, which was set up in collaboration with the Bureau of Labor Statistics (BLS).

Upon coming to power, Roosevelt appointed Frances Perkins as the new Labor Secretary, who as soon as she took over her duties, named Isador

8.2 One of the many pictures of WPA clerical and statistical projects. Here, people are "Summarizing Farm Data" in Des Moines, Iowa. Note the clerks that are both male and female, the calculating machines on the right and behind the man on the left, and the poster on the back wall is a calendar advertising "Armour's fertilizer." The usual statistical order is counterbalanced by the mess of urgency. (ISU Special collection)

Lubin as head of the BLS. Lubin was born in Massachusetts in 1896 to Lithuanian parents who owned a small clothing store. He had studied sociology and economics, in particular under Thorstein Veblen, who was to become one of the principal initiators of economic planning. These studies led him, in the beginning of the 1920s, to take up the position of research fellow in the Brookings Institution, which was attached to the University of Michigan, where he worked on issues related to employment. He then acted as consultant to several elected representatives, including Senator

Robert Wagner, for whom he prepared the famous "Three Bills" (Unofficial Observer 1934). It was on this occasion that Lubin was noticed by Perkins, who was working with Wagner (Wickens 1979), then by Senator Robert Lafollette, a Republican known for his independent views and his liberalism (Schlesinger 1960).

Hardly had he taken office when Lubin immediately got down to work, mulling over prospective unemployment surveys. He sent a circular letter to four advisers asking them how they thought a good survey on unemployment could be organized, then asked one of his assistants, Ewan Clague, to synthesize their answers. Clague was a young economist born in 1896 and educated at the University of Wisconsin—much like several planners in the Bureau of Agricultural Economics (BAE)—who moreover would take over from Lubin as director of the BLS in 1940 when the latter was appointed special adviser to Roosevelt.

What particularly struck Clague was that the four advisers all agreed that the difficulty of a survey on unemployment was twofold. First, the very definition of the term posed a problem, in particular with regard to the range of the category (e.g., how to categorize women who had always been inactive but who because their husbands were unemployed had begun to look for work). Second, although they concurred on the fact that a population census would not be suitable for counting the unemployed and therefore one should stick to carrying out a survey by selecting towns and subunits within these towns, there was complete disagreement on the method of selecting the sample.[9]

The survey, moreover, would definitely be costly. The advisers estimated that it would cost between $125,000 and $500,000 approximately. But Clague had come up with an idea for reducing the cost, which he had perhaps taken from experiments conducted by municipal mutual benefit associations, especially in New York, Philadelphia, and Chicago (Stephan 1935), and which consisted of hiring as canvassers the unemployed registered on the FERA rolls (let us remember that in mid-1933 the CWA had not yet been conceived and wouldn't be formally established until November of that year). If such collaboration was to take place, it would be necessary to take into account the concerned administration's requirements—he clarified—but the survey would only cost between $25,000 and $100,000.

One day as Clague was discussing the project with Lubin, the door to his office burst open; it was Harry Hopkins come to ask him to design projects for white-collar workers. It was as if they were waiting for each other for matters to progress! It did not take long for Clague to send an official report to Hopkins. On November 24, 1933, he submitted to the CWA "tests of various sampling methods for measuring unemployment,"[10] which had a very methodological tone. So problematic was this exercise that Clague had chosen to temporarily set aside not only the unemployment head count but also the definition of unemployment, to instead focus on the more technical matter of sampling, proposing to compare the advantages of the three methods for selecting samples of the unemployed in towns.

By way of response, the CWA noted that "this [is] a worthy project but a more carefully considered formulation of procedure is desirable."[11] The surprise was great in the BLS, and they tried to get more details. According to the information received, "some proposed sampling methods were questionable,"[12] so much so that they did not want to have them in writing. Though we do not exactly know which were being targeted, Clague found out. He persevered and reformulated the project, modifying the principal objective by focusing more clearly on unemployment, which would be measured by means of the familiar *local census* seen as reassuring (by nonstatisticians), and the sampling methods were only outlined secondarily. Finally the new objective was formulated that proposed "a census of unemployment in two or three cities of comparatively similar size: one in New England—probably in Massachusetts or Connecticut; one in the Midwest—probably in Ohio or Indiana; and possibly one in some other section of the country."[13] In this way the statistics project, initially conceived from a methodological standpoint and of interest primarily to statisticians, was reformulated after the intervention of the CWA with the aim of obtaining more information on the unemployed and their interests, through a reassuring method. The accent had shifted from the method to the issue, from the producers to the users of the data, from the statisticians to welfare.

Clague and Lubin, for their part, had confidence in the workers supplied by the CWA. The issue—unemployment—was one of the most problematic at the time, apart from the question of sampling that only a select group of statisticians had worked on, and yet they did not hesitate to entrust the task of this survey to the beneficiaries of the CWA.

This confidence was not fully shared by the statisticians in the universities. Frederick F. Stephan, for example, who had just finished his PhD at the University of Chicago (and would later become a key figure in American statistics) and was the "research coordinator" of the CWA (that is, the evaluator of statistical projects submitted to this administration for funding), considered that the knowledge produced would be secondary in comparison to the objective of hiring the maximum number of unemployed (Stephan 1935). However, Stephan now made a disturbing remark, although a positive one, which unfortunately he did not elaborate: he invoked the gigantic amount of statistics generated by the administrative rolls and wrote: "It is interesting to note that many important statistics are by-products of non-statistical activities" (Stephan 1935, 487). In this instance also, the projects had perhaps not been conceived from a scientific point of view, but this did not necessarily prevent the results from being interesting. Stephan moreover published a list of 743 initial statistical projects classified by category, which he was in favor of. The entire lot was financed to the tune of $10 million:

Type of project	Number of projects reviewed
Comprehensive Planning and Social Surveys	56
Governmental Organization and Taxation	39
Education and Schools	63
Social Welfare and Relief	106
Health and Sanitation	59
Population and Vital Statistics	63
Occupations, Employment, Unemployment	40
Agriculture	52
Prices, Business and Industry	34
Housing, Mortgage and Land Utilization	115
Traffic	74
Historical Research and Records	42
Total	*743*

This episode illustrates several things. First, that the Roosevelt administration was very keen on statistics—the fact that Clague's and Lubin's exploit was repeated more than 700 times is proof enough. Second, that even if the administration initiated these projects—and not the victims of the Depression themselves—those who conceived the idea of turning to this workforce (as far as one can generalize from Lubin and Clague to all the others) had confidence in it. The idea of getting the victims of the crisis to participate in its description did not seem to have shocked them at all.

It is thus worthwhile noting that the actors of this story were all educated in the Upper Midwest where what has been called participationist pragmatism—noticed among agricultural specialists who for a long time entrusted the task of gathering information concerning them to the farmers themselves—was very marked. Dewey had been professor at the University of Michigan where Lubin worked for several years, and the University of Wisconsin where Clague studied was where Richard T. Ely and John R. Commons had taught, two key figures—perhaps *the* central figures—who brought this pragmatic spirit into economics, which deeply influenced American democratic participationism. Their careers were similar to that of the agricultural "planners." In all likelihood, we can say that they believed that the population could take things into its own hands thanks to these administrative tools.

It now remains to be seen how the victims of the Depression reacted. Did they consider these projects as a lesser evil, or did they consider them a means of once again controlling their destiny?

Selection of Personnel

The first question that needed resolution in order to launch the CWA's statistical surveys pertained to the rules of recruitment. We have seen that the CWA projects were on the whole supposed to be useful; therefore staff was hired on the basis of technical competence. But this program continued to be aimed at the needy, who thus had to prove that they were in need. How were these two characteristics, the need for work and scientific competence, articulated?

In view of the urgency, it was decided that the CWA's general rules for hiring would be modeled on those of the PWA, which had been crafted under less extreme conditions. The rule was that the applicant had to be registered on the unemployment rolls of the state where he was residing, and the project directors chose the profiles that they considered interesting from this list. The minimum wages were paid on the hour in accordance with the PWA grid: They depended first on the geographical zone of recruitment—south, center, and north—and second, on the worker dichotomy qualified or unqualified. Third, the workweek was limited to thirty hours (Schwartz 1984, 48).

But these rules had been established for blue-collar workers. They now had to be adapted for clerks and white-collar workers. Three special features had to be taken into account. First, this workforce presented a very delicate problem—the sense of pride, of distinction. The white collars had an "aversion toward applying for aid" (Schwartz 1984, 130); they were ashamed to show that they were penniless. Thus, it was not possible to identify them from the employment rolls alone: "Hiring procedures would have to ensure applicants' qualifications, meet the relief requirement of need, and yet somehow appeal to this 'psychologically sensitive' class" (Schwartz 1984, 132). To do this Hopkins established less intrusive rules of employment: "Although the applicants still had to show definite evidence of need, Hopkins ordered only a minimum of individual investigation and follow-up into the homes" (Schwartz 1984, 139). He preferred to ask professional associations to recommend their most needy members, which, for example, is what the American Statistical Association did. In this way, professional organizations replaced relief organizations for identifying the most impoverished persons.

Second, after several complaints, especially from the professional associations, it appears that, contrary to what had been the earlier practice, it was important that intellectual work be better paid than manual work. It was now decided that, one, the "employees" could work up to thirty-nine hours per week, which also allowed them to increase their weekly wage accordingly, and two, that it would no longer be possible for white-collar workers to earn less than 18, 15, and 12 hours per week in the northern, central, and southern zones, respectively. To conclude, the local CWAs were encouraged to negotiate the issue of salary revision directly with the professional associations.

Lastly, independent of the PWA rules and at Eleanor Roosevelt's behest, Hopkins set up a "Women's Division" in the CWA, the aim of which was to reserve jobs for women who otherwise would have been "excluded" from the relief measures. This division was managed by Ellen S. Woodward, the daughter of a Mississippi senator, who had studied on the East Coast and, after her husband's death, joined the relief sector for poverty alleviation. Most of the jobs that she managed to get funding for came under heading of "piecework," the term used at the time for sewing and quilting, but many of these women were also hired for statistical surveys:

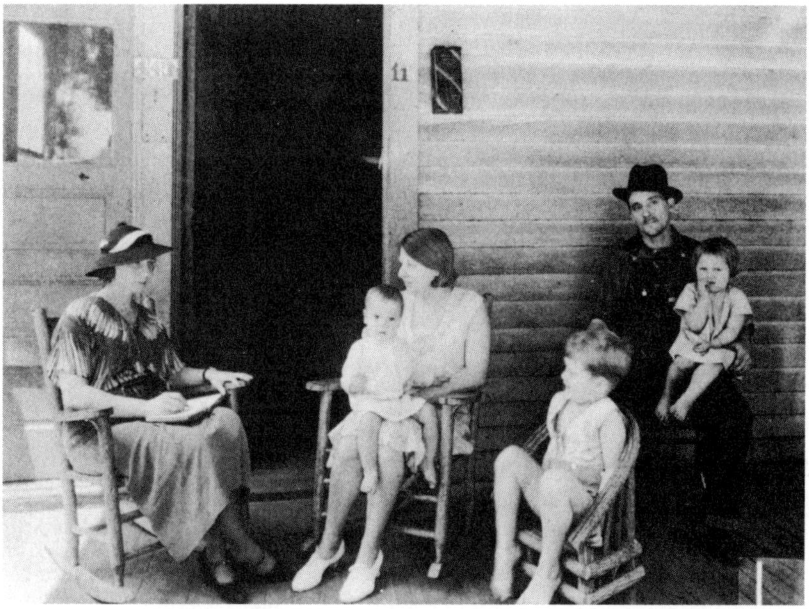

8.3 A woman canvasser at a farm. The caption reads: "Remote rural counties were not forgotten. Interview of a local family in rural Georgia." (Alsberg 1934, 119)

> White collars, professional, and unskilled women all found jobs in statistical programs. Although Washington ordered that at least two thirds of the employees on such projects be women, the order had little effect on supervisory positions, which generally went to men. Girls usually went to work as canvassers or as office staff. (Schwartz 1984, 178)

In a book of photographs published in 1934 as a tribute to the CWA, we find a photograph (see figure 8.3) taken during a statistical survey and showing a woman canvasser on the job. We can now understand why these jobs were more suited to women.

The canvasser employed by the CWA (on the left in figure 8.3) is interviewing a local family from the South. We immediately notice how the situation allows the canvasser to establish a strong asymmetry between her and the family (whereas they both benefit, the family and her, from state aid): she is dressed with care, is wearing a watch, and has her hair done up nicely, whereas the mother is bareheaded, without jewelry, and wearing a rather shabby dress. The statistical survey is thus a situation where the interviewer can distinguish herself from the interviewee, dominate the latter, just like the social worker who dominated the family she came to survey. This asymmetry satisfied Hopkins's endeavor to treat the white-collar workers with sensitivity. But how can one ascertain that there is a survey being carried out? First, we can observe the notebook on the interviewer's lap in which she is about to write the answers. And then there are less direct but just as telling signs: The family is sitting on rocking chairs; the man of the house has given his to the canvasser so that the two women can talk to one another in a situation indicating a certain degree of confidence, even though the husband is present and is listening. The scene is taking place on the *porch*, which no house in the backcountry is without. The porch, as surprising as it may appear, was the public part of the house—so it was a bit like having someone in our living rooms. The canvasser, the outsider, has thus penetrated the family space, the household, in relation to which she is seeking information. We can see in this photograph some advantages that the women interviewers had: the tradition of care and advice given to the most destitute and their familiarity with intimacy.

How were the general recruitment rules implemented in practice? In the case of the TCU, the person hired on December 26, 1933[14] as project director was "Charles E. Persons, a PhD in economics, who served as expert in the Economics of Unemployment, 1930 Unemployment Census and as economist with New York State Joint Legislative Committee on Unemployment, 1931–1932."[15] Persons had considerable experience about these issues and had been a member of the Roosevelt administration when Roosevelt was still governor of New York. He hired a deputy, Raymond V. H.

Gilbert (although nothing more is known of him), and both were paid by the CWA and posted to the BLS headquarters in Washington.

This project involved carrying out a census of three towns. As the manpower would be hired locally, the procedure for selecting the towns played a part in selecting the personnel. This process was quite brief, for time was of the essence, but it was incredibly complicated and is in fact partly obscure—but we will come back to this point later. For now, let us just remember that, finally, Bridgeport in Connecticut, Springfield in Ohio, and Lancaster in Pennsylvania were retained. The supervisors for each of these towns were in effect selected locally. One of them, Thomas L. Easterling, the Springfield supervisor, was formerly "on the staff of Ohio University."[16]

After a brief period of training in Washington, the first task of the supervisors was to hire canvassers and clerks. The field workers (the canvassers) came under the category of qualified workers so that, in the case of Springfield, for instance, a list of candidates was "handed by the Springfield reemployment service" to the supervisor. The candidates had to pass a "test to determine their fitness for the work," which consisted of some dummy questionnaires, but we do not have any further details on this point, except that—and it is certainly worth mentioning—out of the 100 candidates present for the test on January 21 in Springfield, only 21 passed on the first day of examination and 42 on the second day. This induced Lubin to write: "Workers were placed on our payrolls solely on the basis of their experience and training as shown on the Reemployment office records and as determined by examination."[17] We can, moreover, see signs of the effects of feminine voluntarism in this recruitment.[18] In a partial count carried out on January 22, 1934, Persons indicates that, for the towns of Bridgeport and Springfield, 87 people were hired as canvassers and assistants, and further specifies that among them 34 (i.e., 39%) were women. For the rest of the operation, the gender-wise count is missing.

The TCU staff, which soon numbered some 253 persons, was composed of a general supervisor and his deputy, three field supervisors, 70 field workers, 15 stenographic clerical workers in each city, plus three "editors" and 20 staff members in Washington.[19]

The civil administration jobs had thus aroused great enthusiasm, and apparently without the stigma that Hopkins and his administration feared would be associated with them, as more than two people applied for each post at the time of hiring. The population seems thus to have responded massively to the call of statistics, so much so that the designers of the project were able to select candidates, at all hierarchical levels, on the basis of three criteria of equal importance: necessity, competence, and a conscious policy of hiring women. Once the recruitment was done, how did the work proceed?

Filling Out the Questionnaires

Once hired, the interviewers had to go round to the people with the questionnaires. How can one describe the complexities associated with the filling the questionnaire represented? What were the difficulties and what cognitive abilities were required of the CWA staff to bring this task to fruition? To respond to these questions, we will turn to the archives of the TCU experiment.

Before going to the field, the canvassers received the questionnaire along with instructions concerning the survey. These two documents were drafted jointly in advance by the administration sponsoring the project (in the TCU's case, we already know that it was the BLS) and by another administration created by Roosevelt, also at the very beginning of the New Deal, in July 1933: the Central Statistical Board (CSB). The function of the CSB was to "formulate the coordination standards for the statistical services of the federal government." In other words, the CSB advised the government agencies that undertook statistical survey programs on the methodology to be adopted and also played a role that we could call diplomatic: by vouching for the methods, it tried to facilitate relations between different administrative entities. The CSB, which was housed in the Department of Commerce building, next to the Census Bureau, was first headed by Winfield Riefler, an economist-statistician, who was at the time adviser to the National Emergency Council; it comprised both administrators and academics.[20]

In the TCU's case, we were able to locate the instructions for the town of Lancaster,[21] which had been drafted jointly by Persons and E. R. Gray of the CSB, in keeping with the latter's function.[22] The questions asked of the people as well as the principal rules of questioning thus did not depend on the canvassers, but on the interests of the administrations sponsoring the survey and the general statistical rules promulgated by the CSB. What was their content?

The objective was that canvassers, generally persons of "average intelligence," be able to understand the instructions, which were meant to help them elicit responses from a great number of people whose maternal tongue in many cases was not English (see figure 8.4). These instructions covered ten closely typed pages. That is why apart from handing them to the canvassers, they also had to be read, discussed, and commented on together with the supervisors, as is the practice today.

We note that, rather surprisingly, the canvasser's experience of unemployment, similar to that of the interviewee, is neither used nor mentioned in the instructions. It was probably not considered important for the two to share their experience for it to have a positive effect on the quality of the survey. One reason that explains this silence, as we noted earlier, is that the white collars were particularly ashamed to take up public relief jobs. Thus it was probably in an effort not to damage their self-esteem that the project directors tended to overlook this argument which otherwise would have constituted an explicit justification for including this group of people in the list of canvassers.

The first eleven items were "sociodemographic" questions, which even today are standard questions. Then, as in the case of the 1930 census, came three questions that were used to determine if the someone was employed in their "usual occupation"—today we would call it an activity—defined in the instructions as "that which the worker normally follows and hopes to continue or obtain again" (Topalov 1994. In addition, for it to be considered "usual," it was specified that "the person had to spend at least one day per week on this activity," and that it should be the principal source of income of the interviewee: "If the persons were living off their savings,

8.4 Claude Gifford, professor of statistics at Iowa State University, acting as a surveyor, 1947. (ISU Library, University Archives, Special Collections Department)

or if they were helped by other people or institutions," then they were not considered as having a usual occupation.

The work of the canvassers was thus to identify the indicators in the short span of the interview—the normal situation, the minimal frequency, the income source—that would help them to qualify or not qualify the usual occupation. The canvasser was guided by three questions requiring Boolean (binary) answers.

Finally, the questions on the activity were followed by questions on the actual employment of the worker, which determined whether or not the person was unemployed. Consider in particular question 15, which read: "Was the person at work on the last regular working day before the interview?" We first note that the questionnaire limits the period of observation to one working day. This format was not obvious. For example, Gray of the CSB, who had been consulted with regard to the instructions, had proposed to "conduct the test over a period of one week rather than one day"[23] because, according to him, one day was not enough to evaluate the level of occupation of the interviewee. His suggestion was not retained, however, for the situation of the workers was liable to change very rapidly: "For example, if the man lost one day because of sickness, another because laid off and another because of strike, all in the test week, what happens? Do you record all three reasons?"[24]

Contrary to the 1930 census, which left the question open and thereby was a source of major problems (Kleeck 1931), the survey in Lancaster proposed, after three questions permitting the identification of the interviewee, eight modalities of responses to the question of situation regarding work, divided into two sets.[25] The first concerned an interviewee who was at work:

4. The person was at her usual "work."
5. The person was on a "stop-gap" or was employed in another occupation than his usual one to "tide him over."
6. The person was on a relief job.

The second set of questions concerned an interviewee who was not at work at the time of the interview.

7. "The worker has taken time off on his own accord or for personal reasons."
8. "He was idle or lost his job because temporarily disabled by sickness or injury."
9. His family "required" from him that he leave work.
10. "The worker himself is on strike or locked out."
11. "Lack of work, that is the worker is able and willing to work but cannot find work."

By listing the options, this questionnaire asked for dichotomous responses—yes or no. It also adopted Taylor's method of dividing the manual tasks so as to make it easy for the workers to master each step. As such, the intellectual task of the canvasser, as of the interviewee, was simplified to the maximum extent possible.

This work of preparing the questionnaire seems to have borne fruit, as the designers of the TCU felt that the work done by the canvassers was excellent. Thus, as a result of the selection carried out when hiring the canvassers, the clearly and carefully crafted instructions, and the questionnaire given them for interrogating the interviewees with a series of simple questions, the survey on different aspects of the Depression was completed by those who were its victims. We must nevertheless admit that this framework did not leave much initiative with the canvassers. And of course a final element was then added to the process, which seems to have played an important role: hierarchical control.

Control

Statistical work presupposes that the canvassers leave their computing units and go out into the field to collect data. As we have seen in the case of agricultural statistics, this aspect of the profession was what attracted the more independent spirits such as Verne Church (he valued being taken outside, "to the field") but at the same time, as in the case of enumeration, this independence presented a problem as regards the probity of the canvassers because, without any other control, the quality of the data that they produced depended solely on it. During the CWA experiment, the career statisticians, such as Stephan and Samuel Stouffer (who we will introduce later) also referred to this difficulty.[26] How could one ensure that the canvassers would not cut corners?

Morality also depended on another variable: the difficulty of the task. The more difficult it was, the greater the risk of canvassers taking liberties with the instructions. Now, as we have seen with the agricultural statisticians, some units are easier to enumerate than others. It became apparent during the TCU that it was much easier to survey a block of houses, with the block's boundaries clearly demarcated by streets, than to carry out a survey by going to an address indicated by a number, which could be physically hidden or missing and which depended on the administrative organization of the city, which sometimes was rather surprising. To help canvassers be honest, the designers of the survey had to try and give them units that were easy to define.

But the principal techniques that helped to ensure the honesty of the canvassers generally involved hierarchical control. This could be exercised a posteriori, once the questionnaires had been submitted. Stephan, for examples, writes: "Of course, … the enumerator's work could be checked against city directories and rather egregious 'cheating' quickly discovered."[27] But this method was just one way of eliminating the dishonest enumerators from further surveys.

In fact, a major part of the control was traditionally carried out by the hierarchical chain during the survey, whatever the level, with the subordinate submitting an account of the work completed to a superior, often in the form of statistics. The designers of the project had, for example, decided that Persons, the TCU director, had to personally send a progress report of the work accomplished each week to Lubin and to Franck Ross, the coordinator of the joint BLS and CWA projects. Statistical details on the progress of the enumeration work held a prominent place. Thus, on February 17, Persons was able to announce that according to him, the questionnaires would be finished on time; that is to say, on March 15.[28] On February 24, he had to admit that work had been delayed in the two eastern cities because of bad meteorological conditions.[29] However, on March 10, Persons proudly announced that 90% of the surveys had been done, and the chances of completing by the 15th looked good.[30] The amount of time spent in carrying out each task, also inspired by Taylorism, provided the management with the means to react if inexplicable irregularities were noted. Yet the staff's eventual mistakes were not the only problems that compromised the smooth functioning of the project.

The Victory of Federal Procedures on Local Patronage

One of the specificities of the CWA's statistical projects was that they had been planned by the central administrations in Washington but were implemented far from this center, whether in the states, the towns, or the counties. However, the local institutions exercised considerable power in the early years of the New Deal, and particularly in the matter of public relief (we may recall that the FERA, for example, allocated federal money to these local institutions). Inevitably, the CWA's projects gave rise to several conflicts between the federal and local levels. The example of a fierce controversy that took place when the TCU in Springfield, Ohio, was being implemented lets us appreciate the issues involved in the contradictions between the new norms proposed by the federal government and those established locally.

The initial disagreement concerned the salary for enumerators (it also concerned the supervisor's salary, but we will not take this up as it was quite different). The BLS and the CWA had fixed a salary of $110 per month, shortly revised to $100, or $2 per week. But a problem arose with regard to the hours worked. Indeed, for Easterling, the Springfield supervisor, the sum of $25 was valid for a full thirty-hour week. But, for Major Braught, who was the local head of the CWA and responsible for distributing the wages, this sum was valid for a thirty-nine hour week. What's more, the project staff was not allowed to work more than twenty-four hours per week. Their salary of $25 was hence reduced to 24/39 of this amount, or $15.38, which was thus very different. In view of this disagreement, the accountant of the Ohio CWA, A. C. Gray, declined to take any responsibility for the salaries paid and consequently refused to sign the checks. The staff remained without wages for several weeks—from the beginning of January, when most had been hired, until the end of February. The situation remained in limbo.

On February 24, 1934, Isador Lubin, the BLS head, ultimately wrote a very long memorandum to Jacob Baker, the federal director of the CWA (therefore in Washington), where he explained his point of view as evident from the following paragraph:

> This results in our innocently locating in a republican congressional district. Our force was built up, unfortunately for our place in the esteem of state officials, just at the time when state projects were forced to reduce their forces. Workers were placed on our payrolls solely on the basis of their experience and training as shown on the Reemployment office records and as determined by examination. Only one exception to this procedure was reported by Supervisor Easterling. One man—"one good man"—was included on local official recommendation. This procedure as was suggested to Director Persons while in Ohio is contrary to all Ohio political philosophy.[31]

This statement needs clarification. When the TCU, a federal project, was initiated, an independent order was given to reduce the states' expenses (especially those of Ohio). Hence, the Republican protégés of the local authorities could no longer benefit from their largesse. According to Lubin, local authorities therefore tried to put pressure to get the protégés hired in the federal projects, such as the TCU. But again according to Lubin, these practices were not part of the BLS custom (nor, said he, part of "Ohio's political philosophy"—but this strongly resembles a rhetorical argument), although an exception was made for one "good man." The local leaders, who hoped to place many of their cronies, were rather annoyed and, according to Lubin, were likely to put a spoke in the wheels of the federal project, using whatever means they could, by way of revenge. The conflict was not only between the Republicans and the Democrats, but beyond that between two methods of recruiting canvassers: either through patronage, as the local leaders were wont to do, or by following "procedure," taking "experience and training" into account, a method endorsed by the Bureau of Labor Statistics.

We will, however, never know what Baker's reply to his interlocutor would have been, for he did not get a chance to make it. Indeed, Easterling took an initiative that completely changed the course of action. He decided to appeal to public opinion by giving an interview to the *Springfield Daily News*, the local paper, which was published on February 28 under the title "By head of local census: payrolls not met, the accusations hurled by supervisor, T. L. Easterling."[32]

Easterling denounced the local heads of the Civil Works Administration and accused them of not paying their canvassers. There was a big scandal as they were acting against the stated objectives of the CWA. However, Easterling put forward another argument, particularly interesting in this case:

> The same authority was given the supervisors of the Lancaster, Pa., and Bridgeport, Conn., projects as was given to myself. They promised the same rates to their enumerators that I promised the Springfield workers but their state CWA officials cooperated with them and their personnel has been paid with no dispute and delay. … One might assume that our Ohio CWA officials do not consider Ohio workmanship on a par with that of Pennsylvania and Connecticut workers.[33]

For Easterling, the reason that justified the canvassers being paid at the rate they were asking was that they were working within a uniform framework, not only because it was federal, but also because it was statistical and comprised a certain number of issues common to the three cities: the responsibility that devolved on the supervisors, the promises made to the workers, and the agreement between the two administrations. He thus did not see why Ohio should be allowed to renege on the contract based on this common framework.

This matter was finally resolved on March 5, thanks to a compromise reached in Washington. Lubin wrote to Easterling, reprimanding him for giving an interview to the press, then informed Baker of it: "I am fully aware of the fact that Mr. Easterling violated not only the rules and regulation of the Bureau of Labor Statistics, but also certain courtesies that are due to the Civil Works Administration."[34] Indeed, Easterling had not only given an interview, he had also handed the journalists copies of letters exchanged between the two administrations. To ease the situation, Lubin removed Easterling from the CWA but instead took him into the BLS, because of the quality of his work. Eventually, the Springfield enumerators were paid at the same rate as in the two other cities.

As we can see, in Ohio, the relief crews of the CWA and the statisticians had very different views on the correct mode of paying and selecting workers. Two aggregates confronted one another: on one side there was a salary of $15, Major Braught, the state of Ohio and its CWA and patronage, old as the census; on the other, there was a salary of $25, Easterling, the federal administration and Bureau of Labor Statistics, and hiring procedures based on qualifications. The second view eventually prevailed as the employees were selected according to procedure and not because of patronage and paid at the rate fixed by the federal administration.

No doubt the boundary between these two aggregates was not always that clear-cut, and taking advantage of this, TCU Director Persons sometimes practiced favoritism, as he himself admits. Nevertheless, the conclusion according to which the principal norms of the TCU prevailed over Ohio practices can be generalized. This is what Bonnie Schwartz does when she develops in a more than twenty-page chapter the idea that "it drove the politicians wild to find themselves without anything to say about who was going to get a job on public work" (Schwartz 1984, 86). In several CWA projects, whether statistical or not, the local clashed with the federal, which quite often, again according to Schwartz, ended by enforcing its procedures, thus prevailing over patronage. In this enlargement of the federal space, statistics was a particularly effective weapon when there were clear instructions, identical questionnaires, and similar partitioning.

Statistics also offer us a particularly detailed and interesting point of view on this great federal movement of American political life during the New Deal, for they allow us to navigate between levels of analysis: we started with the interactions at work in a locality and, as we followed the evolution of the CWA projects, we arrived, without any suggestion of continuity, in the Washington D.C. offices, to witness what is customarily known as political divergences between administrations. We thus saw politics in the making.

An Experiment for the Unemployed, a Workforce for the Employers

We have seen that the CWA was an experiment designed to provide relief to the victims of the Depression without being condescending (at least as little as possible), because it proposed work corresponding to their abilities, based on a normal wage. The victims of the Depression, satisfied, rushed for these jobs, and for their part, the federal—and local—administrations used this workforce to carry out the many statistical surveys that were needed. With proper supervision, the victims of the Depression seem to have constituted an efficient army of canvassers (Stephan 1935; Myers 1935, 1936). But what was the size of this army? Apart from the question of its quality, it remains for us to examine the question of its quantity—that is to say, the scale of the experiment.

It is extremely difficult to estimate the total number of persons who worked on these projects, among other things, because the counting unit of the relief administrations was the "case," and the beneficiary household could vary from an isolated bachelor to a family with more than two children. In addition, one "case" could occupy successive jobs, moving from project to project—which as we have seen, were of short duration—but would be counted only once. Despite these difficulties, we can estimate that between 1933 and 1937, the period during which projects were undertaken in a major way, the number of such projects, the sums allocated to them, and the number of jobs created were within these certain ranges.[35]

"Research and statistical surveys projects" financed by the relief administrations:

Period	Number of Projects	Total Amount Spent	Number of Jobs Created
Oct. 1933 –	11,435	$50,000,000	3,000,000
Oct. 1937	[9,869–16,253]	[42,883,194–51,127,702]	[2,500,000–35,200,000]

We thus realize that the number of statistical projects alone undertaken in these four years between 1933 and 1937 was nevertheless more than 11,000; and even if we take the lowest estimate, and that too probably is vastly underestimated, the number of statistical positions created amounted to the staggering figure of 3 million (even if this figure does not coincide with the number of individuals employed) for a total of $50 million! Although not as many individuals were hired, this figure is nevertheless edifying. As for the number of questionnaires completed on this occasion, it is not impossible that every American was surveyed during this period. This indicates the massive amount of people who, as a result, had become familiar with the techniques of statistical survey.

In addition, securing one of these jobs sometimes led to people being offered more permanent positions in the administration. Thus, the BLS used this experiment for hiring people.[36] For example, Lubin asked Easterling to recommend staff, which he did in the person of M. Hackenger, "a man of considerable ability … who worked on the project as a consultant," and Miss Mabel Beach, who "was in charge of the editing work during the survey and thus became very familiar with the details of the work and the difficulties that developed. Her help was most valuable."[37]

It is difficult to numerically generalize the observations on the shift from very short term jobs to more stable ones; to our knowledge, no survey on the careers of those who had benefited from civil works positions has been carried out. But Howard Myers, head of research at the CWA, was of the opinion that this happened quite often:

> Social research will profit richly in future years from the experience gained by project directors, supervisors, enumerators and other workers engaged on relief studies and surveys. This profit is, in fact, already being realized; to a steadily increasing extent business organizations and governmental agencies are drawing on the supply of research workers who secured their training through projects financed by the relief administration. (Myers 1936, 777)

The employees of the statistical projects (often called *research workers* at the time) were able to make full use of this experience and enhance their standing on the labor market. At the same time, the number of jobs in the administration open to statisticians continued to increase. Indeed, despite enormous enumeration difficulties, we know that in 1931, 146 positions for statisticians and 628 for economists were counted in the federal administration, and that between January 1935 and October 1936, 129 and 583 new positions, respectively, for statisticians and economists were filled. In other words, the 1931 level practically doubled in the interval separating these two dates. There is no reason to think that it was any different during the other years of the New Deal. So that, by making the basic assumption of a simple doubling of the initial staff every two years, in 1941 (i.e., ten years later), we have 1,460 statistical positions in the federal administration.[38] This does not include nonpublic servant positions: those that depended on the relief agencies, specialist or junior officer positions (like the one for which Brooks was hired in Iowa in 1933), on the basis of lists of suitable candidates. In 1937 there were nothing less than 10,000 applicants for the posts of economists and statisticians (White 1937).

Thus, it is clear to us that one of the first consequences of the statistical relief jobs was to have "statisticized" America (dare we say), both the population as well as the federal administration. An impressive number of persons were able to have direct and professional contact with statistics, which in addition opened up career prospects. Each time a person was hired, statistics made further inroads into America.

Two Causes for Divorce

However, in spite of what may have until now looked like a series of successes, the statistical projects of the CWA—whose name was changed in 1935 to the Works Progress Administration (WPA)—came under increasing criticism. A word in American lingo that came into vogue in 1935, without it being possible to trace its etymology (Algeo 1984), sums up one of the principal reasons for the anger aroused by the increase in the number of civil relief projects for white-collar workers, as they did not have any visible results: *boondoggling* (and its derivative, the *boondoggler*), which even today signifies "a waste of time and money; a project to spend public money" (Spears 1996) (see figure 8.5).

As it happens, this word was specifically applied to canvassers working on statistical projects. Gill thus mentions that "bitter criticism has sometimes been directed at the non-construction projects as 'boondoggling' because the workers on such undertakings do not leave monuments in stone and mortar" (Gill 1939, 193). This public resentment against federal expenditure that did not have visible consequences was so great that the head statisticians, trained as such and already employed in the administrations, ended by taking flight and trying to put an end to the surveys conducted in collaboration with the WPA. Thus, in May 1936, Rice replied to Senator Royal S. Copeland, who had asked him if a special census would

8.5 The legend to this caricature says: "Anyway… the little fellow is queuing up." The criticism is acerbic: Hopkins did nothing more than replace the queues before the soup kitchens with queues before the counters of the relief organizations. The first person is a boondoggler. (*Philadelphia Inquirer*, April 8, 1935)

be conducted in 1937, that in no circumstances would such an operation be carried out as a WPA project for, he explained, there was incompatibility between the legitimate objectives of the public works "and those of sound statistical procedure. This incompatibility is most marked in the case of projects of 'field canvass' type which bring enumerators drawn from relief rolls into direct contact with all classes of citizens."[39] As interviewees were calling the enumerators boondogglers more and more frequently, Rice—no longer wanted the two to come into contact with each other, fearing that it would harm the statistical projects as a whole—therefore preferred to limit the use of this manpower.

This reaction had an institutional consequence that we learned about in a draft letter by Calvert L. Dedrick, dated May 1936, that we were lucky to find in the National Archives, although it is marked "not sent, discussed with Rice."[40] Dedrick, born in 1901 in San Diego, had just finished his studies at the University of Wisconsin. Awarded a scholarship by the Social Science Research Council, which enabled him to work with the prestigious members of the Committee on Government Statistics and Information Services (COGSIS),[41] he joined the research division of the Census Bureau as deputy chief in 1935 and made a career for himself there, leaving the imprint of a great and innovative administrator. In his letter to Rice, he wonders about conducting a census survey of the unemployed prior to the 1940 decadal census and ponders over the difficulties that relations between the Census Bureau and WPA could eventually pose:

> Administrative freedom from the Relief Administration, federal, state, and local, is a *sine qua non* for the securing of data free from suspicion of administrative bias. I am sure that this point will be contested by Mr. Hopkins' organization and since the only apparent source of funds is from relief, it is quite likely that the Relief Administration will set the conditions under which they will cooperate in such an undertaking. I feel that it would be better by far to continue from now until 1940 without

> adequate employment and population data than to subject this inquiry to the Administrative directors and domination of those whose job depend upon proving that there are large numbers of unemployed persons in their communities and to the use of enumerators whose continued support by the Federal Government will be partly contingent upon their findings in their communities on this census. In other words, I believe we are face to face with the presence of measuring social phenomena in which there is considerable vested interest on the part of some of our population and that it would be as unwise to trust relief administrators and relief organizations with the securing of unemployment information as it would be to ask the Chamber of Commerce of the United States to fix the rate of income taxation. It is doubtful whether this point can be effectively presented to the President and the Cabinet; if it can be done, it will have to be done by a man of the point of view of Secretary [Morgenthau of the Treasury Department]. Undoubtedly, the Relief Administrator will ask for almost complete control of the inquiry both because of its nature and the employment opportunity it apparently affords. If complete control is given to the Relief Organization, it is advisable that none of the regular agencies of the government participate directly in this inquiry.

Dedrick's argument was not the same as the one made by the boondogglers. According to him, the problem arose because of a conflict of interests between the WPA and the unemployment surveys—and more generally all the surveys on themes associated with public relief. Indeed, this administration was justified and received funding as long as there existed a large number of unemployed; thus if it was this particular organization that counted the unemployed, by moreover using previously unemployed persons who on this occasion had found employment and who thus had a vested interest in the success of the WPA, it was to be then feared that the interests of this organization would influence the findings. There was danger that the WPA's functioning might render the results of the surveys highly suspect. We note that Dedrick seems to oscillate between his fears of what the public might make of this criticism and his own misgivings about the institution. In any case, for him it was not just a matter of the negative image of the interviewees and the statistical surveys, but also of the validity of the results pertaining to the social problems of the times. We can see the contradiction between a theory of objectivity and a theory of science, in which objectivity translates as disinterestedness and science as a product of public interest (Porter 1995), in relation to which Dedrick's choice is exactly the opposite of the one made in 1921 by the agricultural Statisticians (see, by way of comparison, chapter 3's discussion of the "Individual Farm Inquiry: Objectivity of Informants"). For Dedrick, the bond between the enumerator and the enumerated was no longer a resource but, on the contrary, a very great defect marring the objectivity of statistics.

At the end, the administrator-statisticians felt so threatened that in October 1935 they managed to get the joint committee of the CSB and the WPA to pass a resolution "automatically rejecting all further applications for projects of this type."[42] And in 1936, it was decided that no survey would be financed by relief administration funds, except for those that came under their direct control (USWPA and Harry L. Hopkins 1936).

Thus, after the initial period that many would describe as euphoric, where the underprivileged had regained employment, their lost dignity, and an income allowing them to live, and where the demands of participative democracy for an instant appeared compatible with that of science, a divorce eventually separated them. The victims were no longer considered good enumerators of the scourge affecting them, first, because the public could not really see the utility of the questions they were being asked and began to feel bothered by their intrusiveness and, second, because a conflict of interests surfaced between statistical objectivity and the relief offered by the administration. The fact of entrusting the surveys on the Depression to those that it had affected in the first place had begun to raise questions.

Conclusion: Another Science, Another Democracy

To conclude, we can compare three quite different viewpoints from this experiment. First, we should present Hopkins's perspective, who as head of the relief administrations, continued to believe in the virtues of the statistical projects. He wrote in 1936:

> The largest part of our white collar workers come from the business and not from the professional world. They form a flexible labor supply to undertake on an important scale research basic to future governmental policies. Under the supervision of specialists in the Federal departments they are gathering information to fill gaps in our social knowledge, which previously had to be supplied by small regular staff, or by a few brave scholars and a handful of student investigators. We have only begun as a nation to be self-critical; to learn how we live, what we live by, and how we can improve our lot. Research is popular in the United States. Business pays highly for it and endows research with or without hope of profit. Yet for lack of analysis as to the social significance of this occupation, people are using the WPA investigator as the ultimate boondoggler, his foot in the door, his pencil on his pad. We are examining our social system with the very workers which the system threw out. They are studying, among other things, chronic diseases, facts about housing, occupational characteristics, and unemployment. The return on this investment is such that much of the work is apt to be taken on as a regular function. We can afford to pay to know something about ourselves. (Hopkins 1936, 173)

Several points excited Hopkins. First was the fact that these projects provided specialized manpower to meet the statistical requirements of the government and the companies. Second, he was convinced that these projects made the forces generating these statistics change scale. Third, he was as amazed by the reflexive nature of the experiment as by its democratic aspect: it was the very people who had been rejected by the system who were now analyzing it. Despite the criticism he mentions, for him the experiment was a success both on the scientific and the democratic front.

But the criticism referred to by Hopkins was not insignificant by any means. In particular, the progressive liberals, to designate intellectual non-revolutionary leftist groups of the times, considered that the experiment was nothing more than a democratic failure (Graham 1967). Dewey, for example, was and continued to be extremely critical of the New Deal in general. For him it was simply "vulgar empiricism" … "trying to save the profit system from itself," whereas what he would have really liked it to be was a real experiment in "democratic socialism" (Westbrook 1991). He, who in reality restricted himself to general arguments and had of course never written specifically on the CWA's statistical projects, believed that the New Deal had not led to a redistribution of power in favor of the people, as he had hoped, but had been limited to a series of trials and errors carried out by the government, which took the greater share of the profits in order to re-reinstate itself after the shock of the Great Depression. The fact of entrusting the task of investigating the crisis to its victims did not provide them with an opportunity to produce knowledge related to their own experience, branded with their victim status, but simply reproduced old power relationships.

Between excitement and disappointment, the most complex judgment was made by the professional statisticians. First, let us note that the latter, Clague, Dedrick, and the others we will be encountering in chapter 9, did not themselves go through relief jobs. They were educated in universities and were hired directly by the administration. They seem however to have initially shared Hopkins's enthusiasm (except for some reservations that should be ignored at this stage). The 1933–1935 experiment had two important consequences that they considered positive. First, it allowed them to produce an incalculable number of statistics whose quality, even if it could have been better, was never refuted. After their intervention,

America was much more numerical than before. Second, and this point is crucial for the rest, these experiments resulted in the emergence of a new type of enumerator, which may be qualified as procedural, for the recruitment procedures and their mode of supervision was opposed to patronage. This model was distinct from the three that we have seen earlier—the census agent, the voluntary crop reporter, and the student—but it was the expression that was consolidated in the course of the massive number of experiments that had been conducted.

Yet, little by little, enthusiasm changed into misgivings, then into rejection. It seemed that the people were not able to discern the beneficial effects of all these projects and soon began to call the enumerators vulgar boondogglers. Wary of being associated with the interests of the relief administrations and so have the objectivity of their discipline called into question, the statisticians severed the links with them.

This turning point, which we can pinpoint thanks to Dedrick's unsent letter, seems particularly important to us in the sense that it sounded the death knell of pragmatic participationism on the urban front, which in rural "planning" circles lasted till the end of the 1930s. The practices that allowed people directly concerned with a problem to participate in producing knowledge aimed at its resolution—which was expressly upheld, for example, by an agricultural Statistician such as Nat C. Murray, in the 1920s when he opposed the idea of replacing the crop reporters by the *crop meter*—came to be expressed, on the urban side, in terms of conflict of interests and lack of objectivity.

From this date onward, federal statisticians worked to strengthen the delocalized aspect of the tools of their discipline, the very one that had helped the federal administration to prevail over the local administrations: the detached scientificalness and objectivity associated with numbers. In this sense, one of the key tools that they developed was random sampling.

9

From Participationism to a Government of the Masses

The experiment presented in chapter 8, in which the people actively participated in producing the numbers instead of just replying to the questions put to them, is an example of a statistical "participationist" experiment of which there are several illustrations in this book. Examples include the voluntary crop reporters who gave information on their immediate neighborhood, farmers who used these figures to market their produce, others who used them to optimize land-use strategies, and the unemployed who manifested a desire to be counted. There is a surprising mixture of scientific practice and democratic participationism at the root of American statistical surveys.

However, successive statistical developments that led to the growth of random sampling showed a tendency to curb this participationism, or at least transform it radically. The crop reporters had become superfluous for the Agricultural Adjustment Administration (AAA) and unsuitable for the random selection advocated by Charles Sarle and the Iowa group. The victims of a social problem were no longer considered good canvassers of the problem by those in favor of a more professional statistical enquiry. Experts in the federal agencies were taking over the planning experiments. There was friction between statistical professionalism, the development of government expertise, and the earlier public participationism (Mitchell 2002).

In this chapter we concentrate on the evolution of the random sampling technique in the "urban" administrations of the government to examine, first, how these developments were conceived in that setting—which will help us to understand why, in the aftermath of the war, these administrations succeeded in superseding the Department of Agriculture in statistical innovations—and second, how the data produced by the random method transformed the administrative uses of statistics, and in particular what the effects were in terms of participationism.

Capturing Municipal Lists

As mentioned previously, one of the first problems that Isador Lubin, the new director of the Bureau of Labor Statistics (BLS), had to deal with immediately after his nomination by Frances Perkins, Roosevelt's Secretary of Labor, was to try and measure the rate of unemployment of the country as a whole, as this data was urgently required. He consulted four unemployment specialists and asked them to define the type of survey to be conducted. This consultation resulted in the creation of the Trial Census of Unemployment (TCU), which today is considered to be the first federal experiment on random sampling and generated the most fundamental ideas about random sampling still held today. In chapter 8, we approached this experiment from the angle of the choice of canvassers; we will now see how the method of selection was refined. The first question Lubin faced was the same as Raymond Jessen's,[1] translated to the urban setting: What was the best description, the best frame, to capture American cities?

To start with, let us briefly present the experts that Lubin contacted and Ewan Clague's synthesis of their findings, which painted a panorama of the most advanced surveys on unemployment toward the end of 1933. The first expert was Louis I. Dublin, a statistician at the Metropolitan Life Insurance Company, who conducted a survey on unemployment in forty-six

American towns, for which he had used the same questionnaire as that used for the controversial 1930 census in order to compare the two.

The second expert was Emmett H. Welch, who belonged to the Pennsylvania Relief Committee and had worked at Pennsylvania State University on unemployment and public relief in Philadelphia (Welch 1939). Lubin's third interlocutor was J. Frederik Dewhurst, an employee of the Federal Reserve Bank of Philadelphia, noted for a study that he conducted between 1921 and 1927 (Dewhurst 1928). He established a list of "voluntary" employers (very like the agricultural crop reporters) in different industries and several city zones whose undertakings were of a more or less large size and asked them to send him information regularly so that he could construct a variation index of recruitments. Then, in 1929, he teamed up with Ernest A. Tupper of the Philadelphia Board of Public Education to carry out a survey in which they interrogated the unemployed directly, and for which he obtained the cooperation of the school janitors who went block by block and questioned the families. When Lubin approached him, Dewhurst was employed in the Twentieth Century Fund and was in the process of becoming a member of the Committee on Government Statistics and Information Services (COGSIS).

Margaret H. Hogg, Lubin's fourth expert, must be presented in the greatest detail, for we shall see that though she played a capital role in the history of sampling, she has been completely forgotten. Born in Scotland on October 15, 1894 (she belonged to the same generation as Clague and Calvert Dedrick), she had studied statistics at university and worked at the London School of Economics under Arthur Bowley from 1919 to 1925. In 1925, they jointly published the sequel to the famous *Livelihood and Poverty*, titled *Has Poverty Diminished?* (1925), a defense and illustration of the random selection of samples, which is among the first and the most spirited of its kind. Then, in 1928, for reasons unknown, she left for the United States and was hired by the Russell Sage Foundation. In 1930 she published an article on the research conducted in America in the *Journal of the American Statistical Association*, in which she appealed to statisticians to use rigorous sampling methods—in other words, random sampling. According to Hogg, randomness signified that the units in the sample had an "equal chance of inclusion," and she affirmed that "only if a random sample has been secured can one argue from representativeness, which has been tested, to representativeness where no test is possible" (Hogg 1930, 292). She then conducted a study on unemployment in New Haven, Pennsylvania, publishing the results in a second book (Hogg 1932). The work was so passionately pro-randomness and just as strongly anti-purposive selection that John A. Fitch, a social worker trained by J. R. Commons, who had published a book on metal workers that had attracted a lot of attention, considered the undertaking somewhat "extravagant" and wondered whether strictly methodological issues should not be secondary to the search for truth (Fitch 1910).[2] In spite of this reservation, Margaret Hogg, deemed by both Bowley and the Russell Sage Foundation as an excellent scholar, introduced the random sampling method in the United States right from the late 1920s, much before Jerzy Neyman published his famous 1934 article.

The reports of these experts from varied backgrounds were different—despite the fact that it was Philadelphia that they all gravitated to in the course of their career and not Iowa or the Midwest, as in the case of the agricultural specialists. However, they had an obvious common point, which Clague immediately seized on in his synthesis: all considered towns as the crux of the problem, differentiating between big towns, average-size towns, and rural areas, even if the threshold between the three groups was not always the same. After this the question was, first, to determine whether all the towns from each category had to be taken into account or only some of them and, second, once the towns were selected, if one had to proceed with a general census or select a sample of interviewees. Each one came up with different answers to these questions and, according to Clague, these divergences were explained by the goals pursued by the authors: "There is no one sampling method which is necessary under all circumstances." Whatever it may be, towns were essential to the process of enumerating America as a whole. Hence, Clague proposed enumerating a certain number of small towns to facilitate the survey and to try out different sampling methods for a comparison with the local census results. But which methods?

He began by dismissing the popular idea of voluntary registration of the unemployed (on the invitation of the advertisements of the government, each unemployed person would go on their own initiative to register themselves) because, among other things, of the massive number of relief jobs created (all jobs and not only those related to statistics) that had an ambiguous status and necessarily led to problems of interpretation. (For example, on the question of whether those who were in these jobs should be considered unemployed, there was the likelihood of each one coming up with a different answer.)

The "different sampling methods for measuring unemployment" that Clague wanted to compare were random selection and purposive selection. The advantage of purposive selection, he explained, was that since it was carried out on very small samples, it was the cheaper of the two. Because he did not feel the need to justify the use of random selection, he proposed two "methods" (as he called them), which seem to have been inspired by Hogg's work, and also referred to a third.

First, he thought of using lists of households registered with gas companies as the basis of random selection, the method used by Hogg (1930) in the New Haven study.

Second, he proposed employing another list for the same purpose—the list of taxpayers: "Most towns [must] have a list like this somewhere, and it should definitely be more exhaustive than that of gas subscribers."

Finally, in the place of lists, he proposed a third method—namely, constituting samples of city blocks on the basis of geographical maps. We know that this method was used by J. Frederick Dewhurst (who Lubin had consulted) for his Philadelphia survey in 1929: school janitors were asked to "cover" the blocks—in reality several buildings (Bureau of Labor Statistics 1930). But Dewhurst had never justified this technique, and Hogg regretted this because, although selecting blocks was an easy method, they formed very large units, much bigger than a single household or a single address, and the survey was in danger of losing out on accuracy. She wrote, "The safety of block-sampling, however, has not yet been established, and one may doubt whether the saving of effort would be commensurate with the lessening of security" (Hogg 1930, 291). The experiment would perhaps also enable testing the qualities of this unit.

The problem encountered in testing the random sampling method of the urban unemployed was similar to the one that the agricultural Statisticians would later work on: first and foremost a sample frame had to be found, and the least one can say is that there was no obvious choice. Clague had no other option but to propose one or two small towns (about 50,000 inhabitants), where materials useful in sampling methods were already available, and to carry out an initial experiment, which he then intended to repeat in a half dozen towns of different sizes that "represented different sampling problems," to see if these problems could be resolved at the national level.

It was this initial project that the Civil Works Administration (CWA) had earlier refused (see chapter 8). Clague modified the orientation of his project to be more pertinent for counting the unemployed, but this did not stop it from retaining a methodological character. However, he reversed the order of presentation of the methods envisaged: blocks and purposive selection, which seemed of secondary importance in the first version, now figured as tried and tested methods, and those that interested Clague initially were now regrouped as if they were identical and of lesser importance:

> Thus far three types of sampling methods have been employed in estimating the extent of unemployment … : random block sampling … judicious block selection … It is suggested further that a sample be tested on the basis of addresses secured from the files of local gas companies, tax lists and other sources. (Hogg 1930, 291)

The formulation is strange because first it says that the three methods have already been used and at the same time that the third will be "tested" in the course of the experimental census (as if it had never been used). Clague was of course perfectly aware that they had been used by Hogg, but he minimizes it perhaps because he felt that it may not be to the liking of a potential financier. Thus, the intervention by the CWA had the indirect effect of prioritizing the study on the blocks over the others.

Why were blocks more likely to convince the CWA? As the proposition had not been justified, we are reduced to speculation. We will simply conclude that the block was the urban equivalent of the rural neighborhood that had such a deep impact on agricultural statistics in the initial stages. Here are two examples in support of this thesis. The first is a long article in three parts on the city of Columbus, Ohio, of which the second analyzes the neighborhood as a sociological concept (McKenzie 1921). The author asks his students at Ohio State University, located in Columbus, to define their own neighborhood; he then points out how they all think in terms of *blocks*—a block of houses. The block is the urban neighborhood; that is to say, a space "the limits of which seem to be determined by the extent of [their] personal observations and daily contact." Another example is an article with an ambitious title that examines how a case study on a community should be conducted (Thrasher 1928). For greater accuracy and detail, the author strongly recommends using aerial photographs to map blocks. These two examples suggest that the block was better rooted in the history of American reflexivity than the lists of gas subscribers were (Silver 1990)!

As a result of the emphasis on blocks, this time the project was accepted on December 4, 1933, under the name of "F-74," or "Federal Project No. 74," which the actors unofficially called the Trial Census on Unemployment—TCU, for short. It now remained to effectively test the different sampling methods applicable to cities.

The first difficulty was choosing the cities to test the TCU. This phase was important for the types of lists available in a town would depend on the town selected and hence would also affect the quality of the findings. Though the criteria had been fixed for the project—towns should be of a certain size and located in different regions—circumstances played a primordial role in the first few weeks of the TCU. At the end of several circumvolutions, of which we have only partial details, it was finally Bridgeport in Connecticut, Springfield in Ohio, and Lancaster in Pennsylvania that were selected for enumerating the population (households in the first two cases and only the working population in the third).

The second difficulty was carrying out the sampling experiment initially planned in these towns. Margaret Hogg was entrusted with this task. We do not know how the decision was made to put her in charge, but if we consider the importance of Hogg's ideas in the first version of the project, it is possible that she was roped in early. However the decision was taken, her appointment had important consequences. In her 1930 article, Hogg had announced that for her, the only sampling technique that could claim to be scientifically rigorous was random sampling. So without making any allowances for the initial project, she simply dismissed purposive selection and set up experiments based solely on random sampling. Consequently, her immediate task was to search for sampling frames.

Continuing her earlier work on the gas subscribers list, she started to search for all sorts of municipal lists. But as cities had been selected depending on circumstances and not from this perspective at all, Hogg did not know what surprises were in store for her on the ground. She therefore went personally to the field in February to determine together with the supervisors what solutions were possible.

> I discussed with Mr. Couper and his staff the information that they had obtained regarding local lists, and decided that the [city] directory was the best available list, and that the voter's list was the only other list that could be used in the present circumstances.[3]

Similarly, Hogg "followed up the leads, which Mr. Merkle had prepared, to various local records."[4] The local supervisors acted like spotters, going up and down their town and ferreting everywhere in search of suitable lists to give to Hogg. To assess their degree of exhaustiveness, Hogg used the census that had just been completed (let us not forget that the TCU was initially a census of three towns, coupled with a survey experiment) and invented a small mechanism disarming in its simplicity and effectiveness:

> A system of records has been set up which makes cross reference simple and should, incidentally, be very useful for later analysis of output. … I drew up a form on which households in the ten percent household sample should be checked against both these lists, and myself entered the checking against the directory for the first 25 schedules.[5]

Here Hogg is referring to the Bridgeport example. A 10% sample of households was extracted from the census. These households were listed on the form conceived by her, which made it possible to verify if they really figured on the two municipal lists scrutinized—the address list and the gas subscribers lists.

The exhaustiveness of the lists was however not the only criterion used for grading them. The statisticians also wanted to determine the extent to which each list allowed access to the terrain. Now if, thanks to the census, one could identify households that had been selected in the lists, the reverse was not possible: the lists did not all give direct access to households. The street list, for example, designated addresses or blocks as units, but not households. In fact, each furnished a specific sampling unit.

Sampling Units Tested According to Town

	Bridgeport,	Lancaster,	Springfield,
State	Connecticut	Pennsylvania	Ohio
Census	Population	Workers	Population
In-sample units	Blocks	Households	Blocks
	Households	Buildings	

It still remained for the statisticians to assess the respective qualities of these different units in view of a global survey.[6] It is this job that the "Unemployment Survey Committee" of the Central Statistical Board (CSB) undertook to do. Sitting members included those who had headed the TCU and two new members: Dedrick, who doubted the fallout of unduly long alliances with the CWA, and Samuel A. Stouffer, who later also played an important role in the development of sample surveys.

Stouffer came from Iowa and had completed his doctorate under Professor Thurstone at the University of Chicago. Like Dedrick, Stouffer was granted a scholarship by the Social Sciences National Council, which he used to go to England to work with Karl Pearson; he had also been appointed to the COGSIS. Later, he joined Frederick Stephan and taught in Chicago until the war (Stephan 1960); it was at this time that he participated in *The American Soldier* (Stouffer et al. 1949), a vast and very successful survey on the morale of the American troops.

To accomplish their task, the first criterion that this group of statisticians selected for reviewing the units was the accuracy of the estimators with respect to probable error, which they helped to calculate. Thanks to Hogg's preparatory work, as a result of which random samples could be drawn easily, this test was very easy to conduct, contrary to the one that the agricultural Statisticians were developing at the same time, so that they quickly arrived at a conclusion—a very general one—according to which the size of the sample unit and the size of probable error varied in the same direction. The smaller the unit (i.e., the fewer the individuals that it contained), the smaller the errors that it led to. The blocks, the largest unit, thus led to the greatest error; then came the buildings and finally the households. This rule was theorized in precise terms by Stouffer:

> The precision of an estimate from a sample increases in direct proportion to the root of the number of units on which the sample is based. Therefore, other things being equal, the smaller

> the unit, the better the estimate, if decrease in size of units is accompanied by an increase in their number.[7]

Neyman came to the same conclusion in his famous 1938 article, which makes one wonder whether Stouffer had not got this idea during his stay in England. In any case, the TCU produced its first results in accordance with what would become the legitimate theory of sample surveys. With the best unit being households, lists now had to be found that would facilitate the construction of samples.

But it was not enough for a list to be exhaustive in a town and to contain small units; one also had to be able to use it for a survey on the United States as a whole, and the units that it contained had to be the standard for the whole country. This was the second criterion of evaluation of the units retained by the group of statisticians. Now it was clear from the already-tested TCU city examples that the lists found there produced units that differed from one to another:

> It is possible to approximate this by careful checking of gas meters, water meters, directories, insurance maps, etc., but these sources are not available in comparable forms for all cities. It would seem, therefore, that a household or building sampling technique, while excellent when properly used, would not be feasible for nation-wide application in a sample census of unemployment.[8]

The statisticians, who had not forgotten the end objective of carrying out a nationwide survey on unemployment, consequently concluded that the most feasible partial survey method, clearly seen as a lesser evil in terms of accuracy, would be based on blocks, which they considered the most exhaustive unit at the level of the subcontinent. It would focus on 20% of the population. According to its designers' plans:

> A sample of blocks or street segments will be taken in each city of 100,000 or more; that complete enumeration will be made in a carefully selected group of cities comprising one-fifth of the cities under 100,000; and that complete enumeration will be made in a carefully selected group of rural counties, comprising one-fifth of all rural counties.[9]

With a sample like this, whose principal characteristic was to retain the *blocks* as the most reliable unit for towns because of their countrywide homogeneity, the error committed in each modality would not be greater, according to the authors, than 6% in at least 95% of the cases. Of the units and lists they had examined, they chose the street guide, as this recommendation proves, for they felt it would be most uniformly compiled across the entire country, despite the fact that it gave the most inaccurate results.

Aware of the weaknesses in the unit retained, the TCU officials nevertheless advised their directors to carry out a large-scale intercensal census in 1935 that could serve as the frame for a survey describing all of America and that would help them to avoid the ups and downs that had undermined the process earlier. Without the Holy Grail (i.e., the census), they said, they could not do anything worthwhile. For measuring a variable as crucial as the unemployment rate, a fresh description of the nation in its integrality was perfectly justified.

Capturing America as a Whole?

The TCU team's recommendation to conduct a general census of the population and an intercensal census of unemployment in 1935 immediately struck a chord with the Census Bureau, which was also in the process of reorganization. Although its staff really served as an administrative staff, the directors wanted to turn them into a body of experts (Anderson 1988, 175). They therefore reshaped their employment policy giving preference to young people specializing in statistics or the social sciences: the perspective of surveying a thorny technical problem such as unemployment by means of a census corresponded perfectly with this objective. They managed to convince Representative Ralph Lozier to introduce a draft bill aimed at conducting a census on unemployment and employment as early as 1934.[10] But this project met with no small opposition: on the one hand, such a census would have been costly and, on the other, it seems that President Roosevelt preferred not to make the figures public at this time; he was concerned that the unemployment situation might not have improved since his election and that there would still be too many people on relief. The Lozier project was thus rejected. "No good could be served in mounting an expensive national effort to produce data that would not reflect favorably on the administration," comments Margo Anderson (1988, 177).

This sequence was repeated several times until the war: the statisticians campaigned determinedly for an intermediary census that would have allowed them to measure unemployment and at the same time develop sampling techniques, and each time the "top administrators" shot them down. The road to methodological intransigence was thus paved with disappointment. Four incidents occurred that affected the fate of randomness. Let us present them chronologically.

The Death of Margaret Hogg

First, the most radical voice of intransigence fell silent. At the start of 1935, Margaret Hogg, suffering from an undiagnosed illness, was admitted to Booth Memorial Hospital in New York. There her health declined drastically, so much so that in August 1935 she decided to return to England, despite the discomfort of a maritime crossing, accompanied by her younger sister Winifred and her mother, who had come to fetch her.

Hardly had she stepped on board that her health further deteriorated and on the second night after they had boarded ship, on August 3, she passed away in her sleep, nine days before their scheduled arrival in England.

> The Ship's doctor and the captain advised burial at sea; [Margaret's mother explains in a letter] and as we felt sure that dear

> Margaret, like ourselves, would regard the disposal of the body as a minor matter, and as there were still nine days till our landing, we agreed. They were most kind in making every arrangement and on Monday at 6:30 a.m., before the passengers were astir, we followed her dear body to the deck where the captain conducted a simple and reverent burial service ending with the committal to the deep and benediction. The doctor and nurse were with us, also our stewardess and a few stewards, as well as the four seamen who carried the bier. The doctor and the nurse made a lovely cluster of roses and a beautiful cross of gladioli from flowers that had been sent to Margaret at the boat. Winifred and I carried these and after the committal dropped them into the waves. We think dear Margaret would have been pleased with the simplicity and grandeur of such a burial.[11]

Thus, Margaret Hogg's role, central to the history of random sampling, can practically be said to have sunk with her down to the ocean depths.[12] The further development of random sampling was to continue without her.

Opinion Polls

In comparison, the resounding success of opinion polls is well known in history (Igo 2007). The *Literary Digest*, a publication that traditionally organized "straw polls," asking its tens of thousands of readers to send dummy ballots for a sort of pre-election probe, had, in 1936, predicted that Roosevelt would lose. Against this enormous machinery, three independent institutes headed by George H. Gallup, Elmo Ropper, and Archibald Crossley managed to predict Roosevelt's reelection, thanks to opinion polls carried out on small samples. This event caused a sensation among the public.

Yet the success of the pollsters did not initially spark much of a reaction from the government statisticians (surveyors). This silence can be explained by the fact that, despite appearances to the contrary, there were sharp differences between these two methods as well as between the intellectual references that inspired them. Gallup, who came from Iowa, was a journalist and a keen student of political science. He was especially influenced by the philosopher James Bryce (born 1838), who was in favor of a democracy based primarily on public opinion. Gallup had later studied under S. S. Wilks, a probabilist, at Princeton, who had also imported ideas on sampling from England, but Wilks was not among his principal references. It was from an initial reflection on public opinion that Gallup arrived at statistics and not the reverse, so his theoretical options brought him closer to purposive selection than to random selection (Gallup 1940). His quota sampling method, wherein a sample had to be constructed as a miniature of the total population with respect to a certain number of variables such as sex, age, occupation, or place of residence, did not really use randomness. He talked of it in his publications, for he accorded it scientific legitimacy, but his samples were really selected by surveyors on the basis of quotas and not randomly. In particular Gallup's "sampling base," if we can call it that, had nothing in common with what the surveyors were seeking: it simply consisted of a double-entry table obtained from the previous census—in this case the 1930 one—figuring only the principal variables that interested him. This "miniature America," as Gallup liked to call it (Igo 2007), was thus extremely poor and obsolete with respect to the gigantic "homogeneous form" that the administration was looking for. Gallup had taken the sampling route, but within the framework of this family, he had chosen an option that unemployment specialists had passed over; they thus had nothing much to say to each other.

Despite this, Gallup's feat did not influence the administration any less. By predicting the election result he had managed not only to predict the behavior of public opinion but also to convince people that surveys could be right. Loïc Blondiaux (1998) has given an excellent account of how Gallup was able to stage his opposition to the *Literary Digest*'s straw polls, create suspense right up to the elections, and use that as a cleaver between two incompatible options, which proved him right. Gallup thus publicly showed that his method was reliable. Through a rather incomprehensible reversal, Blondiaux then seems to criticize those who were convinced by such a "superior form of magic" (to use his own words), calling them "simple souls" and "heathens." In other words, Blondiaux wants to tell his readers that he himself is not taken in by opinion polls. But the Roosevelt administration's attitude was very different. It was of course rather put out that the method did not comply with the cabinet departments' methods, but it did not oppose it; much more artfully, Stephan paternalistically qualified it as an example of pardonable amateurism: "The success of the new public opinion polls cannot be traced to any strikingly new principles of sampling. They employ procedures that are relatively simple and depend more on courage, common sense, and hard work than on abstruse scientific theories" (Stephan 1939, 344). In this way he could benefit from Gallup's success. Seen from the outside, the two groups were united in victory. Inside, the situation was more complicated.[13] Despite the deep-seated differences between quotas and randomness, the pollsters had to a large extent rallied victory to the cause of statisticians as a whole by convincing the public of the reliability of sampling in general.

The 1937 "Enumerative Check"

Just after this episode, another highly publicized event gave a clear victory to the proponents of random sampling.

In 1937, Roosevelt's opponents began to show their impatience at being kept in the dark about unemployment (Anderson 1988, 184). After some uncertainty about how to best respond to this situation, President Roosevelt eventually adopted a surprising stand. He reverted to an idea that had been out in the open for some time but which statisticians vehemently opposed. He proposed to organize a "voluntary registration" of the unemployed by launching a massive press campaign to exhort each unemployed individual to fill out and send the government a registration card so that they could be counted. If they were "honest" (a word used by Roosevelt in one of his radio chat programs), which Roosevelt had no doubts about, one would then know how many unemployed there were; above all, if they manifested the desire to be counted, they would at the same time be initiating a grand movement mobilizing people against this scourge.[14] For Roosevelt, the sociopolitical results expected from the registration were as important as the numerical results; moreover, he did not find these two objectives contradictory.

On the contrary, in the government statistics departments, opposition was general. Meanwhile, Howard Myers of the Works Progress Administration (WPA)[15] wrote a long memorandum to Harry Hopkins, head of the Federal Emergency Relief Administration (FERA), listing all the disadvantages of a "mass registration"[16] of this kind—stressing, in particular, that no verification of the validity of the results, although highly suspect, would be possible. Hopkins immediately conveyed this to the Secretary of the Interior. On December 3, 1936, Stuart Rice, now president of the CSB, convened a meeting where all the weaknesses of self-registration were listed, in particular the fact that some unemployed persons did not consider themselves as unemployed (especially white-collar workers, reluctant to acknowledge their situation), while others, unhappy with their work, stated that they were without work whereas they were not. The outcome was a resolution against this plan and an appeal for "a suitable census on unemployment and employment."[17]

The idea of self-registration, which so horrified statisticians, nonetheless continued to gain ground in the President's immediate circles, causing Rice to change strategies radically and publish a *New York Times* column on May 15, 1937, titled "Why Not Have an Unemployment Census!" He explained that it was too late to carry out a large-scale statistical survey because it would require at least two years to process it and this operation would necessarily interfere with the preparation of the 1940 decennial census, which had to be absolutely faultless.[18] As a consequence, he concluded, it was urgent to do nothing, especially not voluntary registration.

However, Roosevelt did not heed the statisticians and finally launched the operation in October 1937. It had to be inexpensive and well organized. He appointed John Biggers, the rich president of the firm Libby-Owens-Ford, at its head, who in his capacity as a successful businessman agreed to manage the $5 million allocated to the mobilization campaign, free of charge. The American Institute of Public Opinion (AIPO), Gallup's firm, showed keen interest and carried out an opinion poll (with technical help from Emil Hurja, Roosevelt's personal adviser on public opinion), according to which 20% of the unemployed thought that they would find work relatively quickly if they filled the voluntary registration card.[19] The press, for its part, compared the registration card to a ballot paper against unemployment or a straw vote like those that were normally associated with the elections. Locally, committees were set up to ensure the success of the operation, which became as much a public action as an enumeration.

Biggers however made sure the team included statisticians—namely, Calvert Dedrick and an even younger recruit, Morris Hansen from the Department of Agriculture (where he had insisted that the Iowa group use aerial photographs); both had been "lent" by the Census Bureau where they were employed. Also forming part of the team were Samuel Stouffer and Frederick Stephan in an advisory capacity. Except for minor variations, this was the same TCU team, except that it was set up in the Census Bureau and not in the BLS. In addition, Frederick Robinson, an employee of the AIPO, also joined the group. The operation thus formed a bridge between the government's enumerators and the pollsters, but forced them carry out a project to which they were methodologically opposed.

The enumerators nevertheless managed to convince Biggers of the weaknesses inherent in voluntary registration for measuring the phenomenon and the necessity of coupling it with an enumerative check, which would verify whether the unemployed, and only they, had responded to the registration. Despite its apparently secondary character, the enumerative check allowed the statisticians to turn the operation around completely and ignore voluntary registration. How did they go about it?

Biggers first announced that they would resurvey certain typically American towns. He immediately received applications. For example, an elected representative from Estherville, Iowa, wrote to him to say that his town was typical and to assure him that they would receive the best assistance possible in their task. But, probably to cut the debate short, Robinson was asked to reply that the units selected would not be disclosed.[20]

The statisticians had decided to draw their sample at random. Therefore they did not look for towns but a sample frame from which they could draw their population. In conformity with the TCU experiment, they conceived various options, such as wards, districts, and blocks. But all these options justifiably needed a lot of time for preparation, which they did not have. Now, to carry out voluntary registration an agreement had been signed with the Post Office Department: its agents were supposed to deposit declaration forms in public locations, then once they had been filled, forward them on to the center. To perhaps resolve the difficult question of the sample frame, the team wondered whether they could reuse a forgotten method devised by the Department of Agriculture: the map of postal routes. This would allow them to connect the whole of America through surveys.

Two main obstacles stood between the statisticians and this map. First, only 82% of the population lived on a postal route—the sections were therefore not exhaustive. Second, postal routes were enormous units, bigger than blocks or the census enumeration districts, such that data would surely lose out in terms of accuracy. But it had certain undeniable advantages. For one, it was quick. It "utilized an established administrative area used by the Post Office Department, and did not require the preparation of maps and other descriptive material" (Dedrick and Hansen 1938, 159). In addition, along with routes, the Post Office provided a good network of canvassers—mailmen—which meant that one could bypass the WPA canvassers. The advantages prevailed over the disadvantages and the statisticians retained this sample base for random surveys to count the unemployed. The mailmen firmly established themselves as the trusted allies of the statisticians.

However, contrary to what Dedrick and Hansen had hoped, it required a major effort on their part to adapt this map to their own method. For example, they had to identify and eliminate postal routes serving only industrial zones. Then they had to regroup them in order to stratify the sample according to towns, which was not a simple process. The solution they finally arrived at (figure 9.1) was described as follows:

> Ten classes of routes were distinguished according to type, and by size of city for cities with 10,000 or more population in 1930. The cities within a State were listed in order of size to assure a direct proportion of sample routes for each city-size group. Cities with a population of 10,000 or more were handled as individual units, and the smaller cities and villages were grouped geographically so as to insure sampling from the routes in a contiguous area within each section of a State. (Dedrick and Hansen 1938, 160)

After having decided that the sample would contain 2% of the routes, they proceeded to draw the sample. They consolidated the routes in each category into groups of 50 and opted for a systematic draw of one route per group: "The exact route from each block of 50 to be used in the enumerative check was selected by the Vice President of the United States in November 10, 1937, when he chose the number '42' from among the 50 numbered disks in a hat" (Dedrick and Hansen 1938, 160). Thus, it was not stochastic chance by which the routes to be surveyed were selected, but *democratic chance*—that is, chance embodied in the person of one of the most eminent members of the government.[21] Lastly, in the less populated western states, several postal routes had to be arbitrarily added to the sample so that each state would have at least ten routes (see figure 9.1).

The list of selected routes was not disclosed until the voluntary registration was complete so that the control procedure (the enumerative check) would not affect the operation. Indeed, it was possible that the people living on an area of a route, on hearing that their registration would be checked afterward, would fill out the registration form better and more precisely. Then, after the cut-off date, each mailman concerned was informed of the

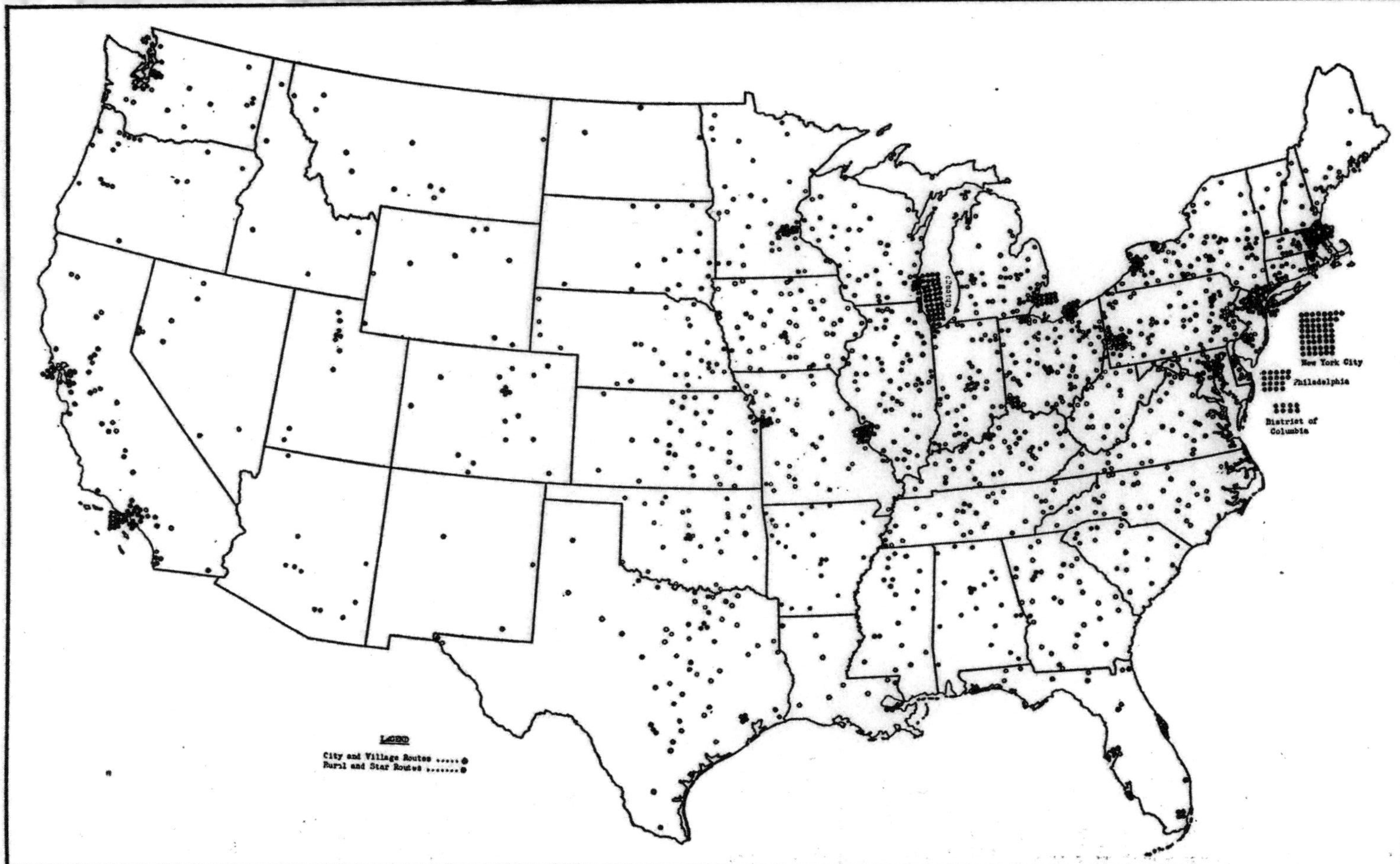

9.1 Situation of postal routes that were selected for the enumerative check. America as a whole reappears. (Dedrick and Hansen 1938, 160)

additional task of giving a questionnaire to each household on his route during the last week of November (let us not dwell on the details of the operation that turned out to be much more complicated than expected, especially when the household was absent).

This questionnaire *did not ask* the interviewees whether or not they had sent a voluntary registration card; this verification would be done in Washington by manually verifying the names. It included, on the other hand, questions to ascertain, independently, whether the interviewees were unemployed. These questions helped to distinguish those who were working from those who were not in the third week of November. As regards those who were working, the questions were used to determine whether it was part-time work and, if this was the case, whether they wanted to work more, or whether it was a relief job; in the case of those who were not working, the aim was to determine whether they worked under normal circumstances or, if they wanted to, whether they were capable of it and actively seeking work.

We understand now—and Biggers too probably understood it in retrospect—that the statisticians had managed to double cross voluntary registration, which became really just an auxiliary of surveys. Indeed, they managed, a little before Christmas 1937, barely a month after the enumeration, to publish an estimate of the rate of unemployment. The speed of the survey's execution prevented any criticism being leveled at the team for acting slowly in comparison to the speed of the phenomenon.[22] The results were valid for the United States as a whole and had been broken down geographically, to apply to the states and some of the bigger cities, and sociodemographically, according to sex, age, "functional categories"—as the authors called them[23]—race, domicile (town/country), large geographical zones (reduced to nine), and distributed according to the "employability" of the interviewees (i.e., according to their immediate availability on the labor market).

The two techniques gave very different results: 10,983,000 unemployed (± 293,000) according to the survey as compared with 7,845,000 counted through voluntary registration. By showing that a large number of unemployed identified in the survey did not appear in the self-registration, the statisticians were able to conclude that only 71% of the unemployed had come forward by means of voluntary registration, and thereby succeeded in greatly discrediting the program.

Just as the advocates of the quota method had prevailed over the straw votes, the proponents of random sampling had prevailed over voluntary registration. The headlines in the *The News*, in Washington, read: "The census controversy won by statisticians."[24] For the first time, the urban surveyors were able to articulate the random sampling technique with a sample base applicable to "America as a whole" and in this way determine the number of unemployed.

Thereafter the relationship between the statisticians and the people was completely transformed. In the minds of the proponents of voluntary registration, the measure of unemployment spearheaded the fight against this calamity and necessarily implied an active partnership between statisticians, politicians, and the people. With random sampling, the strategy was completely different. The people were not informed about the survey; on the contrary, it was kept as secret as possible so that their behavior would not be affected. A sample was chosen randomly from a base whose existence they were not even aware of—in other words, by circumventing the people's will or rather reexpressing it through the fragmented wills of the individuals who were either willing or unwilling to reply. With this victory of the random method, the statisticians had shown that it was possible to objectify the population, but they had in one fell blow broken the old link between the fight against unemployment and popular mobilization that Roosevelt had sought to restore.

However, there were still too many loose ends and the experiment remained fragile because it was isolated. The decennial census provided an occasion for the enumerators to continue the experiment.

The 1940 Census

Preparations for the 1940 decennial census had started at the same time as the initial deliberations on the enumerative check. This operation held special importance for the surveyors, because they hoped that the census would provide them with one of the best bases imaginable, both exhaustive and detailed enough to obtain accurate results. Thus right from their first deliberations, they sought to articulate the survey to the venerable institution. However, on closer scrutiny, they perceived that the procedures used for achieving the exhaustiveness of the census were in reality contradictory to those that were necessary for carrying out a random draw; looking at it more closely, the two procedures were not complementary but incompatible!

At first the complementarity of the two seemed quite obvious. The demand for information was such that the enumerators—especially Dedrick, Stephan, and Hansen—thought they had better prepare a second questionnaire that would be given only to a sample of enumerated individuals. Buoyed by the interest created by the operation, and on the strength of the success of the enumerative check (Hansen 1987, 184), it seems that this time the samplers had no difficulty in convincing the director of the Census Bureau, William Austin, to conduct the experiment. A team of specialists was hired to finalize the sampling method. Among them was W. Edwards Deming, who until now had been working at the Department of Agriculture (it was Deming who had invited Neyman to a 1937 conference), and other young career statisticians who would leave their mark on the history of surveys, in particular Philipp M. Hauser and William N. Hurwitz (Anderson 1988).

To achieve exhaustiveness the census had to be organized in a very systematic manner: In town, for example, canvassers were asked to go from block to block, start from a corner building, do a thorough survey of it, and pass on to the next in serpentine fashion, as done in topographical surveys. When interviewing a household, they always had to start with the head of the family, then if it was required, move on to his wife, their children, and other family members. By proceeding in this way, the chances of missing a person were reduced.

But the effect of this regularity was that "the inevitable results are undulatory" (Stephan, Deming, and Hansen 1940, 622). In particular, the initial problem was that the first person enumerated by each agent was almost always the head of the family, and the second problem was corner buildings in towns: "Corner houses are different from other houses; studies conducted on 'corner influence' show that household characteristics, such as rent, value of home, number of children, number of lodgers, vary from house to house in waves of distinct patterns with peaks or depressions at the corners" (Stephan, Deming, and Hansen 1940, 622). With sampling through systematic drawing, as had been done until now (e.g., one person every ten persons enumerated with only the first person being drawn), which it appears was the only realist solution, there was an unfortunate possibility of the draw being in phase with these undulations, thus leading to systematic errors being committed in the survey. For example, if we draw the first then the tenth then the twentieth person, the enumerators would have at least one family head; the heads of the family would then be represented in the sample in a proportion without any connection with their actual number in the population.

To articulate the surveys with the census, the enumerators had to therefore rethink their theory of selection and devise extremely complex mechanisms in order to avoid the "line biases," which are nowadays typical of sampling theory (Stephan, Deming, and Hansen 1940, 622). At the same time, they had to get the supporters of the traditional census to agree that, contrary to accepted practice, all individuals would not be treated exactly alike; hence some interviewees would be given an additional questionnaire. As we have seen on every occasion until now, the surveys were thus modified by their new sample frame and, in turn, they modified the frame.

The game was worth it, however. By capturing the census, the samplers did not merely possess an exhaustive base—which was already tremendous—but they also acceded to the Constitution itself, along with the Supreme Court, its federal tribunals, and its laws,[25] and to the very foundations of citizenship.

Furthermore, if the census gave access to the country's entire constitutional machinery, it also gave the statisticians access to what was smaller, because it was relatively easy to divide this huge base and work only on portions of the territory, such as regions or states. By joining forces with the census, the America of the surveys infinitely extended its reach, which accordingly increased its solidity.

The census thus put the finishing touches on the structure gradually systematized by the surveys, thanks to which they were able to take stock of America as a whole. But urban specialists, instead of trying like their colleagues in the Department of Agriculture to further refine this vast base and adapt it for use with a larger number of survey issue, enhanced its capacity of passing from one more or less exhaustive sample base to more local bases, articulating the results obtained from each of them with others and with each new research issue. As Frederick Stephan put it so well:

> Modern sampling practice utilizes a variety of devices and methods which have been tested experimentally and incorporated into sampling theory. The aim of modern practice is to select those methods which, when combined in the most appropriate manner, will constitute a sampling system that is economical, convenient, and accurate in the situation for which it was designed. (Stephan 1948, 28)

The option chosen by unemployment specialists for capturing America was thus not to produce a superb, infinitely replicable statistical tool, but to learn to combine diverse frames in keeping with the situation.

True, the advances made in the field of sampling theory had meant sacrificing people's participation, much solicited in the past, by discouraging all popular initiative in the production of data: from this point on, the persons selected by the statistical apparatus had to stick to replying to the questions asked. But the statisticians were able to take up a large number of additional surveys on different issues and of different sizes. Stephan gives several examples in a nearly thirty-page article on the early utilization of random sampling, citing in particular surveys on housing that used samples of blocks, surveys on household consumption patterns that used the street guide, others on health that were based on smaller areal samples, surveys on income that took the households as a sample base, or those on youth that used municipals lists of property assets, and of course, surveys on unemployment (Stephan 1948). They brought out the correlations, which had gone undetected until now, between variables found in American society (Stephan 1948). Thus, by the end of the 1940s, the general feeling was that practically everything could now be counted. The "blindness" of the early 1930s had finally been replaced by a precise and complete vision of American society. The state could, at last, "see" the urban population, but in the very specific frame described here (Scott 1998; Latour 1998).

A New Kind of Political Intervention

During the laissez-faire period, the government regulated relations between peoples and groups with conflicting interests. It published data that was accessible to all. When the surveys stopped using the crop reporters, they became random, and a new type of political interventionism made its appearance.

First, the data produced was no longer for public dissemination, but only for a few interlocutors in the administration. In its 1937 report, COGSIS—sponsored by the American Statistical Association and by the Social Science Research Council—underlined the importance of this evolution (Committee on Government Statistics and Information Services 1937). It regretted the fact that the statisticians' reports were no longer *published* as in the past, but only mimeographed. As insignificant as this remark may seem, it goes to show that statistical data complied with new administrative requirements. According to COGSIS, the use of this reproduction technique no doubt facilitated the "desired economy," but we know that the mimeograph was only economical when it was limited to a small number of copies, approximately a dozen; the reports were thus circulated only among a limited group of administrators. Second, it was also considered an "expeditious method for releasing current reports," which suggests that the pace of data production was more rapid. The COGSIS, however, bemoaned the fact that reports produced this way were "easily lost or misplaced" and that "the figures are apt to be blurred and difficult to read," which shows that the reports were less valued than in the past (Committee on Government Statistics and Information Services 1937, 42). In this way, the stenciled reports were more convenient for the new administration because statisticians were now able to give data, required by political decision makers, more rapidly and at a more sustained pace but with a shorter period of validity. The stenciled reports were the material expression of the "continuous and intimate contact with the problems faced by colleagues in the work of administration, education, and policy formation" yet maintained a greater distance from the general public (Committee on Government Statistics and Information Services 1937, 2).

What type of intervention did this information make possible? First, we have to insist on the fact that surveys had practically no connection with old-age insurance and unemployment insurance, though they were launched during the New Deal. There were several arguments in favor of exploring this line of reasoning and, in particular, the enormous amount of work done by François Ewald on the emergence of the welfare state, in which he accorded a key role to statistics (Ewald 1986). Indeed, for Ewald, the welfare state had replaced the liberal state between the late-nineteenth and early-twentieth centuries because of the development of a particular way of thinking and the practice of insurance that constituted, he felt, a "certain type of rationality":

> Insurance thus is the practice of a certain type of rationality. It does not have a field specific to it. It is defined less by a subject which would be its own than by a somewhat ubiquitous form.

> It provides a general principal objectifying men and their relationships. It is at the same time;
>
> a) An economic and financial technique …
> b) A moral technology …
> c) A technique of reparation and compensation of damages …
>
> All these dimensions turn insurance into a political technology. (Ewald 1986, 180)

According to Ewald, a striking and characteristic feature of the welfare state is thus its relationship with insurance, "the objectivation principle that helps to take cognizance of men and their relationships," that objectifies them and then acts on them. These points are important in our case as it was during the New Deal that insurance was effectively established, and by stretching our vocabulary, we could say that surveys neither express nor capture human beings but objectify them.

In addition, Ewald affirms that insurance cannot do without statistics. He thus devotes an entire chapter to the works of Adolphe Quételet whose conception of the "average man" has, according to him, had a major influence on insurers (Ewald 1986, chap. 1, "Moyenne et perfection"). Furthermore, he imputes to statistics the role of organizing the mutualization of the chance. He refers to Eugène Reboul, author of a book *Les Assurances sur la vie* written in 1863, for whom insurance is "the compensation for the play of chance by the mutual principle organized according to the laws of statistics" (Ewald 1986, 176). Like us, Ewald gives a central place to statistics to explain the transition from a liberal state to a more interventionist one, because for him it is statistics that enables the organization of mutual insurance so characteristic of the welfare state. Because surveys appeared more or less at the same time as unemployment insurance, the linkages between them are very strong.

However, when we go into greater depth, we cannot really say that surveys served to establish social insurance. First, the law on unemployment insurance was passed in the summer of 1935, and we have seen that on this date sampling theory and techniques were still in a state of flux. In fact, if we examine the history of the Social Security Act in detail, we realize that the sampling experts we have encountered until now only played a marginal role in its development. If Corrington Gill, Hopkins's deputy at the CWA, Howard Tolley of the Bureau of Agricultural Economics (BAE), and Winfield Riefler of the CSB intervened in the debate, they also dropped out very soon (Witte 1936).

In reality, it is other statisticians who played a major role. Substantially all the statistical sources that served to constitute a social insurance plan were taken from the administrative records at hand: "These studies were not directed primarily toward the collection of new information, but toward the summation and evaluation of the vast amount of data available in all of these fields." (Witte 1936, 161) Once the initial surveys were completed, the service used regular administrative data:

> With minor exceptions, the statistical materials of the new program will be secured automatically from the routine administrative records which will be kept incident to the collection of contributions and taxes, the registration of eligibles, the payment of benefits and other phases of administration. (Givens 1935)

Unemployment insurance was thus introduced simply on the strength of administrative data—in other words, it ignored the exact level of unemployment as well as its different features. Although it may seem surprising that unemployment insurance could have been introduced without clarity on the phenomenon itself, the paradox is explained when we realize that it was implemented on the basis of data used by actuaries,[26] whose skills were very different from those of the enumerators, more suitable for calculating premiums and deductions. In fact, actuaries had been long since working on administrative data, the limitations and advantages of which they were fully aware of. That is to say that the system was not based on just any statistics, as

Ewald would have us believe in his chapter on Quételet (averages are to be found everywhere in statistics), but on very specific actuarial skills.

But if the surveys did not have any direct connection with the creation of this New Deal symbol that unemployment insurance constitutes, what purpose did they serve?

To answer this question, we have to turn to two other major government measures pertaining to the New Deal: relief and public employment policies. We have seen that these measures were initiated as early as 1933 (and even earlier in the case of relief), so the surveys were therefore not a necessary condition.[27] On the other hand, from 1940, when they became standard practice, surveys helped the government to decide where, when, and what kinds of public employment and relief measures should be developed and how to make them much more effective. Gill severely criticized the data taken from the administrative records on unemployment and in 1939 wrote:

> Now that I have urged extreme caution in the use of unemployment statistics, I may add that I am heartily in favor of taking periodic censuses of the unemployed.... In order to plan for re-employment and to frame our relief policies intelligently we should know whether a substantial group of the jobless are older workers, whether young workers with very little experience are an important element, and whether women are in need of jobs. (Gill 1939, 109)[28]

The categories mentioned by Gill here, which he learned about from the surveys, are situated at the periphery of the working population or "employable" persons. The first problem faced by people managing relief jobs was to outline the characteristics of the target population. Now Myers, the director of research at the WPA, again with the help of a survey, showed in 1941 that this population evolved at a very rapid pace: "They demonstrate that the supply of labor, far from being fixed, in fact fluctuates sharply during short periods of time" (Myers 1941, 179). Why? The causes are diverse, but once again they are accessible through surveys:

> It is clear that one important cause is the closing of schools during the summer months, resulting in both permanent and temporary additions to the labor supply. Other shifts are caused by illness or accident, desire for retirement, changes in family income or family responsibilities, desire for further education, and so on. The decision of many persons to enter or leave the labor force probably is based largely on their judgments as to their market prospects—their chances of getting a job or of reemployment once a job has been lost, and the wages they may expect to receive. Some of these causes are pretty clearly seasonal in nature, others are probably related to cyclical fluctuations in economic activity, and some appear to be irregular in their influence. (Myers 1941, 183)

The characteristics of the working population changed constantly, depending on the *conditions* in which the workers found themselves and the *behavior* that these conditions occasioned. The surveys helped to rapidly measure these variations and identify their causes.

Thus, the induction of surveys in the administration—more specifically, the development of random sampling techniques—completely modified the role of statistics and of statisticians in governmental action. During the liberal phase, it chiefly consisted of making people's voluntary efforts visible—which is why people were invited to contribute to the production of data, even during the technical phases. After the war, the situation changed completely. The population was frozen in the sampling bases, from which masses of data on the relations between variables was extracted, which provided the government with a lever for action: it could act on a particular variable that constituted a problem (for example, unemployment), and then identify another that was easier to manage (for example, the school timetable), which would affect the former.

Charles Wright Mills, whose work we will discuss in a moment, showed about ten years after the war that this new type of action was based on the idea that surveys enabled the *prediction* and *control* of the masses (Mills 1959). Indeed, by having such an enormous amount of data and social correlations so easily at one's disposal, the government could hope to predict people's behavior (i.e., knowing that a variable B depended on a variable A, if it knew how A behaved, it could deduce B's evolution) and, consequently, think that it could control B, to the extent that it was able to act on A. Thus, with the chains of causation at the government's disposal, which were similar to the laws of nature but applied to the masses, it could actually perceive itself as a "human engineer," an idea evoked in the late 1930s (Davis 1937), manipulating people like engineers manipulate natural objects.

Therefore, the emergence of the welfare state does not merely amount to setting up different insurance systems, as it has been at times claimed; rather it refers to the vast transformation of government action into social engineering, thus replacing the old liberal participationism. The Great Depression had forced the government to realize that people, if left to themselves, even within a framework optimized by the state, could create a dangerous situation that could lead to national disintegration. The surveys had shown that it was materially possible for the government to turn to social engineering and repair the damages incurred by society as revealed by the surveys, in the same way that engineers learned through the natural sciences to repair the damage to roads and bridges. To translate this idea into contemporary terms, the focus had shifted from *empowerment* concerns to technocratic expertise on the population with statistics as the plotter.

Obviously, this new conception of governance resulted in a radical transformation in politics to the extent that many wondered if democracy itself was not being questioned.

The Question of Democracy

The reconfigurations of the role of statisticians in the government and the types of actions undertaken as a result were not without effect on the place occupied by the people in the functioning of American democracy. To understand this, we are going to refer to the work of Charles Wright Mills, a sociologist who is not much read today despite his success in the 1950s, but whose work interests us for two related reasons. The first is that he is easily the last of the pragmatist sociologists, before the revival of this current in the 1980s (Gross 2007). In fact, Mills was very largely influenced by William James and John Dewey, so much so that he wrote a book, published posthumously, on the sociology of the pragmatist current in philosophy (Mills 1964), and throughout his career retained a democratic imperative inherited from this current—which he also combined with a neo-Marxism of his own (Horowitz 1964). The second reason is that one of his recurring questions, stemming precisely from pragmatism, was on the political consequences of the utilization of the social sciences. As we noted previously, he had deliberated on the relationship between the proponents of "abstract empiricism" (in other words surveys) and the government (Mills 1959). Even if the question of the effects of surveys on the people is not explicitly asked by Mills, the interpretative grid that he developed can still be useful to us.

His description of the transition from the America of the 1930s, which he characterized as being a "community of publics," to the postwar era, which he defined as a "mass society," in fact corresponds to the history of the people captured by the surveys as a tool of government. Thus, Mills provides us with a guideline and a vocabulary to describe the American population as it was described by the surveys.

According to him, until the war, American democracy was founded on a "community of publics" within which each individual was part of a series of intermediary groups small enough to foster a sense of belonging and where each individual could see the effect of his own decisions and actions (Mills 1956). Mills describes these publics in a manner which Dewey himself would not have disowned: "The people are presented with problems. They discuss them. They decide on them. They formulate viewpoints. These viewpoints are organized, and they compete. One viewpoint 'wins out.' Then the people act out this view, or their representatives are instructed to act it out, and this they promptly do" (Mills 1956, 306). One essential characteristic of these publics was that each individual acted voluntarily and could personally see that he influenced the course of things and participated in the production of a winning "point of view."

As we have seen, initially statistics was linked to a public so conceived—the voluntary participation of individuals and the product of their own actions. The very name "voluntary crop reporters" suggested that it involved a method based on the association of autonomous wills. The "straw votes," scoffed at today because they failed the test of the 1936 elections, were nothing more than voluntary declarations, the beginnings of the constitution of a public, which was supposed to be reenergized by the politicians; the statistical public works programs were first, at least in Hopkins's mind, the voluntary mobilization by the victims of the crisis of all the means available to them to combat its effects. As for the planners from the Department of Agriculture, they wanted the survey results to be given to the local associations so that farmers could use them. All these examples show that until the war, surveys were a tool associated with policies for publics. Their *technical* characteristics (the role of the informants, selection of enumerators, status of users) participated in the creation or the consolidation of publics in the sense given to it by Mills and Dewey.

However, according to Mills, the 1930s and 1940s witnessed the transformation of the community of publics, which had become increasingly phantomatic (he writes citing Walter Lippmann), into a democracy or "mass" society (Mills 1956, 305). The appearance of a mass society is a correlative to a new "power elite"—made up of members of the armed forces, politicians (less and less), and captains of industry—that has the power, rarely in so concentrated a form as until now, to control the variations in the population. The mass is the form taken by the people in this power configuration. Mills did not conceive population either from an antifascist denunciatory perspective, as a group easy to deceive and manipulate through propaganda, or from an aristocratic perspective, often associated with aesthetic theory and the Frankfurt school, as a new form of kitsch vulgarity emanating from the industrialization of art (Hayden 2006).

Two features characterize the mass, which is the converse of the public and which Mills sometimes calls the "public of public opinion" (to denigrate the public brought into being by opinion polls). First, as part of the mass, the individual finds it increasingly difficult to effectively respond to the opinions emitted by the government in a way that bears results. Second, "the formation of opinion to its realization in social action" has become more and more difficult; it is increasingly rare that the opinions that the individual shapes are followed by material, concrete effects, which he can observe himself (Mills 1956, 310). As a part of the mass, the individual has mainly become a "receiver" of actions and of opinions, and no longer their source, as when he was part of the public. This is the big difference: as part of the mass, the individual is "exposed," "passive," "manipulated" by the powers that be and can only react in a significant manner with difficulty.

According to Mills (1956, chap. 13, "The Mass Society"), this transition from the community of publics to the masses is explained through structural evolutions. Most important, for him the "growth of metropolises" results in the segregation of individuals in restricted environments (e.g., an individual is part of a neighborhood, a block), and it is extremely difficult to extract oneself from it, which however is necessary for individuals to get an overview of the processes at work in the city and so participate actively in their transformation. Second, he identifies the "decline of the voluntary association as a genuine instrument of the public." These associations, like churches and trade unions, which were previously the form taken by the public, became huge. Elites then emerged in their midst who took over the decision-making process, especially the important decisions, so that ordinary members lost both their sense of belonging—the bigger the group (i.e., constituted of strangers), the more difficult it is to have a sense of belonging—and above all the capacity to influence the fate of the group.

If Mills does not mention surveys among the other factors of the massification of the society that he describes, we feel that they played a major role in this process. This remains to be specified.

Some people, including Sarah Igo (2007), have defended the idea that surveys played a part in "fabricating" a mass society by producing the *Averaged American*. Igo's reasoning, which she partially borrows from Olivier Zunz (1998), does not in reality pertain to government surveys but mainly opinion polls, as well as the survey on sexuality conducted by Professor Alfred Kinsey, which was published after the war. In particular, Igo demonstrates the extent to which American society was affected by surveys—so much so that they took to bombarding survey producers with letters, in which, she remarks, their principal demand was to participate. Most of these letters came from people who had not been interviewed and felt that they should have been, or who had been interviewed and wanted to continue the dialogue.

But according to Igo, the results of these statistical surveys were all descriptions of the average American, for, she argues, statistics always works on the basis of averages. The surveyors seem to have devoted all their efforts to averaging the population, coming out with discourses on the majority that equate it with "America," and if it was not the surveyors, then it was journalists who distorted the statistical discourse and simplified it further (Igo 2007, 142). Because these surveys met with great success, the averages that they presented to the population as being the equivalent of America "reconstructed the space of possibilities for personhood," she writes while citing the works of Ian Hacking (1986); they limited the type of individual that each and every one could conceive of becoming. According to her, surveys delimited all the various ways of "being" American so that everyone ended by resembling one another and the population became a "mass" of averages.

Still it seems to us that this interpretation of the survey method is limited. We consider Igo an ally, in particular designating the appearance of mass society as the outcome of the evolution of surveys, but we differ from the route she has taken.

First, the surveys did not influence Americans in just their way of "thinking" of themselves, but also materially. For example, they participated in the redistribution of wages, in redefining the areas of state intervention, in the grouping of categories benefiting from government aid. In short, the surveys resulted in tangibly redistributing public action.

Second, it seems to us that one should not mix up the "sample bases" on which surveys depend and the averages that they help to calculate. The surveyors developed the famous bases to identify a series of identical units over the entire territory: sampling units in the case of the Master Sample, postal routes for the enumerative check, and enumeration districts for the census survey. But these bases, these vast homogenous grids, served precisely to highlight not the averages but the differences, the contrasts, the variations in the population. The earlier agricultural surveys of the 1920s helped to estimate the total crop yield to enable a comparison of the different production zones (we recall that the Board's estimation sheets were based on large geographical areas). Similarly, the surveys realized on the basis of the Master Sample helped to distinguish, for example, the abandoned farms from the productive farms. For their part, the employment surveys strived to differentiate the unemployed from the non-unemployed. Finally, in politics, the sole aim of pre-electoral polls was to distinguish and compare the political forces to find out who would win and not to ascertain the so-called average opinion. In short, the surveys effectively developed homogenous forms covering the entire territory, but they had nothing do with an average: these forms were units, quite small and extremely concrete, that are replicated over the entire territory (hence it is difficult to identify them) and that help to highlight the contrasts between the various subpopulations. The problem of the government was to refine its actions, not to act in an indistinct manner.

Far removed from the averages, it seems to us that the amazing feat realized by the surveys was to a large extent the induction of random sampling in the place previously occupied by voluntary associations in the community of publics. As we have seen, until the 1930s, statistics was only one among other such kinds of associations: the public just as easily congregated around trade unions or churches as around statistical projects to make itself heard. After the war, with the emergence of new sampling techniques, statisticians simply short-circuited these associations (to take a critical stand) and replaced them (to say it in a more positive tone) with tools compatible with this mass society described by Mills.

In a "mass society," the power elites exert an influence on the population. But what about the reverse movement, from the masses to the elite? Mills is not interested in this and has us believe that it has simply disappeared, as if the people had become mere "objects of manipulation," as he writes elsewhere while citing Marx. And yet the proliferation of surveys, which Mills highlights in *The Sociological Imagination*, clearly demonstrates that bottom-up movements—from the public to the leaders—did not simply vanish (Mills 1959).

Surveys first served to provide information regarding the population to the government: in this case, the changes affecting the population, whether involving variations in the conditions of agricultural production, the unemployment rate cycles, or schools of thought. On the condition that it not influence the course of things in any way, the sample selected testified to these changes. The sample was purely (as purely as possible) epistemic: it merely responded to the questions asked, without trying to change anything. It is precisely this characteristic—the absence of all volition—that made the masses and sampling compatible, especially random sampling. As Mills (1956, 312) says, it was a question of recording "public opinion as a mere reaction—we cannot say 'response.'" The participation of the population was thus not nil, but it was henceforth limited to reacting to government stimuli. Thanks to the sample, the canvassers could describe phenomena and identify the levers for the government to act on. The population, as a mass, was consequently conceived merely as an object following natural laws and government action; it no longer needed to be the source of this action.

At the same time, if the government was informed of popular movements, the population had to remain as immobile as possible from the moment it was observed up to the moment when the action took place so that the information did not become stale. Concretely, this precaution took the form of a new economics of secrecy.

Of course, once there is a public sphere, there is secrecy (Didier 2005). We have seen ever since the Crop Reporters' method, confidentiality had been concretely implemented by means of curtains, lockers, and secret codes, which made access to information more equitable. But after the war, the recourse to secrecy changed matters completely. We can date this turning point to 1937, when the experiment to count the unemployed was carried out. For the first time, the statisticians—including Dedrick and Frederick Mosteller, among others—hid the fact that they were conducting a survey from the people so that it would not affect their behavior.

This new confidentiality factor exercised a deep influence on the American imaginary, which is illustrated in Robert Riskin's 1947 film *Magic Town* starring James Stewart. He tells the story of a pollster discovering a village in the Midwest perfectly representative of the United States. His first reflex is to impose total secrecy on his two collaborators. Thanks to the secret complicity of the village schoolmaster, who is an old comrade-in-arms (this point by itself merits a complete analysis), the pollster goes about the surveys very discreetly. Why this secrecy? For, he insists, if the village knew that it was representative, it would completely change its behavior and would cease to be representative. And as a result, once the secret is out, the village is radically transformed.

Four years later, in 1951, Isaac Asimov published the first volume of his series *Foundation*, of which the first part is a meditation on the power of statistics to predict human behavior—which the "psycho-historians" feel is perfectly possible. Now, the express condition of this power is to keep the results secret. Failing which, human beings would react to the predictions and distort them.

The secret thus also contributed in making the masses passive, as under pressure from the government and the natural forces, they were prevented from reacting to the information provided by statistics. Of course, this massification of the population put off some souls who, like Mills, expressed doubts about the democratic character of this mode of government:

> To act in the as-if-I-were-a-human-engineer manner might be merely amusing in which human reason were widely and democratically installed, but the United States is not such a society. Whatever else it is, surely this is evident: it is a society in which functionally rational bureaucracies are increasingly used in human affairs and in history making decisions. … Ours seems to be a period in which key decisions or their lack by bureaucratically instituted elites are increasingly sources of historical change. (Mills 1959, 122)

On the other hand, a Lippmann, for example, one of the most complex figures of this period, or even a Dewey, who on this point concurs with him, considered that leaving it to the administration to settle everyday problems encountered by the people was perfectly consistent with the normal functioning of a democracy (Marres 2005). For them, an administration that acted for the people, in the place of the people, remained within the bounds of democracy. The public only voiced its opinion in exceptional circumstances, when the technicians in the administration were overwhelmed by a new problem that they had to deal with, which, we may add, did not happen very often after the war, specifically because of the surveys. With this new statistical technique, the issue of the relationship between social expertise and democratic government was set aside for many years.

Conclusion: Random Sampling as Democratic Expertise

At the end of the 1940s, statisticians specializing in urban problems had finally managed to impose the use of random sampling in the administration. The method not only transformed survey techniques, but also their uses. Over and above this, it transformed the relationship of the government with the people.

Whereas in the past, the government relied on public participation, including in statistics, which we have qualified as pragmatist with reference to Dewey's conception of democracy, it now placed its hopes in the hands of expert statisticians who observed society like an object. If the sole aim was to act for the good of the people, it was nevertheless a very different conception of democracy (Rosanvallon 2011, 1998).

Now, it seems to us that the crux of this change is to be found in the *random selection of the sample*. In addition to the fact that henceforth statisticians resorted to esoteric knowledge—in this case the theory of probability for calculating intervals of confidence—that legitimized the exclusivity of their expertise, they also replaced people's participation with randomness. By accelerating the pace of data production, this method also established a much more direct and immediate relationship between the statisticians and political leaders, which is illustrated by the development of mimeographed reports. Inversely, the links that the statisticians had with the public weakened: not only did they not turn to the will of people for gathering data, but they also hid from the public the fact that they were conducting the survey so that the results would not be affected. Thus, government action was from now on guided by the social sciences based on facts that could rightly be termed "neutral," in the sense that they were factual and free from all contamination by public opinion.

We have here a new example of this oft-highlighted mechanism (Gigerenzer et al. 1989), wherein statistical objectivity is not a way of forgetting politics, of distancing oneself from partisan arguments, of letting nature eventually settle disputes between human beings. On the contrary, each method of producing objectivity brings with it a certain manner, in opposition to others, of bringing together the population, the government, and the means of knowledge—an operation that constitutes a political ideal (Daston 1992).

Some feel that the objectification of the public sphere was responsible for the disappearance of the pragmatic spirit, which had until now prevailed in American politics. In support of this thesis, they emphasize the decline of this philosophical current after the war (Gross 2007). But on the contrary it seems to us, as Edward A. Purcell puts it, that "pragmatism blended into the broader naturalism that dominated American thought" (Purcell 1973, 273). Pragmatism had not disappeared, but on the contrary, another of its dimensions had prevailed over its participationism: its belief in science as a practice requiring "more labor to acquire the ability to use and understand it than to get skill in any other instrumentalities possessed by man" (Dewey 1991, 163). In other words, the egalitarianism favored by the pragmatists had not withstood the expertise that their conception of science required.

Conclusion to Part III

Series and Consistency

After having explored a second approach—the urban one—to the development of sample surveys, it is now possible, by comparing and contrasting it with the agricultural one, to highlight the specific contribution of sample surveys to the consistency of America.

Statistics in general, from census surveys to random sampling, captures certain types of elements that contribute to the consistency of social aggregates (i.e., series). Over and above individual differences, distinctiveness, and local specificities, statisticians seek to identify the similarities, repetitions, and regularities that cross the space that they are studying at a particular moment in the history of statistics. We have seen, for example, a great number of *lists* that were used in statistics and as many simple checkboxes provided in questionnaires for filling by respondents, areas indicated on maps, and photographs.

As Gabriel Tarde had pointed out at the end of the nineteenth century, we can only enumerate something that has been serialized: "Quantity in reality is the possibility of infinite series of similarities and infinitely small repetitions" (Tarde 1999, 57). For statistical enumeration to be feasible, similarities in the population, where this tool is used, should necessarily be constituted into series. The specific contribution of statistics to an aggregate not only refers to the numbers that it produces, which can come from a source other than statistics, it also and above all consists of identifying and capturing series that are repeated in an aggregate to measure their evolution.

But series can be so different that a single method cannot capture them all. The old census survey enabled us to input demographic series varying very slowly, but to comprehend these new, pervasive, and rapid repetitions, such as unemployed or impoverished individuals, a novel and special method—that of sample surveys—was needed.

This method was not devised by statisticians using a linear and predetermined approach. Quite the contrary. We have thus been able to observe differences between bureaus specializing in urban problems and those specializing in rural problems. These differences can be summed up by the contrast between the environment of the rural statisticians, characterized by the Midwest and the universities of Iowa, Wisconsin, and Michigan, and the environment of the urban statisticians, situated in New England and, in prospect, in England, where Arthur Bowley and the London School of Economics were to be found (Gilbert 2000). This shows the importance of the globalism of the thinking on employment already vouched for (Topalov 1994). These differences moreover allowed urban specialists to achieve their aim more quickly and become the most innovative domain in statistics by developing random sampling.

In this task, the statisticians we have studied had a trump card identified by Tarde, which helps us to understand why sample surveys became popular in the United States and not elsewhere: the colossal size of the country. Indeed, Tarde remarks that "statistics develop more easily when States are big," for the larger the state, the easier it is for the series to present "as a voluminous mass and capture the minds of statisticians with greater clarity" (Tarde 1999, 57). In other words, the number of unemployed and impoverished and bankrupt farmers was so obvious in the United States that the initial enumeration took off as if on its own.[1]

This point is also an explication why the earlier statistics assumed a form that we have qualified as participationist. Everyone felt the need to count the victims of the crisis and did not foresee any major difficulty in carrying out the task, to the extent that it seemed natural to allow them to count themselves.

This phase of the first enumerations, the first series, was very important and made it possible to take stock of the scale of the phenomenon. In 1933, after Corrington Gill and the Federal Emergency Relief Administration (FERA)—whose employees were no great specialists of statistics—completed a survey at top speed and announced that 3 million families received government assistance, it triggered real awareness of the magnitude of the problem needing a solution (Gill 1934).

As and when it became necessary for counting to become more accurate, this participationism was undermined by the technical nature of the tools of measurement, the professionalization of the interviewers, and the different relationship that now existed with the users of the data, who henceforth were limited to government executives. This is an instance of the officialization of statisticians (Dewey 1991). At the same time, by becoming random, surveys contributed to the massification of the population, for the specific series that they tried to capture to pull the country out of the slump—mass unemployment, mass poverty, mass consumerism, mass democracy—could only take place in a population that was stable, immobile, objectified, and purged of any collective will.

Grand Conclusion

What America Consists Of

The usual practice is to differentiate between warm-hearted, compassionate, and lyrical individuals, epitomized in the period that we are concerned with by the duo of James Agee, the novelist, and Walker Evans, the photographer, who went to the remotest corners of Alabama to depict the lives of the sharecroppers and expose the debilitating conditions the Depression had reduced them to (Agee and Evans 1969), and cold-hearted, rational, and classificationist individuals, sitting in the capital's icy buildings, measuring a disembodied social reality through the yardstick of abstract figures. But at the end of our American saga, is this what we have seen? Were the cold hearts really cold? It seems to us that we have said no at least a hundred times. Statisticians were not using the same tools as Agee and Evans (although they too used photographs), but they were not indifferent to the lot of the people they were studying, whose humanity they fully appreciated.

Throughout this book we have tried to show the part played by the men and women behind the numbers, the equations, and the methods to which the history of statistics is often limited. While putting a face to them, describing their trajectories, underscoring their personal innovations, and highlighting the circumstances of their discoveries, we have tried to avoid getting caught in a causal analysis of social change in which the actors are made to act in a manner predetermined by history.

If statistics eventually came to embody this very causal and determinist model from about the 1960s, we have seen that it was not always so (Abbott 2001). Until the 1930s, the purpose of statistics was not to bring to light the mechanisms through which society was organized and its members subjected to the effects without being able to do anything about it, but on the contrary to mobilize the population to combat these effects: the ruined farmers took the statistics that the planners were offering to try and once again make a living, the unemployed undertook surveys themselves to participate in the creation of new jobs, and the impoverished made use of them to recover their dignity. Statistics was not, as is generally the case today, a tool for identifying the causes; on the contrary, it was a vehicle for mobilization through which the people could eventually transform the world.

Over and above the sociology of statistical practices, we have tried in this book to highlight the links between a population, the instruments of reflexivity, and a mode of political action in order to show how their articulation brought consistency to a nation at a particular period of its history.

Representation and Reflexivity

In a democracy, people's representation cannot be limited to voting and to parliaments; other forms of representation should be appended to them. Pierre Rosanvallon (1998) gives a broad outline of the subject, including the function that unions and political parties fulfill in this regard. We have detailed here the role of the cognitive representation of the population, ensured by a social science in the service of the government.

This method of representation is just as important as the others. The most compelling proof is not only the universal development of statistical surveys in the administration of President Franklin D. Roosevelt, as we have just studied, but even more specifically, the appeal made by politicians to statisticians. Government members (for example, Henry Wallace's staff in the Department of Agriculture) and representatives (such as Senator Robert Wagner) asked for data on the population, specifically statistical, in order to govern better.

One of the flaws in the theoretical reflection on *State-Building* of a certain Francis Fukuyama—that is, on the most effective way to rebuild a state after the failure of decolonization or after its defeat by an external power (an issue central to the United States today)—is that he did not take into account the problems of cognitive reflexivity that face a country in the process of reconstruction (Fukuyama 2004). According to Fukuyama, there is no universal theory of the state, for the state must adapt to its context, and foreign reconstructors (in this instance American) should not impose institutional forms on the conquered countries but leave the natives to rebuild themselves, for they alone are familiar with the local context to which their country must adapt. Now we have just seen all along in this book that the America of the Great Depression, when its structures were especially weak, *did not know itself*. The administrators in the Department of Agriculture never stopped demanding statistics or complaining that they were not good; Senator Wagner asked for funds to measure the scale of unemployment even before Roosevelt's election; and all the federal relief agencies under Commerce Secretary Harry Hopkins in 1933 also asked for numbers. In other words, although all were Americans born and bred, they still *lacked* knowledge of their country. America *itself* did not stop asking what it was, and it had to strive hard to rediscover itself once it emerged from the Depression.

The fact of being a native in no way confers immediate knowledge of the context (no more today than it did yesterday) that can be used by the government. To rebuild a deliquescent democracy (whether because of an economic crisis or because the country was destroyed by war), democracy has to be equipped with the tools of reflexivity that can facilitate knowledge of society, which indigenous as well as nonindigenous people desperately lack. Statistics has historically constituted a special means of generating information for all democracies: that is why one of the first measures taken by the French government after the Second World War was to create a national institute of statistics (the INSEE) in 1946. It remains for us to understand the specific relationship that statistics has with the government.

Statistical Chains

If, during the period that we have studied, the executive branch of government always resorted to such data, it did not use it to enforce the same policies before and after the crisis. On the contrary, we would be more inclined to radically compare the liberalism that preceded the crash to the interventionism that followed.

Before the crisis, statistics was used by the government to stabilize markets (especially the agricultural products and labor markets) by correcting the information asymmetry between the different stakeholders. After the crisis, it served to guide state intervention in the public works and social welfare sectors.

Did statistical methods also undergo drastic change? Initially, they depended on the voluntary Crop Reporters' method—whose title insists on the active participation that was expected of the individuals conducting the surveys. At the end of the 1940s, statistics followed the random sampling method—from active involvement in the survey earlier, the population, an anonymous mass, now became a simple object of study.

If methods have evolved along with the policies, the characteristics of the population whose data was input have also been modified. Whereas the first series depended on political divisions (counties and communes) and quantified agricultural outputs or strikes, the second series was constructed on the basis of sampling units that enabled the quantification of completely different series, such as rural exodus, unemployment, and social despair. Each method collected facts, but not exactly the same; the new method served to capture those that were missed out by the earlier one.

In other words, the swing from political liberalism to state interventionism occurred with the rupture of the initial chain as constituted by three elements, *Jeffersonian liberal citizen* → *Voluntary crop reporters* → *Market cleansing*, and the formation of a new chain: *Mass society* → *Random sampling*

→ *Public works and social welfare*. This shift corresponds perfectly to the general model described by Alain Desrosières, according to which statistical methods are part of the following chain: *Characteristics of society → Statistical method → Mode of political action* (Desrosières 1998).

For each policy option there are specific tools of reflexivity for recording certain characteristics of society necessary for action. To govern is to act on certain realities, and statistics makes it possible to capture them in the form of series. To implement a policy of interventionism, one has to know certain specific series pertaining to population and ignore others, and some statistical techniques are best able to capture them. Thus, as long as the government's objective was to combat market asymmetries, it was important to mobilize the stakeholders around statistics so that they could make use of them, and the best method was to effectively establish lists of voluntary crop reporters. To pursue an unemployment control policy, one had to know and manipulate very varied elements, and statisticians demonstrated that random sampling was the most reliable method for this task. There is thus congruence between the political actions proposed, cognitive methods, and relevant characteristics of society.

Statistics has a "mirror" function, as Rosanvallon (1998, 390) insists on, for which "the multiple forms taken by the deciphering of society, accompanies, extends and corrects the search for figuration which is at work in the process of political representation." But they are not reduced to a general, abstract function as he means it when classifying statistics among "not political means of representation." On the contrary, statistics take concrete forms (called methods), each more or less compatible with a particular type of policy to capture the relevant social aspects of a specific action.

The fact that statistics is linked to politics in no way signifies that its scientific nature has been polluted, distorted, and skewed by partisan interests, as several critics have affirmed. On the contrary, statistics hold great interest for politicians who can draw on their results for their own use. An incorrect statistic would only be good, at best, for misleading the public, but this was not what the American government had in mind, for it needed reliable data to serve as a source of action and policy formulation. It is the paradox of this history: *statistics is all the more political as it produces indisputable facts*. The sociology of statistics is thus not the study of the ways in which scientists distort the rules of their discipline toward a more or less legitimate end; the sociology of statistics means understanding how statistics and politics come together to create a society.

Today, it would be easy to show that benchmarking methods, which have been imported to government and public administrations from the corporate world and developed in Europe as spelled out in the Lisbon Strategy, help to make a new chain. By seeking to establish performance indicators for states, social systems, and economic models so that each country aligns itself with the highest ranked, these methods subscribe to a generalized competition logic, radically foreign to the measures adopted in the 1940s and 1950s. As a result, the characteristics that contemporary statisticians attempt to capture, in response to the political demand for competitiveness of the modes of governance, are very different from those that the pollsters of the New Deal sought at the time to quantify (Bruno and Didier 2013).

All the same, a thorough analysis of the present financial crisis could highlight the necessity of constructing new series about the prices of innovations such as financial options and the risk undergone by investors, which public statistics has difficulty capturing—in much the same way as was done in the 1930s by the American Bureau of Labor Statistics during the Great Depression.

But if building a society, developing a statistical method, and defining a policy are not independent processes, can we then say that they are linked to each other in the same way as cause and effect are related? And if it is so, what is the significance of this causality? Our analysis of the situation before and after the 1929 crisis makes us consider things from a completely different angle.

From One Chain to Another

To understand the transition from one chain to another, we started from the chain seen in the United States in 1920. The chain was so solid that it was difficult to distinguish the characteristics of the population, the statistical method (the voluntary Crop Reporters' method), and the government policy that composed it. This chain suddenly broke under the impact of the Great Crash of 1929, which at the same time, as it plunged the nation into an economic slump, made the liberal policy enforced till then ineffective and rendered the tools of analysis guiding action obsolete as well.

To tackle this situation, statisticians and politicians initially worked separately, more or less independently of each other. The Roosevelt government launched the New Deal without waiting to perfect sample survey techniques, and statisticians began their work on random sampling without guidelines from the executive. Relations nevertheless were soon established between them, thanks to which statistics and political action gradually came to fall into step and mutually transform each other.

The transition from one chain to another did not take place at the instigation of either of these groups—politics is no more the cause of the reinvention of sampling by statisticians than sampling is the basis of interventionist policies. To avoid these two determinisms while conserving the idea of mutual articulation, we have described this process as a new consistency. Politics and statistics have together redeveloped consistency and, through it, the players have managed to reorganize a society that was in complete meltdown.

This way of describing things allows us, moreover, to avoid another alternative: the one that sets radical constructivism, according to which sample surveys create their reality from nothing, against absolute realism, which tends to disregard the fact that statistics is not limited to entering data but produces important social effects.

Other authors—Rosanvallon, in particular—also resort to similar vocabulary that we can compare to ours. Without, unfortunately, going into detailed explanations of his use of these terms, we note that he writes, for example, that "it is all the more necessary [for the modern world] … to institute people as an artificial judicial person as the latter no longer has its own consistency." Or, that we need to seek to "give form to society and consistency to the power of the collectivity over itself." Or, that in the recent past, we have witnessed a "liquefaction of the representations of the future," or yet again that France has become "soft" (Rosanvallon 1998, 19, 137, and 425).

Throughout this book we have on our part defined a set of concepts that we can now recapitulate in the form of a glossary—in which terms are not presented alphabetically but, as in a movie cast, by order of apparition—to synthesize the theory of consistency (Didier 2012).

Glossary of Consistency

Plasma: The plasma is a fiction referring to the beginnings of statistical activity. It is the set of elements available to statisticians when they embark on their work and that they are likely to use to capture the characteristics of the population.

Consolidation: Consolidation is an act aimed at ensuring the regular production, in time and space, of a given series of steps when capturing an aggregate. In a counterintuitive manner, it is done by inserting an additional step between two already defined ones. It is also the consequence of this act; that is to say, the capacity of an aggregate to resist the shock triggered by an unexpected event or new circumstances. The solidity of an aggregate is the result of the consolidation process.

Deliquescence: Deliquescence is the opposite of consolidation. It results from the loss of predictability of the coordination of earlier sequences.

Fragilization: Fragilization is the weakening of the links between the aggregate and one of its earlier components, which might result in the exclusion of this one or several other components and increase the risk of rupture of the whole. It applies both to the solid as well as the deliquescent aggregates.

Expression: Expression is the process by which something new is produced. Two elements initially distinct are brought together and articulated with each other, and this articulation produces new properties belonging to each of the associated elements.

Capture: Capture is an expression considered from the specific perspective of the aggregate with which is articulated an additional element.

Series: Series are elements specifically captured in the plasma by statistics to consolidate the aggregates. They contain analogous elements that are repeated and can be counted; all these elements have a specific characteristic in common such that a series can be distinguished from another series.

Consistency: The consistency of an aggregate is the combined product of a set of elements that it has captured and the degree of solidity (or deliquescence) of the links that hold them together.

Weak Links as Extension

Zooming in on these three components of America—namely, population, statistics, and government—we have witnessed the appearance of a very large number of other elements: the Constitution, urbanism, automobiles, the press, federalism, the myth of the frontier, political and philosophical conceptions, values, traditions, a way of life, an economic system, and a multitude of other features.

However, America undeniably encompasses many other things and it might seem illusory to attempt an exhaustive description of what it consists of. America would, moreover, have appeared differently to us if we had looked at it through the eyes of writers such as Agee, Hemingway, or Dos Passos and not those of a statistician. What importance should we give those features that do not appear here but that also constitute America?

John Dos Passos, whose words we used in this book's introduction, also deployed infinite energy to understand what his country was all about, before setting down his reflections in a novel spread over more than a thousand pages, titled *U.S.A.*, published in 1938. We can well imagine that this America too, even though it was produced by a single man, had a very solid consistency, but it was literary, textual, containing narratives, press cuttings, scenes captured by a "camera-eye," and deep melancholy and mostly rugged spaces (Dos Passos 2002).

Dos Passos continued this interrogation in another of his novels, *The Great Design*, published in 1949, on the New Deal administration, and in which statistics also plays a role. We come across Paul Graves, a character who leaves his home state to work in the federal Department of Agriculture. When for the first time he turns to Miss Washburn, his new secretary, he says to her while continuing with his work:

> I want some figures ... I suppose you know your way round this place ... I don't ... Farm tenancy ... any significant figures ... every ten years back to 1836 or thereabouts. Relation of farm population to industrial population during the same century. Never mind if you can't get them for the particular decades I mention. (Dos Passos 1949, 69)

Thus, even with this other America, the literary one, supposedly indifferent to sample surveys, links can be forged. These are weak links not yet consolidated because there is barely any mention of numbers in Dos Passos' America, but it is enough to cross from the America of surveys to his, as over a flimsy bridge.

These weak links connect the various Americas that come to mind. The "America as a whole" of the surveys grabs a piece of the legal, constitutional America, which in turn grabs a piece of the postal, communicating America, which grabs the cartographic America of the geographers, and so on. All these Americas, each with its own consistency, are linked to each other through admittedly tenuous links but could, if the actors got down to the job, in their turn be consolidated and so form an aggregate with an original consistency.

Notes

Introduction

1. This study is based in particular on the analysis of the National Archives Record Group 29, Bureau of the Census; Record Group 51, Central Statistical Board; Record Group 69, Works Progress Administration; Record Group 83, Bureau of Agricultural Economics; Record Group 257, Bureau of Labor Statistics; National Archives Building, Washington, D.C.; as well as the Iowa State University Library, University Archives, Special Collections Department; Clark County Public Library, Ohio; Connecticut State Library; and the personal archives of Richard Allen, former director of the National Agricultural Statistical Service, U.S. Department of Agriculture.

2. This ternary division was mainly inspired by Alain Desrosières (2008).

3. Gabriel Tarde compared archaeology, the science of past innovations, with statistics, the science of repetitions. According to his interpretation, here we are involved in the archaeology of the science of repetitions (Tarde 1903).

Chapter 1

1. In 1933, the Division boasted about publishing 65,000 estimates and forecasts each year (USDA 1933, 12).

2. The Division as a government institution had the immense advantage of having its archives preserved in the National Archives, Record Group 83, Bureau of Agricultural Economics (hereafter cited as RG 83), National Archives Building, Washington, D.C.

3. This extract is from a 300-page, unpublished biography of a statistician from the Department of Agriculture. It was kindly made available, as was the photograph, by his descendants, Gregg Wager and his family.

4. Fabien Locher clearly shows, with regard to nineteenth-century French meteorology, that the networks operating on the basis of obligation, as in the case of schoolteachers compelled to note meteorological observations, gave very different results (Locher 2004).

5. RG 83, entry 85, "Schedules." We find in this archival entry the notebooks of the section responsible for posting the documents to the Reporters. Let us raise our hat to Miss Skinner who had to put them all inside the envelopes, for it meant a lot of work—14,000 questionnaires were sent in July 1929!

6. RG 83, entry 74, Advisory Committee on Grain Crop Reports, "Grain crop reports," unpublished article without mention of author or date.

7. RG 83, J. A. Becker, "Analysis of assumptions underlying the various indications of change in crop acreage," *Class of the Division, March 9*, Washington, D.C., 1928.

8. RG 83, entry 75, "Schedule," December 1923.

9. There were in fact two kinds of Reporters: One was in contact with the statistical head of his state and the other with the central department of the Division in Washington D.C. We will follow the longer path but will revert to the other at the appropriate moment.

10. We are using a capital "S" to separate the agricultural Statistician from all the other statisticians, practitioners of statistics in general, whom we may also encounter later.

11. In the small East Coast states, one Statistician headed several states. Since 1959, the Union has comprised 50 states with the addition of Hawaii and Alaska. In 1933, there were only 41 Statisticians.

12. RG 83, entry 36, G. D. Clarck file, "Estimating the commercial vegetable acreage in Texas," February 1, 1932.

13. RG 83, entry 36, G. D. Clarck file.

14. Ibid.

15. RG 83, "Comments on crop reports," Iowa report, March 1, 1932.

16. RG 83, entry 83, "Comments on crop reports," L. Carl's letter to W. Callander, May 27, 1932.

17. RG 83, entry 83, "Comments on crop reports," Ohio report, April 5, 1923.

18. The Peg strip was explained by Richard Allen, at the time head of the NASS. His office does not only contain rare archives but has a small museum of the most innovative objects in the history of agricultural statistics.

19. RG 83, entry 83, J. A. Becker, "Comments on crop reports," Wisconsin, October 1, 1922.

20. Unfortunately for him, it seems that in the end the research failed to show results. It had not been possible to find a formula for linking the weather to the condition.

21. Even today the Board operates practically in the same manner. Upon learning that I was working on the subject, the director of the Division said that he would make an exception and let me observe the Board at work. I made an appointment, and the guard let me in, which was a real favor. But once inside the premises, there was no way I could go out before the publication of the figures. I had to stay inside the Board's premises for a couple of hours, until the figures were released—in a way that will soon be explained.

22. RG 83, entry 74, J. A. Becker, "Production forecasts and estimates," unpublished, n.d.

23. March 4, 1909 Act. Senate Bill 2982. See USDA (1969, 52–53).

24. RG 83, entry 74, J. A. Becker, "Practical problems in crop estimating," *Weather-Crop Seminar*, Kansas State College, 7, n.d.

25. RG 83, entry 74, J. A. Becker, 7.

26. Ibid.

27. RG 83, entry 74, J. A. Becker, 1.

28. Brooks likes to talk of him in the third person.

29. It is remarkable that, in the beginning of the period that is of interest to us, the chain of construction of meteorological data rested on voluntary reporters, very much like the agricultural crop reporters (Fleming 1990).

30. RG 83, entry 74, J. A. Becker, 1.

31. RG 83, entry 74, J. A. Becker.

32. This method of deciding through consensus is reminiscent of—and I thank Lorraine Daston for pointing it out—the Congregationalist and Quaker caucuses (Walker 1893). It is another indication that politics can just as well be a resource, and not a source of contamination, of science.

33. The median is the value that separates a statistical series into two sets of equal cardinal numbers; as there were five Board members, it was thus equal to the value for which there were two members below and two above. It had the advantage over the average of never showing results that were not integers, which would have been inappropriate.

34. RG 83, entry 74, J. A. Becker, "Production forecasts and estimates." The quantities are actual yields. Is it not fascinating to learn than in July 1921 the condition was 68% in comparison to the normal?

35. I did not find proof of this in the archives, but the Board members explained that this is how they worked nowadays.

36. The United States as a whole is the very symptomatic expression used by the Board.

37. RG 83, entry 74. In practice, it seems that it was really the deputy secretary of the Department of Agriculture who signed the reports, as in the example we have given here. However, this ceremony was of crucial importance. Allow me to share an ethnographer's mistake to prove this point: When I was invited to observe the Board, I presented myself in informal dress—jeans, running shoes, and no tie. At the time of the signing of the report, the chairman, who had invited me, was forced to justify my clothes before the acting secretary, stating, "This person, who looks like a student, is indeed a student" (*laughs*).

38. RG 83, entry 74. Notes 38 and 39 come from the same entry; it was a text standing alone in the cardboard.

39. This race for data no longer takes place today—to my eternal sorrow, I must admit. At present, journalists are ushered inside the premises of the Board where terminals await them. The Board gives them its results as soon as they are ready, and the journalists type their own reports—but with no possibility to send them. When at 3 p.m. all the numbers have been determined, the terminals are reconnected to the Internet, and the journalists just have to click on the icon to *Send message*.

40. RG 83, entry 74, L. M. Estabrook; see also Estabrook 1915, 9.

41. The speculator is a person who too has a history. W. Cronon (1992) dates the emergence of speculators at around 1850. They appeared along with the *corner* technique, which could not exist without the birth in the nineteenth century of a great number of institutions. To *corner* someone is to buy grains before they are harvested (by means of a contract that stipulates the date on which the seller has to supply his buyer) and, at the same time, to buy up all grain available on the market. So that, to honor his contract, the person who has contracted to supply grains has to buy it, virtually at any price, from the one who has it.

42. This word is the translation of the French word for "intercalation," used by Dupréel (1933).

43. Our solidity can claim a link with statistical "robustness." Statistics is said to be robust if it is insensitive to outliers. For example, the median is robust because it does not change if one of the values observed is very different from the others, whereas the average, which is less robust, will change. Our solidity can thus seem like a generalization of the concept of robustness applicable to the entire chain of data collection (Didier et al. 2009).

Chapter 2

1. And yet there exists a striking counterexample showing that such studies are possible, in which two entire chapters are devoted to showing that the production of a new spirit of capitalism (which the New Deal also was) was associated with the destruction and weakening of the working world's rights during the 1980s (Boltanski and Chiapello 2005).

2. Henry Wallace's diagnosis depended on the works of "economist statisticians" Hugh Johnson and George Peek (Wallace 1945). This equality has posed numerous problems, in particular that of fixing a base period.

3. Pork and corn were merged into one "crop," for corn was used nearly exclusively to feed stock hogs. The link between the two activities was too strong to undo it.

4. Brooks (1977, 5) recalls that Wallace was subjected to very violent public opposition at the idea of slaughtering the piglets. The Secretary of Agriculture was surprised by what he considered sentimentality compared to the suffering of the farmers and mocked his adversaries in a sentence too juicy not to be quoted. Addressing his adversaries, he said, "*Every little pig has the right to attain, before slaughter, the full pigginess of his pigness*" (Wallace 1935). According to Brooks again, it was Charles S. Sarle who, when appointed to the AAA, played a key role and was successful in implementing the mass slaughter program. And, indeed, 6.2 million piglets were sacrificed in 1933 and their flesh was distributed to soup kitchens.

5. (Bourguet 1988) describes another—very different—instance of statistics produced by prefects that completely failed.

6. American planning thrusts its roots even deeper into history. In particular, as early as the 1920s, research on this subject was initiated in the National Bureau of Economic Research attached to the Commerce Department (Alchon 1985).

7. It is equally important to note that, following the Mount Weather agreement (a July 1938 agreement between the federal administration represented by Wallace and twenty five state officials representing state Extension services, aiming at establishing harmony in the intergovernmental balance), the task of the extended BAE was to also handle the relations of the Agriculture Department with the "Land Grant Colleges," a network of agricultural universities financed by the states and the federal Extension Service.

8. Some authors have insisted on the fact that if this objective was the real aim of the players, it remained at the fantasy stage, and in fact all the farmers did not participate at the time (Gross 1943) and later (Gilbert and Howe 1991).

9. Actually, this image does not fit the United States of the 1930s, and for a reason that is too comical to ignore. During the 1920s, the Agriculture Department needed more office space. The Secretary of Agriculture, Henry C. Wallace (the father of the Wallace that we are concerned with here), submitted a budget to the Congress that, as frequently happens, only granted half the funds asked for. Wallace took umbrage, and to force the Congress to give him the totality of his budget, he decided to construct only the right and left wings of the building, leaving the space intended for the main building between the two wings, empty! Congress ultimately relented, but only after the war, so that during the period that we are dealing with here, the central structure of the Department remained a vast uncultivated field. Farmers, academics, and administrators no doubt met, but in the sludge!

10. According to Kirkendall (1966, 185), M. L. Wilson wrote to Lynd about the success of his book in the Department in the following terms: "Tolley has made it mandatory to read your book in the BAE."

11. The merger of the newly renamed Division with the BAE took place in December 1941, after Wallace left the Department of Agriculture and the planners had lost a great deal of their influence.

Part II

1. Raymond Lévy-Bruhl, whom we pay homage to, was sent to the United States in 1946 by the newly created INSEE to learn about the sampling methods. Impressed by the *Master Sample*, he conducted the first survey on the living conditions in households, drawing directly from it. We have employed the term "échantillon maître" and also certain illustrations used by him here. By generously sharing his personal archives with us, he allowed us to present some features that served in the construction of the Master Sample.

Chapter 3

1. Henry C. Taylor, the author of this reference (Taylor and Taylor 1952, 176), was the founder of the Bureau of Agricultural Economics, to which the Division was immediately assigned in 1921. He was also, during the early years of the twentieth century, its tutelary figure, something like the tribe elder, guardian of the great legends. That is why we talk of "story" and could even talk of a legend.

2. It is interesting that, according to Taylor and Taylor (1952), Judd's surveys are inspired by the Prussian agricultural workers example, which, we might add, have been studied by Max Weber (Pollak 1986). Also, Martine Mespoulet (2001) has shown that agricultural crop reporters, very similar to those described in this book, can be found in many countries, especially Russia, France, and Italy, toward the end of the nineteenth century. But nowhere have we come across the mutual influence between these practices.

3. In his brilliant book *The Principles of Representative Government*, Bernard Manin (1997) shows that, during the drafting of the American Constitution, there were two opposite conceptions of democratic representation. One, the anti-federalist, held that the representative should match his electorate as much as possible (a farmer should represent a farmer), for only knowledge of the situation would ensure true representation of the general will. The federalist view, on the contrary, held that the representative had to be the best of the group being represented—that is, he had to be different, as much as possible, for only the best could best discern the general will. His demonstration ends with a description of

the Federalists' victory in the United States, where the representatives are considered as being the best of their group.

4. National Archives, Record Group 83, Bureau of Agricultural Economics (hereafter RG 83), entry 75, letter of February 5, 1922, from the Committee to Taylor.

5. There is a certain irony in the fact that the initial surveys considered psychology as harmful when we know that later they became one of the primary instruments of research. See, for comparison, Converse (1987).

6. RG 83, entry 75, letter from Murray to Yeager, January 15, 1922.

7. T. M. Porter (1995) defends the very powerful argument that mechanical objectivity (i.e., resorting to mechanical rules and machines) is the product of the weakening of groups charged with producing numbers. When a body responsible for numbers is attacked, one way for it to strengthen itself is to mechanize its methods, which *ipso facto* becomes less open to criticism. We note here that the beginning of the process conforms exactly to this theory, but that it finally ends in a contrary decision.

8. RG 83, entry 74, "November Crop Schedule," USDA, November 1923.

9. We must stress that this definition of objectivity and the manner of obtaining it is one option among others. One alternative, for example, would be to consider that objectivity is the product of the greatest detachment possible and that, to obtain reliable data, it would have been better to keep the crop reporter away from the fields—that is to say, only retain *non*agricultural representatives, who would thus not have risked being influenced by the interests and strategies in play between neighbors. Statisticians opted for *one of the possible conceptions* of objectivity.

10. RG 83, entry 85.

11. The problem of getting *sufficient* returns appears at this time. Initially, the difficulty bore on having *not too many* crop reporters, who could contradict one another and put too heavy a workload on the Division. "The number of such correspondents should *not exceed* one for an ordinary sized county," according to the USDA in 1863 (Taylor and Taylor 1952).

12. The *Omnibus* was a small newspaper brought out by one of the Division's agricultural Statisticians. He would photocopy the paper and send it to his colleagues. It was not in any way official, just small comments on the salient facts of this profession, poems that one of them had written, and jokes. Copies of this paper were kindly shown to me by Richard Allen.

13. Such postal distribution maps would indicate that "Districting of States for Crop reporting purposes is a modification of the system used by the Post Office Department in handling the mails."

14. RG 83, entry 74, "Special hog report," December 1, 1923.

15. Ibid.

16. Ibid.

17. Ibid.

Chapter 4

1. There is a controversy over Keynes's role in the formulation of Roosevelt's policies. Some affirm that the New Deal is a recovery policy inspired by Keynesian thought, while others affirm that, on the contrary, inspiration is impossible as the New Deal was launched in 1933, whereas *General Theory*, Keynes's seminal book, was only published in 1936. This is the reason why it is necessary here to emphasize the fact that Keynes undoubtedly influenced the group behind the first New Deal, directly, without intermediaries, but through his theory of probability, which was repeatedly cited by the actors during this period. On the other hand, his works on economics are not mentioned at all. Keynes thus played a direct role in the first Roosevelt government's policies: he participated, as a resource, in the reformulation of statistical tools without which the New Deal would not have been innovative.

2. Sarle had made an approximate calculation in his first article, which he corrected in the second paper.

3. In addition, we concur with the "internalist" history of sampling that systematically cites this reference. We will come to it in the next chapter.

4. National Archives, Record Group 83, Bureau of Agricultural Economics, entry 36, "Manuscripts" box 119, is the archives that records this controversy. The discussions on the first article are in the same archives group, box 179.

5. One example among a thousand, their influence is recognized by A. J. King (1945).

Chapter 5

1. A fact generally unknown is that Henry Wallace's passion for statistics was genuine. Invited in 1935 to Iowa State University, he told the students present: "I merely want to say that I once believed in statistics" (Wallace 1944, 97).

2. We have already met the Iowa Statistician Leslie Carl in chapter 1 and observed him processing his questionnaires.

3. The "Farm Credit Administration" was set up by the New Deal to grant farmers low-interest loans under certain conditions.

4. In a third talk, Sarle compared the qualities of the different interviewers—tax assessors or postmen—and thus does not focus on the method of selecting the population to be interrogated.

5. M. L. Wilson called this option the "Jeffersonian model" of agriculture: family-based agriculture, comprising a great number of farms, each owned by a family working its own land. According to him, the protection of this model was one of the fundamental tenets of the New Deal, which enabled the preclusion of collectivism and latifundism. For him, the New Deal was justified only if one accepted that land should be fragmented into a multitude of diverse and family-owned holdings (Wilson 1936).

6. The common source of the two meanings of "surveying"—statistical and topographical—can be found here.

7. The committee responsible for this issue was composed of John D. Black, Harvard University; Dr. Charles Sarle, U.S. Department of Agriculture; Dr. Oscar C. Stine, U.S. Department of Agriculture; and Professor Theodor C. Schultz, Chairman, Iowa State College. Schultz was on the editorial board of the journal and therefore welcomed his colleagues despite some slight differences. We note that Sarle has doctor affixed to his name, although no doctorate has ever been mentioned in connection with him.

8. A rigorous and broad definition of internalism is difficult to give. For example, Shapin (1992) has shown that no one has ever claimed to be an externalist and that the word is sheer anathema. However, the definition we have given here applies at least to the surveyors.

9. This is an important difference between the works of internalists and ours: they don't take into account the fact that events change characteristics when they are considered in the making or afterward.

10. Gigerenzer et al. (1989) tell the story of the war that took place during the second half of the 1930s between Fisher, on the one hand, and Neyman and Egon Pearson, on the other.

11. This tradition is prolonged nowadays by Fienberg and Tanur (1996), whose work, following Snedecor, tries to show that the two camps can be reconciled.

Chapter 6

1. Let us again clarify that the last two states, Hawaii and Alaska, had not yet become part of the Union.

2. https://senate.universityofcalifornia.edu/_files/inmemoriam/html/RaymondJessen.htm.

3. At the time of the topographical survey and the sale of lands, the United States, contrary to Canada, had not set aside tracts of land for roads. But this did not constitute a major problem because the farmers readily gave a part of their land for the construction of roads, as they were useful for them.

4. Stuart A. Rice, the president of the American Statistical Association at the time, had already complained about this deficiency: "The fact is little known that the geographical units to which enumerations of the census type relate are often unmapped and inexactly described" (Rice 1934, 4). Then in 1937, John D. Black, wrote: "The main obstacles have been that suitable base maps have not been available for considerable sections of the country (especially in the South)" (Black and Allen 1937, 462).

5. Practically at the same time, but otherwise unconnected with our subject, this survey method was implemented in France by Paul-Henry Chombart de Lauwe, who after the war was to play a key role, generally ignored today, in the development of French sociology (Chombart de Lauwe 1948).

6. Statistical Laboratory, *Annual Report, 1946–1947*, Ames: Iowa State College, 1947, mimeograph. According to this report, the Laboratory's total budget came to $234,000.

7. Even today, when one goes to Iowa, one hears that several insurance companies are installing their head offices there because they can find a meticulous and cost-effective female workforce made up of the wives and daughters of WASP agriculturists, who serve the bureaucracy wonderfully well (interview with J. Prusacki, agricultural Statistician for the state of Iowa, May 2007).

8. Area sampling has become canonical worldwide. For example, it is used in France for the official Survey on Employment.

9. Goodsell, Jessen, and Wilcox (1940, 758) also write that "this body of data would especially be useful for measuring year to year changes and for the analysis of probable effects of alternative government policies on various farm groups."

Chapter 7

1. Falkner (1898, 36) further clarifies that "in the absence of an adequate supervision of the work of the enumerators, it is to be feared that this provision was not strictly carried out. As late as 1860 it was not infrequent that in the rural regions the census was filled out on court days. The story of the man who took a census in a 'boom' region by announcing that he wanted to buy real estate, and counting the crowd which gathered about the hotel, is not wholly improbable."

2. Till then there was no permanent Census Bureau, and a superintendent was appointed for each operation.

3. National Archives, Record Group 51, Bureau of Agricultural Economics (hereafter RG 51), e144a, box e44, "Why Not Have an Unemployment Census?," published in 1937 by the *New York Times* in the Letters to the Editor.

4. It is remarkable that in England the constructor of an early index (1910) was the same Arthur Bowley who had so actively participated in the discussions on sampling at the International Institute of Statistics during the 1920s and who was a great inspiration to Charles Sarle.

5. This remark has been deepened and systematized; see Bruno, Didier, and Prévieux 2014; Bruno, Didier, and Vitale 2014; Didier 2018.

Chapter 8

1. It should be noted that here "social control" is to be understood in a very positive sense, in line with John Dewey's thinking: society will control the forces descending on it so pitilessly.

2. Preparing the projects took a certain amount of time, but there is another explanation for why the PWA projects took so long. Roosevelt, hoping that economic recovery would take place before the launch of the project, which would have economized public money, would ask the PWA not to proceed any faster (Schlesinger 1958, 287).

3. S. F. Charles (1963, 21) cites Roosevelt's famous statement of 1932: "The country needs and, unless I mistake its temper, the country demands bold, persistent experimentation. It is common sense to take a method and try it: If it fails, admit it frankly and try another. But above all, try something."

4. Keynes's *General Theory* was in fact published in 1936, three years after the creation of the CWA.

5. It is here, and not on the agricultural side, that we come across the planning tradition started by Taylor (see Alchon 1985).

6. Perhaps it should be explained here that the FERA was a light administration; it gave grants to local relief services for the destitute who were employed by the local authorities. The CWA, on the contrary, was a federal service that not only hired people on relief temporarily but also its entire administration. But to gain time, very often the same people worked under two different heads for the two administrations at the same time (Hopkins 1936).

7. However, Ross (1934, 293) specifies that "by far the most significant studies were those carried out by the various agencies of the federal government, financed by Civil Works Grants and supervised by the federal civil works administration and the central statistical board."

8. Today, it is not statistical studies that are the most famous but the artistic projects. CWA gave grants to abstract expressionists completing their training and authors of realist theater, among others.

9. We will take up in detail the four technical questions connected with sampling in chapter 9.

10. National Archives, Record Group 51, Central Statistical Board (hereafter RG 51), entry 144b, folder E37.

11. RG 51, entry 146a.

12. National Archives, Record Group 257, Bureau of Labor Statistics (hereafter RG 257), entry 44a, letter of November 27, 1933, from Joy to Lublin.

13. RG 51, entry 146a, box 5.

14. RG 51, entry 146a, box 5, memo of January 16, 1934, from Persons to Lubin.

15. RG 51, entry 146a, box 5, letter of April 26, 1936, from Lubin to Ross.

16. RG 51, entry 146a, box 5, letter of January 6, 1934, from Lubin to Braught. Unfortunately the archivists of this university, despite their incredible helpfulness, did not enable us to find out more, and the same applies to the other universities of the state with similar names.

17. RG51, entry146a, box 5, memo of February 24, 1934, from Lubin to Jacob Baker.

18. B. F. Schwartz (1984, 178) states moreover that in a project that consisted of enumerating the unemployed in Pennsylvania, 2200 women were hired: "Mostly white collar and professional unemployed [women] found jobs. Since many had no previous experience, a two-day training course on techniques of interviewing and the use of schedules was offered and followed by an exam."

19. RG 51, entry 146a, memo from Lubin to Bartlett (CWA), December 8, 1933.

20. Among the original members of the CSB were Modecai Ezekiel, agricultural economist one of the chief planners; Isador Lubin; Meredith B. Givens from the Committee on Government Statistics and Information Services (COGSIS); Corrington Gill, who was Hopkins's deputy; and Stuart Rice ("The Central Statistical Board," 1933).

21. RG 51, entry 146b, box 5.

22. RG 257, entry 33, letter of January 14, 1934, from Persons to Gray.

23. RG 257, entry 33, letter of January 14, 1934, from Lubin to Gray.

24. RG 51, entry 146b, box 5.

25. Ibid.

26. RG 257 entry 44a, memo written by Morris Copeland, the executive secretary of the CSB, dated December 4, 1934.

27. Ibid.

28. RG 51, entry 146a, February 17, 1934, report.

29. RG 51, entry 146a, February 24, 1934, report.

30. RG 51, entry 146a, March 10, 1934, report.

31. RG 51, entry 146a, box 5.

32. Ibid.

33. Ibid.

34. RG 257, entry 22, letter of March 5, 1934, from Lubin to Baker.

35. The estimates were calculated the following way. First, it is possible to know precisely certain information concerning the projects between 1933 and 1935, according to the report of the WPA published in 1939 (Brown 1939). Among the public projects, there is a line dedicated to "research and statistical projects." The CWA (1932–1934) has financed 8,800 such projects for a total amount of $28,952,000. Another report of 1936 (USWPA 1936) sums up all the public projects that have been financed in all the relief administrations between the close of the CWA and December 31, 1935. During this period, a total of 1,069 "research and statistical surveys" have been financed for a total of $13,931,194. The minimum of the number of projects and their cost is the sum of these figures (number of projects: 8,800 + 1,069 = 9,869; cost: $28,952,000 + $13,931,194 = $4 2,883,194). This being said, projects continued to be launched and financed after 1935 until the end of 1937, even though it is harder to estimate how many. US WPA (1938) says that the WPA financed 1,566 "research and statistical surveys" between its creation and October 1, 1937—but with no monetary information. So we can estimate that the number of projects was 9,869 + 1,566 = 11,435. But this addition might not be valid because during 1935, the WPA and FERA coexisted; thus there might be double counts. But we can estimate the maximum number of projects. US FERA (1942) says that between 1933 and 1937 the total amount of white-collar projects (in which are diluted the statistical projects) was $39,894 for a total amount of $147,700,814. Then from the two first cited sources we learn that there were 14,600 + 9,041 = 23,641 such projects that were not statistical for a total amount of $25,675,000 + $70,898,112 = $96,573,112. By subtraction, we get our higher estimates (number of projects: 39,894 – 23,641 = 16,253; cost: $147,700,814 – $96,573,112 = $51,127,702).

Finally, we can try and estimate the number of positions created through these projects. The duration of these jobs was quite short (a few months) and one person could occupy several positions successively. Hence a position cannot be equated with an employed person. Nevertheless, it is an additional estimator of the workforce employed in statistical work in this case. We know that in the TCU, a CWA venture conceived as a small project, which we will be discussing later, 250 positions were offered (including supervisors). Schwartz (1984), moreover, talks of a CWA project called the "Census of Pennsylvania," described as "the largest nonworker project in Pennsylvania," for which 2,200 young women were hired. We estimated the number of statistical positions offered with relief money by multiplying 250 by 10,000 (a figure rounded off to the minimum number of projects estimated) and 2,200 by 16,000 (rounded off to the maximum number of projects).

36. RG 257, entry 22.

37. RG 257, entry 22, Letter of May 12, 1934.

38. Calculated as $146 \times 2 \times 5 = 1{,}460$.

39. RG 257, entry 44a, Stuart Rice's letter of May 14, 1936, to Senator Royal S. Copeland.

40. National Archives, Record Group 29, Bureau of the Census (hereafter RG 29), entry 210, Calvert L. Dedrick's correspondence, May 18, 1936, Dedrick's letter to Rice—addressed as *chairman* of the CSB.

41. Financed by the Rockefeller Foundation, the COGSIS was founded in June 1933 at the behest of the secretaries of Labor, Agriculture, Commerce (under which came the Census Bureau), and finally Harry Hopkins, to advise them on statistical matters. For an exhaustive list of the COGSIS members and the dates of the period of their membership, see Committee on Government Statistics and Information Services 1937. We notice mainly, other than the two successive chairmen, Stuart Rice and Edmund Day, the names of Murray R. Benedict and Robert E. Chaddock, both of whom we encountered when they were involved in agricultural statistics. Among the names that we came across afterward, let us mention Ewan Clague (Community Council of Pennsylvania), Morris Copeland (Michigan University), J. Frederick Dewhurst (Twentieth Century Fund), and Samuel Stouffer (Wisconsin University).

42. RG 51, entry 144a.

CHAPTER 9

1. Raymond Jessen was the statistician from Iowa State University.

2. We note that Hogg *opposes* a social worker's representative, trained what's more at the Wisconsin participationist school, traditionally the spokespersons for the underprivileged and the unemployed. A big thank you to the Rockefeller Foundation and to Bethanie Anton to have so graciously given us the file on Margaret Hogg from the Russell Sage Foundation, which contains all the previously unpublished information presented here.

3. National Archives, Record Group 51, Central Statistical Board (hereafter RG 51), entry 144a, box E37, memorandum of February 16, 1934, from Hogg to Emerson Ross.

4. RG 51, entry 144a, box E37, memorandum of February16, 1934, from Hogg to Charles Persons.

5. RG 51, entry 144a, box E37, memorandum of February 16, 1934, from Hogg to Ross.

6. National Archives, Record Group 257, Bureau of Labor Statistics (hereafter RG 257), entry 44a.

7. RG 257, entry 44a.

8. Ibid.

9. Ibid.

10. This project was titled "A bill to provide for a census in continental United States of unemployment, employment, occupations, population and agriculture, and for other purposes."

11. Archives of the Russell Sage Foundation. Copy of a letter by Mrs. Hogg to Mrs. Hurlin, August 8, 1935. Despite the tragic circumstances, by strange coincidence Margaret Hogg was admitted to a hospital founded by the Booth family, one of whose members, Charles, played a key role in the definition of unemployment. See, for example, Desrosières (1998).

12. Only F. F. Stephan (1948) recalls the important role that Margaret Hogg played.

13. The ambiguity was dispelled in 1948 when opinion polls were not able to predict that the majority of voters would vote for Dwight Eisenhower. A parliamentary inquiry was ordered that came to the conclusion that the quotas were faulty. Since then, American opinion polls always use random sampling and quotas are no longer considered reliable (Mosteller 1949).

14. National Archives Record Group 29, Bureau of the Census (hereafter RG 29), entry 262, "Scrapbook of press clippings," pp. 37–38. The press campaign was extremely well-orchestrated, so that the archives on this experiment filled up more than four boxes containing books in which each double page spread contained 12 articles. To go through them, I drew a random number on my computer: I got 0,175626. I multiplied this by 12 and took the integral number which came to 2. I then read the second article on each page.

15. Let us recall that the WPA, the relief administration, was the successor to the FERA (Federal Emergency Relief Administration) and the CWA. It should not be mixed up with the Public Works Administration (PWA). Stuart Rice, rather amused, talked of an "alphabetocracy"—a government of initials!

16. National Archives, Record Group 69, Works Progress Administration (hereafter RG 69), entry 27, Myers to Hopkins, December 22, 1936.

17. RG 257, entry 44a, "Minutes of a special meeting of the CSB, resolution 1," sent on December 16, 1936, to President Franklin Roosevelt himself.

18. RG 257, entry 44a.

19. RG 29, entry 256, "1937 unemployment census, general records."

20. RG 29, entry 256.

21. The vice president in question was John N. Garner. Unfortunately, for historical consistency, H. A. Wallace acceded to this post only in 1941.

22. M. H. Hansen (1987, 184) relates that he still remembers, fifty years later, how they worked even on New Year's Eve: "I called my wife at midnight to wish her for the new year." This shows how important it was for the group to proceed at a rapid pace.

23. The nomenclature distinguished the seven following categories: (1) workers; (2) part-time workers wanting additional work; (3) part-time workers not wanting more work; (4) workers with a relief job; (5) unemployed; (6) those indisposed due to illness; (7) nonworkers.

24. RG 29, entry 262, "Scrapbooks of press clippings," *The News*, December 21, 1937, 37–38.

25. M. J. Anderson and S. E. Fienberg (2000) show that today's surveys threaten to do to the decennial census what they did to the 1937 voluntary census—namely, to supersede it in terms of accuracy and to replace it.

26. On the role of actuaries in sampling history, we can consult Lie (2002). As regards their relations more specifically with the American Social Security Administration, see Givens (1935), Witte (1936), and Perkins (1946).

27. M. J. Anderson (1988), however, highlights the capital role played by Arthur Bowley, the English statistician, in formulating civil works projects as early as 1909 by participating in the *Report of the Royal Commission on the Poor Laws*. The connection between surveys and civil works was thus established in Great Britain by Bowley at the very beginning of the twentieth century.

28. It should be pointed out that Gill does not use the word "surveys," but "periodic censuses." The word census was repeatedly used by the supporters of surveys accompanied by adjectives such as "periodic," "repeated," and "partial" because they did not want to frighten away the public, which might not be ready to be surveyed. But in practice, the expression definitely corresponded to surveys. Here, for example, between two phrases, Gill talks of the enumerative check experiment. Not for an instant did Gill think that it would be possible to undertake "periodic censuses" of unemployment in the strict sense, but surveys.

Conclusion to Part III

1. There is an opposition on this point between Tarde and Michel Foucault. Foucault argues that "statistics first developed in small countries" or under military occupation. He presupposes that statistics are always the result of a "domination" (to use his word). But we have seen all along that this is all but necessary (Foucault 2007, 280).

Bibliography

Abbott, Andrew. 2001. *Time Matters: On Theory and Method.* Chicago: University of Chicago Press.

Abbott, Edith. 1940. *Public Assistance. American Principles and Policies.* Vol. II, 2 vols. Chicago: University of Chicago Press.

Agee, James, and Walker Evans. 1969. *Let Us Now Praise Famous Men: Three Tenant Families.* Boston: Houghton Mifflin.

Akerman, James R. 1993. "Selling Maps, Selling Highways: Rand McNally's 'Blazed Trails' Program." *Imago Mundi* 45: 77–89.

Alchon, Guy. 1985. *The Invisible Hand of Planning: Capitalism, Social Science, and the State in the 1920s.* Princeton, N.J.: Princeton University Press.

Algeo, John. 1984. "Etymologies Unknown: Boondoggle." *American Speech* 51 (1): 93–95.

Alsberg, Henry G. 1934. *America Fights the Depression. A Photographic Record of the CWA.* New York: Coward-McCann.

American Farm Bureau Federation. 1937. *The Nation's Agriculture.* October, 6–7.

Anderson, Margo J. 1988. *The American Census.* New Haven, Conn.: Yale University Press.

Anderson, Margo J. 2015. *The American Census: A Social History.* 2nd ed. New Haven, Conn.: Yale University Press.

Anderson, Margo J., and Stephen E. Fienberg. 2000. "Partisan Politics at Work: Sampling and the 2000 Census." *PS: Political Science and Politics* 33 (4): 795–799.

Bauman, Zygmunt. 2000. *Liquid Reality.* Cambridge: Polity Press.

Becker, Joseph A. 1937. "Crop Reports Are Hot News." *The Nation's Agriculture*, 6–9.

Becker, Joseph A., and C. L. Harlan. 1939. "Developments in Crop and Livestock Reporting since 1920." *American Journal of Agricultural Economics* 21 (4): 799–827. https://doi.org/10.2307/1231786.

Ben-David, Joseph. 1984. *The Scientist's Role in Society: A Comparative Study*. Chicago: University of Chicago Press.

Beveridge, William H. 1907. "The Pulse of the Nation."*Albany Review* 2 (8):160.

Beyleveld, A. J. 1929. "Determination of a Precise Indication of Change in Crop Acreage." *Journal of the American Statistical Association* 24 (168): 405–411. https://doi.org/10.2307/2277086.

Bjelic, Dušan. 1996. "Lebenswelt Structures of Galilean Physics: The Case of Galileo's Pendulum." *Human Studies* 19 (4): 409–432. https://doi.org/10.1007/BF00188851.

Black, J. D., and R. H. Allen. 1937. "Estabrook Counting of Farms in the United States." *Journal of the American Statistical Association* 32 (199): 439–463.

Blaisdell, Donald C. 1940. *Government and Agriculture: Franklin D. Roosevelt and the Era of the New Deal*. New York: Da Capo Press.

Blondiaux, Loïc. 1998. *La fabrique de l'opinion : une histoire sociale des sondages*. Paris: Éditions du Seuil. http://catalogue.bnf.fr/ark:/12148/cb367017028.

Bloor, David. 1991. *Knowledge and Social Imagery*. 2nd ed. Chicago: University of Chicago Press.

Blum, Alain, and Martine Mespoulet. 2003. *L'anarchie bureaucratique: Statistique et pouvoir sous Staline*. Paris: La Découverte.

Blumer, Herbert. 1969. *Symbolic Interactionism: Perspective and Method*. Englewood Cliffs, N.J: Prentice-Hall.

Boltanski, Luc, and Eve Chiapello. 2005. *The New Spirit of Capitalism*. London: Verso.

Boltanski, Luc, and Laurent Thevenot. 2006. *On Justification: Economies of Worth*. Translated by Catherine Porter. Princeton, N.J.: Princeton University Press.

Boorstin, Daniel J. 1973. *The Americans: The Democratic Experience*. New York: Random House.

Bourguet, Marie-Noëlle. 1988. *Déchiffrer la France: La statistique départementale à l'époque napoléonienne*. Paris: Éditions des archives contemporaines.

Bowley, Arthur Lyon. 1915. *Livelihood and Poverty: A Study in the Economic Conditions of Working-Class Households in Northampton, Warrington, Stanley and Reading*. London: George Bell & Sons.

Bowley, Arthur Lyon. 1926. "Measurement of the Precision Attained in Sampling." *Bulletin de l'Institut International de Statistique* 22 (3): 6–62.

Bowley, Arthur Lyon, and Margaret H. Hogg. 1925. *Has Poverty Diminished? A Sequel to "Livelihood and Poverty."* London: King & Son.

Box, Joan Fisher. 1978. *R. A. Fisher: The Life of a Scientist*. Wiley Series in Probability and Mathematical Statistics. New York: Wiley.

Brooks, E. M. 1977. *As We Recall: The Growth of Agricultural Estimates, 1933–1961*. Washington, D.C: U.S. Department of Agriculture Statistical Reporting Service.

Brown, Josephine Chapin. 1940. *Public Relief 1929–1939*. New York: Henry Holt.

Brown, P. 1939. *Analysis of Civil Works Program Statistics*. WPA. Washington, D.C.: Government Printing Office.

Bruno, Isabelle, and Emmanuel Didier. 2013. *Benchmarking: l'État sous pression statistique*. Zones (Paris, France). Paris: Découvert.

Bruno, Isabelle, Emmanuel Didier, and Julien Prévieux. 2014. *Statactivisme: comment lutter avec des nombres*. Paris: Zones.

Bruno, Isabelle, Emmanuel Didier, and Tommaso Vitale. 2014. "Statactivism: Forms of Action between Disclosure and Affirmation." *Partecipazione & Conflitto* 7 (2): 198–220. https://doi.org/10.1285/i20356609v7i2p198.

Bucki, Cecelia. 2001. *Bridgeport's Socialist New Deal, 1915–36: The Working Class in American History*. Urbana: University of Illinois Press.

Bureau of Agricultural Economics. 1936. "Proceedings of Conference on Statistical Methods of Sampling Agricultural Data, July 14–17, 1936, Iowa State College, Ames, Iowa," microform. In *Conference on Statistical Methods of Sampling Agricultural Data (1936 : Iowa State College)*. Washington, D.C: Bureau of Agricultural Economics.

Bureau of Labor Statistics. 1930. "Unemployment Surveys of Philadelphia and Buffalo." *Monthly Labor Review* 30 (2): 17–39.

Callander, W. F., and Joseph A. Becker. 1923. "The Use of 'Pars' and 'Normal' in Forecasting Crop Production." *Journal of Farm Economics* 5 (4): 185–197. https://doi.org/10.2307/1230295.

Callon, Michel, and Fabian Muniesa. 2003. "Les marchés économiques comme dispositifs collectifs de calcul." *Réseaux* 122 (6): 189–233. https://doi.org/10.3917/res.122.0189.

Cassin, Barbara. 1995. *L'effet sophistique*. NRF Essais. Paris: Gallimard.

"The Central Statistical Board." 1933. *Journal of the American Statistical Association* 28 (184): 438.

Chaddock, Robert E. (Robert Emmet). 1925. *Principles and Methods of Statistics*. Boston: Houghton Mifflin.

Chapoulie, Jean-Michel. 2001. *La tradition sociologique de Chicago: 1892–1961*. Paris: Éditions du Seuil.

Charles, Searle F. 1963. *Minister of Relief: Harry Hopkins and the Depression*. Syracuse, N.Y.: Syracuse University Press.

Chew, Arthur P. 1937. *The Response of Government to Agriculture*. Washington, D.C.: Government Printing Office.

Chombart de Lauwe, Paul-Henry, ed. 1948. *La Découverte aérienne du monde*. Paris: Horizons de France.

Church, Verne H. 1944. *Personal History and Recollections of the Government Crop Reporting Service*. Washington, D.C.: National Agricultural Statistical Service.

Clark, Florence M. 1935. "Unemployment Survey of Bridgeport, Conn. 1934." *Monthly Labor Review* 40 (3): 626–635.

Committee on Government Statistics and Information Services. 1937. "Government Statistics." *Social Science Research Council Bulletin* 26 (April).

Converse, Jean M. 1987. *Survey Research in the United States: Roots and Emergence 1890–1960*. Berkeley: University of California Press.

Cox, Gertrude M., and George W. Snedecor. 1936. "Covariance Used to Analyze the Relation between Corn Yield and Acreage." *Journal of Farm Economics* 18 (3): 597–607. https://doi.org/10.2307/1231220.

Cronon, William. 1992. *Nature's Metropolis: Chicago and the Great West*. New York: W. W. Norton.

Curti, Merle. 1955. "Intellectuals and Other People." *The American Historical Review* 60 (2): 259–282.

Daston, Lorraine. 1988. *Classical Probability in the Enlightenment*. Princeton, N.J: Princeton University Press.

Daston, Lorraine. 1992. "Objectivity and the Escape from Perspective." *Social Studies of Science* 22 (4): 597–618.

Daston, Lorraine, and Peter Galison. 2010. *Objectivity*. New York: Zone Books.

Daston, Lorraine, and Elizabeth Lunbeck. 2010. *Histories of Scientific Observation*. Chicago: University of Chicago Press.

David, H. A. 1984. "The Iowa Statistical Laboratory : Antecedents and Early Years, 1914–1947." In *Statistics, an Appraisal: Proceedings of a Conference Marking the 50th Anniversary of the*

Statistical Laboratory, Iowa State University, Ames, Iowa, June 13–15, 1983, edited by H. T. David, H. A. David, and Iowa State University Statistical Laboratory, 1st ed., 3–18. Ames: Iowa State University Press.

Davis, Joseph S. 1937. "Statistics and Social Engineering." *Journal of the American Statistical Association* 32 (197): 1–7.

Debaise, Didier. 2006. *Un empirisme spéculatif. Lecture de Procès et réalité de Whitehead*. Paris: Vrin.

Dedrick, Calvert L., and Morris H. Hansen. 1938. *Final Report on Total and Partial Unemployment, Vol. IV: The Enumerative Check Census*. Washington, D.C.: Government Printing Office.

Deleuze, Gilles. 1990. *Spinoza et le problème de l'expression*. Paris: Éditions de Minuit.

Desrosières, Alain. 1993. "Le territoire et la localité : deux langages statistiques." *Courrier des statistiques* 65 (March): 59–59.

Desrosières, Alain. 1998. *The Politics of Large Numbers: A History of Statistical Reasoning*. Cambridge, Mass: Harvard University Press.

Desrosières, Alain. 2003. "Managing the Economy: The State, the Market, and Statistics." In *The Cambridge History of Science*, edited by Theodore M. Porter and Dorothy Ross, 553–564. Vol. 7, *Modern Social and Behavioral Sciences*. Cambridge: Cambridge University Press.

Desrosières, Alain. 2008. *Gouverner par les nombres*. Paris: Presses des Mines.

Dewey, John. 1927. *The Public and Its Problems*. Athens: Ohio University Press.

Dewhurst, J. 1928. *Employment Fluctuations in Pennsylvania 1921–1927*. Harrisburg: Pennsylvania Department of Labor and Industry.

Diaz-Bone, Rainer, and Emmanuel Didier. 2016. "Introduction: The Sociology of Quantification—Perspectives on an Emerging Field in the Social Sciences." *Historical Social Research/Historische Sozialforschung* 41 (2): 7–26.

Didier, Emmanuel. 1996. "De 'l'exclusion' à l'exclusion." *Politix* 34 (n.d.): 5–29.

Didier, Emmanuel. 2000. "De l'échantillon à la population : sociologie de la généralisation par sondage aux États-Unis avant la Seconde Guerre mondiale." Thesis, ENSMP. http://www.theses.fr/2000ENMP0964.

Didier, Emmanuel. 2002. "Sampling and Democracy: Representativeness in the First U.S. Surveys." *Science in Context* 15 (3): 427–445.

Didier, Emmanuel. 2005. "Releasing Market Statistics." In *Making Things Public—Atmospheres of Democracy*, edited by Bruno Latour and Peter Weibel, 638–642. Cambridge, Mass.: MIT Press.

Didier, Emmanuel. 2007. "Do Statistics 'Perform' the Economy?" In *Do Economists Make Markets? On the Performativity of Economics*, edited by Donald MacKenzie, Fabian Muniesa, and Liucia Sue, 276–310. Princeton, N.J.: Princeton University Press.

Didier, Emmanuel. 2012. "La consistance du futur. La prévision statistique aux États-Unis et la Grande Dépression." *Raisons politiques* 48 (4): 65–83. https://doi.org/10.3917/rai.048.0065.

Didier, Emmanuel. 2018. "Globalization of Quantitative Policing: Between Management and Statactivism." *Annual Review of Sociology* 44 (1): 515–534. https://doi.org/10.1146/annurev-soc-060116-053308.

Didier, Emmanuel, Sophie Névanen, Philippe Robert, and Renée Zauberman. 2009. "La solidité des institutions. Les statistiques de 'victimation' de l'Insee (1996–2006)." *Genèses* 74 (1): 128–144. https://doi.org/10.3917/gen.074.0128.

Dos Passos, John. 1949. *The Grand Design*. Boston: Houghton Mifflin.

Dos Passos, John. 2002. *U.S.A.* Paris: Gallimard.

Duncan, Joseph, and William Shelton. 1976. *Revolution in United States Government Statistics, 1926–1976*. Washington, D.C.: Government Printing Office.

Duncan, Joseph W., and William C. Shelton. 1992. "U.S. Government Contributions to Probability Sampling and Statistical Analysis." *Statistical Science* 7 (3): 320–338.

Dupréel, Eugène. 1931. "Théorie de la consolidation. Esquisse d'une théorie de la vie d'inspiration sociologique." *Revue de l'Institut de sociologie* 3: 473–530.

Dupréel, Eugène. 1933. "La cause et l'intervalle ou ordre et probabilité." *Archives de la société belge de Philosophie* 5 (2): 1–51.

Dupréel, Eugène. 1961. "La consistance et la probabilité constructive." *Mémoires de la classe de lettre de l'Académie royale de belgique* 55 (2): 1–38.

Ebling, Walter H. 1935. "The Field of Agricultural Data." *Journal of Farm Economics* 17 (4): 659–668.

Ebling, Walter H. 1936. "Some State Problems in Agricultural Statistics." *Journal of Farm Economics* 18 (1): 107–130.

Ebling, Walter H. 1939. "Why the Government Entered the Field of Crop Reporting and Forecasting." *Journal of Farm Economics* 21 (4): 718–734.

Espeland, Wendy Nelson, and Mitchell L. Stevens. 1998. "Commensuration as a Social Process." *Annual Review of Sociology* 24 (August): 313.

Estabrook, Leon M. 1915. *Government Crop Reports: Their Value, Scope, and Preparation*. Washington, D.C: Government Printing Office.

Ewald, François. 1986. *L'Etat Providence*. Paris: B. Grasset.

Falkner, Roland P. 1898. "The Development of the Census." *Annals of the American Academy of Political and Social Science* 12 (November): 34–62.

FERA (Federal Emergency Relief Administration). 1942. *Final Statistical Report of the Federal Emergency Relief Administration*. Washington, D.C.: Government Printing Office.

Fienberg, Stephen E., and Judith M. Tanur. 1996. "Reconsidering the Fundamental Contributions of Fisher and Neyman on Experimentation and Sampling." *International Statistical Review/Revue Internationale de Statistique* 64 (3): 237–253. https://doi.org/10.2307/1403784.

Fisher, Sir Ronald Aylmer. 1958. *Statistical Methods for Research Workers*. 13th ed., rev. Edinburgh: Oliver and Boyd.

Fitch, John A. (John Andrews). 1910. *The Steel Workers*. Pittsburgh Survey. Vol. III, 6 vols. New York: Charities Publication Committee. http://nrs.harvard.edu/urn-3:FHCL:679750.

Fitzgerald, D. A. 1935. *Livestock under the AAA*. Washington, D.C.: The Brookings Institution. http://hdl.handle.net/2027/mdp.39015021938298.

Fleischhauer, Carl, and Beverly W. Brannan, eds. 1988. *Documenting America 1935–1943*. Berkeley: University of California Press.

Fleming, James Rodger. 1990. *Meteorology in America, 1800–1870*. Baltimore: Johns Hopkins University Press.

Foucault, Michel. 2007. *Security, Territory, Population: Lectures at the Collège de France, 1977–78*. New York: Palgrave Macmillan.

Frankel, Martin, and Benjamin King. 1996. "A Conversation with Leslie Kish." *Statistical Science* 11 (1): 65–87.

Fukuyama, Francis. 2004. *State-Building: Governance and World Order in the 21st Century*. Ithaca, N.Y.: Cornell University Press.

Fuller, W. A. 1984. "The Master Sample of Agriculture." In *Statistics, an Appraisal: Proceedings of a Conference Marking the 50th Anniversary of the Statistical Laboratory, Iowa State University, Ames, Iowa, June 13–15, 1983*, edited by H. A. David, H. T. David, and Iowa State University Statistical Laboratory, 1st ed., 584–594. Ames: Iowa State University Press.

Galison, Peter. 1987. *How Experiments End*. Chicago: University of Chicago Press.

Gallup, George. 1940. *The Pulse of Democracy: The Public-Opinion Poll and How It Works*. New York: Simon and Schuster.

Garfinkel, Harold. 1967. *Studies in Ethnomethodology*. Englewood Cliffs, N.J: Prentice-Hall.

Gigerenzer, Gert, Zeno Swijtink, Theodore Porter, Lorraine Daston, John Beatty, and Lorenz Krüger. 1989. *The Empire of Chance : How Probabilities Changed Science and Everyday Life*. Cambridge: Cambridge University Press.

Gilbert, Jess. 2000. "Eastern Urban Liberals and Midwestern Agrarian Intellectuals: Two Group Portraits of Progressives in the New Deal Department of Agriculture." *Agricultural History* 74 (2): 162–180.

Gilbert, Jess. 2001. "Agrarian Intellectuals in a Democratizing State." In *The Countryside in the Age of the Modern State*, edited by Catherine McNicol Stock and Robert D. Johnston, 222–238. Ithaca, N.Y.: Cornell University Press.

Gilbert, Jess, and Carolyn Howe. 1991. "Beyond 'State vs. Society': Theories of the State and New Deal Agricultural Policies." *American Sociological Review* 56 (2): 204–220.

Gill, Corrington. 1934. "A Study of the Three Million Families on Relief in October 1933." *Annals of the Academy of Political and Social Science* 176 (November): 25–36.

Gill, Corrington. 1939. *Wasted Manpower*. New York: Norton.

Givens, Meredith B. 1935. "Statistical Implication of the Social Security Program." *Journal of the American Statistical Association* 30 (192): 651–661.

Goodsell, Wylie D., Raymond D. Jessen, and Walter W. Wilcox. 1940. "Procedures Which Increase the Usefulness of Farm Management Research." *Journal of Farm Economics* 22 (4): 753–761.

Graham, Otis L. 1967. *An Encore for Reform: The Old Progressives and the New Deal*. New York: Oxford University Press.

Gross, Neal C. 1943. "A Post Mortem on County Planning." *Journal of Farm Economics* 25 (3): 644–661.

Gross, Neil. 2007. "Pragmatism, Phenomenology, and Twentieth-Century American Sociology." In *Sociology in America: A History*, edited by Craig Calhoun, 183–225. Chicago: University of Chicago Press.

Gruchy, Allan G. 1939. "The Concept of National Planning in Institutional Economics." *Southern Economic Journal* 6 (2): 121–144.

Guibert, B., J. Lagagnier, and M. Volle. 1971. "Essai sur les nomenclatures industrielles." *Economie et statistique* 20: 23–36.

Hacking, Ian. 1984. *The Emergence of Probability: A Philosophical Study of Early Ideas about Probability, Induction, and Statistical Inference*. 1st pbk. ed. Cambridge: Cambridge University Press.

Hacking, Ian. 1986. "Making Up People." In *Reconstructing Individualism: Autonomy, Individuality, and the Self in Western Thought*, edited by Thomas C. Heller and Christine Brooke-Rose, 222 et seq. Stanford, Calif.: Stanford University Press.

Hansen, Morris H. 1987. "Some History and Reminiscences on Survey Sampling." *Statistical Science* 2 (2): 180–190.

Hansen, Morris H., and H. G. Madow. 1976. "Some Important Events in the Historical Development of Sample Surveys." In *On the History of Statistics and Probability: Proceedings of a Symposium on the American Mathematical Heritage, to Celebrate the Bicentennial of the United States of America, Held at Southern Methodist University, May 27–29, 1974*, edited by D. B. Owen, 80–91. Vol. 17, *Statistics, Textbooks, and Monographs*. New York: Marcel Dekker.

Harrison, Robert W. 1954. "Public Land Records of the Federal Government." *Mississippi Valley Historical Review* 41 (2): 277–288.

Hayden, Tom. 2006. *Radical Nomad: C. Wright Mills and His Times*. Boulder, Colo.: Paradigm Publishers.

Heffer, Jean. 1991. *La Grande Dépression. Les Etats-Unis en crise (1929–1933)*. Paris: Gallimard.

Hill, E. B. 1941. "Comments on Sampling to Increase the Usefulness of Farm Management Research." *Journal of Farm Economics* 23 (2): 499–501. https://doi.org/10.2307/1231650.

Hogg, Margaret H. 1930. "Sources of Incomparability and Error in Employment-Unemployment Surveys." *Journal of the American Statistical Association* 25 (171): 284–294. https://doi.org/10.2307/2278191.

Hogg, Margaret H. 1932. *The Incidence of Work Shortage*. New York: Russell Sage Foundation.

Holmes, Irvin. 1939. "Results of Four Methods of Sampling Individual Farms." *Journal of Farm Economics* 21 (1): 365–374.

Hopkins, Harry L. 1936. *Spending to Save: The Complete Story of Relief*. Seattle: University of Washington Press.

Horowitz, Irving Louis. 1964. "Introduction: The Intellectual Genesis of C. Wright Mills." In *Sociology and Pragmatism: The Higher Learning in America*, edited by Charles Mills, 11–31. New York: Oxford University Press.

Huthmacher, J. Joseph. 1968. *Senator Robert F. Wagner and the Rise of Urban Liberalism*. New York: Atheneum.

Igo, Sarah E. 2007. *The Averaged American*. Cambridge, Mass.: Harvard University Press.

Jatteau, Arthur. 2018. "Random Experiments, the 'Gold Standard' of Impact Evaluation?" *Regards croisés sur l'économie* 22 (1): 184–194.

Jensen, A. 1926a. "Report on the Representative Method in Statistics." *Bulletin de l'Institut International de Statistique* 22 (3): 359–380.

Jensen, A. 1926b. "The Representative Method in Practice." *Bulletin de l'Institut International de Statistique* 22 (3): 381–439.

Jessen, Raymond J. 1939. "An Experiment in the Design of Agricultural Surveys." *Journal of Farm Economics* 21 (4): 856–863. https://doi.org/10.2307/1231790.

Jessen, Raymond J. 1942. "Statistical Investigation of a Sample Survey for Obtaining Farm Facts." Agricultural Experiment Station, Iowa State College of Agriculture and Mechanic Arts.

Jessen, Raymond J. 1945. "The Master Sample of Agriculture: II, Design." *Journal of the American Statistical Association* 40 (229): 46–56. https://doi.org/10.2307/2280453.

Jessen, Raymond J. 1947. "The Master Sample Project and Its Use in Agricultural Economics." *Journal of Farm Economics* 29 (2): 531–540.

Johnson, Hildegard Binder. 1976. *Order upon the Land: The U.S. Rectangular Land Survey and the Upper Mississippi Country*. London: Oxford University Press.

Keynes, John Maynard. 1921. *A Treatise on Probability*. London: Macmillan. http://pi.lib.uchicago.edu/1001/cat/bib/523857.

King, A. J. 1945. "The Master Sample of Agriculture: I, Development and Use." *Journal of the American Statistical Association* 40 (229): 38–45. https://doi.org/10.2307/2280452.

King, A., and G. Simpson. 1940. "New Developments in Agricultural Sampling." *Journal of Farm Economics* 22: 341–349.

Kirkendall, Richard S. 1962. "Franklin D. Roosevelt and the Service Intellectual." *Mississippi Valley Historical Review* 49 (3): 456–471.

Kirkendall, Richard S. 1966. *Social Scientists and Farm Politics in the Age of Roosevelt*. Columbia: University of Missouri Press.

Kleeck, Mary van. 1931. "The Federal Unemployment Census of 1930." *Journal of the American Statistical Association* 26 (173): 189–200.

Kruskal, William, and Frederick Mosteller. 1979a. "Representative Sampling, I: Non-Scientific Literature." *International Statistical Review/Revue Internationale de Statistique* 47 (1): 13–24. https://doi.org/10.2307/1403202.

Kruskal, William, and Frederick Mosteller. 1979b. "Representative Sampling, II: Scientific Literature, Excluding Statistics." *International Statistical Review/Revue Internationale de Statistique* 47 (2): 111–127. https://doi.org/10.2307/1402564.

Kruskal, William, and Frederick Mosteller. 1979c. "Representative Sampling, III: The Current Statistical Literature." *International Statistical Review/Revue Internationale de Statistique* 47 (3): 245–265. https://doi.org/10.2307/1402647.

Kruskal, William, and Frederick Mosteller. 1980. "Representative Sampling, IV: The History of the Concept in Statistics, 1895–1939." *International Statistical Review/Revue Internationale de Statistique* 48 (2): 169–195. https://doi.org/10.2307/1403151.

Labrousse, Agnès. 2010. "Nouvelle économie du développement et essais cliniques randomisés : une mise en perspective d'un outil de preuve et de gouvernement." *Revue de la régulation. Capitalisme, institutions, pouvoirs*, no. 7 (February). https://doi.org/10.4000/regulation.7818.

Lange, Dorothea, and Paul Taylor. 1939. *A Record of Human Erosion*. Cornwall, N.Y.: Cornwall Press.

Lascoumes, Pierre, and Patrick Le Galès, eds. 2004. *Gouverner par les instruments*. Centre de recherches politiques de Sciences-po Et University of Oxford. Vol. 1, Collection académique. Paris: Presses de Sciences.

Latour, Bruno. 1987. *Science in Action: How to Follow Scientists and Engineers through Society*. Philadelphia: Open University Press.

Latour, Bruno. 1988. *The Pasteurization of France*. Cambridge, Mass.: Harvard University Press.

Latour, Bruno. 1998. *Paris ville invisible*. Collection Les empêcheurs de penser en rond. Paris: La Découverte.

Latour, Bruno. 1999. *Pandora's Hope: Essays on the Reality of Science Studies*. Cambridge, Mass.: Harvard University Press.

Latour, Bruno. 2012. "Paris, Invisible City: The Plasma." Special issue, "Traceable Cities," *City, Culture and Society* 3 (2): 91–93. https://doi.org/10.1016/j.ccs.2011.11.002.

Leparwsky, Albert. 1948. "Government Planning in the South." *The Journal of Politics* 10 (3): 536–567.

Lester, Richard A. 1934. "Emergency Employment in Theory and Practice." *Journal of Political Economy* 42 (4): 466–491.

Lie, Einar. 2002. "The Rise and Fall of Sampling Surveys in Norway, 1875–1906." *Science in Context* 15 (3): 385–409.

Likert, Rensis. 1940. "Democracy in Agriculture—Why and How ?" In *Yearbook of Agriculture, 1940*, edited by Department of Agriculture, 994–1002. Washington, D.C: Government Printing Office.

Locher, Fabien. 2004. "Le nombre et le temps: la météorologie en France (1830–1880)." PhD diss., École des hautes études en sciences sociales, Paris.

Lord, Russell. 1947. *The Wallaces of Iowa*. Boston: Houghton Mifflin.

Lunt, Edward C. 1888. "History of the United States Census." *Publication of the American Statistical Association* 1 (2/3): 63–93.

Lynd, Robert S. 1939. *Knowledge for What? The Place of Social Science in American Culture*. Princeton, N.J.: Princeton University Press.

Maas, Harro, and Mary Morgan. 2012. "Observation and Observing in Economics." *History of Political Economy* 44 (supplement): 1–24. https://doi.org/10.1215/00182702-1631761.

Mackenzie, Donald. 1991. "Comment faire une sociologie de la statistique. . . ." In *La Science telle qu'elle se fait*, edited by Michel Callon and Bruno Latour, 200–261. Paris: La Découverte.

Mackenzie, Donald. 2006. "Is Economics Performative? Option Theory and the Construction of Derivatives Markets." *Journal of the History of Economic Thought* 28 (1): 29–56. https://doi.org/10.1080/10427710500509722.

Mackenzie, Donald A., Fabian Muniesa, and Lucia Siu. 2007. *Do Economists Make Markets?: On the Performativity of Economics*. Princeton, N.J.: Princeton University Press.

Manin, Bernard. 1997. *The Principles of Representative Government*. Themes in the Social Sciences. Cambridge: Cambridge University Press.

Marks, Harry M. 1997. *The Progress of Experiment: Science and Therapeutic Reform in the United States, 1900–1990*. Cambridge: Cambridge University Press.

Marres, Nortje. 2005. *No Issue, No Public: Democratic Deficit and the Displacement of Politics*. Amsterdam: University of Amsterdam.

Martuccelli, Danilo. 2005. *La consistance du social. Une sociologie pour la modernité*. Rennes: Presses Universitaires de Rennes.

Maynard, Douglas W., ed. 2002. *Standardization and Tacit Knowledge: Interaction and Practice in the Survey Interview*. New York: Wiley.

McKenzie, R. D. 1921. "The Neighborhood: A Study of Local Life in the City of Columbus, Ohio. II." *American Journal of Sociology* 27 (3): 344–363.

Mespoulet, Martine. 2001. *Statistique et révolution en Russie. Un compromis impossible (1880–1930)*. Rennes: Presses Universitaires de Rennes.

Miller, Shepherd. 1933. "Cooperation in Agriculture, Livestock Marketing." *Iowa Experiment Station Bulletin* 26 (306): 76–95.

Mills, C. Wright. 1956. *The Power Elite*. New York: Oxford University Press.

Mills, C. Wright. 1959. *The Sociological Imagination*. New York: Oxford University Press. http://www.archive.org/details/sociologicalimag00mill.

Mills, C. Wright. 1964. *Sociology and Pragmatism: The Higher Learning in America*. New York: Paine-Whitman Publishers.

Mills, Frederick C. 1924. *Statistical Methods Applied to Economics and Business,*. American Business Series. New York: Henry Holt.

Mitchell, Timothy. 2002. *Rule of Experts: Egypt, Techno-Politics, Modernity*. Berkeley: University of California Press.

Mitchell, Timothy. 2005. "The Work of Economics: How a Discipline Makes Its World." *Archives Européennes de Sociologie* 46 (2): 297–320. https://doi.org/10.1017/S000397560500010X.

Mosteller, Frederick. 1949. "The Pre-Election Polls of 1948." *Social Science Research Council Bulletin* 60: 396.

Moulton, F. R. 1938. "Scientific Events: Reorganization of the U.S. Department of Agriculture." *Science* 88 (2285): 347–348.

Murray, Nat C. 1939. "A Close-up View of the Development of Agricultural Statistics from 1900 to 1920." *Journal of Farm Economics* 21 (4): 707–717. https://doi.org/10.2307/1231781.

Myers, Howard B. 1935. "The General Development and Present Status of the Fera Research Program." *Social Force* 13 (4): 477–481.

Myers, Howard B. 1936. "Research with Relief Funds—Past, Present, and Future." *American Sociological Review* 1 (5): 771–780.

Myers, Howard B. 1941. "Dynamics of Labor Supply." *Journal of the American Statistical Association* 36 (214): 175–184.

Myers, Howard B. 1946. "Corrington Calhoun Gill 1898–1946." *Journal of the American Statistical Association* 41 (235): 393–394.

Neyman, Jerzy. 1934. "On the Two Different Aspects of the Representative Method: The Method of Stratified Sampling and the Method of Purposive Selection." *Journal of the Royal Statistical Society* 97 (4): 558–625. https://doi.org/10.2307/2342192.

Neyman, Jerzy. 1938. *Lectures and Conferences on Mathematical Statistics.* Washington, D.C.: Graduate School of the United States Department of Agriculture.

Nourse, Edwin G., Joseph S. Davis, and John D. Black. 1937. *Three Years of Agricultural Adjustment Administration.* Washington, D.C.: The Brookings Institution.

O'Muircheartaigh, C., and T. Wong. 1981. "The Impact of Sampling Theory on Survey Sampling Practice: A Review." *Bulletin de l'Institut International de Statistique* 44: 465–493.

Pearson, Karl. 1911. *The Grammar of Science.* 3d ed., rev. London: Adam and Charles Black.

Perkins, Frances. 1946. *The Roosevelt I Knew.* New York: Viking Press.

Pitkin, Hanna Fenichel. 1972. *The Concept of Representation.* Berkeley: University of California Press.

Pollak, Michael. 1986. "Un texte dans son contexte [L'enquête de Max Weber sur les ouvriers agricoles]." *Actes de la recherche en sciences sociales* 65 (1): 69–75. https://doi.org/10.3406/arss.1986.2351.

Porter, Theodore M. 1986. *The Rise of Statistical Thinking, 1820–1900*. Princeton, N.J.: Princeton University Press.

Porter, Theodore M. 1995. *Trust in Numbers: The Pursuit of Objectivity in Science and Public Life*. Princeton, N.J: Princeton University Press.

Purcell, Edward A. 1973. *The Crisis of Democratic Theory: Scientific Naturalism and the Problem of Value*. Lexington: University of Kentucky Press.

Raper, Arthur F. 1943. *Tenants of the Almighty*. New York: MacMillan.

Rice, Stuart A. 1934. "Statistical Opportunities and Responsibilities." *Journal of the American Statistical Association* 29 (185): 1–10.

Rosanvallon, Pierre. 1998. *Le peuple introuvable: Histoire de la représentation démocratique en France*. Bibliothèque des histoires. Paris: Gallimard.

Rosanvallon, Pierre. 2011. *Democratic Legitimacy: Impartiality, Reflexivity, Proximity*. Princeton, N.J.: Princeton University Press. http://nrs.harvard.edu/urn-3:hul.ebookbatch.PMUSE_batch:PMUSE426520151124.

Ross, Emerson. 1934. "Research and Statistical Program of the Federal Emergency Relief Administration." *Journal of the American Statistical Association* 29 (187): 288–294.

Roux, Jacques, and Thierry Magnin. 2004. *La condition de fragilité*. Saint Etienne: Presses Universitaires de Saint Etienne.

Sarle, Charles F. 1927. *Reliability and Adequacy of Farm Price Data*. USDA Bulletin. Washington, D.C.: Government Printing Office.

Sarle, Charles F. 1932. *Adequacy and Reliability of Crop-Yield Estimates*. Technical Bulletin 311. Washington, D.C.: U.S. Department of Agriculture.

Sarle, Charles F. 1938. "Methods in Sample Census Research." *Journal of Farm Economics* 20 (3): 669–672.

Sarle, Charles F. 1939. "Development of Partial and Sample Census Methods." *Journal of Farm Economics* 21 (1): 356–364. https://doi.org/10.2307/1230662.

Sarle, Charles F. 1940. "The Possibilities and Limitations of Objective Sampling in Strengthening Agricultural Statistics." *Econometrica* 8 (1): 45–61.

Schlesinger, Arthur M., Jr. 1957. *The Crisis of the Old Order: The Age of Roosevelt Vol. I, 1919–1933*. Boston: Houghton Mifflin.

Schlesinger, Arthur M., Jr. 1958. *The Coming of the New Deal: The Age of Roosevelt Vol. II, 1933–1935*. Boston: Houghton Mifflin.

Schlesinger, Arthur M., Jr. 1960. *The Politics of Upheaval: The Age of Roosevelt Vol. III, 1935–1936*. Boston: Houghton Mifflin.

Schultz, Theodore W. 1933. "Testing the Significance of Mean Values Drawn from Stratified Samples." *Journal of Farm Economics* 15 (3): 452–475. https://doi.org/10.2307/1231065.

Schultz, Theodore W., and George W. Snedecor. 1933. "Analysis of Variance as an Effective Method of Handling the Time Element in Certain Economic Statistics." *Journal of the American Statistical Association* 28 (181): 14–30. https://doi.org/10.2307/2277999.

Schutz, H. H. 1937. "Test of Various Sampling Methods." *Journal of Farm Economics* 19 (2): 464–467.

Schwartz, Bonnie Fox. 1984. *The Civil Works Administration, 1933–1934: The Business of Emergency Employment in the New Deal.* Princeton, N.J.: Princeton University Press.

Scott, Ann Herbert. 1968. *Census U.S.A.* New York: Seabury Press.

Scott, James C. 1998. *Seeing Like a State: How Certain Schemes to Improve the Human Condition Have Failed.* Yale Agrarian Studies. New Haven, Conn.: Yale University Press.

Seng, You Poh. 1951. "Historical Survey of the Development of Sampling Theories and Practice." *Journal of the Royal Statistical Society. Series A (General)* 114 (2): 214–231. https://doi.org/10.2307/2980977.

Shapin, Steven. 1992. "Discipline and Bounding: The History and Sociology of Science as Seen through the Externalism-Internalism Debate." *History of Science* 30 (4): 333–369. https://doi.org/10.1177/007327539203000401.

Shapin, Steven, and Simon Shaffer. 1985. *Leviathan and the Air-Pump: Hobbes, Boyle, and the Experimental Life.* Princeton, N.J.: Princeton University Press.

Shepard, J. B. 1937. "Selection of Areas for Sample Agricultural Enumerations, with Discussion." *Journal of Farm Economics* 19: 454–469.

Silver, Allan. 1990. "The Curious Importance of Small Groups in American Sociology." In *Sociology in America*, edited by Herbert J. Gans, 61–74. American Sociological Association Presidential Series. Newbury Park, Calif.: Sage Publications.

Simmel, Georg. 1894. "Comment les formes sociales se maintiennent." In *Sociologie et épistémologie*, 171–206. Paris: PUF.

Skocpol, Theda, and Kenneth Finegold. 1982. "State Capacity and Economic Intervention in the Early New Deal." *Political Science Quarterly* 97 (2): 255–278.

Snedecor, George W. 1939. "Design of Sampling Experiments in the Social Sciences." *Journal of Farm Economics* 21 (4): 846–855. https://doi.org/10.2307/1231789.

Spears, Richard A. 1996. *NTC's Dictionary of American Slang.* Lincolnwood, Ill.: NTC Publishing Group.

Stapleford, Thomas A. 2009. *The Cost of Living in America: A Political History of Economic Statistics, 1880–2000.* Cambridge: Cambridge University Press.

Stephan, Frederick F. 1935. "State and Local Statistical Studies Conducted as Work Relief Projects." *Social Forces* 13 (4): 485–490.

Stephan, Frederick F. 1939. "Representative Sampling and Large-Scale Surveys." *Journal of the American Statistical Association* 34 (206): 343–352.

Stephan, Frederick F. 1948. "History of the Uses of Modern Sampling Procedures." *Journal of the American Statistical Association* 43 (241): 12–39.

Stephan, Frederick F. 1960. "In Memoriam: Samuel Andrew Stouffer." *The Public Opinion Quarterly* 24 (3): 545–546.

Stephan, Frederick F., W. Edwards Deming, and Morris H. Hansen. 1940. "The Sampling Procedure of the 1940 Population Census." *Journal of the American Statistical Association* 35 (December): 615–630.

Stewart, Lowell O. 1979. *Public Land Surveys*. New York City: Arno Press.

Stigler, Stephen M. 1996. "The History of Statistics in 1933." *Statistical Science* 11 (3): 244–252.

Stott, William. 1973. *Documentary Expression and Thirties America*. New York: Oxford University Press.

Stouffer, Samuel A., Arthur A. Lumsdaine, Marion Harper Lumsdaine, Robin M. Williams Jr., M. Brewster Smith, Irving L. Janis, Shirley A. Star, and Leonard S. Cottrell. 1949. *The American Soldier*. 2 vols. Princeton, N.J.: Princeton University Press.

Struve, A. W. Von. 1940. "Geography in the Census Bureau." *Economic Geography* 16 (3): 275–280.

Sukhatme, F. N. 1966. "Major Developments in Sampling Theory and Practice." In *Research Papers in Statistics: Festschrift for J. Neyman*, edited by F. N. David, 367–409. London: Wiley.

Tarde, Gabriel de. 1903. *The Laws of Imitation*. Translated by Elsie Worthington Clews Parsons. New York: H. Holt.

Tarde, Gabriel de. 1999. *Monadologie et sociologie*. Collection Les empêcheurs de penser en rond 1. Le Plessis-Robinson: Institut Synthélabo.

Taylor, Henry C. (Henry Charles), and Anne Dewees Taylor. 1952. *The Story of Agricultural Economics in the United States, 1840–1932: Men, Services, Ideas*. Ames: Iowa State College Press.

Thévenot, Laurent. 2006. *L'action au pluriel: sociologie des régimes d'engagement*. Vol. 1, Textes à l'appui. Paris: Éditions la Découverte. http://catalogue.bnf.fr/ark:/12148/cb40098972m.

Thorp, Willard L. 1934. "Statistics as Public Works." *Journal of the American Statistical Association* 29 (185): 157–185.

Thrasher, Frederic M. 1928. "The Study of the Total Situation." *Journal of Educational Sociology* 1 (8): 477–490.

Tolley, H. R. 1939. "Contribution of Agricultural Economics to the General Welfare." *Journal of Farm Economics* 21 (1): 8–21.

Tolley, H. R. 1943. *The Farmer Citizen at War*. New York: MacMillan.

Tolley, H. R., and Conrad Taeuber. 1944. "Wartime Developments in Agricultural Statistics." *Journal of the American Statistical Association* 39 (228): 411–427.

Tooze, J. Adam. 2001. *Statistics and the German State, 1900–1945: The Making of Modern Economic Knowledge*. Cambridge Studies in Modern Economic History. Cambridge: Cambridge University Press.

Topalov, Christian. 1994. *Naissance du chômeur : 1880–1910*. L'évolution de l'humanité. Paris: A. Michel. http://catalogue.bnf.fr/ark:/12148/cb357364620.

Unofficial Observer. 1934. *The New Dealers*. New York: Simon and Schuster.

USDA (United States Department of Agriculture). 1925. *Annual Report of the Department of Agriculture*. Washington, D.C.: Government Printing Office.

USDA (United States Department of Agriculture). 1933. *The Crop and Livestock Reporting Service in the United States*. Washington, D.C.: Government Printing Office.

USDA (United States Department of Agriculture). 1969. *The Story of U.S. Agricultural Estimates*. Washington D.C.: Government Printing Office.

USWPA (United States Works Progress Administration). 1936. *Report on the Works Program, Works Progress Administration*. Washington, D.C.: Government Printing Office.

USWPA (United States Works Progress Administration). 1938. *Inventory: An Appraisal of the Results of the Works Progress Administration*. Washington, D.C.: Government Printing Office.

USWPA (United States Works Progress Administration), and Harry L. Hopkins. 1936. *Guide to Project Eligibility*. Vol. 8, Circular. Washington, D.C.

Vogel, Frederic A. 1995. "The Evolution and Development of Agricultural Statistics at the United States Department of Agriculture." *Journal of Official Statistics* 11 (2): 161–180.

Walker, Williston. 1893. *The Creeds and Platforms of Congregationalism*. Charles Scribner. http://hdl.handle.net/2027/nyp.33433084969934.

Wallace, Henry A. 1934. "Research and Adjustment March Together." *Science* 80 (2066): 105–106.

Wallace, Henry A. 1935. *New Frontiers*. New York: Reynal & Hitchcock.

Wallace, Henry A. 1944. *Democracy Reborn*. New York: Reynal & Hitchcock.

Wallace, Henry A. 1945. "The Use of Statistics in the Formulation of a National Full Employment Policy." *Journal of the American Statistical Association* 40 (229): 11–19.

Wallace, Henry A., and George W. Snedecor. 1925. "Correlation and Machine Calculation." *Official Publication: Iowa State College of Agriculture and Mechanic Arts* 23 (35).

Warren, Stanley W. 1936. "Statistical Analysis in Farm Management Research." *Journal of Farm Economics* 18 (1): 169–179. https://doi.org/10.2307/1231321.

Weber, Florence. 2013. "Le Calcul économique ordinaire." In *Traité de sociologie économique*, edited by Philippe Steiner and François Vatin, 2nd ed. Paris: PUF.

Welch, Emmett H. 1939. "Various Government Provisions for the Unemployed." Special issue. "Appraising the Social Security Program." *Annals of the Academy of Political and Social Science* 202: 36–44.

Wells, O. V. 1938. "Agricultural Planning and the Agricultural Economist." *Journal of Farm Economics* 20 (4): 753–764.

Westbrook, Robert B. 1991. *John Dewey and American Democracy*. Ithaca, N.Y.: Cornell University Press.

White, Leonard D. 1937. "New Opportunities for Economists and Statisticians in Federal Employment." *American Economic Review* 27 (1): 210–215.

Wickens, Aryness Joy. 1979. "Isador Lubin 1896–1978." *The American Statistician* 33 (4): 207.

Wilson, M. L. 1936. "Validity of the Fundamental Assumptions Underlying Agricultural Adjustment." *Journal of Farm Economics* 18 (1): 12–58.

Wilson, Milburn L. 1940. "The Democratic Process and the Formulation of Agricultural Policy." *Social Forces* 19 (1): 1–11.

Witte, Edwin E. 1936. "An Historical Account of Unemployment Insurance in the Social Security Act." *Law and Contemporary Problems* 3 (1): 157–169.

Yule, G. Udny (George Udny). 1911. *An Introduction to the Theory of Statistics*. Griffin's Scientific Series. London: C. Griffin.

Zunz, Olivier. 1998. *Why the American Century?* Chicago: University of Chicago Press.

Index

Abandoned lands, 62, 185, 330
Accuracy
  of crop reports, 34, 100, 127, 132, 135, 138, 143
  and frequency of statistical reports, 220
  of individual farm reports, 134, 142, 148
  in Master Sample, 206, 213, 221–222, 224
  probable error affecting, 149, 302
  in random sampling, 186, 191, 222
  of representative surveys, 221–222
  sample size affecting, 138, 179, 183, 191, 302–303
  serviceable, 100, 116, 222
  of unemployment data, 298, 299, 302, 303, 304, 311, 316
Acreage measures, 7, 8
  of cultivated areas. *See* Cultivated acres
  of harvested areas, 62, 81
  of yield. *See* Yield per acre
Adjustment programs, agricultural, 89–103
  abandoned lands affecting, 185
  contracts on, 92, 93f, 94
  quotas in, 91–103
Aerial photography
  of city blocks, 299
  road maps combined with, 202, 206
Agee, James, 341, 349
Aggregation methods in agricultural statistics, 22, 126
Agricultural Adjustment Act, 87
  repeal of, 102, 103
Agricultural Adjustment Administration, 89–103, 176–177, f293
  Bureau of Planning in, 105, 107
  county reports in, 218
  creation of, 89, 251
  quota system of, 91–103
Agricultural Marketing Service, 112

Agricultural planning, 104–117, 119–121, 361ch8n5
- deliquescence process in, 110–116, 117, 120–121
- farmers in, 107–110, 111, 114, 120, 224, 226, 355n8
- Master Sample in, 222–225
- number involved in, 109
- phases in, 107–108, 109

Agricultural prices
- adjustment programs on, 89–107
- compared to industrial prices, 90, 214
- in corner technique, 354n41
- farmer knowledge of, 19, 79–80
- and insider trading, 58–59
- paid by cooperatives, 80–81
- reducing production for increase in, 90–103, 129
- speculation on. *See* Speculation on agricultural prices
- Statistician interviews on, 37–38

Agricultural production
- crop reports on. *See* Crop reports
- cultivated acres in. *See* Cultivated acres
- harvested acres in, 62, 81
- reduction of, for price increase, 90–103, 129
- yield per acre in. *See* Yield per acre

Agricultural Statisticians
- on accuracy of data, 221–222
- and agricultural planning programs, 110–112, 119, 120
- area confabs of, 37
- in area sampling, 209
- calculating average of questionnaire results, 46–48, 50–54
- coded telegrams sent by, 54, 55f, 58, 59–60
- comments on crop reports, 54–58
- consolidation of data from, 83–85
- crop meters used by, 130
- editing questionnaire responses, 42–46, 66, 85
- evaluating questionnaire responses, 135
- and farmer interactions, 25, 32, 33, 37, 66, 97, 98, 100, 101, 102
- field surveys of, 23–26, 32–38, 39, 40
- initial experiences of, 23–25
- and Master Sample, 209, 210, 211, 212, 223, 225–226
- Neyman as influence on, 195
- number of, 352n11
- and politics, 87–88
- prefect role of, 96, 102
- in quota system, 92, 95–103
- on random and purposive selection, 187, 190, 191–192
- random sampling by, 126, 197
- sample selection experiments of, 176–177
- smoothing questionnaire results, 48–50, 51f, 85, 100
- summary sheets provided by, 52–54, 53f, 58
- territorial divisions and reporting districts of, 33–37
- training on probable error, 160
- and voluntary crop reporters, 26–32. *See also* Voluntary crop reporters

and Washington, D.C. office
interactions, 39–40, 41, 42, 63
weighting questionnaire data, 50–54
Agricultural statistics, 9–10, 12–13
aggregate of elements in, 82–83, 120–121
aggregation methods in, 22, 126
of Agricultural Adjustment Administration, 97
from Board of Crop Estimates, 58–78
coded telegrams on, 54, 55f, 58, 59–60
consolidation of, 48, 54, 83–85, 119
control or check data in, 81–82, 133, 134, 173, 177, 181
County Reporters as source of information in, 67–68
on cultivated acres. *See* Cultivated acres
districts in. *See* District crop reports
estimations in, 12, 20, 28–30, 69–72
expression in, 140–143
farmer criticisms of, 25
fragility of, 97–103, 112, 120–121
frequency and rhythm of reports on, 220–221
geographic variables in. *See* Geographic variables in agricultural reports
on harvested acres, 62, 81
from Iowa State University Statistical Laboratory, 163–196
from Master Sample, 197–226. *See also* Master Sample
objectivity in, 128–136, 140–143, 185, 292, 357n9n
in planning, 104–117, 119–121
plasma stage of, 22–23, 227, 228
political representatives as source of information in, 127–128
probable error in, 145–161
questionnaires as source of information for. *See* Questionnaires on agriculture
quota system based on, 91–103
release of new reports, 75–78, 83–84, 353n21
representativeness of, 152–157. *See also* Representativeness
sampling in. *See* Sampling on agriculture
solidity of, 83, 117, 119, 120–121, 354n43
sources of information for, 127–128
in speculation problem, 19–20
standardization of, 41, 42, 114
from state Statisticians. *See* Agricultural Statisticians
on ten year period, 68, 81
use of, 58–59, 78–82, 226, 327, 344
voluntary crop reporters as source of information in, 26–32. *See also* Voluntary crop reporters
on yield per acre. *See* Yield per acre
Agricultural Statistics Division, 112
Agriculture Department, 4, 20, 343
academics and intellectuals in, 104–105, 110
Board of Crop Estimates in, 58–78
Bureau of Agricultural Economics of, 89, 105–107

Agriculture Department (cont.)
creation of, 127
crop reporting districts of, 34, 35f, 36
economists in, 105
Extension Service of, 89
planning programs of, 104–117
quota system of, 91–103
state Statisticians in, 23–26, 32–58. *See also* Agricultural Statisticians
Statistical Office of, 9–10
voluntary crop reporters to, 226. *See also* Voluntary crop reporters
Agriculture Secretary, 136, 168
and Agricultural Adjustment Administration, 89, 90, 91, 92, 93f, 95, 107
approval of crop reports, 75, 354n37
Wallace as, 87, 166, 216
Agriculturist, The, 127
Alabama, 176, 179, 182
Alaska, 199, 359n1
American Economic Association, 242, 248
American Farm Economists Association, 178, 184
American Institute of Public Opinion, 310
American Soldier, The (Stouffer), 302
American Statistical Association, 113, 178, 248, 255, 268, 319, 360n4
Anderson, Margo J., 249, 305, 366n25, 366n27
Arbitration by Board of Crop Estimates, 64–67
Area confabs of agricultural Statisticians, 37
Area sampling, 360n8
in Master Sample, 209–211
Arkansas, 211f
Asimov, Isaac, 332
Asymmetrical comparison of random and purposive sampling, 192
Austin, William, 316
Average calculations
in agricultural questionnaire processing, 46–48, 50–54
probable error in, 148–149, 150

Baker, Jacob, 279, 280, 281
Bankhead-Jones Act, 167
Bauman, Zygmunt, 120
Beach, Mabel, 284
Becker, Joseph, 55f, 56, 57, 62, 63, 67, 77, 145
Behavior patterns and conditions, 215–216, 324
Beveridge, William, 246
Bias
of crop reporters, 56–57, 64–66, 101, 209–210
in individual farm inquiry, 133–134
and probable error, 157, 158
in sample selection, 185
in tax assessor data, 177
in unemployment data, 287–289, 317
Biggers, John, 309–311, 314
Black, A. G., 112
Black, John D., 359n7, 360n4
Blaisdell, Donald, 108–109

Block-sampling on unemployment, 247, 295, 297–299, 301–304, 319
Blondiaux, Loïc, 307–308
Bloor, David, 187, 192
Blue-collar workers, CWA assistance to, 260–261, 267
Blumer, Herbert, 8
Board of Crop Estimates, 58–78, 119, 228
  arbitration by, 64–67
  archives of, 63
  Becker as director of, 67, 145
  calculation methods of, 72–75
  chairman of, 60
  comparison of reports by, 67–69
  on cultivated acres, 73–74
  education and training in, 61–63
  estimation process of, 69–72
  experts in, 60–63
  individual decisions in, 69–70
  nonnumerical information used by, 64
  release of information from, 75–78, 83–84, 353n21
  secrecy of, 59–60, 84, 353n21
  sources of information used by, 64–69
  transfers of professional staff in, 62–63
  on yield per acre, 74
Board of Review in adjustment program, 95
Boondoggling, 285, 286f, 287, 288, 290, 292
Bowley, Arthur, 338, 366n27
  and Hogg, 295, 296
  on probable error, 145–159
  on purposive selection, 170
  on representativeness, 188
  unemployment index of, 361ch7n4
Brain Trust, 2, 104, 145, 163
Braught, Major, 278, 281
Bridgeport CT, Trial Census of Unemployment in, 271, 280, 300, 301
Brooks, E. M., 285
  on Area Confabs of Statisticians, 37
  crop reporting districts used by, 36
  invited to join Washington office, 63
  on quota system, 97, 98, 99, 100, 102, 355n4
  on systematic draw of sample units, 207
Brown, Josephine Chapin, 252
Bryce, James, 307
Buchanan, Pat, 168
Bureau of Agricultural Economics, 9, 105–107, 110–113, 121
  education of planners in, 105, 263
  founding of, 89, 111, 187, 356ch3n1
  Middletown read in, 110, 356n10
  and Mount Weather agreement, 355n7
  Sarle presentation to, 213
  Tolley in, 105, 107, 110, 111–113, 184, 322, 356n10
Bureau of Crop Estimates, 21
Bureau of Labor Statistics, 10, 346
  founding of, 244
  hiring practices of, 283–284
  Lubin as director of, 253, 262, 263, 279, 281m283, 294
  salary paid by, 278

Bureau of Labor Statistics (cont.)
  Trial Census of Unemployment in collaboration with, 261, 272, 277, 279–280, 281
  on unemployment sampling methods, 264
Bureau of Planning in AAA, 105, 107
Bureaus of Labor, 243, 244, 245

Callander, William F., 91, 102, 145
Capture, 349
  and expression, 229, 349
Carl, Leslie M., 36, 43–44, 46, 56, 166–167, 176, 358ch5n2
Case study approach
  to agriculture, 214, 215
  to poverty, 215
  to unemployment, 251, 259, 299
Cattle reports, 43, 183, 220
Census Bureau, 10, 73–74, 81, 169, 178, 205
  financial support of Iowa Statistical Laboratory, 204
  Geography Division of, 199
  patronage in, 241
  unemployment statistics of, 240–243, 304–305, 316–319
Census data, 4, 5, 10
  of 1780, 240
  of 1840, 187
  of 1880, 241, 242
  of 1890, 242
  of 1910, 242, 243
  of 1920, 243
  of 1930, 6, 52, 248, 275, 295
  of 1940, 309, 316–319
  as check or control data, 81, 133, 134, 173, 177, 181
  compared to sample data, 173, 175, 177, 178, 181, 183, 191
  on cultivated acres, 73–74, 81, 133, 134
  on harvested acres, 81
  on income, 214
  in Michigan, 25
  probable error in, 150
  on unemployment, 13, 236–237, 240–243, 247, 248, 304–305, 316–319
  weighted averages from, 52
  in Wisconsin, 133
  on yield per acre, 74
Central Statistical Board, 178, 272–273, 275, 289, 322
  original members of, 362n20
  Rice as president of, 309
  Unemployment Survey Committee of, 302
Chaddock, Robert Emmet, 146, 364n41
Chaptal, Jean-Antoine, 96
Charles, S. F., 361n3
Check or control data
  on agriculture, 81–82, 133, 134, 173, 177, 181
  on unemployment, 310–315, 316
Chicago IL, 235, 236
Chicago School, 113
Chicago University, 246
Church, Verne H., 23–26, 32–33, 37–42, 62, 276
  crop meter invented by, 129
  on quota system, 92, 98–100, 102

survey of pickling cucumber crop, 38–42, 67, 182
Civil Works Administration (CWA), 257–272, 277–282, 285
administrators of, 259–260
artistic projects of, 361n8
compared to FERA, 361n6
local and federal conflicts in, 278–282
number employed by, 363n35
salary paid by, 278–279
selection of personnel in, 267–272
statistical projects of, 260–272, 291, 298, 299
women in, 268–270, 272
Clague, Ewan, 263–266, 291, 294–299, 364n41
Clarck, G. D., 34, 36
Coded telegrams on agricultural statistics, 54, 55f, 58, 59–60
Collins, H. L., 131f, 176
Commerce Secretary, Hopkins as, 343
Committee of Consulting Statisticians, 128–129, 140
Committee on Government Statistics and Information Services (COGSIS), 287, 295, 302, 319–320, 364n41
Commons, John R., 266, 296
Conditions and behavior patterns, 215–216, 324
Confidence intervals in sampling, 189, 222, 334
Confidentiality, 332–333
of agricultural statistics, 54, 55f, 58, 59–60, 332
of unemployment surveys, 332
Connecticut, Trial Census of Unemployment in, 271, 280, 300, 301
Consistency, 347
of aggregates, 13, 121, 126, 337, 349
of America, 12, 85, 126, 225, 227, 237, 337
expression and, 227–231
glossary of, 348–349
and reflexivity, 12, 342
series and, 337–339
solidity and, 119–121
theory of, 117, 126, 348
Consolidation process, 230, 348
in agricultural statistics, 48, 54, 83–85, 119
Contracts signed on agricultural quotas, 92, 93f, 94, 97
Control factors
in sampling, 170–171, 177, 185–186
in unemployment surveys, 276–278
Control or check data
on agriculture, 81–82, 133, 134, 173, 177, 181
on unemployment, 310–315, 316
Converse, Jean M., 114
Cooperatives, sale of crops to, 80–81
Copeland, Royal S., 285
Corn crop
for pork production, 93f, 99, 355n3
production and demand for, 90
quantity stocked on farm, 51–52
quotas on, 93f, 98
Cornell University, 145, 164, 167, 185, 214

Corner houses in unemployment sampling, 316–317
Corner technique, 354n41
Cost considerations
in aerial photography, 202
in choice of sampling unit, 178, 179, 181, 183, 191
in unemployment survey, 263–264
Costigan, Edward P., 249
Cotton crop, 68
estimation error on, 128–129
insider trading on, 58–59
Mexican ball weevil affecting, 67, 228
production and demand for, 90
quotas on, 92, 98
reduction of, 98, 128–129
Counting units in Master Sample, 206–209, 218
County Control Committee, 94, 98–99
County divisions
agricultural planning in, 107, 109
crop production estimates for, 34, 56, 100
cultivated acres in, 34, 56, 73–75, 98–99, 128–129, 185
Extension Service in, 89
growth condition of crops in, 49, 50
in Master Sample, 218
number surveyed, 181, 182, 197
quotas on production in, 91–103, 218
random and purposive samples of, 181
road maps of, 201f, 202
sampling experiments in, 176, 177, 179
subsidies to, 94, 218
tomato production in, 36
township samples of, 176, 177
weighted averages from, 156
County Reporters, 67–68
Cox, Gertrude, 165
Crisis, government response to, 250–251
Cronon, W., 235, 354n41
Crop meters, 129–130, 131f, 164, 292
Crop reporters
County, 67–68
voluntary. *See* Voluntary crop reporters
Crop Reporters' method
and census data, 134
consolidation in, 84, 119
elements of, 141
expression in, 229
and fragilization, 103
and Master Sample, 217
neighbor influences in, 130
Sarle on, 148
secrecy in, 332
statistical chain in, 344, 347
Crop Reporting Board, 66
Crop Reporting Service, 91, 100
Crop reports
and agricultural planning, 111, 112, 115
average picture in, 139
bias in, 56–57, 64–66, 101, 133–134
from Board of Crop Estimates, 75–78, 83–84
from County Reporters, 67–68

crop meters as source of data in, 129–130, 131f, 164, 292
by district. *See* District crop reports
on entire locality, 133
errors in, 128–129, 130, 134
from farmers, 26, 27, 66, 128–143, 266
geographic variables in. *See* Geographic variables in agricultural reports
from individual farms, 132–135, 140, 148, 195, 198, 202
journalists waiting for, 77–78, 354n39
objectivity in, 128–136, 140–143, 292, 357n9n
from political representatives, 127–128
probable error in, 145–161
quota system based on, 91–103
statistical expression in, 140–143
Statistician comments on, 54–58
utilization of, 78–82
from voluntary reporters. *See* Voluntary crop reporters
Crossley, Archibald, 306
Cultivated acres
abandonment of land affecting, 62, 185, 330
accuracy of estimates on, 28, 34, 128–129, 134, 183
bias in reports on, 56–57
Board of Crop Estimates on, 73–74
census estimates on, 73–74
County Reporters on, 68
farmer reports on, 128–129, 131–136
and harvested acres, 62
judgment of changes in, 132
percentage of change from previous year, 28, 30, 56
of pickling cucumbers, 39–40
reduced for production quotas, 92, 94, 98–99, 128–129
on sample farm, 135
in soil conservation program, 103
subsidies for, 92
validity of data on, 81
CWA. *See* Civil Works Administration

Davis, Joseph S., 114
Decomposition of links between statistics and politics, 87–117
Dedrick, Calvert L., 287–289, 292, 302, 310, 316
and Hogg, 295
on postal route sampling of unemployed, 311–312
university education of, 291
Deleuze, Gilles, 141
Deliquescence process, 348
in agricultural planning, 110–116, 117, 120–121
in unemployment statistics, 250
Deming, W. Edwards, 194, 316
Democracy, 326–335
agricultural adjustment program in, 92, 94, 99
agricultural planning in, 104, 107, 109, 224–225
reflexivity and representation in, 343
surveys in, 11, 224–225
Democratic Party, 5, 249, 253, 280

Deputies, federal, census data collected by, 240–241
Desrosières, Alain, 12, 345
Dewey, John
and agricultural planning, 105, 109, 223, 226
criticism of New Deal, 291
on democracy, 333, 334
on government response to crisis, 250
Mills influenced by, 326, 327
pragmatism of, 105, 266
on service intellectual, 105, 229
Dewhurst, J. Frederick, 295, 297, 364n41
Disintegration, 116–117
District crop reports, 27, 34, 35f, 36, 136
benefits to farmers, 79
homogeneity in, 36, 136, 152
mail carrier distribution of questionnaires for, 136–140
probable error in, 148
representative sample in, 152
shingling of, 47, 48
smoothing of, 48–50
weighting of, 52–54
Division, the, 89
and agricultural planning, 111, 112, 114, 120–121
agricultural questionnaires of, 27–32, 38–42, 136–140. *See also* Questionnaires on agriculture
archives of, 21
and Board of Crop Estimates, 58–78
and Bureau of Agricultural Economics, 105, 111, 356ch3n1
Callander as head of, 145
coded telegrams sent to, 54, 55f
control data used by, 81–82
County Reporters to, 67–68
crop reporting districts of, 136
cultivated acreage estimates of, 73, 74
initial experiences of agricultural Statisticians in, 23–25
and Iowa State University Statistical Laboratory, 161, 163–196
list of names compiled by, 25–26, 27
loss of relationship with crop reporters, 101–102, 103, 116, 120, 185
loyalty of crop reporters to, 26, 68, 130, 137
name changes of, 21
number of reporters to, 101, 135–136, 137–138, 357n11
objectivity in reports of, 133, 134, 140–143
probable error in data of, 145–161
production quotas based on data from, 91–92, 96, 97, 102–103
random sampling by, 125–126
release of new reports, 75–78
transfers of professional staff in, 62–63
utilization of reports, 78–82, 116
voluntary crop reporters of, 26–32. *See also* Voluntary crop reporters
Division of Crop and Livestock Estimates, 21, 89
Division of Crop Estimates, 21
Division of Markets and Crops Estimates, 21, 125
Division of Program Surveys, 114

Dos Passos, John, 1, 349–350
Dublin, Louis I., 294–295
Duncan, Joseph W., 236
Dupréel, Eugène, 84

Easterling, Thomas L., 271, 278, 279, 280–281, 283
Ebling, Walter, 101
Economic development, 224, 230
Economic zones and boundaries, 218–219
Edinburgh model, 72
Editing of agricultural questionnaires, 42–46, 66, 85
Eisenhower, Dwight, 365n13
Elite farmers as crop reporters, 26, 27, 57, 64, 185, 214
Ely, Richard T., 266
Empiricism, 291, 326
Employees of statistical projects
  as boondogglers, 285, 286f, 287, 290, 292
  hiring of, 267–270, 283–284
  number of, 283–285, 363–364n35
  as research workers, 284
  salary of, 278–281
Empowerment, 11, 325
Enumerative check on unemployment data, 310–315, 316
Enumerators of unemployment statistics, 255–292
  beneficiaries of CWA as, 265
  as boondogglers, 285, 286f, 287, 290, 292
  confidence in, 265, 266
  local informants as, 243–244, 247
  number of, 283–285
  objectivity of, 289, 292
  patronage appointments of, 279–282
  salary of, 278–281
  selection of, 267–272
  students as, 246
  training of, 246, 256, 271, 279, 280
  women as, 268–270, 271, 272, 362n18, 363n35
"Equality for agriculture," 90, 214
Errors
  in agricultural questionnaire responses, 43
  in crop reports, 128–129, 130, 134
  probable, 145–161. *See also* Probable error
  risk of, 150
  in sampling, 148–149, 158
Estabrook, Leon M., 20, 32
Estimations in agricultural statistics
  by Board of Crop Estimates, 69–72
  on cultivated acres, 28, 34, 73–74, 128–129, 134, 183
  probable error in, 149
  on yield, 20, 28–30
Estimation theory, 4
Evans, Walker, 3, 341
Ewald, François, 320–321, 323
Experimentation, Sarle on, 174, 175
Expert members of Board of Crop Estimates, 60–63
Expression, statistical, 140–143, 159, 227–231, 349
Extension Service, 89, 91, 96, 167, 355n7

Falkner, Roland P., 360n1
Farm Credit Administration, 169, 358ch5n3
Farm Economists, 167, 170, 187
Farmers
  in agricultural planning, 107–110, 111, 114, 120, 224, 226, 355n8
  and agricultural Statistician interactions, 25, 32, 33, 37, 66, 97, 98, 100, 101, 102
  benefits of crops reports for, 79–81, 226
  bias in reports of, 56–57, 64–66, 101, 209–210
  criticisms of agricultural statistics, 25
  elite, 26, 27, 57, 64, 185, 214
  in Great Depression, 1, 2, 88
  income of, 90, 177, 213–217
  influences on production estimates of, 45–46, 66, 129, 130
  in Jeffersonian model of agriculture, 225–226, 359n5
  knowledge on agricultural prices, 19, 79–80
  mail carriers in contact with, 136–140
  objectivity of, 141, 142
  price paid for agricultural materials by, 68
  prices paid to. *See* Agricultural prices
  questionnaires answered by; Questionnaires on agriculture
  quotas reducing production of, 91–103
  random selection of, 226
  representative, 57, 128, 138–139, 140
  speculators targeting, 19
  subsidies to, 90, 92, 94, 97, 99, 102, 218
  as voluntary crop reporters. *See* Voluntary crop reporters
Farms
  in counting and sampling units of Master Sample, 206, 207
  cultivated acres of. *See* Cultivated acres
  growth condition of crops on. *See* Growth condition of crops
  individual, as sample unit, 132–135, 140, 148, 198
  mail carrier selection of, 136–140
  in multiple counties, 74–75
  quantity of corn stocked on, 51–52
  random selection of, 171, 181
  representative, 57, 139, 140, 171
  tax assessors collecting data on, 177, 183, 199
  in type-of-farming areas, 219
  variations between, 170–171
  yield per acre of. *See* Yield per acre
Farm Security Administration, photographs of, 2–3
Federal Emergency Relief Administration (FERA), 257–258, 259–260, 278, 339
  compared to CWA, 361n6
  number employed in projects of, 363n35
  paternalism of, 258
  survey canvassers hired from unemployed registered with, 263–264

Federal marshals and deputies, census data collected by, 240–241
Federal Project No. 74, 299. *See also* Trial Census of Unemployment
Federal Reserve Bank of Philadelphia, 247, 295
Field surveys
of agricultural Statisticians, 23–26, 32–38, 39, 40
interviews in. *See* Interviews
for Master Sample, 210–211, 211f
of unemployment enumerators, 276–278
Fienberg, S. E., 366n25
Financial assistance to unemployed, 251–254
Fisher, Ronald, 146, 164–165, 169, 170, 190, 359n10
Snedecor influenced by, 165, 172, 188, 195, 196
Fitch, John A., 296
Foucault, Michel, 366n1
Foundation (Asimov), 332
Fragilization, 348
of agricultural statistics, 97–103, 112, 120–121
Frictional unemployment, 245, 250
Fukuyama, Francis, 343
Fuller, Wayne, 193
Futures market, insider trading in, 58–59

Gallup, George, 4, 113, 306–308
Garner, John N., 366n21
Gas company lists for unemployment sample selection, 297, 298, 299, 300, 301
General Theory (Keynes), 361ch8n4
Geographic variables in agricultural reports, 34, 36, 41, 133, 151–152, 156
in growth condition, 134
smoothing of, 49–50
and stratification, 151–152, 155, 156, 186
in township sections, 199
Geographic zones in Master Sample, 199, 210, 217, 223
Gifford, Claude, 274f
Gifford, Walter S., 249
Gilbert, Raymond V. H., 270–271
Gill, Corrington, 259–260, 260f, 285, 322, 323, 339, 362n20, 366n28
Gosnell, Harold, 246
Grain crops
questionnaires sent to Reporters on, 27–32, 43, 50, 51f
transport of, 235
Gray, A. C., 279
Gray, E. R., 273, 275
Great Depression, 1–2, 3, 341
agricultural statistics during, 12, 85, 87, 88, 116, 117, 121, 125, 213, 225–226
conditions and behavior patterns after, 216
frequency of statistical studies during, 220
government response to, 221, 325
New Deal program in. *See* New Deal
and reflexivity, 12

Great Depression (cont.)
representative surveys during, 6, 7
unemployment during, 231, 236–237, 239–254, 255–292, 343, 346
Great Design, The (Dos Passos), 350
Growth condition of crops
bias in reports on, 56–57, 64–66
Board of Crop Estimates decisions on, 70
County Reporters providing information on, 68
in exceptional years, 30
in neighborhood, 134
normal condition in, 29–30, 74
smoothing of reports on, 49–50, 51f
voluntary Reporters providing information on, 27, 28–30, 56–57, 64–66, 74
weather affecting, 29–30, 57–58

Hackenger, M., 283
Hacking, Ian, 329
Hansen, Morris, 204, 310, 311–312, 316, 366n22
Harvested acres, 62, 81
Has Poverty Diminished? (Bowley & Hogg), 295
Hauser, Philipp M., 316
Hays, Willet M., 59, 60
Heffer, Jean, 249
Highway system. *See* Roads
Hiring policies
of Bureau of Labor Statistics, 283–284
of Civil Works Administration, 267–270
Hogg, Margaret H., 295–296, 364n2
death of, 305–306, 365n11
on sampling methods, 295–296, 297–298, 300, 306
and Trial Census of Unemployment, 300–302
Hogs. *See* Pork production
Holmes, Edwin S., 58–59
Holmes, Irvin, 182–183, 184, 190, 191, 198
Homogeneity, 151–152
in crop reporting districts, 36, 136, 152
and stratification, 151–152, 157, 159
Hoover, Herbert, 2, 4, 87
on unemployment rate, 247–248, 249
Hopkins, Harry L., 257–261, 290–291, 327
Brown as assistant to, 252
and COGSIS, 364n41
as Commerce Secretary, 343
Gill as deputy of, 322, 362n20
on hiring procedures of CWA, 268
Myers memorandum to, 309
and relief work projects, 272, 286f, 287
and voluntary registration of unemployed, 309
on white-collar workers, 264, 268, 270, 291
on Women's Division in CWA, 268
Households
consumption patterns in, 319
in corner houses, 316–317

as sampling unit on unemployment, 297, 300, 301, 302–303, 316–317
Hurja, Emil, 310
Hurwitz, William N., 316
Hyde, John, 73

Ickes, Harold L., 258
Igo, Sarah, 11, 329–330
Income
of farmers, 90, 177, 213–217
of industrial workers, 90, 214
Indexes on unemployment rate, 245–248, 250, 361ch7n4
Indiana, 207
Induction problem, 147, 148
Industrial prices, compared to agricultural prices, 90, 214
INSEE (Institut National de la Statistique et des Études Économiques), 126, 356n1
Insider trading, 58–59
Institut National de la Statistique et des Études Économiques (INSEE), 126, 356n1
Insurance
old-age, 320
unemployment, 320–323
Interactionism, symbolic, 8
Interior Secretary, 258, 309
Internalism, 187, 193, 195, 359nn8–9
International Institute of Statistics, 3, 154, 170, 188, 227
Interventionism, 10, 344, 345, 347
agricultural planning programs in, 110, 113
agricultural quota system in, 90, 92, 97, 103
Master Sample data in, 214, 216, 221
in poverty, 216
surveys in, 10–11, 216–217, 219, 221, 224–225, 320–325
in unemployment, 251–254, 319–325
Interviews, 9
with farmers, 33, 34, 114, 199, 200, 209, 210–211, 211f
probable error in data from, 147, 150
on unemployment, 241, 242–243, 269–270, 269f, 272–278
Iowa
Brooks as agricultural Statistician in, 97
Carl as agricultural Statistician in, 36, 43–44, 46, 56, 166–167, 176, 358ch5n2
counting and sampling units in, 208f
road map of, 200, 201f
Sarle as agricultural Statistician in, 145, 166
township sections in, 198–199
Iowa State University, 197, 202, 223
Statistical Laboratory of, 161, 163–196, 198, 204

James, William, 326
Jeffersonian model of agriculture, 225–226, 359n5
Jensen, Adolph, 147, 188
Jessen, Raymond, 198–202, 203f, 204–206, 209, 215, 294, 364n1
Journal of Farm Economics, 187, 189, 198
Judd, Orange, 127, 356n2

Kansas, 50, 51f, 131f, 176
Keep, Charles H., 73
Keep Commission, 73
Kentucky, 34
Keynes, John Maynard, 146, 259, 358ch4n1, 361ch8n4
Kiaer, Anders, 3, 147, 188
King, A. J., 193, 204, 210, 212f
Kinsey, Alfred, 329
Kirkendall, Richard S., 104–105, 106f, 356n10
Kish, Leslie, 216, 236
Kruskal, Frederick, 163, 193

Labor Department, 10, 248
Labor Secretary, Perkins as, 2, 261, 294
Labor statistics
  on demand and supply of labor, 245, 247
  models of, 240–251
  on number hired, 146
  paradoxical decomposition of, 239–254
  in random sampling, 293–335
  unemployment rate in. *See* Unemployment rate
  victims of Depression as enumerators of, 255–292
Labor strikes, unemployment in, 243, 245
Labor union statistics on unemployment, 240, 244–246, 247
Lafollette, Robert, 263
Laissez-faire period, 10
  agriculture in, 12, 22, 88, 117, 221
  unemployment in, 240–247, 319
Lancaster PA, Trial Census of Unemployment in, 271, 273, 275, 280, 300, 301, 363n35
Land grant colleges, 355n7
Land prices, questionnaire responses on, 43–44
Land-use planning, 107–109, 116–117, 119–121, 226
Lange, Dorothea, 3
Latour, Bruno, 141, 142, 190
Lee, Russell, 3
Lévy-Bruhl, Raymond, 356n1
Libby-Owens-Ford firm, 309–310
Liberalism, 10, 344, 347
  corporate, 259
  of Lafollette, 263
  of Locke, 133, 230
  participationism in, 11, 325
  progressive, 291
  of statisticians, 260
  and transition to welfare state, 10, 320, 321
Likert, Rensis, 114, 216, 224–225
Lippmann, Walter, 327, 333
Lisbon Strategy, 346
Lists
  of County Reporters, 67–68
  on price paid by farmers for agricultural materials, 68
  of voluntary Reporters, 25–26, 27, 42
Literary Digest, 306, 307
Livelihood and Poverty (Bowley), 295
Livestock reports, 43, 131, 183, 220
  on pork production. *See* Pork production

Local informants, unemployment data collected by, 243–244, 247
Locke, John, 133, 230
London School of Economics, 338
Lozier, Ralph, 305
Lubin, Isador
as Bureau of Labor Statistics director, 253, 262, 263, 279, 281, 283, 294
on Central Statistical Board, 362n20
and Civil Works Administration, 263–266, 281
experts working with, 294–295
and Three Bills of Wagner, 253, 263
and Trial Census of Unemployment, 271, 277, 279–280
Lynd, Robert, 110–111, 114, 356n10

Magic Town (film), 332
Mahalanobis, P. C., 212f
Mail routes. *See* Postal routes
Manin, Bernard, 356n3
Maps
of Census Bureau, 199
of city blocks, 297, 299
Master Sample based on, 199–209
of postal routes, 311, 313f
of roads. *See* Road maps
Market prices, 37
in corner technique, 354n41
farmer knowledge of, 19, 79–80
and insider trading, 58–59
paid by cooperatives, 80–81
speculation on, 19–20, 58–59, 78–79, 90
Marshals, federal, census data collected by, 240–241
Martuccelli, Danilo, 120
Massachusetts, 240, 242
Mass democracy, 11
Mass society, 344
Igo on, 11, 329–330
Mills on, 326, 327–329, 331
Master Sample, 13, 126, 197–226, 356n1
accuracy of, 206, 213, 221–222, 224
area sampling method in, 209–211
conditions and behavior patterns in, 215–216
counting units in, 206–209, 218
geographic zones in, 199, 210, 217, 223
grant funding of, 204
history of, 212f
observation units in, 209–211
in planning, 222–225
reliability of, 223
representativeness of, 210, 214–215, 225–226
sample units in, 206–211, 223, 330
selection mechanism in, 210, 211
speed of surveys with, 221, 224
staff working on, 205f
strata in, 205–206
systematic draw of sample in, 207
variety of issues studied with, 217, 218
willingness of respondents in, 210, 211
Meat products, transport of, 235
Median value, Board of Crop Estimates on, 70, 71, 353n33
Mespoulet, Martine, 356n2

Meteorological data. *See* Weather
Metropolitan Life Insurance, 294
Metzger, Sam, 37–38, 57
Mexican ball weevil, 67, 228
Michigan
  Church as agricultural Statistician in, 23–26, 32–33, 37–42, 98–99, 182
  pickling cucumber crop in, 38–42, 67
Middletown (Lynd), 110, 356n10
Mills, Charles Wright, 325, 326–329, 331, 333
Mills, Frederick C., 146, 150
Mimeographed reports on unemployment, 319–320, 334
Mirror function of statistics, 345
Missouri, 180f
Mitchell, Timothy, 8
Montana, 109
Mosteller, William H., 163, 193
Mount Weather agreement, 355n7
Municipal lists for unemployment sample selection, 300–301
Murray, Nat, 130, 292
Myers, Howard, 284, 309, 323–324

National Agricultural Statistical Service (NASS), 21
National Board of Trade, 73
National Meteorological Agency, 64
Nature's Metropolis (Cronon), 235
Neighborhoods, rural, agricultural reports on, 226, 293, 299
  accuracy of, 99, 129, 130, 143
  compared to entire locality, 132–133
  compared to individual farm, 136
  from elite farmers, 26, 57, 155
  on growth condition of crops, 34, 134
  psychological influences on, 129, 130, 134
  in questionnaire responses, 48
  territorial limits in, 148
  from township, 135
Neighborhoods, urban, 299, 328
Nevada, 207
New Deal, 3, 346, 347, 350
  Agricultural Adjustment Administration in, 87, 89–103
  agricultural planning in, 104–117
  Brain Trust in, 2, 104, 145, 163
  Central Statistical Board in, 178, 272
  Civil Works Administration in, 278, 282, 291
  Dewey on, 291
  frequency of statistical studies in, 220
  and government interventionism, 221
  Keynes influence on policies in, 358ch4n1
  links between statistics and politics in, 87–117
  Master Sample created in, 213
  number employed in statistical projects of, 283–285, 363–364n35
  proposals on employment programs in, 253
  relief programs in. *See* Relief programs
  representative surveys in, 5, 10, 11, 220
  unemployment insurance in, 320–321, 323
New Haven PA, Hogg study on unemployment in, 296, 297

New Mexico, 108–109
New York Times, 309
Neyman, Jerzy, 163, 164, 189, 193–196, 212f, 296, 316, 359n10
Nonresponse rate
  in agricultural questionnaires, 135–136, 185
  in Master Sample, 211
Normal condition of crops, 29–30, 74
Normal distribution, 149

Objectivity, 324
  in crop reports, 128–136, 140–143, 185, 292, 357n9n
  in expression, 230
  in unemployment data, 287–289, 292
Observation units in Master Sample, 209–211
Occupation, as factor in unemployment rate, 242, 243, 273–275
Ogburn, William F., 246
Ohio
  Trial Census of Unemployment in, 271, 278–281, 300, 301
  West as agricultural Statistician in, 45–46, 56
Old-age insurance, 320
Omnibus, 135, 357n12
Opinion polls, 4, 5, 113, 114, 306–308, 328, 365n13

Par method in yield per acre calculation, 74
Participationism, 11, 105, 266–267, 292, 293–294, 327, 339
  and pragmatism, 266–267, 335
  of voluntary crop reporters, 105, 266, 293, 327, 344
Patronage appointments of unemployment enumerators, 279–282
Pearson, Karl, 146, 302
Peg strip, 48, 49f, 352n18
Pennsylvania
  Hogg study on unemployment in, 296, 297
  Trial Census of Unemployment in, 271, 273, 275, 280, 300, 301, 363n35
  women as unemployment enumerators in, 362n18
Perkins, Frances, 2, 247–248, 249, 261, 263, 294
Persons, Charles E., 270, 273, 277–278, 279, 281
Pettet, Z. R., 202, 204
Photographs
  aerial, 202, 206, 299
  of Farm Security Administration, 2–3
Pickling cucumber crop, 38–42, 67, 182
Planning, agricultural. *See* Agricultural planning
Plasma stage, 348
  of agricultural statistics, 22–23, 227, 228
  of unemployment statistics, 250
Politics, 345–346, 347
  decomposition of links between statistics and, 87–117
  representation in, 219, 342, 345, 356–357n3
  zones and boundaries in, 218–219

Population, 6
  homogeneity in, 151–152
Pork production, 90
  corn used in, 93f, 99, 355n3
  quotas on, 92, 93f, 98, 101, 355n4
  reduction of, 98, 355n4
  and transport, 235
Porter, T. M., 357n7
Postal routes
  agricultural questionnaires distributed in, 136–140
  map of, 311, 313f
  purposive sample selection in, 182–183
  unemployment questionnaires distributed in, 311–315
Potato crops, 37–38
Pottawattamie County IA, 201f, 208f
Poverty, 213
  case studies on, 215
  interventions in, 216
  urban, 236
Pragmatism
  Dewey on, 105, 266
  and participationism, 266–267, 335
Prediction and control functions of surveys, 325
Prices
  of agricultural products. *See* Agricultural prices
  industrial, 90, 214
  of land, 43–44
  paid by farmers for agricultural materials, 68
Principles of Representative Government, The (Manin), 356n3
Probability, theory of, 4, 143, 149, 159, 229, 334
Probable error, 145–161, 183
  application of formula for, 158–161, 164
  assumptions in, 150–151, 159
  homogeneity and stratification in, 151–152, 159
  publication of articles on, 160
  representativeness in, 151, 152–157
  restricted interpretation of, 157–158, 160
  Sarle on, 145–161, 195, 228
  in unemployment data, 302
Psychological influences on crop reporters, 129, 134
Public and Its Problems, The (Dewey), 250
Public works, statistics as, 255
Public Works Administration (PWA), 258, 267, 361n2
Purcell, Edward A., 335
Purposive sampling, 154, 155, 156, 170, 174
  compared to random selection, 175–196
  control factors in, 185–186
  experiments on, 178
  in opinion polls, 307
  representativeness in, 188, 189
  sample units in, 154, 155, 174, 190
  Snedecor on, 188–189
  stratified, 155, 156
  on unemployment, 297, 298

Questionnaires on agriculture, 27–32, 38–42, 136–140
average picture from, 138, 139
averaging of results in, 46–48, 50–54
bias in responses to, 56–57, 64–66
coded telegrams on results of, 54, 55f, 58
contradictory data in, 46
editing of, 42–46, 66, 85
on entire locality, 133
on grain crops, 27–31, 43, 50, 51f
on individual farm, 133, 135, 136
inducements for replies to, 137
initial processing of, 32
on livestock, 43
mail carriers in distribution of, 136–140
for Master Sample, 210, 215
nonresponse rate in, 135–136, 185
number of responses to, 101, 135–136, 137–138, 357n11
pickling cucumbers as category in, 38–42
shingling technique in handling of, 47–48
smoothing of results in, 48–50, 51f, 85, 100
social theory on interpretation of, 46, 56
standardized, 114
summary sheets on, 52–54, 53f, 58
weighting data in, 50–54, 156
Questionnaires on unemployment, 316, 317
of Bureaus of Labor, 243
of Census Bureau, 240–243, 295
of Civil Works Administration, 259
mail carriers in distribution of, 311–315
of trade unions, 244–245
in Trial Census of Unemployment, 272–276
of universities and private firms, 246
Quételet, Adolphe, 139, 321, 323
Quota sampling method, 307, 315
Quota system agricultural production, 91–103
contracts on, 92, 93f, 94, 97
problems in timing of, 97, 98
reduction targets in, 95
subsidies in, 92, 94, 97, 99, 102
voluntary participation in, 92, 94, 101

Rand McNally Road Atlas, 200
Random sampling, 3, 4–5, 344
sample frame in, 6–7
stratified. *See* Stratified random sampling
Random sampling on agriculture, 125–126
accuracy of, 186, 191, 222
advantages of, 186
Bowley on, 146, 150, 152
census data compared to, 191
Master Sample in, 13, 126, 197–229
probable error in, 146, 150, 152–157
purposive selection compared to, 175–196
representativeness in, 13, 126, 152–157, 188, 189, 198, 229

Random sampling on agriculture (cont.)
sample units in, 154, 155, 172, 173, 174, 190, 193
Sarle on, 152–157, 174, 186, 187, 190
Schultz on, 170–172
Snedecor on, 172–173, 188–189
voluntary response compared to, 146
Random sampling on unemployment, 13, 236, 237, 293–335, 345
as democratic expertise, 333–335
Hogg on, 295–296, 300, 306
and participationism, 293
postal routes as basis of, 311–315
representativeness in, 296
Stephan on, 319
voluntary response compared to, 315, 334
Reboul, Eugène, 321
Reflexivity, 1–13, 299, 342, 345
concept of, 11–12
and consistency, 12, 342
and representation, 3–13, 342–344
Release of statistical reports
on agriculture, 75–78, 83–84, 353n21
journalists waiting for, 77–78, 354n39
on unemployment, 319–320
Reliability
of census data on unemployment, 241
of Master Sample, 223
of sampling method, 178–179, 181
Relief programs, 2, 251–254, 323
administration of, 257–260
boondogglers in, 285, 286f, 287, 288, 290, 292
of CWA. *See* Civil Works Administration
of FERA. *See* Federal Emergency Relief Administration (FERA)
number of persons in, 282–283, 284, 305
of PWA, 258, 361n2
white-collar workers in, 267–268, 273, 285
women in, 268–270
of WPA, 285–289, 290
Reporters, voluntary crop. *See* Voluntary crop reporters
Representation, political, 219, 342, 345, 356–357n3
and local crop reports, 127–128
Representativeness, 126, 152–157
Bowley on, 188
concept of, 5
conference proceedings on, 169–175
of crop reporting district, 152
expression of, 143
importance to Division, 167
Kiaer on, 3, 147, 188
mail carrier determination of, 138–139
of Master Sample, 210, 214–215, 225–226
in purposive selection, 188, 189
of random sample, 13, 126, 152–157, 188, 189, 198, 229, 296
and reflexivity, 3–13, 342–344
of sample farms, 128, 135, 138–139, 140
Sarle on, 152–157, 173–175
Schultz on, 170–172

Snedecor on, 172–173, 188, 189
of voluntary crop reporters, 26, 57, 128, 140, 148, 155–156
Representative sample, 3, 4
compared to opinion polls, 4, 5
conference proceedings on, 169–175
control factors in, 170–171
of farms, 128, 135, 138–139, 140
and probable error, 151, 152–157
Sarle on, 174
Representative surveys, 3–13, 26
accuracy of, 221–222
administrative units in, 9–10
Buchanan bill on, 168
conference proceedings on, 169–175
in interventionism, 10–11, 216–217, 219, 221
logistics of, 7
in mass democracy, 11
Master Sample in, 13, 197–226
opinion polls compared to, 4, 5
political debates on, 5
sample frame in, 6–7
speed of, 221
Republican Party, 5, 249, 263, 280
Research workers, 284
Retrospection in expression, 229–230
Rice, production and demand for, 90
Rice, Stuart A., 241, 255, 285–287, 309, 360n4, 362n20, 364n41
Riefler, Winfield, 272, 322
Riskin, Robert, 332
Road maps, 199–202
aerial photography combined with, 202, 206
of Census Bureau, 199
counting and sampling units based on, 206, 207
limitations of, 200, 360n4
standardization of, 200
Roads, 109
construction in rural areas, 199, 359n3
sample unit based on, 179, 183, 190, 191
and travel of agricultural Statisticians, 33–34
Robinson, Frederick, 310, 311
Robustness in statistics, 354n43
Roosevelt, Franklin, 2, 342, 361n3
Agricultural Adjustment Administration of, 251
Brain Trust of, 2, 104, 145, 163
on census of unemployment, 305
Central Statistical Board of, 272–273
Civil Works Administration of. *See* Civil Works Administration
Keynes influence on, 358ch4n1
New Deal programs of. *See* New Deal
as New York governor, 247, 257, 270
number of statistical projects under, 265–266
Perkins as Labor Secretary of, 261
prediction of reelection of, 4, 113, 306, 307
Public Works Administration of, 258, 361n2
unemployment statistics at time of election of, 255
voluntary registration of unemployed under, 297, 308–315

Roosevelt, Theodore, 73
Ropper, Elmo, 306
Rosanvallon, Pierre, 342, 345, 347
Ross, Emerson, 260, 361n7
Ross, Franck, 277
Rural areas, 12–13
  agricultural planning in. *See* Agricultural planning
  agricultural Statisticians in. *See* Agricultural Statisticians
  agricultural statistics on. *See* Agricultural statistics
  compared to urban areas, 338
  voluntary crop reporters in. *See* Voluntary crop reporters
Russell Sage Foundation, 295, 296, 364n2

Salary of unemployment enumerators, 278–281
Sample frame, 6–7, 223, 224
  on unemployment, 298, 300, 304
Sample units, 344
  costs associated with, 178, 179, 181, 183, 191
  geographic zones as, 199
  individual farm as, 132–135, 140, 148, 198
  in Master Sample, 206–211, 223, 330
  purposive selection of, 154, 155, 174, 190
  random selection of, 154, 155, 172, 173, 174, 190, 193
  Sarle on, 191
  size and accuracy of, 183, 191, 302–303
  systematic draw of, 207
  topographical survey sections as, 179–181, 180f, 198–199
  townships as, 176, 177, 179, 198–199
  on unemployment, 247, 295, 297–299, 301–304
Sampling, 4, 182
  error in, 148–149, 158
  in opinion polls, 306–308
  population in, 6
  purposive. *See* Purposive sampling
  random. *See* Random sampling
  reliability of, 178–179, 181
  representative. *See* Representative sample
Sampling on agriculture, 152–157, 169–196
  bias in, 185
  comparison of methods in, 175–196
  confidence intervals in, 189, 222
  control factors in, 170–171, 177, 185–186
  costs associated with sample units in, 178, 179, 181, 183
  homogeneity in, 136, 151–152
  individual farm as sample in, 132–135, 140, 148, 198
  mail carriers role in, 136–140
  objectivity in, 185
  probable error in, 147, 151, 152–157
  purposive selection in, 154, 155, 156, 170, 174. *See also* Purposive sampling

random. *See* Random sampling on agriculture
reliability of, 178–179, 181
Sarle on, 173–175
Schultz on, 170–172
Snedecor on, 172–173, 176
subjective, 185, 186
topographical survey sections as sample unit in, 179–181, 180f
Sampling on unemployment, 263, 264–265
blocks as basis of, 247, 295, 297–299, 301–304, 319
postal routes in, 311–315
purposive, 297, 298
random. *See* Random sampling on unemployment
in Trial Census on Unemployment, 294–304
Sarle, Charles S., 164, 209, 355n4, 358ch4n2, 359n7
on accuracy of data, 221–222
as agricultural Statistician for Iowa, 145, 166
on Master Sample, 213
on probable error, 145–161, 195, 228
on random and purposive selection, 178–179, 181–182, 184–187, 191, 293
on representativeness, 152–157, 173–175
and Statistical Laboratory at Iowa State University, 166, 167, 169
on stratified random sampling, 186, 187, 190
on township sections, 181, 198
School janitors, collaboration with unemployment survey, 247, 295, 297
Schultz, Theodor C., 359n7
Schultz, Theodore W., 170–172, 173
Schutz, H., 176, 177, 178, 179
Scott, James, 7–8
Seasonal workers, 242, 324
Secrecy, 332–333
in agricultural statistics, 54, 55f, 58, 59–60, 84, 332
in unemployment surveys, 332
Self-employed workers, 242
Self-registration of unemployed, 297, 308–315
Series, 349
and consistency, 337–339
Serviceable accuracy, 100, 116, 222
Service intellectual, 105, 229
Shapin, Steven, 359n8
Shelton, William C., 236
Shephard, J. B., 176, 177, 178, 179, 220–221
Shingling technique, 47–48
Shipping points as source of agricultural information, 34, 36
Simmel, Georg, 227
Simpson, G., 210
Smoothing
by agricultural Statisticians, 48–50, 51f, 85, 100
by Board of Crop Estimates, 75
Snedecor, George, 166
Fisher as influence on, 165, 172, 188, 195, 196

Snedecor, George (cont.)
and Iowa state University Statistical Laboratory, 165, 168, 212f
on random and purposive selection, 172–173, 187–189
on sample units, 176, 179
Schultz influenced by, 170
Social control era, 255, 361n1
Social engineers, 113, 114, 115
Social Science Research Council, 319
Social Security Act, 322
Social Studies of Knowledge model, 71
Social theory on questionnaire responses, 46, 56
Social workers, 251–253
Sociological Imagination, The (Mills), 331
Sociology, 9, 110, 125
of statistics, 21, 342, 346
Soil conservation, crop adjustment for, 103
Solidity of agricultural statistics, 83, 117, 119, 120–121, 354n43
Specificity of expression, 230
Speculation on agricultural prices, 19–20, 90
history of, 354n41
in insider trading, 58–59
prevention of, 59–60, 78–79, 80, 111
Springfield Daily News, 280
Springfield OH, Trial Census of Unemployment in, 271, 278–281, 300, 301
Standard deviation, 151
Standardization
of agricultural statistics, 41, 42, 114
of road maps, 200
State agricultural Statisticians. *See* Agricultural Statisticians
State Allotment Committee, 91
Statistical chains, 344–347
Stephan, Frederick F., 265, 277, 302, 308, 310, 316, 318–319, 365n12
Stigler, Stephen, 166
Stock market crash (1929), 11, 87, 88, 347
agricultural planning after, 104, 111, 120
unemployment after, 247
Stouffer, Samuel, 277, 302–303, 310, 364n41
Stratification of data, 151–152, 156–157
accuracy in, 222
geographical, 151–152, 155, 156, 186
and homogeneity, 151–152, 157, 159
Stratified random sampling, 163, 164, 172, 190, 192
Neyman on, 193, 196
representativeness in, 189
Sarle on, 186, 187, 190
Snedecor on, 188–189
Strikes, unemployment in, 243, 245
Stryker, Roy, 2–3
Subsidies to farmers, 90, 92, 94, 97, 99, 102, 218
Summary sheets on agricultural questionnaires, 52–54, 53f, 58
Surveys on agriculture, 12, 338
agricultural Statisticians in, 32, 34, 37
Buchanan proposal on, 168
check data from, 81

comparison of random and purposive selection in, 175–196
on conditions and behavior patterns, 215–216
conference proceedings on, 169–175
on cultivated acres, 73–74, 134
on entire locality, 132–133
and government interventions, 10–11, 216–217, 219, 221, 224–225
individual farmers in, 133
individual farms in, 134, 135, 195
Master Sample in, 13, 197–226. *See also* Master Sample
objectivity in, 143
on pickling cucumbers, 39–42
probable error in, 148, 150, 157, 158
questionnaires in. *See* Questionnaires on agriculture
speed of, 221, 224
in statistical research, 114
topographical sections in, 178–181, 180f, 198–199
variety of issues studied in, 217
voluntary crop reporters in, 27, 30–32, 101, 143, 146, 185
Surveys on unemployment, 338
by Bureaus of Labor, 243
by Census Bureau, 240–243
by Civil Works Administration, 260–272
on conditions and behavior patterns, 324
and government interventions, 320–325
by local individuals, 243–244
in prediction and control, 325
questionnaires in. *See* Questionnaires on unemployment
selection of personnel for, 267–272
by trade unions, 244–245
in Trial Census of Unemployment, 13, 236–237
Symbolic interactionism, 8
Symmetry, 192, 230

Tammany Hall, 253
Tarde, Gabriel de, 254, 337, 351n3, 366n1
Tax assessors, farm data collected by, 177, 183, 199
Taxpayer lists for unemployment sample selection, 297, 298
Taylor, Henry C., 111, 138, 187, 259, 356ch3n1, 361ch8n5
Telegrams, coded, on agricultural statistics, 54, 55f, 58, 59–60
Texas, 34, 36
Thorp, Willard L., 255
Three Bills, 253, 263
Tobacco, 90
Tolley, Howard, 106f, 217
in agricultural planning, 107, 109, 111–113, 114–115, 222–223
in Bureau of Agricultural Economics, 105, 107, 110, 111–113, 184, 322, 356n10
in Bureau of Planning of AAA, 105
criticism of statistical data, 114–115
Lynd as influence on, 110, 356n10
on Master Sample, 222–223
Tomato production, 36

Topalov, Christian, 239
on indexes of unemployment, 245
on indicators of unemployment, 241–242
on local individuals conducting unemployment surveys, 243–244
Topographical survey sections as sample unit, 178–181, 180f, 182, 198–199
Townships
Reporters representing, 27, 30, 135
as sample unit, 176, 177, 179, 198–199
supervisor reports on, 127–128
systematic draw of samples from, 207
topographical survey sections of, 179–181, 180f, 182, 198–199
Trade union statistics on unemployment, 240, 244–246, 247
Training
of agricultural Statisticians, 61–62, 63, 113, 160
of social engineers, 113, 114, 115
of unemployment enumerators, 246, 256, 271, 279, 280
Travel of agricultural Statisticians for field surveys, 32–38, 39, 40
A Treatise on Probability (Keynes), 146
Trial Census of Unemployment, 13, 236–237, 261, 270–281
number employed in, 363n35
quality of data from, 276–278
questionnaires in, 272–276
sample selection in, 294–304
staff of, 270–272, 310
Tugwell, Rexford, 105, 106f
Tupper, Ernest A., 295
Unemployment insurance, 320–323
Unemployment rate, 2, 236–237
bias in data on, 287–289, 317
case study approach to, 251, 259, 299
census data on, 13, 236–237, 240–243, 247, 248, 304–305, 316–319
conflicting reports on, 247–251
cost of survey on, 263–264
demand and supply of labor affecting, 245
duration of unemployment in, 241–242
enumerative check on, 310–315, 316
Federal Reserve Bank of Philadelphia study on, 247, 295
FERA survey on, 259–260, 263–264, 339
fluctuations in, 245–246
frictional, 245, 250
indexes on, 245–248, 250, 361ch7n4
local informants on, 243–244
number employed in statistical projects on, 283–285
number of unemployed in, 242
objectivity in data on, 287–289, 292
occupation as factor in, 242, 243, 273–275
paradoxical decomposition of, 239–254
personal responsibility as issue in, 251–253
private firms on, 240, 246–247, 295
questionnaires on. *See* Questionnaires on unemployment
and relief administration, 257–260

sampling on. *See* Sampling on unemployment
seasonal variations in, 242, 324
selection of personnel for surveys on, 267–272
of self-employed workers, 242
social workers on, 251–253
time lost by workers in, 242
Trial Census of. *See* Trial Census of Unemployment
union statistics on, 240, 244–246, 247
university statistics on, 240, 246–247
victims of Depression as enumerators of, 255–292
from voluntary registration of unemployed, 297, 308–315
and Works Project Administration, 285–290
Union statistics on unemployment, 240, 244–246, 247
United States Employment Service (USES), 247–248, 250
University of Michigan, 262, 266
University of Wisconsin, 105, 170, 263, 266, 287
University statistics
on agriculture, 161, 163–196
on unemployment, 240, 246–247
Urban areas
compared to rural areas, 338
neighborhoods in, 299, 328
unemployment rate in. *See* Unemployment rate
Veblen, Thorstein, 262
Voluntary crop reporters, 26–32
in adjustment program, 92, 93f, 94, 101, 102–103
bias of, 56–57, 64–66, 101, 209–210
compared to random sampling, 146
on cultivated acres, 28, 56–57
editing of information provided by, 42–46
elite status of, 26, 27, 57, 64, 185, 214
errors in information from, 43, 128–129, 130, 134, 146
on growth condition of crops, 27, 28–30, 56–57, 64–66, 74
inducements for cooperation, 137
limitations of, 185
list of, 25–26, 27, 42
local prominent individuals as, 243
number of, 101, 135–136, 357n11
objectivity of, 128–136, 292
opinions and judgments of, 131–132, 155–156
paperwork filed by, 31f
participationism of, 105, 266, 293, 327, 344
psychological influences on, 129, 134
public spirit of, 57, 129, 130
questionnaires sent to, 27–32. *See also* Questionnaires on agriculture
relationship with the Division, 26, 101–102, 103, 116, 120, 130, 137, 185
representativeness of, 26, 57, 128, 140, 148, 155–156
selection of, 26–27, 127–128, 130–131, 138, 145

Voluntary crop reporters (cont.)
solidity and consistency of data from, 119
in statistical chain, 344, 345, 347
and transition to random selection, 125, 226
on yield per acre, 28–30, 64–66
Voluntary registration of unemployed, 297, 308–315, 365n14
enumerative check on, 310–315

Wagner, Robert, 253, 263, 343
Wallace, Henry A., 342, 366n21
and agricultural adjustment programs, 87, 90, 92, 94, 96, 355n4
and agricultural planning, 104, 105, 107, 112
on "equality for agriculture," 90, 214
at Iowa State University, 166, 358ch5n1
and Mount Weather agreement, 355n7
as Secretary of Agriculture, 87, 166, 216
Wallace, Henry C., 65f, 355n9
Warren, Stanley W., 167
Washington, D.C. office of Division
Board of Crop Estimates in, 58–78
coded telegrams sent to, 54, 55f
County Reporters in communication with, 67–68
state Statisticians interacting with, 39–40, 41, 42, 63
transfers of professional staff to, 62–63
Weather
Board of Crop Estimates reviewing data on, 64, 72
and growth condition of crops, 29–30, 57–58
voluntary reporters of, 353n29
Webbink, Paul, 260
Weber, Max, 356n2
Weighing-scale model of comparisons, 175, 187, 189, 190–191
Weighting data from agricultural questionnaires, 50–54, 156
Welch, Emmett H., 295
Welfare assistance for unemployed, 251–254, 257–260
Welfare state, 10, 320–321
Wells, O. V., 107, 108, 111, 115
West, C. J., 45–46, 56
Wheat crop
cultivated acres of, 28
production and demand for, 90
quotas on, 92, 98
smoothing of growth condition reports, 50, 51f
transport of, 235
yield per acre of, 74
White-collar workers
as boondogglers, 285
CWA projects for, 264, 267–268, 269, 270
Hopkins on, 264, 268, 270, 291
salary paid to, 268
sensitivity toward, 270, 273
unemployed, 239, 261, 309
WPA projects for, 285

Whitehead, Alfred N., 229
Wilks, S. S., 307
Willingness of respondents
  in agricultural adjustment programs, 92, 94
  in agricultural reports, 26, 57, 101, 125, 156, 327
  compared to random selection, 146, 315, 334
  in Master Sample, 210, 211
Wilson, Elmo, 216
Wilson, John, 100
Wilson, Milburn L., 105, 106f, 107, 108, 109–110, 113–114
  on Jeffersonian model of agriculture, 226, 359n5
Wisconsin, 55f, 56, 67, 101
Women
  agricultural statistics compiled by, 205f, 262f
  in census data collection, 241
  in insurance companies, 360n7
  as unemployment enumerators, 268–270, 271, 272, 362n18, 363n35
  unemployment of, 263
Wood products, transport of, 235
Woodward, Ellen S., 268
Works Progress Administration, 262f, 285–289, 290, 363n35, 365n15
  Myers at, 309, 323–324
Wright, Carroll D., 10, 244

Yield per acre, 62, 330
  Board of Crop Estimates calculations on, 74
  crop reporters on, 28–30, 64–66
  growth condition of plants as indicator of, 28–30, 74
  of harvested acres, 62
  Master Sample on, 211
  par calculation method, 74
Yule, George Udny, 146

Zones
  economic, 218–219
  geographic, 199, 210, 217, 223
  political, 218–219
  tenure type as basis of, 219
  type-of-farming areas in, 219
Zunz, Olivier, 329